D1504459

W
Ne

Other Books by Edward Kiersh

WHERE HAVE YOU GONE, VINCE DIMAGGIO?

Where Are You Now, Bo Diddley?

THE STARS WHO MADE US ROCK AND WHERE THEY ARE NOW

Edward Kiersh

PHOTOGRAPHS BY

Stephen Wallis

A Dolphin Book
DOUBLEDAY & COMPANY, INC.
GARDEN CITY, NEW YORK   1986

We would like to thank the following people for permission to reprint the song lyrics used in this book.

"Sock It to Me, Baby" by Bob Crewe and L. Russell Brown, copyright © 1966 by Saturday Music, Inc. All Rights Reserved. Used by permission of Saturday Music, Inc. "The Jon" by Mitch Ryder, K. Levise, and W. Gabriel, copyright © 1978 by American Jade. All Rights Reserved. Used by permission of Mitch Ryder, K. Levise, W. Gabriel, and American Jade.

Library of Congress Cataloging-in-Publication Data
Kiersh, Edward.
    Where are you now, Bo Diddley?
    1. Rock musicians—Biography.   I. Title.
ML394.K53   1986   784.5'4'00922 [B]   85-31092
ISBN 0-385-19610-5

To my wife, *Nancy*.
Without her loving support this book would
not have happened.

Contents

Where Are You Now, Bo Diddley?

Robbie Robertson of the Band

Leaving the Bus to Ride with Martin Scorsese

His key influences were once the tribal chieftains of the Iroquois Nation, the fearless Hurons and Mohawks, who dared to climb skyscrapers and bridges. Between jobs these men would visit his mother in her Toronto home, and while they sat around playing music, the youngster would be asked to "come here, we'll show you another chord . . . another boogy-figure." Watching their fingers dance across guitars and mandolins, the ten-year-old dreamed of playing his own tunes. And this fascination inevitably led him to other sages, like the "Hawaiian Hula Master" Billy Blue, rockabilly's Ronnie Hawkins, and of course, Dylan.

Under their tutelage, Robbie Robertson matured into one of rock's most gifted songwriters/guitarists. Teaming up with the Band, he fashioned such classics as "The Weight," "The Night They Drove Old Dixie Down," "Up on Cripple Creek," "Rag Mama Rag," and "Ophelia." Robertson's earthy, country-gospel-inspired songs, which probe various facets of Americana with rich, unrelenting zeal, brought the group folk-hero stature for almost a decade. Once known simply as Dylan's backup band (hence their name), these four Canadians and a Southerner (Levon Helm) made their own headlines with *Music from Big Pink*, featuring the novel use of two keyboards. That work was followed by the equally

innovative and insightful albums, *The Band* and *Stage Fright,* albums
that are still celebrated for their searing, powerful vocals.

Shaped by Iroquois wisdom, Robertson knew the fame would be
fleeting. One day the music stops, the cheers suddenly fade. So ever the
realist, searching for knowledge, he looked for a new teacher, another
mentor with wondrous secrets to impart.

In the same manner that Butch Cassidy sidled up to the Sundance
Kid, Robertson became bosom buddies with Martin Scorsese, the director of *Taxi Driver, The King of Comedy,* and *Raging Bull.* The two men
met in 1976, during the filming of *The Last Waltz,* the rock concert
documentary about the Band's final appearance on Thanksgiving night,
1976, in San Francisco. Seven years earlier, they had spotted each other
at Woodstock, where Scorsese was working on the Warner Brothers
movie.

By 1976, Robbie had become convinced that "the group's ideals had
strayed." He was saddened and disgusted by the way the others were
abusing themselves with drugs, reckless driving and alcohol. There was
a feverish, "berserk need to do self-destructive things . . . to ride it on
the edge," *à la* James Dean, Jimi Hendrix, and Marilyn Monroe. So
before splitting, he urged the group to do *The Last Waltz,* with the
"only man I could think of who understood music in a way that trans-
lated into magic."

With the success of *The Last Waltz*—critic Pauline Kael calls the film
"the best of all rock documentaries"—Robertson's relationship with
Scorsese flourished. Together, they had produced the musical arrangements, so a mutual respect was engendered. They wouldn't collaborate
again until *Raging Bull* (1980), when Robbie did some of the scoring.
But a connection had developed between them, a common vision or
link, that even survived Robertson's acting in the 1980 Jodie Foster–
Gary Busey film *Carny,* about carnival life (Kael said of him, "his
twitches and druggy Garboesque expressions don't connect with anything").

This hardly bothered Robertson. He gravitated toward the mean and
twisted. In 1982, at Scorsese's urging, he produced the score for another
irreverent, black-humored film, *The King of Comedy* (starring Jerry
Lewis). Drawing on the talents of such diverse artists as Rickie Lee
Jones, B. B. King, Van Morrison, Ray Charles, and the Pretenders,
Robertson won raves for his musical statement. Subsequently turning
those plaudits into a nonexclusive, high-six-figure deal with EMI for
sound tracks. He's been working on several projects since 1984. Fore-

most among these are more films with Scorsese, whose violent, haunting themes best echo Robertson's world view.

"Scorsese's as good as it gets," says Robertson triumphantly. "He's my best friend. It's hard to get excited about working with anyone else. His movies are about passion, obsession, people who just rip through life with their guts . . . who do it until it explodes. He's a little stick of dynamite, and he's sometimes hard to deal with, but he's so vivid, so intense, and alive. He uses the heart and gut stuff. He takes chances, going against what's fashionable, and that's what I want to do . . . I've got to prove that I can do this. Hollywood's a rough game. Maybe that makes him a tough guy, delving into the underside of life; whores, gang members, drug dealers. But who should I like? Disney characters, little guys in space suits?"

In Hollywood parlance, Robertson is certainly a comer. He's gotten off the proverbial bus of endless touring and record promotion, to become one of the celluloid jungle's most promising creative forces. Unlike most of the Band members (Helm has been acting in films such as *Coal Miner's Daughter,* and *The Right Stuff),* he hasn't been wedged into one career mold. He's evolved, dared to be different, grappled with challenges. Even if it's meant periods of inactivity, self-reassessment, or flirtations with disaster.

As a result of this dicey, high-powered life-style, there's a tough-guy Hemingwayesque edge to him. He evokes images of De Niro, puffing on a long, illegally obtained Havana cigar, in between swigs of a double extra-dry martini. Gangster style, his voice is gravelly. It has a raw, demanding quality, that suits his rugged, pock-marked face.

Now a devotee of boxing matches, and the "forbidden passions of *Police Gazette* style writing," Robertson has made a sharp U-turn from his days with Billy Blue, the ukelele teacher who gave him his first music lessons. The boys in the Pink Robots wouldn't know him either, nor would the Hawk. And what about the Band's Garth Hudson, Rick Danko, and Richard Manuel? While their joint endeavors had a fiery American Gothic ring, they too would find Robbie transformed.

In the mid-1950s, Robertson was just like any other kid, entranced with the early stirrings of rock 'n' roll. After leaving Billy Blue because "I didn't want to hold any instrument on my lap," Robbie became "obsessed" with the manic, a wop-a-bam-boom sounds of Little Richard. Most of his friends were shaking to Everly Brothers tunes, but, as he laughingly remembers, "even as a twelve-year-old I didn't want to play cowboy music. I didn't think they [the Everlys] were shit compared to Chuck Berry, Jerry Lee Lewis, Bo Diddley, Elvis. They were playing real rock 'n' roll; their stuff was happening; it was like this disease taking over the world. I started to comb my hair like Little Richard. I'd get home from John Wayne movies, and I'd immediately close the door, and stay in front of the mirror."

Before turning thirteen, Robertson started his own band, Robbie and the Robots. Wearing pink-and-black futuristic outfits, they played the Sweet Sixteen circuit, and quickly realized that the music offered fringe benefits. "There was a definite connection between playing rock 'n' roll and girls. At my age I wasn't thinking about getting lots of women. I wasn't at that lust stage. But I was working up to it."

Encouraged by his mother, he spent most of his early teens writing songs. Still "overwhelmed" by rock, he met Ronnie Hawkins at a school dance, and was soon mingling with the Hawk's friends, most notably, Carl Perkins and Conway Twitty.

"I wasn't old enough to get in those clubs, but I hung around, until Ronnie took an interest in me," says Robertson, perched on a stool in a Los Angeles recording studio. No longer the awestruck kid who was bedazzled by these above-named greats, he calmly continues, "Hawkins introduced me to James Brown and Bo Diddley, and after a while, when I was sixteen, I started to play with him" (along with Helm, Hudson, Danko, and Manuel, who were already in the Hawks).

"Ronnie was very good at pushing you to seek out your potential. He made you work very hard. Yeah, he was very good at giving you a street education . . . What he was doing at that time particularly appealed to me because it was very violent rock 'n' roll. That was exciting, and he was almost like an ape up there. He's got a hunched back, not in a sense that it was grotesque or anything, but he'd bend over, and growl, and they played so fast, and explosive. It would get so quiet, and then BOOM! Was he a character, very funny, innovative, and very Southern, very crude. Geez, was he crude. It was almost embarrassing to me."

On the road constantly with Hawkins, even at the tender age of sixteen, Robertson needed a friend, someone he could talk to about music, and his missing home. "Levon and I got to be very close, since we wound up running the show, musically. We also got to be good together . . . so our dreams went from the ordinary to *flash stardom.* Then all of this became boring in our minds. We became kind of sophisticated. We wanted to be really good, we wanted to play really exceptional music.

"So the first thing we did was to leave Ronnie Hawkins [in 1963, after a three-year association]. That was a very emotional thing, because he was like a father figure, and we were all still kids. It was painful to him, and to us, but we had grown musically, to a point where the stuff that we produced was much more fun to do, and more satisfying. Doing his songs became more like a novelty. We just surpassed that musically . . . and his evolvement just stopped. I still see him whenever I go to Toronto for a film festival, but, back then, he got this musical inferiority complex. Unfortunately, Ronnie felt everyone was better than him."

Looking weary and glum, Robertson slides off his chair to get a cigar. That cache of dark panatelas brings a brief, faint smile to his face. But talking about Levon and the mid-sixties still seems to disturb him. His responses are less assured, more clipped; while some questions go totally unanswered, as he pretends not to hear them.

He and Helm were once "brothers." When Levon and the Hawks started to do their own thing in small Ozark Mountain honky-tonks, there was a camaraderie born of mutual suffering. They went through the mill together, playing a funky brand of rock 'n' roll, to rowdy, beer-guzzling backwoodsmen. So now that their relationship has soured, Robertson speaks reluctantly about the past, in a pained, faltering voice.

"Eventually we made it to Jersey [1965], near Atlantic City, a summer resort. We played there for a couple of months, and while we were there, Bob Dylan got in touch with us . . . Supposedly, he heard of us through John Hammond, Jr. But I don't know. We got this phone call . . . Some time before that I'd been in New York, and Hammond said, 'Do you want to go and hear Bob Dylan, he's recording at this studio? Do you want to go by and hear what he's doing?' So we went by, and he was recording 'Like a Rolling Stone.' It wasn't much of a meeting.

"But this next time I went to meet him we sat and we talked about music. And then we played music, just him and me, with two guitars. And he sang, and I played, and he said 'This is wonderful, let's do it.' He said 'I'd like you to play with these other guys that I've got.' So I said, 'No, I don't do that, I'm working with some people. I'm not interested in leaving this band, we've been working together for a while.'

"Well, he wanted me to do these two jobs with him, one at Forest Hills, and one at the Hollywood Bowl. I said okay, but I didn't think much of the drummer he had, so I told him Levon was better . . . We played those two jobs, and I said 'See ya around.' It was kind of exciting [playing with him], but it was also ridiculous. It [referring to the Forest

Hills concert, where Dylan was booed by folk purists for using an electric guitar] had nothing to do with music, and that was frustrating too. The whole thing was just screaming, and throwing things at him . . . he didn't really know what he was doing, so it was kind of *rang-ngy* and *chang-ngy* (he made these sounds through pursed lips), and you couldn't hear very good. We were just hacking away at the music, I don't blame them for booing. We weren't very good. So we just said goodbye."

Dylan stubbornly refused to be put off. Visiting the Hawks in Toronto a few months later, he offered the group a slot on his world tour. The Hawks accepted; not because of any desire for greater fame—that impulse never motivated them—but because they reasoned that backing him up was far better than another stint in the boondocks.

To Robbie's chagrin, however, Dylan continued to provoke controversy. And instead of fame, there were only bananas, and more bananas.

"We took the guy [Dylan] seriously; he was intent on doing something good," says Robertson, savoring the first puff of his cigar. "It was just hard to figure out how to present the songs, how to settle him down. Unfortunately, he didn't have the patience to learn the songs; we had to do that while we were on tour. So we discovered the strangest way in the world of making a living. We'd pack up our equipment, go to a place, set up, play, they'd boo and throw things at us; we would tear down our equipment, go to the next place, they'd boo, and we did it all over the world, from Australia to Stockholm. And we'd say, what a weird way to make a buck! We'd go out there, people were throwing bananas at you, booing . . . and we acted like they're wrong and we're right."

At this point, a hint of enthusiasm creeps into Robertson's voice, as he continues with spirit, "After a while, though, the banana throwing stopped. Not on this tour, but on this other tour years later, no one booed, nothing . . . So it was interesting, the world changed, we didn't change, people came around . . . all of a sudden people's ears became keen to our sounds.

"But when we were playing, and people were booing, when we'd finish, we'd go back to the hotel, and listen to a tape of ourselves . . . it sounded quite good, very powerful and dynamic, the songs sounded strong, and the arrangements were really starting to become tight and good. There was a spontaneous quality to them. We got very proud of what we were doing.

"Dylan must have felt that way too. For everyone around him was saying, 'Get rid of these fucking guys, they're killing your career. Get rid of them.' And he wouldn't do it. I'll always commend him for that. He just laughed off the booing, as he said 'Fuck 'em, they don't understand,' or something like that . . . We were going to do another tour, but that's when he had his motorcycle accident."

So began their Big Pink sojourn. Or the adventure that would catapult them into the forefront of 1960s music.

The Hawks played nursemaid to Dylan. They rented a large pink clapboard house close to him on the outskirts of Woodstock, New York, dubbed the place Big Pink, and as soon as Dylan recovered from his injuries (a broken neck, facial cuts, a concussion, and partial paralysis), began work on *The Basement Tapes.* Some of Dylan's most critically acclaimed pieces were produced during those easygoing recording sessions, songs like "This Wheel's on Fire," and "Tears of Rage." But Robbie and the boys weren't thinking of making history. They were too busy having a good time.

"Big Pink was like a clubhouse. Everybody would go there every day like the Bowery Boys and we'd shoot pool, talk dirty, and write songs," chuckles Robertson. And then Dylan started hanging out with us, he played pool, talked dirty, and wrote songs . . . You have to remember, there weren't too many people living up there at the time. It was only a little art colony, with a few writers, so we just hung out, it was an ideal existence."

But contrary to most reports, Robertson emphatically insists, "We were never Bob Dylan's band. We were just this group that played with Dylan on a tour. That's all we ever did with him, then. People thought that there was a whole thing going on, we only cut a few singles with him, obscure singles. And I played on *Blonde on Blonde,* that was the extent of it. The band never had a real involvement with him except this bizarre tour."

Though the group used a Dylan painting on the jacket of *Music from Big Pink,* this debut album (1968) was an assertion of their independence on several levels. Unlike the era's other rock stars, members of the newly named Band didn't wear flashy psychedelic clothes, tour, or seek wider popularity. Content to remain anonymous, even if that made them seem mystical and mysterious, they "got past the goofiness of wanting to be celebrities." As Robbie proudly announces, they styled themselves after fifties rebels—and rebelled against the "counterculture revolutionaries."

"At the time it was burn the flag, stab your mother and father (he starts laughing), wear goofy clothes, all those things were happening but we loved our mothers and fathers. After the Ronnie Hawkins thing, everybody was listening to a very corny kind of music. It was the Frankie Avalon period . . . while we were playing obscure music, musical music. We were never interested in trends. Our launching period was that time of fifties discontent. We were all really vulnerable to oppression—that's part of it.

"And also we didn't like psychedelic things. I wasn't interested in wearing paisley pants [chortling again]. We wore suits and ties [in their leather vests, western derbies, and thick mustaches, they resembled the Jesse James gang]. When we played with Bob Dylan, we wore jackets and ties. He hated it. He kept telling us, 'You guys gotta do something with your clothes.' "

While they continued to live like hermits in Woodstock, *Music from Big Pink* became an underground cult favorite. It was hip to have a copy. And when their second release, *The Band* (1969) received even more favorable reviews, the pressure mounted for them to go public. Rock promoter Bill Graham, pleading "the case for the people," visited the Band in Woodstock, and persuaded them to do two concerts, San Francisco's Winterland and the Fillmore East. They then turned up at the Isle of Wight festival with Dylan, and in their own backyard for that epochal weekend of "Peace and Music."

"Woodstock was an invasion of our privacy," says Robertson, his eyes narrowing into a look of disgust. "They gave us this whole rigmarole about, you know, 'you're this and that . . .' They wanted us to close, to be the last group that played, and Jimi Hendrix flipped out. He said, 'No, you promised that I'd close.' He made a big pissing and moaning thing about it. I didn't give a shit, because it looked to me like that would mean we'd go on at four or five o'clock in the morning. So we played at eight o'clock at night, when there were five hundred thousand people there. And by the time he played three hundred and fifty thousand had left.

"Woodstock wasn't very good. It was hard to play for that many people. The people were there for the people, the music thing was really secondary. That's why we didn't participate in the movie, or the record. It didn't seem like our calling, we didn't feel like this is where we belonged. We felt 'This is a happening of another kind, it's not a musical happening. It's a thing of people taking acid, getting naked, and getting muddy. What does that have to do with us? Nothing.' We wanted to do a film, we just wanted to do it properly, by ourselves."

The Last Waltz is a testament to that idealism. It has a joyousness, a clarity of vision that celebrates the nobler qualities of rock. But in a sense, the film is deceiving. For it's only a parting tribute to the Band. As would be expected, it doesn't focus on the turmoil and ugliness that destroyed their family spirit.

According to Robertson, a few members of the Band went stir crazy in the early seventies. Together for several years, in the hermetic environs of Woodstock, they needed some sort of outlet, a release from the pressures of success. And, when finding these pleasures, they started to act like the rock celebs they once had scorned.

"Everything started out very creative, real family-oriented," recalls Robertson, "but then things went berserk. Though we had been together for so long, success didn't come smoothly, comfortably. Different guys went crazy. I don't know what happened, it's so difficult to understand. It was self-destructive things. It was drugs, or just a way of life, or driving fast . . . It's a fever . . . a riding of things to the limit . . .

"Maybe people think that they don't really deserve success, that they don't believe in it. So they start fucking with it, start sticking their hand in the fire.

"Yeah . . . yeah," he responds, when asked if he played similarly dangerous games. But as he adds, soberly, "It was different for me, I had already started a family [Robertson now has two teenaged daughters and a ten-year-old son]. I had a commitment that prevented me from leaping off, I had an anchor. If I hadn't had a family I could've gotten as goofy as anybody. My family was like a protective device. The other guys' lives were just more available. I had to go home to change diapers."

Robertson roars with delight. And now that his daughters are beginning to think of their own careers, he talks animatedly about them, and how "they've grown so fast."

But these memories of the Band still upset him. In a moment, he ruefully continues in a voice that's grown strained and hoarse, "The other guys' availability was definitely an alienating factor. It tested our relationship and it was scary for everyone, since we were concerned about one another. So that place of leisure turned into a snake pit, because everyone was bored. Now what? Now we're successful, now we're making money. But so what? I was afraid of someone dying; they were getting into car wrecks—I mean all the time. Rick [Danko] broke his neck very very bad. Richard [Manuel] had several severe accidents. It wasn't unusual to get up in the morning and say 'Richard's out here, upside down, in a car somewhere.' Everything played a part, drugs, drinking, anything that was taboo."

So Big Pink, the house that was synonymous with sounds of a rural, more innocent America, turned into a nightmare for Robertson. Fearing the place would destroy them all, Robbie moved to Malibu, believing "it was time to do something creative for myself. I had never hung out with an ocean before."

He still communicated with the other band members, often telling them the sun-kissed beach locale was "paradise." They subsequently joined him there in 1973, in another Big Pink-styled retreat, called Shangrila.

The magic returned for a while. Once Dylan relocated there, they collaborated on *Planet Waves,* and also toured together again. Now the Band was welcomed into the musical establishment. They were no longer seen as outlaws for eschewing psychedelia—or as the purveyors of what Robbie calls, "Judas music."

"Suddenly, everybody accepted us. They acted like the whole thing from before, which was just taboo, was always accepted [Robertson does admit that *Stage Fright,* the Band's third album, reflected the Woodstock horror period]. Everything was now terrific."

That tour with Dylan was captured on *Before the Flood,* which Robertson produced. He also wrote all the songs for the Band's *Northern Lights–Southern Cross* (1975). This latter work was generally well received, as it broke new ground with Garth Hudson's organ and synthesizer instrumentals. Robertson also won praise for such tunes as "Ophelia," "Hobo Jungle," "Arcadian Driftwood," and "Forbidden Fruit."

But the joys of recognition were tempered, as the old problems continued to surface. Life at Shangrila was anything but peaceful. And Robertson grew progressively disenchanted.

"It was very annoying to me that some of the guys were still having difficulties keeping their head on straight," bristles Robertson, the passage of time having done nothing to soothe his irritation. "Just dealing with it all the time was a pain. We couldn't be consistent, not to the point that it [the band's creativity] was dependable. So that's when I drifted off. I wanted to do something more positive.

"Neil Diamond talked me into doing this album *[Beautiful Noise* in 1976] with him. I didn't understand the idea at first, but he's a very nice person, and he genuinely wanted to do a good album. It was kind of strange [their collaborating], everyone thinks he has a very pretentious style, and that it's kind of square. He wanted that album, though, because he had never gotten a good review in his life, probably. And that's why he bought it, he wanted a good album, and he got it. The album came out, it's the biggest studio album he ever did, and he got rave reviews. We did some very musical things, we took some chances, and now they're talking of making a movie out of *Beautiful Noise.*"

The Band was still Robertson's first love. But since he wanted the group to live up to his image, to his expectations, he was bound to be disappointed. "It *was* heartbreaking, to see people you care about abusing themselves. I'm no saint, I wasn't the goody-goody in the thing. But I could never take it to the degree that other people could . . . Levon kept telling me, 'Don't worry about it, I'll be fine, I won't let you down.' He always did a great job, it's just that our ideals and philosophies strayed. I just became more productive. And, eventually, I saw there was nothing I could really do about it, or wanted to. You don't want to run someone's life . . . these were my friends, my brothers . . . the best thing you can do is to walk away. I wasn't Mr. Wonderful, not at all. I just didn't want to play this game."

None of the other band members realized Robbie was so unhappy. When he talked about doing *The Last Waltz,* they simply thought it was a good idea, that would be followed by other joint ventures. Only later, after the film was finished, did they get a clearer message from Robertson. He had had it with "ptomaine burgers." He wanted out. Totally.

Admitting it was initially difficult to end a fifteen-year relationship, Robertson explains how the confusion arose. "Well, I told everybody I wasn't interested in going on the road anymore. I'm off the bus. I told them I was sick of Howard Johnson's in the middle of nowhere, that I had nothing to learn anymore. And everyone said 'Me too, me too.' Everyone really felt that way too. But . . . but we weren't breaking up, we said we'd still record, we'd write, we'd do projects. So everyone agreed; we did the film and the album to go with it.

"It's only later on that I think it sunk in. Everyone said, 'well gee, does this mean that we'll never, ever do this again.' So I said, 'Yes, yes, *this* is what we've been talking about."

"I didn't want to know about anything except finishing the project. Everyone was doing their solo thing, while I had to complete the movie, the triple album. So that brings us up to the stage where we had all the intentions in the world of recording and doing more things, but time went on and people were like, 'Ah, I'm doing this and you know, I have to concentrate on my own songs.' So after that I got involved in movies, I did the music for some films, and wrote a couple of stories that are now being made into movies."

Hollywood marquees didn't light up overnight for Robertson. Like anyone else making a career change in midlife, he had to make certain adjustments and sacrifices. There were disappointments. It took him a couple of years to land a part in *Carny,* and, afterward, he was typecast as a washed-up, drug-crazed rock star. Instead of taking him seriously, directors viewed him as a caricature of a world they didn't really understand. Predictably stung by this treatment, Robbie lost interest in acting. And while he can now jokingly attribute various role rejections to inexperience, the hurt is still evident in his eyes.

"I was offered lots of parts in movies, but I either hated them, or I'd meet with directors and I'd get this feeling that was a nightmare to me. I'd have these dreams where I'd have to dress in a cowboy outfit with fur chaps, a cowboy hat, and a guy would tell me, 'Go over there in the corner, and take your pants down, drop your chaps.' I'd say to myself, 'What's my motivation for this?' and the guy says, 'Just do it.' So I had a big problem just going along with this acting thing. I'm not starving. I'm not a waiter who's hoping the phone will ring. I don't need the money; I don't need the aggravation either. It's a funny job [acting], you sit around and wait until you go crazy. It's like an island that you can't get off."

Robertson didn't even want to do the music for *The King of Comedy.* Disgusted with Hollywood, he wasn't interested in writing movie scores. That is, until he was charmed by Scorsese. Viewing this often-criticized director as a genius, Robbie worked on the film simply to be close to him. He now praises Scorsese for giving him "the freedom to create," adding, albeit immodestly, "Look at what I was able to do [on the soundtrack]! Look at the people I got—all this stuff except the Ray Charles piece was new. There's no other album where there's that kind of conglomeration of artists, and it absolutely works. There's no problem going from B. B. King to the Talking Heads."

Equally excited about the future, Robertson is currently collaborating with Scorsese on two other prospective movies—films that have completely changed his perspective on acting. "Now I'm really doing what I want to do," says the forty-two-year-old Robertson. "I'm working on the first movie that I really want to act in. It's called *Goodbye.* You see, my problem was that I started with Martin Scorsese, so it was hard to get excited with anybody else, and the projects weren't strong enough to excite me. The two things Marty and I are talking about doing together I'd do anytime, anywhere. No problem at all. The other project is *The King Lives,* which is a music-oriented film. I get to invent a whole new kind of music for it."

No wonder Robertson is rarely in contact with the other Band members. In terms of post-seventies achievements, the gulf between them seems to be constantly widening. What could they talk about? While he's experimenting with new musical formulas, they (with the exception of Helm) are still on the roadhouse circuit, playing the same tired songs.

Robertson doesn't gloat over this. Still professing great love for them, he sadly notes, "They don't know what else to do, they need to do it." The "guys" might have been swept away by the roars of the crowd, to the point that they didn't prepare for the future. But not wanting to sound too critical, Robertson squelches these thoughts in midstream, opting instead to talk about himself.

"I've been lucky, I've been able to fulfill some of my dreams. I don't know what my dream is now, I only know I want to do great work. I want to take those chances, evolve, grow. I don't want to play in Milwaukee, at the Country Club, or in New York at the Lone Star. Are you joking? It upsets me just to think about it.

"I made my big statement *[The Last Waltz].* I did the movie, I made a three-record album about it—and if this is only my statement, not theirs, I'll accept that. They're saying, 'Well, that was really his trip, not our trip.' Well, fine. I'll take the best music film that's ever been made, and make it my statement. I don't have any problems with that. None at all. Why should I? What the fuck would *I* learn by playing those clubs again?"

Without answering, Robertson snickers derisively. This laughter is so shrill, so devilish, it echoes through the recording studio, making his listeners shiver. Not because Robertson is mocking the other guys. Or even himself. No, that's not it.

Coupled with a cold, hard stare, this outburst is another "final statement," an emphatic break with the past. Robertson must go on. He can't be trapped by his memories, even if it means playing the tough guy. But that laughter is still haunting. Like *The Last Waltz,* it's a goodbye to the sixties, to the "guys," and to a friendship we all benefited from.

John Sebastian of the Lovin' Spoonful

A Case of Betrayal

The magic was not supposed to end this way, with a drug bust, and with the band members denounced as "police informants." Almost overnight, the Lovin' Spoonful went from cornerstone of the counterculture to the Benedict Arnolds of the music world. Their records were boycotted, the spirit that held them together disintegrated in an ugly spate of acrimony. No wonder their "good time" music stopped. With deportation and countless other lawsuits hanging over them, it wasn't a time to believe in magic.

For a true child of the 1960s, the ever-romantic John Sebastian, this besmirching of the group's reputation was "a shocking, painful fall from grace that made all of us very cynical." He was angry with the other band members: they were arrested for possessing an ounce of marijuana in 1966 and were "conned" into cooperating with the police (Canadian-born lead guitarist Zal Yanovsky was threatened with deportation). But Sebastian's biggest gripe was with the Spoonful's once adoring public. The counterculture, according to him, "just deserted us . . . fans were all too quick to believe the worst." His voice quaking, even though the "bust" occurred over nineteen years ago (1966), Sebastian ruefully adds, "I couldn't believe it, they even lumped me in there as an informer, too."

Sebastian has experienced other hurts since then. Although he made peace with the counterculture in a 1969 Woodstock appearance, he's only had one hit ("Welcome Back" in 1976) since his legendary "Do You Believe in Magic?" and "Summer in the City." Now a marginal figure on the rock circuit, he's forced to appear in small clubs and theaters as an opening act—and has even been hooted off stage on occasion. Despite these setbacks, Sebastian has not despaired, or become cynical. Ever faithful to the spirit of the 1960s, he's still the gentle idealist, dedicated to finding "universals" that will promote another "greening" of America.

In the mid-sixties, Sebastian's dreamy, upbeat music mirrored the mood of America. There was an optimism in the air, a sense of Manifest Destiny that was largely generated by our astronauts walking in space. Consequently, we felt we could overcome all obstacles; heal the divisions in our society; and build a more perfect democracy. Intent on this Great Society, the LBJ White House fueled our hopes with a raft of civil rights laws, as well as Medicare, tax reforms, and new spending for education. Since this "social revolution" transfixed us, we didn't pay much attention to the ever widening war in Southeast Asia. Those battles were too far off, too ambiguous to throw the nation into convulsions. This was a time for faith, unfettered expectations, and magical mystery tours. So young people put flowers in their hair, tuned in to groups like the Mamas and the Papas, and marched to the strains of "good time" music.

But before "California Dreamin' " awakened our wanderlust, Sebastian stayed close to home and went through his folk period. Raised in Greenwich Village, he was influenced by his father, a noted classical harmonica player, to study the guitar. When his fingers were still small, he was "intrigued" by a musician's globetrotting life-style, and he began to hang out in Washington Square with other budding folk stars such as Bob Dylan. These contacts led to appearances at hoots, as he wound up playing for tourists "making the artsy Village scene," in clubs like Gerdes Folk City and the Café Bizarre.

"I had a terrific advantage, I could go to get the tortellini for my mother, and I'd run into all sorts of great music people," exclaims Sebastian, standing by a refrigerator in his Woodstock, New York, home. Surrounded by two hungry, yelping dogs, Boza and Ralph, he's wearing a faded T-shirt and patched jeans. Characteristically, his long sandy-hair grazes the wire rims of his glasses. Looking much as he did in the 1960s, the forty-two-year-old Sebastian continues, "I was allowed to participate in a scene about two years before any of my contemporaries. The mere fact of going to the Village horrified most parents [raising his voice] 'My son, the college student, is now going to the seedy Village.' Well, in my situation, there was no fear involved. I started working with Tim Hardin, John Hammond, running around with Lightnin' Hopkins, carrying his guitar, playing with Mississippi John Hurt—all at a time when most people my age were not allowed to go downtown.

"I was there every night, five hours a night, walking those streets, walking into every single club and basket house that existed because I knew where everyone was, and that was crucial. I had the advantage of familiarity on that street. I knew which streets to go to, which clubs were just for tourists, which were reserved for jazz—there was no point in my going into *them* . . . unless, of course, John Hurt was playing there. It was such an ecstatic time! No doubt about it, I felt blessed."

Putting aside his romantic notions of being a New England sailmaker ("The paint made me swell up like a balloon"), Sebastian parlayed that "advantage" into meeting Cass Elliot. In late 1963, the celebrated "Earth Mother" was playing with a group called the Mugwumps, a folk quartet that included Zal Yanovsky. John became pals with Cass ("There was no avoiding it, you had to love her"), and eventually was an item on the street with Zal.

John was cool in those days. He wore granny glasses and long sideburns; a variety of hucksters wanted to manage him. Yet all of these offers were rejected; John didn't feel it was time to make his move.

"I was waiting for a little more electric music to penetrate the scene," explains Sebastian matter-of-factly, as he moves into the living room to sit in front of a roaring fireplace. "At fourteen, fifteen, I'd been in doo-wop groups with an electric guitar. So I was already very comfortable with electricity at a time when my contemporaries were saying, 'Oh, that's all Frankie Avalon, Fabian, and we don't want to have anything to do with that . . .' I already understood that this music was going to go into a mulching phase, it was going to ferment and exchange juices.

"I didn't want to get in now, when it was Dickie Dee time, it was just not the right moment. I upped my ante by turning these offers down. I said to myself, 'Hey, I've gotten better since being offered something. So, that means they're going to have to pay me more the next time. So, what if I wait even longer?' "

He grins, content that the right decision was made.

"The Beatles were my signal to jump in. Their success showed that America was ready to accept a four-piece electric band that was self-contained, and did its own composing. Then it was time for Zally and me to use the 'drum system.' The word went out, people knew that there were these two guys wandering around looking for a bass player and a drummer. We went to see this group called the Sellouts, and while they had this unbelievable tape-delay system, they weren't right . . . We wanted to do a strange potpourri of electrified jug band music, that was our point of departure. And we learned from the guitarist in the Sellouts that he had a brother who played bass, and was a bit whacko.

"We said, 'Hey, you gotta have this guy [Steve Boone] come visit us.' So later on we staged a little rehearsal, and interviewed him. But, in fact, when he walked in, Zally and I were standing at the far end of the hall, and we saw this guy—real tall, red hair, and just bones. He looked like Mr. America, he was so frontier American, so Zally and I knew right away that he was our guy."

After the newly christened Spoonful found a drummer (Joe Butler) who was blowing the walls out, they were ready for the big time. In early 1965, this meant a three-month stint at the Café Bizarre, which paid them thirty-five dollars a week each, and all the tuna-fish sandwiches they could eat. During that engagement, Joe and Steve lived in the nearby Albert Hotel, in a cubbyhole-sized room that was also used to store the group's equipment. Before they could leave the room in the morning, Zal and John would have to drag the stuff into the hall. The entire group practiced at the Hotel Albert—in the basement alongside the cockroaches.

This dues paying netted them a gig at the Nite Owl café, where they were spotted by Artie Ripp of Kama Sutra Records. In a few weeks, after turning down offers from several other execs (including Phil Spector), the Spoonful had their first recording deal.

Recalling these innocent days with a boyish smile and an earnest, unyielding seriousness that apparently comes from studying at a Catholic high school, Sebastian says, "I knew right from the start that it was going to happen. I knew we were going to make it. I felt it in my gut. Maybe it was youthful enthusiasm, but we knew we had something other groups didn't have. Even in the face of the publicity that some of the early West Coast groups were getting, we knew we were okay. They weren't doing original material and they hadn't paid the dues we had. Really, our only fear in those days was the Rascals, because they were the only other group that had been together a long time, and had, you know, serious musicians. I mean Felix and Dino were both killers. Dino

Danelli to this day is a fabulous drummer, and Felix Cavaliere could do stuff with an organ . . .

"This isn't hindsight. I said the same thing when 'Do You Believe in Magic?' came out [1965]. The wild thing is that I hadn't even begun to compose yet. We just knew, or felt, that we were doing something distinctly American, that it was original, and that it was motivated by an entire life-style that we had been participating in. I'm sure that everybody from the young romantics to the punkers have the same story to tell. If you have something to offer, that distinct and strong, you realize very quickly how much of the industry is based on hype, and that all you have to do is outlast some of that—and you'll have your time in the sun.

"Look, we felt that we were ahead of our time. That's why we didn't embrace the growing hippie mentality; we had already been through that freedom thing at fifteen. So when we went to California, and saw all of these people that were blissed out, I mean, it was only more encouraging to us. We said, 'Jesus, these people are completely out of it, these people are pussycats, we are from New York. This drummer from the Byrds came up to us and said, 'Gee, you guys are so great, I wish I was with your band.' Well, we were shocked! In New York, if you belonged to a band there was real chauvinism; you'd never cop to admiring another group. If this was not true of the heaviest band out there, with all this publicity, let us out there. So we felt ahead of it. We weren't worried. We knew we'd make it. We were so confident that Zal would even parody the hippie sixties, the everything-is-groovy mentality. He was hilarious on the subject."

Despite this feeling of uniqueness, the Spoonful's fate was inextricably tied to the social currents around them. They became synonymous with the rising flower-power phenomenon as a result of their ebullient, fresh-sounding music. And their disintegration can be seen as a metaphor for a more complicated, high-pitched epoch, in which alienation and angry protests predominated. Basically, rhapsodic melodies about goofing off and youthful sexual stirrings didn't make sense in the face of Charles Manson's horrors and the violent excesses of the Chicago police.

But up until the drug bust, and the subsequent internal bickering, the nation played to the beat of the Spoonful, as evidenced by their stream of tuneful classics, "Summer in the City," "Daydream," "You Didn't Have to Be So Nice," and "Darlin' Be Home Soon." The group dominated the charts in 1966. Innocent and pure, they were a rock version of a teddy bear. We cuddled up to them, lulled by their soft refrains. And, while they seemed to be mocking hippiedom by dressing in folky jug-band vests, ridiculous hats, and long, flowing raccoon coats, no one was offended. Their music was so sweet, we lapped it up.

"This was our time to exult, that time in the sun we're all looking for," says Sebastian, a hint of melancholy in his voice. "It was thoroughly enjoyable, but an artist always wonders, 'What's next, what's next, what's next.' Really, there's very little time to sit back and enjoy it all, especially during that fast surge. I was only twenty, twenty-one. I thought it would go on forever. It was very hard to imagine a fall from grace [he laughs sardonically]. But I was, nonetheless, conscious of the fact that I did not dare sit back, and pat myself on the back.

"I still get a rush from 'Do You Believe'. It was only the fifth or sixth song I'd ever written. It came in a flash, and it was the first tune to give me any degree of recognition. There was a joyousness in it, and while I wasn't an active participant in the full-out hippie mentality, success allowed me to subscribe to the theory that 'everything is possible now.' Particularly because in my own life everything *was* becoming possible. Yes, it was a very optimistic period. You have to remember, we wrote 'Do You Believe' in a two-bit nightclub. We were playing it in a topless club in San Francisco, and we had to break up our set and play for Topless Maria. That's when everything started to break. Now we wanted to blow all these protest singers off the map. Even though people lumped us with them, it annoyed us no end. We were just out for a good time."

Since they had this aura of innocence and youthful purity, their finking to the police was all the more shocking. Cops were then the Enemy, the pigs the counterculture lustfully scorned. No self-respecting hippie would talk, much less do business with the men in blue. So when Zal and Steve ratted on a San Francisco drug dealer, even though it was done under coercion, the Spoonful's fans felt betrayed. Sebastian and Company had been so revered, so emblematic of a free-spiritedness, they seemed to be violating the trust that had sprung up. And accordingly, these transgressions demanded swift and severe punishment. Their former admirers wouldn't have accepted anything less.

"My worst suspicions were proven right; that event cut a minimum of three to four, maybe five to six, years off the group," rues Sebastian, after initially refusing to speak about the incident. "If this hadn't happened, we could've functioned well into the seventies . . . I was absolutely enraged. It was a typical Zally-and-Steven-go-off-for-a-good-time type of evening that went completely wrong. I was mad at them, but I didn't have any quick, easy answers. Because, in the course of one evening, they went from being members of the hottest group worth talking about, except maybe for the Beatles, to being threatened with that group's demise—that's all in an hour. They'd been taken out of their car, the police sat them down, and in one hour [he angrily snaps his fingers] they had to make a decision: would they cooperate with the police?

"The cops said, 'Look, you have to name the guy you bought the pot from, and from him, we'll go to Mr. Big. If you don't, Zally, you're out of the country, you're immediately deported, you can't come back to the United States.' So they're faced with the end of the band, and this is where you do anything for the guys in the band. This was very much a part of our togetherness—during the course of the Spoonful each guy had an opportunity or felt a necessity to do something for the guys in the band. We had to pull Joe away from some girl he had gotten pregnant. We had to get me married at one point to keep me out of the Army. So here was the Big One, either you tell me where you got this pot or you get deported."

Sebastian's voice is barely audible now, while his face suddenly looks tired. Although these events have been replayed in his mind countless times, talking about them never gets any easier.

"Well, given the choice, they had to tell. The rock press got hold of it, and, almost overnight, I was an informer too. There were all kinds of problems. Zally not only felt betrayed by the police but also by this counterculture that had supported him as an icon. They were so quick to believe he was an informer, rather than look at the thing in a compassionate way. He had no choice.

"I felt betrayed too. Not that I was concerned about our future, it just wasn't a big factor at that point. What I was much more aware of was how this was affecting Zal. The uproar affected our interaction, our spontaneity, we were simply different people after this happened. I didn't know what was going to happen to us. Zal became very difficult, very cynical about what we were doing, and, eventually, I went to him and said, 'Zally, you've been trying to break the group up, it's not going to work, we're kicking you out.' He was dumbfounded, but I had to do it. He was ruining what the Spoonful had done; our chemistry was disintegrating."

Staring into the fireplace, with that mournful look still engraved on his face, Sebastian mutters, "Talking to Zally that way was the hardest thing I ever had to do in my life. I always felt I made the right decision, and even Zal agrees that I did. But I wasn't quite prepared to play the heavy, to do the Michael Corleone thing.

"Eventually I put a lot of energy into overcoming this very unhappy turn of events. During the course of the last seven years, I've seen Zally at least every six months, and most of those visits were spent yelling at each other, sort of ventilating. I feel pretty good that we've recaptured our friendship. It had to be done; we didn't get together for nearly ten years, but now I'm very glad we're communicating. There's a genuine warmth between us."

In 1967, however, Sebastian was only interested in saving the group. He replaced Zal with Jerry Yester, the onetime producer of the Association, and the Spoonful were able to chart a few more hits. But there was no more magic. As the bust got more publicity, the public began to boycott the Spoonful. Seemingly blacklisted from the choicer venues, the band members quarreled bitterly among themselves. And as their love for each other went sour, Sebastian sadly realized that the group's dynamic had totally changed. Only paychecks were important now, so instead of living out a lie, he split—and essentially said goodbye to the sixties.

Intent on a total break, he then divorced his wife, and rebelliously moved out of his Long Island house for a tent in "Chicken Flats," California, outside Burbank. For a while Sebastian was "quite happy," living next to a chicken coop with a 160-pound dog named Bear. "I felt perfectly capable and content." But, as he soon discovered, there was one aspect of his life that defied simplification. Contractually tied to MGM Records, he was a veritable prisoner of the past—they wanted Spoonful albums, not John Sebastian solos.

He tried to break the impasse by signing with Reprise, but that only complicated matters further. A protracted legal dispute with both companies ensued, and the skirmishing delayed the release of his new album, *John B. Sebastian* (recorded with David Crosby, Stephen Stills, and Graham Nash), for over a year.

Amid these uncertainties, Sebastian made his now-legendary appearance at Woodstock. Invited there as a guest, he played around backstage, getting stoned on a triple dose of acid. So when the promoters unexpectedly asked him to perform, Sebastian admittedly got caught with his "pants down." Instead of focusing on the music, he delivered a flowery sermon, extolling the crowd and the joyousness of the event. It was an embarrassing display, an overemotional paean to the sixties that he still regrets.

"It's very ironic to me that *this* was the highest visibility thing I ever did, and that I'd wind up looking like a hippie-dippy. I'm very sorry about that. I had no idea I'd be performing; if I had, I just wouldn't have gotten so smashed."

Woodstock also signaled the end of a more universal innocence. Rock suddenly became a commercial enterprise, the music that was "co-opted," in Sebastian's view, "to launch a million natural yogurt companies."

Recognizing that the advent of the Alice Cooper Era would make his hippie-mellow music passé, Sebastian tried to fend off the seventies with cocaine. Frustrated by the heavy-metal sound and his sudden loss of popularity, he did a year's worth of coke, believing this would lead to new inspiration. After leaving "Chicken Flats," and marrying his present wife, Catherine, in 1971, he renounced the drug. The early seventies were a chaotic period of "creative dearth" for Sebastian, except for having a son. "I immersed myself in the joys of being a parent." He was constantly moving around from one Californian locale to another ("From 1970 to 1975, selling houses gave me a better income than my music"), and he couldn't find a niche in the business. "The West Coast recording industry was going strictly Alice Cooper," Sebastian recalls. "They had no use for me."

Not until "Welcome Back," the 1975 single that made Sebastian a star again. It propelled him onto the charts after an eight-year absence, and was soon adopted as the theme song for the TV comedy "Welcome Back, Kotter." Coming at a most opportune time, these successes quieted some of Sebastian's financial worries, and enabled him to buy his rambling Woodstock house.

"Reprise had just about written me off, when they called and said I had a monster hit," explains Sebastian. "They were damn near ready to let me out of the last record I owed them, just to get me out of their hair. Now, they had the second biggest single of that year on their hands, and they didn't eat crow gracefully either. They simply took the money that came from the single and put no money into publicizing the accompanying album. While the song was very lucrative for me, my future was far from secure. I had a son now, and was trying very hard to expand my horizons.

"I was trying to interest people in a casual musical talk show. I did a lot of work with this Canadian animation firm. In that time period I had a couple of children's TV shows that asked me for music. I was trying to write for film, and also had an opportunity to write for a prospective Broadway musical, *Charlotte's Web*. That project looked dead for several years, but recently I've been dealing with a publishing company that wants to release this as a children's musical for churches and schools."

Lamentably, most of these endeavors haven't borne fruit. While Sebastian has done a few movie scores with Robin Williams, he's still struggling for wider acceptance in the entertainment community. This often means working on "cheapo, cheapo" films, since Sebastian isn't a high-priced headliner anymore. "I'm viewed in some quarters as an old, irrelevant rock star," he concedes. "But I'm proving myself again. Gradually I'm building up my credentials." It's disturbing to hear him talk this way, but that's the reality of his life. To support his family, he opens for more current pop idols—and must silently tolerate other indignities.

The worst of these humiliations occurred in 1983, when Sebastian opened for Rodney Dangerfield at Radio City Music Hall. Appearing after the promoters failed to put his name on the marquee, Sebastian was immediately greeted with an unrelenting chant of "get off the stage." He tried to pacify the crowd with witticisms. But the booing continued, and he was forced to abbreviate his act.

Time has softened the sting of that incident, as Sebastian is able to quip, "I had fun just surviving the show." Since he speaks easily, in a dry, emotionless voice, it's impossible to tell if there's any lingering hurt. Should we believe him when he says, "These types of audiences strengthen you; there's a knack in turning them around"? Or is this calm symptomatic of deeper wounds? The overheated sixties left him— and many of us—bruised and battered. So, perhaps stoicism is his only defense against the chilling winds of the eighties.

Whatever is going on in his head, Sebastian is not about to quit his "concertizing." He can't. He still has something to prove.

"I want people to know that the stoned-out guy that they saw in the movie in Woodstock was an item of that period, and not necessarily a continuum in my life," says Sebastian. "I was a part of that era there, but if you go see Sebastian now, you're not going to see the performance that you saw on the film. He's grown."

After throwing a few logs into the fire, Sebastian addresses the equally emotional issue of being an opening act.

"It doesn't make me ecstatic; I can't take my clothes off and run naked with joy. But I'm working. Lightnin' Hopkins, a blues legend, was opening for Valentine Pringle when I was working for Val. I have to take the benefits of that information as well as the sadness. I'm a musician who's going to do this till I drop, and I'll do it however I can do it.

"It's not a constant battle. Sure I'm frustrated that so many contemporaries of mine, even those with fewer contributions, have managed to keep their visibility a little higher. But I have an awful lot of things that outweigh the approval, the rather fleeting approval, that comes from success in the world of pop music. I don't think, even at the height of popularity, that I ever made the mistake of thinking that this was the end-all, be-all achievement that I might have."

Mentioning his thirteen-year-old son, Ben, as the prime example of these priorities, Sebastian continues, "He's rolling right along. That's far more satisfying to me than my music. I can look around at my contemporaries, and I don't see them having as much fun with their kids as I do."

Wanting to be there for Ben, Sebastian has spurned the temptation to go back onto the road with a reformed Spoonful. Already away from home a third of the year, he fears a reunion would keep him traveling for more extended periods.

And while these enticements have meant million-dollar-plus offers, he's not too sure the sixties can be recaptured. Or that they even should be.

"The Spoonful was a very uncompromising group. I'm cheered by the feeling that we never did anything for the bucks," says Sebastian, his face reflecting the glow of the fireplace.

"We used to go out there with love in our eyes. That's hard to duplicate . . . We were a gang, it really was one for all, and all for one. Thankfully, we're all very capable of expressing love for each other. No problem there. Even Zally and Joe, who have the most adversarial relationship, can yell at one another, and, in the next breath, say 'I love you dearly.' Yeah, I really miss them, that's my gang."

Mary Wilson of the Supremes

Where Did All That Love Go?

It was a dream fulfilled.

Three girls rising out of the Detroit ghetto, to notch twelve number one hits, and to be heralded by Dick Clark as "the group that put Motown on the map."

They were indeed Dreamgirls—Diana Ross, Florence Ballard, Mary Wilson—and they reigned Supreme.

"Where Did Our Love Go?" was their first spectacular success. It bumped the Beatles out of the number one slot in 1964, and immediately catapulted the girls into the bright lights. Then came "Baby Love," "Come See About Me," "Stop! In the Name of Love," and assorted other songs which gave them a particular sound we'll never forget.

They were big, all right. Only the Beatles and Elvis eclipsed them.

And, remarkably enough, the heady flight to the top didn't spoil them. At least, not in the beginning. For three wonderful years, they didn't forget their roots. They came out of high school together, had to grudgingly accept backup work at Motown for two dollars and fifty cents a session, and even after their starship took off, the bonds between them remained strong. They were truly soul sisters.

Tragically, though, the dream took a wicked turn in 1967. Once Diana became the darling of Motown boss Berry Gordy, the group was suddenly renamed Diana Ross and the Supremes. The other two girls drifted out of the spotlight, and the group's inner strength disintegrated into an ugly wrestling match among three competing egos. Florence ultimately left the group in late 1967. She was flat broke a few years later. Upon her death in 1976, at the age of thirty-two, the following inscription could've been chiseled on her tombstone: WHERE DID OUR LOVE GO?

Diana Ross hasn't answered that question yet. She rarely talks about the Supremes (her children weren't even allowed to see the play *Dreamgirls),* and apparently wants to put the past far behind her.

That's understandable. Move beyond the glitter and the stream of golden oldies, and the Supremes' story is a depressing one. It's a tale of greed, jealousy, and vindictiveness. There was once something beautiful there, but, as Mary Wilson says, "Things got so confused, so heavy and twisted. We did have a dream. Only in this crazy [music] world, life is so fast, you lose sight of what's really important, and for Diana that meant going after everything she could, with an aggressiveness that was out of control."

Choking off a sigh, Mary squirms in a chair on the patio behind her mother's Hollywood home, and continues, "By 1969, it was no longer beautiful. You had to contend with egos, and people telling you what to do. It became more of what was good for Diana, not for the group. I knew right then, you either fought it, or gave the business up. The whole thing was geared to Berry and Diana—they had their own dream . . . no matter what it took, Diana was going to have a great solo career."

Though the Detroit ghetto toughened her, Mary finds it difficult to talk this way. She still agonizes over the breakup, and when she discusses either Diana or Flo, her radiant dark eyes become a little misty. She misses the fun they shared. The Supremes were adulated all over the world; while Mary's life today is far more mundane. At forty-two, she sings at supper clubs, does occasional revival shows, and is trying to be "the best mother in the world" to three young children.

But she doesn't just miss the accolades, or the Hollywood galas. There's a more profound gap in her life. Two dear friends are gone. One can only be eulogized, while the other is so far removed from her that Mary feels "very, very alone" these days. Flo and Diana weren't only her singing companions. They were "partners in a great adventure, a flight into fantasy." As Mary says, "We were a team. We didn't need anyone to tell us how good we were. We knew we were special.

"I can't put it into words, but there was something unique about us.

In the old days we thought we'd be friends for life, that whatever happened affected all of us equally. We were so together, so really together. When someone spoke about 'the girls' it meant all of us.

"And I think that spirit, even more than the music, had a terrific impact on people. For black America especially, we became everyone's sister or daughter. We were heroes to people. We were sweet little girls who belonged to them. Blacks didn't have too many heroes in those days, but we gave people pride in themselves. We made their lives a little sweeter."

In the beginning, these three Dreamgirls did provide a measure of hope. Everything about them, and their coming together, had the ring of a beautiful fairy tale.

Fantasizing wasn't easy, not in Detroit's Brewster Housing Project. But as a child, Mary ignored the grayness around her by lip-synching to the radio. She especially liked Doris Day, and would spend hours in front of the set imitating her.

In the eighth grade in 1959, Mary joined the school glee club, and was soon asked to sing at a neighborhood variety show. For that auspicious first solo appearance, she got dressed in her brother's black leather jacket, tight-fitting blue jeans and did a "mean black" version of Frankie Lyman's hit single "I'm Not a Juvenile Delinquent." The crowd loved it. They cheered lustily for a few minutes, and when Mary got backstage, she started to think, "Wow, that was me out there, I can do it. Singing in front of a crowd is as easy as breathing."

On that triumphant evening, she also met Florence. Mary was taking congrats from people backstage, when "this typical 1950's street-wise girl" came up to her to say a few kind words.

"Flo said that she really liked my singing, and that really thrilled me, for I already knew how ba-a-ad she was," recounts Mary wistfully. More relaxed now, she smilingly watches one of her sons playing nearby. He and a playmate have been up to all sorts of mischief, but, unperturbed, Mary only warns him to "watch the sprinkler hose," before she drifts back to her bittersweet memories.

"Was Flo tough! She was the Aretha Franklin of the 1950s. Even in elementary school, I remember her as being wild and aggressive. Soulful, that was Flo. It was a wonderful feeling to be respected by her. She had such a great voice. I looked up to her, and when she asked me later on to sing with her, I was flattered. It was a real honor."

About six months after their initial meeting, Florence formed a "sister" group to the Primes, a male quintet that would later become the

Temptations. At this time, Flo was also friendly with Diana, so she was asked to join, and the three girls (along with two other neighbors, Betty Travis and Barbara Martin) were soon singing at local record hops, as the Primettes.

Yet the group didn't stay together very long. The other two girls pursued different interests; while Florence's mother, feeling her daughter's schoolwork was being neglected, insisted that she leave the group. Diana and Mary were "heartbroken," but they didn't stand idly by. They begged Flo's mother to reconsider, and their "sister" was eventually allowed to return after she promised to get good grades.

Heartened by this development, the three teenagers began to perfect a certain look. Bouffant hairdoes in place, they'd stand in front of the mirror for hours, experimenting with different shades of mascara and eyeliner. They wanted to seem older, sexier, for as Mary says, "We checked out the other girls, the ones that were already making it, like Mary Wells, the Shirelles, and we knew what other people were looking for. We weren't thinking about records, or dreaming about being stars, not right then. But we did know we wanted to get out of the ghetto."

Helped by Diana's neighbor, Smokey Robinson, the Primettes auditioned at Motown in early 1961. While they impressed Berry Gordy, he felt they were too young for a recording contract, and offered them some session work instead. He finally signed them later in the year, and the Primettes got more than a new name. Sensing they were still raw and unfinished talents (the Supremes' first two records, "Your Heart Belongs to Me," and "Let Me Go the Right Way" never went higher than number ninety on the charts), Gordy sent them to what's become known as "the Motown finishing school."

This was Gordy's own dream factory. Here, he shaped mere singers into charming, poised entertainers, by giving them months of dancing, modeling, and acting lessons. Only the prized members of Gordy's stable—like the Temptations, Martha Reeves and the Vandellas, and the Marvelettes—got such training. But these classes led to a special stage presence, an aura that meant one hit after another.

The Supremes were also up to this rugged test. Though they had to work during the day at various odd jobs, they satisfied Gordy's demands, and upon "graduation" were given a special reward. Their songs would now be written by Eddie Holland, Lamont Dozier, and Brian Holland, the three producers who had pushed Martha Reeves and the Vandellas to the top of the charts.

From the outset, it was a match made in heaven. The H-D-H team gave the girls a strong new beat, highlighted Diana's tender vocals against a background of resounding pianos, and the resulting mix was "Where Did Our Love Go?" (mid-1964), the first of the Supremes' million-plus sellers. Mary was only twenty at the time. They'd have two more number one hits that year ("Baby Love" and "Come See About Me"), and before their streak ended in the summer of '65 ("Nothing But Heartaches" only made it to number eleven), the girls would hold on to the top spot with "Stop!" and "Back in My Arms Again."

The H-D-H triumvirate had certainly hit upon a magical formula, and as Mary says of this dizzying time, "We were like little girls in a candy store, we were going so fast, even the money we made didn't hit us. It was a dream coming true, but the successes were so accelerated, so phenomenal, we didn't even know we had the dream. Wow! It was something, something very unique!"

International celebrities by 1965, the Supremes swept into England as the "American Invasion," were fixtures on "the Ed Sullivan Show," and along with dominating the Las Vegas scene, turned up in some highly unlikely places—Like the time they were invited to the Beatles' hotel room and discovered marijuana.

"It was very exciting to meet them," recalls Mary, "but when we first saw them, they were stretched out on the floor smoking pot. The Beatles thought we were these hip black girls and we really got all made up for the occasion. You should have seen us in all that makeup. But they were just lying around smoking, and I thought the whole thing was terrible. I grabbed the girls, and told them, 'Let's get out of here fast.' "

The two groups were also jockeying for the top slot on the charts—and in late 1965, the Supremes took that vaulted position with "I Hear a Symphony." Their follow-up song, "My World Is Empty Without You," didn't do as well. But they came back, with a flourish. For starting with "You Can't Hurry Love," they ran off another remarkable streak of four consecutive number one singles from 1966 into 1967.

These successes, though, were tinged with problems. Their work schedule got extremely hectic, and without consulting them, Motown made all of their business decisions. This irked Flo, and she started to complain. She ostensibly wanted more free time to be with her family. But there was a more crucial reason for her bitterness. Though she had a better voice, the music was being written to showcase Diana.

Ugly fights were inevitable, and while it is still unclear whether Flo was asked to leave or voluntarily quit, Gordy replaced her with Cindy Birdsong in 1967. While the "new" Supremes went on to more hits, like

"Love Child" and their much maligned psychedelic-influenced "Reflections" (critics felt they were becoming too middle-of-the-road), Flo stumbled badly as a solo artist. She told *Ebony* magazine in 1969, "I believe I can make it. I wonder if people know how many flops the Supremes had before we made it big?" But the bookings never came. Forced to pawn jewelry to feed her children, she desperately tried to sue Motown for throwing her out of the group (1971). This lawsuit was quickly dismissed, and she subsequently went on welfare. Her life in a shambles, she died of a heart attack in 1976.

Mary is still mourning that loss. Her eyes fill with tears when she is talking about Flo, and she's no longer the poised, ever-confident product of Motown. Instead, she speaks hurriedly, even frantically at times, as if the rush of words will wipe away the pain, or at least provide new insight into what Mary calls a "senseless tragedy."

"I think of Flo every half second; she's not dead as far as I'm concerned. I see her and talk with her all the time. She had the biggest heart you ever wanted to see . . . what a laugh she had, it was a Santa Claus laugh . . . I'm sure Diana thinks of her, too. She has to, I'm sure of it. There were conflicts, their relations were always strained. Flo wasn't willing to do certain things in the business, that Diana would do. The entertainment world is very dirty, but even though they had their differences, they loved each other.

"They never really got together, because we were all so young to be thrown into this caldron. Diana thought Flo would come up to her standards, but after a while I knew Flo would be leaving—I knew she would. She didn't want to do it anymore. It had become too unbearable. We were supposed to be smiling at one another, but we just couldn't. Once Flo made up her mind, you knew she'd go through with it. And when she left, it was all over. I didn't want to admit this at the time, but our group was more than a musical trio, there was a special chemistry between us."

Anguish rising up in her face, Mary suddenly snaps, "Can't we stop talking about this stuff? That's it, let's move on to something else."

Mary then excuses herself, and walks a few yards away, to watch her son's antics in the family swimming pool. After giving him some cautionary advice, she returns saying, "My boys are really something, they have to be watched, and I mean *all* the time."

Apparently resigned to a less glamorous life, she chuckles, and emphatically shrugs her shoulders. Sounding almost apologetic, she then volunteers, "With all that stuff going on, people might wonder why I stayed with the Supremes. Well, you have to realize I loved what we were. I still love it. I was part of the beginning, and I wanted to persevere. I grew during those years and I learned so much, even if I was in the middle of those fights.

"We shared a dream, and even if your hopes change, you still hold on to the dream. At least *I* couldn't give it up. I wanted to go for it; I wanted to do what I felt. Sure, Diana's success came first, but her aggressiveness also made us great. We made a lot of money because of her, and giving that up isn't easy. Once you quit and live off it, it gets to the point where you don't have enough to cover expenses. Look at Flo; she wasn't destitute, she just had nothing coming in.

"But I didn't stay on just for the money. Once Flo left, I had to give the group more of myself. If you have something that's admired throughout the world, you can't just let it die. So my commitment became even more complete. The Supremes were too beautiful to give up."

So the Supremes went on. They performed with the Temptations at times, and had a major success with "Love Child," their ode to life in the ghetto. But despite its sales, the song was a bit phony. They were much more pop than soul. Gordy had styled them this way to reach white audiences. And curiously, after they did "Someday We'll Be Together" in 1969, the Motown maestro pulled another switch. He gave Diana the okay to go solo.

Fearing she'd end up like Flo, Mary continued with the Supremes for the next seven years. Alongside Birdsong and Jean Terrell, she led the group to several minor hits during this period, and even had a number one song (the Supremes' last), "Stoned Love" in 1970. But her "commitment" to the Supremes had faded. Feeling little kinship to these new girls, she performed solely to make money, and that was also a problem. She started to argue with Gordy over royalties, and after a while it became apparent that she was fighting a losing battle.

Their verbal battles finally resulted in a lawsuit (1977). It was a traumatic affair for her, and the mudslinging was worthy of the *National Enquirer*. But unlike Flo, she was able to prove that she hadn't gotten her fair share of the Supremes' receipts, and won a 50 percent slice of all future revenues accrued from the group's records, or name.

While she denies she's still bitter, that lawsuit prompts her to say, in a defiant, acerbic tone, "I built Motown, but did that matter? Forget it! We assumed we were being taken care of, because that's what everyone was telling us. We should've gotten the right lawyers, for what company cares about your interests? We let Motown handle everything for us, so how can I be sad about what happened? Let's just say I spent a few million, and it's all gone. What bothers me is that I grew up thinking everything was good, and this burst my bubble. Motown, Flo,—I certainly learned the world wasn't pretty."

Mary learned even more about life after she went out on her own. Her marriage fell apart. She didn't fare that well on the touring circuit, and with less money coming in, severe changes had to be made in her life-style. No longer a superstar, she had to give up "those splashy things, the big million-dollar house, the expensive dresses, the constant partying." It was extremely difficult. For years, she hadn't known anything else. But after the first shocks, she entrusted her three children to her mother, and began a process of self-exploration that is still continuing.

"I had to get in touch with myself, I had to be a normal person again," says Mary emphatically. "I couldn't be *the* Mary Wilson anymore, I had to just be Mary Wilson. You get hung up in that crazy world, and you lose your real self. I wasn't able to buy three- to four-thousand-dollar dresses, and that of course made people talk 'Oh, she's not living in a mansion anymore.' But for once I had to live in a way *I* wanted, not the way people thought I should be living."

Confident that she's grown a lot these past few years, Mary feels it's the right time to look back at the Supremes, and to write a book. She promises, "I'm not going to keep anything back." But these memoirs won't be another Hollywood "kiss and tell" diary. For despite her saying "the dream lasted long enough for all three of us," that dream lives on. The Supremes are still a vital part of her.

"We were the nineteen sixties with the Beatles and Elvis," she asserts, when asked why she's writing the book. "We made people forget their prejudices. Before we came along, when people thought of black singers, they thought of prostitutes. The Supremes changed that. We opened some doors, but even more importantly, we made *lots* of people smile."

Peter Noone of Herman's Hermits

Dreamin' of Pacino, Brando, and Redford

The dueling swords have been put away, along with the black eye patches, menacing-looking knives, and red bandanas. They're of a different time, when swashbuckling pirates flitted through the air, wired to adventure. Now, though, there are no fiery sea battles, no treasure boxes laden with pieces of eight, or duets with Linda Ronstadt. Life has become far less charged. No one's cheering. The curtain calls are only a memory.

Instead of leading a charmed existence as the "new toast of Broadway," Peter Noone is home in Hollywood, waiting for the phone to ring. Since starring as Frederick in *The Pirates of Penzance,* he hasn't gotten much work. While the blond, impish, graduate of Herman's Hermits is as bubbly as ever, joking in an exaggerated Cockney accent, "A good Shakespearean part is bound to come my way," he's hardly living like Laurence Olivier. Besides worrying about the mortgage, he spends most of his time reading *Variety* or *Backstage,* going to auditions, and attending drama school. Lately, these efforts haven't paid off.

"It doesn't matter that acting's rough, if you think you'll be good, you should do it," insists the thirty-nine-year-old Noone, bursting into a bar of "Mrs. Brown, You've Got a Lovely Daughter" to emphasize the point that he'll always be theatrical. Noone has chosen a Hollywood café for this performance, and a few nearby patrons eye him curiously. But, undaunted, he adds in a more serious vein, "I want a career, something to work on all the time. I don't care if this demands hard work, a lot of dues paying, I want a reason to get up every day. That's why I'm doing these classes. I want to create, movies, plays . . . It's just a desire to perform, to get on stage and jump around. I enjoy the business, and now I know I can do Shakespeare. Getting a part won't be that easy, but what do you want me to do, be an accountant? Sell used cars?"

Heavens!

That would be too disappointing for the folks back in Manchester, England. Especially for Noone's musically inclined family. In the 1950s various household members would place young Peter (known then as Davy Hulmes) on their lap, and let him sing such ditties as "The Milkman's Song." No one could have suspected that this early frolicking would lead to international fame and such teenie-bopper classics as "Can't You Hear My Heartbeat?" "I'm Henry VIII, I Am," and record sales totaling over 40 million. These songfests made such an impression on the little boy that he lost interest in school. Precociously, he learned to play a half-dozen instruments, and was soon staging his own living room concerts, much to the delight of relatives.

With everyone agreeing "The kid's a natural," Peter's future was clear. The youth with a choir-boy face would become an entertainer.

The family got him an agent, and before you could say Shirley Temple, he was on British TV, in a show called "Carnation Street." This setting was a bit strange for a fourteen-year-old. The 1961 BBC drama was a sexier version of "Peyton Place," yet as Peter boyishly recalls, "It didn't matter what the show was about, I now saw myself as an actor. I met people who were a lot more interesting than my schoolmates. They were so fascinating, they knew so much. Right then I decided to broaden my horizons."

This new sense of purpose ultimately led Peter to the Manchester School of Music. A great citadel of learning, MSM was "an eye-opening, mind-blowing experience" that irrevocably changed him. Not that he spent a lot of time with his studies, they were simply "an excuse," so Peter "wouldn't have to go home."

So if it wasn't the classics and trigonometry, what turned this young boy's head?

Like others his age in the early sixties, he discovered the jukebox, got his first taste of rock 'n' roll, and realized, "a guitar wasn't just this thing some guy in a Spanish restaurant used when they brought paella to the table."

Noone was so inspired, he started buying records, forty-fives, of Buddy Holly, Roy Orbison, Sam Cooke. As his collection increased, he began to impersonate these people, and this gift was eventually parlayed into a DJ job at a local club. A rising star now, with a heightened sense of what was cool, the fourteen-year-old changed his name to Peter Novak.

"I'll admit, I was the furthest thing from cool. I wore this purple shirt, winkle-picker shoes, and had this suitcase record player. God, was it heavy. I'd take it under this tunnel at night and mimic the people I liked. I never bought Cliff Richard records, he was British. It was the Americans who were happening, Gene Vincent, Orbison, Elvis, and I found I could do their songs real easy."

That talent was put to a supreme test in early 1962. Without any warning, Peter was asked to leave his seat in a small Manchester club, to sing lead with a bunch of friends in the Heartbeats. Their lead singer had mysteriously disappeared, and they knew Peter had split from the Cyclones, another local band that was more interested in meeting girls than in making music. So they persuaded him to do a few numbers— and as a reward for joining the group, Peter soon got another name.

"We started to get a lot of decent gigs, bar mitzvahs, weddings, but I wanted us to be really unique, to have real style," laughs Peter, who was then outfitted by his mother in secondhand, ill-fitting satin and lamé suits. "We knew we couldn't impersonate the Beatles, so we got more Bobby Rydellish; we became a fun band. Well, if we were going to sound different, we also had to have a far-out name. So one night, in this Manchester club, while we were watching the Bullwinkle show on TV, this guy yells out 'Why don't you call yourselves the bloody Hermits?' That stuck, and since everyone thought I was saying Herman, instead of Sherman (one of the Bullwinkle characters), I wasn't a Peter anymore."

While the switch brought them more money—their fees rose from five to twenty pounds a night—none of the five Hermits were satisfied with the ballroom circuit. They yearned for a record contract. Yet in the face of mounting competition, netting such a deal wasn't easy. To get companies to look at them, they agreed an edge had to be established, something that was even more distinctive than their names, or the potato sacks they wore on stage.

Initially, Peter thought the Hermits could gain that advantage if they had a reliable means of transportation. Believing out-of-town gigs were an impossibility as long as the group was dependent on hitchhiking with mounds of equipment, he equated "all sorts of bookings" with a van or truck. It didn't faze him that the group couldn't afford such a luxury. Admitting "I was completely mad back then," he did construction jobs during the day, and "borrowed" company vans at night.

Worried that these escapades could lead to a jail term, Karl Greene, Keith Hopwood, and the other Hermits eventually convinced Peter to go straight. With their concurrence, he adopted a more conventional strategy, hiring "a manager with good business sense," Harvey Lisberg, and wooing an established hit-maker, Animals producer Mickie Most.

"Once we sent Most a plane ticket, and put him up in a hotel. We got a load of girls into the club we were in, and told them to scream," says Noone, proudly thrusting his head and shoulders up in the air. After congratulating himself for concocting this "ingenious" ruse, he continues, "Unfortunately, though, the whole show was quite pathetic and it didn't work. Most wasn't too impressed at first. He told Harvey he liked us, but only wanted to sign this Herman guy, not his mates. I couldn't do that."

"We worked a bit more, got ourselves a new drummer, and when Most finally agreed to help us, he found this Carole King song, 'I'm into Something Good.' Once we recorded it, and I heard it on the radio, I said 'That's it, my life's complete.' "

"Then we did some TV shows, and in three weeks we were number one. It was unbelievable, the whole damn thing. I was sixteen, taking the bus into Manchester, and these old ladies would come up to me and say 'Hey, you got a number one record! My, you're so young and cute . . .' "

Chuckling, Noone finally discovers the cup of tea that's been getting cold on the table. Once refreshed, he pointedly exclaims, "I had no star training; I didn't know what was going on. I got a check for four thousand seven hundred pounds and blew the whole thing on a Jaguar. I wasn't even old enough to drive it, so this roadie drove me around for five years. He'd also pick up girls for me after a show. Eventually I gave the car to my brother, who introduced it to a tree."

After selling over a million records in a month, Peter also sent his grandfather on a trip to Italy. "I gave him two hundred quid, and he gave me change when he came back." He bought his parents a hotel, but his own life-style didn't change, at least not initially. Still living at home, he ate with his grandmother, listened to her scoldings, and dutifully took out the garbage. "I kinda lived it day to day. I never thought of who I was, or of the success I was having."

Yet 1965 brought big changes. The Hermits released "Can't You Hear My Heartbeat," and quickly supplanted the Beatles at the top of the charts. That, however, was only the beginning of what Peter calls "a mind-boggling, dizzying trip into never-never land." For as soon as "Heartbeat" went gold, the boys giddily took off on their first U.S. tour, knowing that their follow-up, "Silhouettes," had already notched over 400,000 orders in advance sales. The tour meant appearances on the Ed Sullivan, Dick Clark, and Danny Kaye shows, and on these telecasts the group did one of their old Heartbeats' songs, "Mrs. Brown You've Got a Lovely Daughter." Issued as a single by MGM in April, the song sold 600,000 copies in a few weeks, and held down the number one spot for over a month. Then the Hermits finished off the year with three more smash hits, "Wonderful World," "Just a Little Bit Better," and of course, "I'm Henry VIII, I Am," bringing their 1965 box score to a remarkable six gold singles, plus one gold album, *Introducing Herman's Hermits.*

Amid all this early excitement, there was only one sour note. The Hermits weren't taken very seriously by rock critics. Frequently compared to more sophisticated-sounding groups like the Stones or Beatles, they were dismissed for doing "novelty" songs—records that basically had trivial themes. These media attacks infuriated Peter, and, instead of reacting in a more diplomatic manner, the eighteen-year-old often stormed out of interviews, especially when the press drifted into such subjects as the Vietnam War, or the American racial crisis.

"I didn't want to be compared to other groups, or to talk about things I knew nothing about. I was constantly being told I was a kid who did meaningless songs, so why did they want my opinion on these other issues? The whole thing really got on my nerves . . .

"The Hermits were different, sure they were. But we were also successful, almost as much as the Beatles or Dave Clark. But because our records were different, they became 'novelty.' We were a lot more than a novelty band. A lot more."

At the height of the group's popularity in 1965–66, there were other pressures, most particularly, the unmanageable crowds of hysterical adolescent girls, and the nonstop touring. On the road for most of that two-year period, the Hermits were trailblazers, as they opened up several Far Eastern locales for western rock groups. Yet these jaunts were exhausting, and would magnify, or exacerbate, the tensions that always exist when five teenagers are compelled to live together.

Scowling, when remembering this down side of celebrityhood, Noone says, "By the middle of 1966, the whole spirit of the group had disappeared. We were running into a corridor that was progressively narrowing.

"The life was so insane. I had been on a *Time* magazine cover, and a guy brought it over to me a few years later, and I never knew I'd been on it. The people drawing fifteen hundred dollars a week for patting me on the back were saying how great the band was, but I felt kinda trapped. The whole thing became a lot of pressure.

"After a while I felt an obligation to do better records, to move away from the purely pop stuff, maybe to acid rock. But by '67 I knew we were stuck, and started to think 'Let's break it.' You can't stop, though, you can't stop. You have all these obligations: mortgages, insurance, houses. Music was just a way to make money. And once that happens, you lose it, it's all over."

While Peter contrived to tour with the group for the next three years, legal battles with MGM sharpened his disenchantment. The record company didn't pay the group any royalties for over a year, and consequently "No Milk Today" and "There's a Kind of Hush," singles Noone calls "some of my best stuff," weren't originally released in the United States. Forced to work, to pay bills, Peter was on the road for three hundred days in 1967. But this grinding schedule, which saw the Hermits playing in sleazy Las Vegas nightclubs, didn't disturb him as much as his recurring image problem.

"No matter what we did, or how we changed our music, the press always looked on us as a joke," complains Noone, grimacing. "We didn't get a bit of respect. Because we seemed to be having fun, or to be saying, 'Come to the party,' no one thought our music could be any good. What a . . . Maybe the only way to get any respect is to be serious, maybe like Dylan."

Disgusted by their bad rap, Noone temporarily left the group in 1968, to work on a TV show with the future director of *A Chorus Line*, Michael Bennett. According to Peter, this devastated the Hermits. Not getting as much work, they "flipped out" and pressured him "with all sorts of guilt trips." Eventually bowing to what Peter calls "mind games," he returned to the fold, only this time, their collaboration became an on-again, off-again arrangement. Sensing "we were just a corporation out to make some bucks," he did sporadic, "joyless" European tours with them, knowing his "Herman" days were as numbered as the sixties.

Once the Hermits officially disbanded in 1970, Peter recorded David Bowie's "Oh You Pretty Things," with the soon to be famous "glitter rocker" on piano. They continued to work together for the next few years, though the success of their first collaboration was never repeated. With his solo career floundering, Noone went "middle of the road," hosting a British TV show. That, too, proved disappointing, so Peter tried to recapture the "good ole days," on a 1973 revival tour with the Hermits.

"I'm twenty-five then, and I'm in an oldies package, just think how crazy that is," says Peter, his now tired-looking eyes conveying a deep sense of desperation. "I always knew you couldn't go back; there was no joy. That's not to say I didn't enjoy myself on the stage, I did. I liked doing the old songs, and the guys on the tours were a lot of fun: Gerry and the Pacemakers, Wayne Fontana, the Searchers . . . we'd drink, stick our asses out of the window."

"But every conversation was about money. We weren't fifteen anymore, and while I wanted to talk about the old days, how we used to make records, no one wanted to listen. It was a much different world. Me and the Hermits were brothers at one time—now we were mangled."

Dispirited by these new realities, Peter switched off, by living a solitary existence in Southern France for three years. Describing this traumatic period as "a time I went back to being thirteen," he sourly adds, "I didn't know what the fuck I was doing. I certainly wasn't writing my masterpiece. I'd go into a record store, and wouldn't even ask about my own records. I was just waiting around to see who'd call me, who my real friends were. As it turned out, most of them happened to be Americans. So I went to the States, to L.A."

The sun-drenched, fabled land of make-believe worked wonders. His life became "a giggle" again. Especially after a few appearances with Cheap Tricks led to his hosting "Saturday Night Live." No longer seeing himself as only "Herman of the Hermits," Peter felt confident enough to give singing another try. Combining with the "new wave" Tremblers, he did thirty-five-dollar-a-night gigs, produced an album, *Twice Nightly,* and was basically "high on life again."

Frederick, Noone's frolicking, sweet-voiced *Pirates of Penzance* character, was a product of this new energy.

Putting aside fears of returning to the theater that had understandably formed during his long absence, he successfully auditioned for the part in 1981. Obviously impressing the show's creator, the much-heralded Joseph Papp, Peter remained with the show for two years, first appearing on Broadway, then triumphantly returning to England for a long-desired stint on a London stage.

And while a Shakespearean role hasn't yet materialized—perhaps people would then take him seriously—he s no intention of ever becoming "Herman" again. Convinced "it's downright sad that the guys have to do these rip-off gigs, they're ruining what the Hermits stood for," he recently took his old buddies to court to prevent them from using the name Herman. The judge ruled against him. But Peter still argues, "When I left, it was agreed that the whole thing was over, that the Hermits would be put into a locked time capsule. We had our time, we were one of the most successful bands around. No one came near us for a while, not even the Beatles. We had a monopoly on the charts, hell, 1965 was only the Hermits. But what are these guys doing now? They're peddling their ass in the street, just to make a buck. Look, if you want to create the Coasters all over again, you can always get two guys here, two guys there. But that's a rip-off, and it destroys what the group once had. That's sad, very sad."

Once his anger cools, Peter remembers that he has to drive his wife, Marie, to the health club. Married to her for sixteen years, he proudly announces, "I did all my screwing around when I was fifteen, now I have one of the greatest relationships in the world." They don't have any children, but as Peter calls for the check, he cheerfully says, "When I do have kids, I know exactly what I'll tell them about the Hermits. All in all, being a rock star was a joy. Every day I had another horizon. That kinda spoiled my life. If I don't have something to do now, I panic. But the sixties were a great time to be in rock 'n' roll. There was so much going on, back then it was meant for kids my age.

"And best of all, I'd tell them that I was the only one to come out clean."

David Crosby of Crosby, Stills and Nash
The Loss of an American Hero

All looks tranquil.

The country road winds through rich, verdant farmland, past grazing cows and sheep. Clapboard barns, their red paint peeling from too much California sun, dot the hillside. An occasional tractor lumbers by, with a hand jutting out from the cab, waving hello. While off in the distance, the Olompali Mountains jut into the sky, casting a majestic shadow over the Cotati Valley.

About fifteen miles outside Novato, in a particularly deserted spot, a gravel driveway bends off that backwoods road, leading to a house fortified with security cameras. Except for these cameras, which silently rotate back and forth, there's a mournful stillness in the air. The cheerless, nondescript ranch house shows no signs of life. A small backyard pool is littered with brown-stained leaves, while rotting lemons lie abandoned on the ground, buried in clumps of weeds.

Repeated knocks on the front door bring no response. Though the occupants expect visitors, shouts go unanswered. Nothing stirs . . . not until a cat jumps onto a window ledge, to peer through the Levolor blinds.

The hush goes unbroken for several minutes, leaving the visitors troubled and confused. But perhaps one should be prepared for the eerie silence. From the very outset, this "meet" has smacked of a cloak-and-dagger yarn. Previous arrangements have abruptly changed, or fallen through. Heavy-voiced intermediaries speak cryptically of "circumstances" beyond their control. There've been warnings not to disclose certain details about the meeting or its exact location. And when these "rules" are questioned, the crisply worded replies are pointedly clear. One either plays the game or the interview can be forgotten.

That's the way it is, getting to meet the elusive David Crosby. Everything is carefully choreographed, various safeguards must be in place. He has to be protected, from the outside world and from himself.

David has been arrested four times on various drug and weapons charges since 1982. Invariably escaping long-term incarceration, he's retained an aura of sixties lawlessness, a romantic bad-boy image that boosts his value on the revival circuit.

But David's continued freedom is always in doubt. He was busted in a Dallas rock club in 1982 for possession of a quarter gram of cocaine and a loaded .45. His 1983 conviction on these charges was later overturned on a legal technicality, but in June 1984, a Texas appeals court reinstated the original verdict. A five-year jail sentence now hangs over his head while his case is again appealed, but attorneys' fees, coupled with years of expensive drug use and repayment of a 3 million-dollar debt to the IRS, have plunged David into murky financial waters. A group of shadowy financial backers supports him, and during the Crosby, Stills and Nash 1985 tour, they carefully monitored all interviews to promote the notion that the "new" David is drug-free. Yet, on several occasions he has barely escaped torching himself to death while freebasing.

"When David set fire to his hotel rooms, I paid the bills out of my pocket. I just wanted to keep everything going," says Michael Gaiman, president of the Cannibal Agency, who booked a Crosby tour in 1984. "I didn't want David to get arrested. People would say half kiddingly that he's down from seven grams to two grams a day, but he and his girlfriend Jan Dance were going to hell arm in arm. I'll never forget, after he torched his suite in the Vista International (in New York), Jan was sitting there shaking, the wall was scorched, the sheets burnt, and David looked like he hadn't bathed in weeks. He said, 'You gotta help me, man, you gotta help me, man.' "

The waiting drags on. A burly man, identifying himself as Crosby's manager, Jack Casanova, finally appears at the door. Without apologizing, he announces, "Come on in. David will be out in a few minutes, he's getting dressed." The consummate host, he then throws a video cassette into a VCR. And as he disappears again, into a rear bedroom, pornographic images flicker across the screen.

For about forty minutes, not a sound is heard. Eventually, a Mercedes pulls into the driveway, and a yuppie-looking couple enters the house through the garage. They also vanish. And in the growing twilight, the plush, oriental-influence living room is enveloped by shadow. It's grown so dark, in fact, the tabby has curled up in a corner, contentedly asleep.

In this bizarre context, one's imagination runs wild. With Crosby mysteriously closeted, for what seems an inordinate amount of time, the mind is destined to play various tricks. Some hellish scheme might be afoot. Maybe David is seriously ill, not even here, or perhaps this meeting is just part of a cruel hoax. Who knows? The fact remains, Crosby is inexplicably missing.

Suddenly a door bangs shut, and a disheveled, unshaven figure walks into the living room. His stomach is bloated; thinning frizzy hair leaps wildly into the air. A few of his front teeth are missing, his pants are tattered and his red plaid shirt has a gaping hole. The most frightening thing, however, is his pale, swollen face, riddled with thick white scales, deep, encrusted blotches that don't seem to be healing. Looking at him is painful. A fourteen-year addiction to heroin and cocaine has caused David to resemble a man at the end of his rope. The spiritual leader of the Woodstock nation has come to this.

David slumps into a chair. "Do you know that each-man-is-an-island thing? That's no joke man, everybody is. I'm alone a lot, I don't handle it well at all. I'm not good at it. Getting sad and missing people who aren't there anymore is the worst. I've lost a lot of friends, musicians, I've lost an old lady too, Chris, Christine Hinton. She was killed in an auto accident. I wrote a number of things that refer to her—'Guinnevere,' 'Where Will I Be . . .'—I miss so many people, Cass Elliot, Jimi Hendrix, Janis, Lowell George was a dear friend of mine. There's an enormous list of folks . . .

"I'm sad, very sad, but I don't have the urge to go over the edge. The French have a phrase, *raison d'être,* a reason for being, and I have several strong reasons for living. There's my music, look at what they gave me to work with [a reference to his voice]. My daughter, sailing, all the adventures I haven't been on yet, all the music I haven't written or sung yet. Almost nothing makes people happy, man, there's very little in this world that can really make people happy, and I can. I can pull off that magic trick by myself sometimes. I love doing that, I love lessening the distance between people. I love it when we sing 'Teach Your Children,' and get twenty thousand people singing it. They all walk out feeling different, they're all touched by it, and moved by it. It changes them, it changes how they feel. They're less alone."

Belying this message of self-affirmation, there's the reality of Crosby's life, the devastation wrought by drugs that hangs heavy in his hoarse voice, which has been reduced to a whisper. Where there was once hope, or the promise of a new age, there is now the vocal equivalent of coarse sandpaper, a dull, flat rasp.

"I quit completely," says the forty-four-year-old Crosby as he grabs for a bag of Pepperidge Farm cookies.

"You gave up coke?"

"Yeah!"

"Heroin?"

"Yeah!"

"You were doing coke and heroin?"

"I'd rather not talk about that. Coke I'll admit to. And I did quit, completely. It changed things considerably. I'm not into it at all on the level I once was. I don't . . . for the most part I don't do it. I agree with them [Graham Nash, Jackson Browne, and others who came to David's house in 1983 to persuade him to seek help]; I was too much into it."

Looking pained, David stares vacantly ahead. Disregarding the laughter in another room, he resumes, "I do good work. I want to work with those guys [Stephen Stills and Graham Nash]. I love them . . . Drugs wouldn't hurt my working with them now. Things have changed."

Suddenly a note of exasperation creeps into his voice. He cries out, "Do we have to talk about drugs? Can you believe it, five years for less than a gram. I won't get out of that state alive. I'll die in one of those jails. I don't want to talk about drugs. It's been used against me so many times. I just want to talk about my music."

David's eyes close; his head drifts into a slow nod. One eye barely opens when he's asked to describe how the Byrds broke up. He mumbles a few words and quickly falls back into a stupor.

Prodded several times, he comes to, and without a word rises and stumbles to the door separating the two wings of the house. He pauses for a moment, smiles wanly, then disappears. And his guests are left sitting there, stunned.

Death and ruptured friendships have made David a lonely, wrenchingly sad figure. Tragic or premature losses dog him. His mother died of cancer. Christine Hinton, the twenty-one-year-old woman he was passionately in love with, died in a violent car crash in 1969. Since the late sixties, he has been estranged from his father, Floyd Crosby, the Academy Award-winning cinematographer who worked on *High Noon* and *Tabu.* Embroiled in a child-support battle with former girlfriend Debbie Donovan, he rarely sees his eleven-year-old daughter, Donovan Ann. And while David was once surrounded by such artists as Grace Slick, Elvis Costello, and Jackson Browne, his closest friends have either severed ties or don't want to talk about him.

Alienated from his friends, David has drifted in and out of a netherworld where only the next fix is important. Desperate for drugs, he has sold musical instruments to raise cash for cocaine. And while this belies his oft-repeated claim that music is his primary concern, his so-called *raison d'être,* freebasing is a sickness that has often rendered him helpless.

David's friends have repeatedly tried to admit him to hospitals, lent him money, and brought drug counselors to his Mill Valley, California, house. But David has disappointed them by rejecting their efforts with contempt or by agreeing to seek help and then fleeing from clinics.

"We've tried to do everything short of imprisoning him, but David looks down on almost all of his friends. He thinks he's the king of the world," said Jefferson Airplane co-founder Paul Kantner in 1984. Suggesting that people shouldn't feel sorry for David, Kantner continued, "If you take a thoroughbred horse, pamper and feed him all the fat grains and wonderful milks all day, pretty soon he'll be a big fat horse who can't run . . . and the same with musicians. If you put them in mansions, feed them steaks, you're going to have some big fat guy *à la* David Crosby pushing shit into his arm and doing nothing but dying."

Yet in 1969 CSN&Y were the heralded leaders of the Woodstock Generation.

And David Crosby was the group's driving force.

Though arrogant and volatile, he had been a leader before, with the Byrds. There had been trouble, ugly spats with the other Byrds. But he moved on, became Joni Mitchell's producer, her guiding spirit, and even her lover.

In those halcyon days, David only smoked marijuana and dreamed of owning a sailboat. Friends saw him as an innocent yet committed musician. When Bobby Kennedy was assassinated, he was shocked into writing "Long Time Gone." To John Sebastian, Grace Slick, and Eric Clapton, David was an inspiration, the long-mustached, flowing-red-haired figure they adoringly called "Yosemite Sam."

Winning such esteem was a struggle for David. Both as an adolescent and as an early-sixties rocker, he faced innumerable obstacles. And the torments on the way to Woodstock left their scars.

His childhood was especially tormented. The son of a celebrated cinematographer, David felt the pressure to succeed—or to "match up." Hurt by his parents' divorce and unable to conform in school, he became the quintessential fifties juvenile delinquent. As a teenager in Santa Barbara, he broke into cars and houses and, most troubling of all to his father, played folk music at beatnik coffeehouses.

In 1960, hoping to pacify his father, David enrolled at the Pasadena Playhouse acting school. Compelled to "kiss ass" and to "fake" his true feelings, the outspoken, quick-tempered David soon dropped out to play blues guitar at the Unicorn in Los Angeles. After getting his Hollywood girlfriend, Cindy, pregnant, he fled to New York, learned a new playing style from folksinger Fred Neil, and hitchhiked around the country. He lived with Dino Valenti, later of the Youngbloods, on a houseboat in Sausalito, but finally returned to Los Angeles in 1963. At a Troubadour club hoot, Roger McGuinn and Gene Clark were impressed with David's "fresh, energetic voice" and asked him to join their group, the Jet Set, which later became the Byrds.

In 1964, the Byrds recorded Dylan's "Mr. Tambourine Man" and took off. But as their stature grew, David began competing with McGuinn for control of the group.

"There was always a rub between me and David. He had to be on top, and this rivalry often turned ugly in the studio," sighs McGuinn, recalling the time drummer Michael Clarke was angered by David's "shit" and punched him in the face. "The tension hurt the Byrds terribly. We'd be searching for material and fights would break out. They got physical, and David was often at the center of them."

David was experimenting with cocaine by the mid-sixties, and emblematic of this interest, he collaborated with McGuinn to write "Eight Miles High." But hostilities peaked in 1967, when the Byrds refused to record David's song about a *ménage à trois,* "Triad." McGuinn said the lyrics were "immoral." Angered, David complained that the Byrds were "canaries" who stunted his musical growth.

" 'Triad' was simply a bad song, and David had simply become too tough to deal with," says McGuinn. "There was bad blood between us, so Chris Hillman and I asked him to leave. David said, 'Come on, guys, we make good music together.' But I told him, 'We make good music *without* you.' "

David was already hanging out with Stephen Stills. The Byrds gave him a fifty-thousand-dollar settlement, and with it he bought a boat, the *Mayan.* Inspired by idyllic trips on the *Mayan,* David teamed with Stills and Paul Kantner to write the revolutionary anthem "Wooden Ships." It was the beginning of the historic group that would become CSN&Y.

In 1968, David fell in love with a wispy blonde California girl named Christine Hinton. Luxuriating on beaches or swimming naked in Monkee Peter Tork's Laurel Canyon pool, the couple epitomized the Aquarian Age. They enjoyed life, and in this beatific spirit, David sang harmonies with Stills and Nash at Joni Mitchell's house. "We knew we'd locked onto something so special," David told biographer Dave Zimmer.

The world soon felt the same way. In 1969, their debut album, *Crosby, Stills and Nash,* featured "Long Time Gone," "Suite: Judy Blue Eyes," and "Marrakesh Express." It sold 2 million copies. The album had a lilting, soothing quality that was a stark contrast to the frenetic politics of the era. CSN was likened to the Beatles by the American counterculture, and Jimi Hendrix raved, "These guys are groovy . . . Western sky music. All delicate and ding-ding-ding-ding."

The euphoria persisted all the way to Woodstock. Together with Neil Young, who joined the group shortly before the festival, the group made their second live appearance as Crosby, Stills, Nash and Young at Max Yasgur's farm, and the "music and arts" fair cemented their reputation as love children.

Still enraptured by Christine Hinton and hailed as the group's driving spirit, David was excited by life. Happier than he'd ever been, he didn't use "peace and love" as mere buzzwords. To him, the phrase had real meaning as he stood poised to lead the Movement to an even higher consciousness.

As the wait for David grinds on, that Novato house becomes more eerie—thirty minutes have passed . . . forty . . . fifty . . . and the stillness forces one to wonder—what happened to him and the revolution? During that apocalyptic era, protestors marched to the new music and echoed calls for freedom. David and the forces of rebellion were intertwined. Then and now. For his weakened condition, which has forced him into a back room to revive, is symbolic of the lost Revolution.

David reappears, mysteriously rubbing the edge of a large brass bowl with a wooden cylinder. His slow, circular strokes make the bowl reverberate, and a shrill, piercing hum fills the room.

"That's nice, eh," says David. "It's Tibetan. It drives the bad Mojo out of the room." His eyes are bleary; the sound is annoying. "Anyone who's bad has to leave. I haven't been to Tibet, but I've seen pictures of the people's faces. They're all happy, they're still free, they haven't been conquered. That's why I'd like to get there."

"Woodstock was also an uplifting experience," he cheerfully exclaims. "That was good, man, real good. We didn't realize at the time what was going on quite as much as we did later. But it was amazing for us, because we were just starting out. Everyone in the entire music business that we respected was standing all around us, looking to see what we were going to be. And we were nervous. Everybody was there, the Who, Hendrix, everybody, the Airplane . . . it was quite something. It was good, man.

"We [CSN&Y] were all good writers. We had this incredibly wide palette to paint the albums from. Those days were the best, man. We were doing work that we thought was absolutely the best of our lives, and it probably was. We were tight buddies. I love Stills, and Nash has been my best friend for many, many, *many* years, and still is. He's one of the best men I know in the world. We played for the right reasons, because we loved it. Music was our whole life, the main joy in our life. It gave us purpose . . ."

David's voice trails off mournfully, and he moves to the window to stare at a lone farm worker on a distant hillside. He's trying to hide the tears glistening in his eyes. But like the shadows creeping over the surrounding fields, David is enveloped by darkness, the darkness of a past suddenly clouded by tragedy.

On September 30, 1969, only a month after his Woodstock "high," David was frolicking with Christine Hinton, and other friends by the pool in back of his Marin County home. Chris rolled a few joints. Carefree and high, she gathered up their four cats and put them in David's '64 VW bus and drove off to the veterinarian. On the way, one of the cats suddenly jumped onto her lap. The VW swerved into the path of an oncoming school bus. On impact, Chris flew through the windshield. She died a short time later in a hospital emergency room.

That loss dragged at David's spirit like a ball and chain. The inspiration for "Guinnevere," Christine represented David's nondrugged, creative side. He eulogized her in "Laughing" and "Déjà Vu." David made the arrangements for Christine's cremation. Afterwards, he carried a deep guilt over her death.

David is standing forlornly by the window. " 'Déjà Vu' was my song, and I'm proud of it. This was a different experience for me. After Chris died I'd go to the studio and just sit on the floor and cry."

David was in a stupor for months. He didn't regain his sense of purpose until May 1970, when four Kent State students were killed during a campus demonstration. Calling that incident a nightmare, he speaks with new clarity, a passion that's reminiscent of the old David.

"I remember handing Neil [Young] *Life* magazine, and he looked at the pictures of the girl kneeling over the guy dead on the pavement, looking up with that 'Why?' expression on her face. I saw the shock of it hit him. I handed him his guitar and helped him write 'Ohio.' I got him on a plane, took him to L.A., and we recorded that night. By one o'clock in the morning we passed the tape to Ahmet Ertegun, the president of Atlantic Records, and got on a plane to New York. It was out in three days. And we point the finger at Nixon, the military establishment, the generals who were sending innocent boys into war. That was right on. We could feel that 'Ohio' was important to people.

"It was a bitch, and to be able to put that song out, man, right away [his voice rises again] and have it stand for *something,* have people stop us in the street and say, 'Man, right-fucking-on.' That was exciting. It was good stuff."

But this mood couldn't be sustained, and an atmosphere of mistrust and acrimony enveloped the group. The main battle raged between Stills and Nash, who bitterly vied for the affections of Rita Coolidge. Stills fought with Young for the greater share of lead vocals. Young finally settled the issue by going solo. The group flew apart. David left to rejoin the Byrds. CSN&Y regrouped at other times during the late seventies, but, muses David sadly, "When we got big, music was sacrificed on the altar of ego again and again and again."

While his eyes remain pained, David fervently insists, "Music is magic, man. There hasn't been a major magic on the planet since the caveman danced around his fire going 'ugga-bugga, ugga-bugga.' Music is what people do when they feel good. It's a magic, it's an elevating force in our lives, in our consciousness. It makes us not alone.

"Issues were crystallizing that polarized the country in the sixties and made everyone think they had to stand up and be counted. Music was a unifying force. 'Long Time Gone' seemed to mean a lot to people. 'Almost Cut My Hair' seemed to mean a lot. So did 'Teach Your Children.'

"Apathy overtook everything," says David, "There are big divisive issues that are tearing the country up. The same people are still running the country, and they're getting ready to get us into another war. They'll sacrifice one hundred thousand people in the blink of an eye. You can smell the new war acoming.

"It's sort of a guerrilla warfare I play, where I try to spot one of those moments when you can affect everything hugely by just one small act, one human being standing up and sticking up for the right thing. I look for those moments. I'm praying I'll come across one."

His voice cracks with emotion. Standing up again, he clenches his fists. He then stares at his guests and in a barely audible tone says beseechingly, "I don't harm anybody, I don't steal, lie or cheat, or mess with other people's old ladies or anything. I've tried really hard to be a decent human being. All I do is go around and make people feel good— that's my whole life's work, to make people happy. I try really hard to be a positive force."

But, like that of many flower children, David's revolutionary ardor cooled in the 1970s. He continued to mourn Christine's death and retreated to a more private world.

The word spread quickly. In Los Angeles and Marin County, David's closest friends heard that he had a drug problem. In early 1981, the story traveled like a brushfire that while on tour David had twice fallen unconscious after freebasing.

Some members of the music community doubted David would survive the year. Cynics wagered among themselves on *when* he'd finally do himself in.

Others wanted to help him, but what could be done?

As David drove to an antinuclear rally on March 28, 1982, cocaine and a .45 revolver were concealed by his side. Nodding off en route, he crashed into a divider on the San Diego Freeway. When the police searched his car he was arrested for possessing methaqualone, cocaine paraphernalia, and the gun, as well as for driving recklessly. He was allowed to plead guilty to the driving violation, while the other charges were dropped, and was sentenced to three years' probation, fined $751, and ordered to enroll in a drug program.

A few weeks later, David was again in trouble. Big trouble.

Desperate for money, even if it meant playing in sleazy bars, on April 13, 1982, David turned up at Cardi's, a now defunct rock club in Dallas. Around midnight, two cops responded to a fight that had broken out in the parking lot outside the club. One cop entered the club and went backstage. He saw David holding a propane torch in one hand and a pipe in the other. As the policeman approached, David flung aside a green bag that contained coke and a loaded .45 and screamed, "Don't do this to me, don't do this to me!"

David made other emotional appeals in court. "Jail is no joke," he told Judge Patrick McDowell. "Handcuffs are no joke. It's real serious stuff. It's been very lonely. I spent a lot of nights lying there thinking about it. Those bars are very real. It certainly frightened me. I don't want to do anything ever again, *ever,* that puts me in jeopardy. I want to feel proud of myself and stand for something again."

Cold and dispassionate, the Dallas D.A., Knox Fitzpatrick, wanted David to do hard time, five years, in a state prison. And on June 3, 1983, David was found guilty. But the legality of the search was disputed in Texas courts and David was freed on bond during the appeal. As he said, "For a thumbnail's worth of pipe residue they sentenced me to five years. I guess they wanted to make an example of me."

Despite his fears, David continued to freebase on his 1984 solo tour. In October of that year, David was arrested again for recklessly driving his motorcycle in the Marin County town of Ross. Police found in his possession heroin, cocaine, marijuana, a rubber hose tourniquet, a spoon, a torch, a pipe with coke residue, two daggers, a knife, white-powder residue on two of the knives, and other narcotics paraphernalia. He later pleaded guilty to the driving charge, and received three years' probation and a fine of $1,325.

In Texas, Knox Fitzpatrick heard of David's rearrest. He intensified his campaign to get David put away. Another hearing was held before Judge McDowell in December 1984, and David was ordered into the drug rehabilitation program at the Fair Oaks Hospital in Summit, New Jersey.

When David entered the hospital, he immediately refused to take part in any of the therapy sessions. He repeatedly begged his manager to take him back to California. According to his counselor, Dr. Stephen Pittel, David would belligerently reject the staff's overtures, then sob uncontrollably for help, then turn hostile again. He suffered from several illnesses, including edema (his ankles were swollen to four times their normal size), apnea (a condition where breathing stops for twenty to thirty seconds during sleep), and dental abcesses.

During the fifth week of confinement David began to participate in the program. He met with other drug abusers and talked about how addiction had ruined his life. He'd cry grievously during these traumatic sessions. He began composing music for the first time in three years, organized a hospital band, and asked for permission to bring in a synthesizer. The request was denied, but David continued to cooperate with the doctors. Hospital staffers believed David had "turned a corner." He acted like a man transformed, strolling happily on Fair Oaks lawns.

On February 24, 1985, during one of these walks, a car driven by an unidentified old girlfriend of David's pulled up to the hospital, and he jumped in. He wasn't seen for the next twenty-six hours—not until the New York police arrested him near Greenwich Village for possession of cocaine.

Unable to post a ten-thousand-dollar bond, David was held at the Tombs and on Rikers Island. Eventually, he was assigned an attorney from the public defender's office, but he remained in jail for four days. He appeared at hearings wearing torn and badly stained clothes and barely spoke. From Texas, Knox Fitzpatrick assigned two deputies to bring David back for having again violated his bond. David meekly submitted to Fitzpatrick's demands for his extradition.

After another Texas hearing, where it was disclosed that David was addicted to cocaine and heroin, he was given a set of white coveralls and locked up in the "tank" that housed seven other inmates. He was made a trustee in the medical ward. For a week he swept and mopped floors in the infirmary and assisted guards in the cafeteria. He was granted other privileges, including the freedom to walk around a dayroom and to eat in the general dining room.

Yet the guards soon had trouble with him. On March 15, David was warned about eating food off the cafeteria carts as he served the other inmates. The following day he missed work and was reprimanded. Complaining about not feeling well, he came late to work the next four days. David was stripped of his privileges and put in a more restrictive setting.

Confined for most of the day to a forty-square-foot cell, David spent the next month in virtual isolation. He constantly telephoned Casanova, hoping his manager could get him released. As Casanova recounts, "[Jail] It scared the shit out of him. He tried to get hold of me every day. He was afraid he'd never get out. He'd just plead with me and say, 'Jack, you gotta get me out of here, please, please, man. I've been good, I did everything people told me to do. I took off for a little while, I know that was wrong. Please, get me out of here. I'm going crazy, I'm going to kill myself.' "

Philadelphia, July 13, 1985. It is an emotional benediction. Joan Baez, the Mother Teresa of the sixties counterculture, moves onto the Live Aid stage and dramatically proclaims to the crowd, "Welcome children of the eighties, this is your Woodstock." As she sings "Amazing grace, How sweet the sound . . ." Baez seems to be trying to evoke ghosts of that rain-soaked, three-day conclave. But that's a long time gone, and Live Aid isn't Woodstock II. Too much has changed in America, in the music industry, and especially in David Crosby to justify such a comparison. In 1969, skinny-dipping hippies were taking LSD and chanting obscenities at Nixon, while at JFK Stadium short-haired preppies were waving the Stars and Stripes. Back then rock raged against the Establishment; today it's a multimillion-dollar enterprise, a cornerstone of the American mainstream.

Here, David is interviewed by MTV's Alan Hunter, and talks about an unfinished album, and the 1985 CSN tour. Barely able to keep his eyes open, he tells Hunter, "I'm a happy man, I'm a very happy man. If I was put here on this planet to do anything, it was this [singing]. Things are looking great. You saw what we do, you saw how well we're doing, you see my friends are still my loyal friends. I'm just overjoyed to be back doing exactly what I'm supposed to be doing. I'm a very happy man."

But onstage, David Crosby, the counterculture's "Yosemite Sam," was hardly able to stand upright. His face was covered with makeup, yet the scars from his staph sores are still visible. His stringy, thinning hair and bloated stomach were kept from the TV audience. Yet David is still more evocative of Altamont's savagery than of "Teach Your Children."

As Graham Nash said that day, "I'm amazed that he's still alive. He'll eventually die—it's only a question of when. He won't want to hear that. He'll read that and despise me for a while. I've armored myself, but it's heartbreaking."

Arlo Guthrie
In the Shadow of a Curse

The rebellion began in a garbage dump on Thanksgiving. It soon spread to an army induction center in New York City, and wound up at Alice's, a ramshackle restaurant in the heart of the Berkshires.

It was a picaresque journey, one that gave Arlo Guthrie a unique heroic aura. From the twenty-five-dollar fine he incurred for dumping trash, to his confrontations with the draft board, he was the Little Guy daring to question Authority. We loved him for it. He was *our* kind of patriot, an innocent, sweet Don Quixote type, who bumbled his way to becoming one of the most effective antiwar spokesmen of the 1960s.

Protest was in the Guthrie family tradition. Woody, Arlo's father, was an avowed Communist, who challenged the Establishment with fiery folk songs. Wandering across America with a guitar in hand, he endured poverty, a crippling disease (Huntington's chorea, a disorder of the nervous system), and faced vicious attacks from right-wing critics. At journey's end, though, he had gotten his message across. Woody Guthrie's songs are a body of literature unto themselves, reference works which have influenced Pete Seeger, "Rambling" Jack Elliott, Bob Dylan, and a host of other folk singers.

Clearly, Woody was a hard act to follow. His shadow was so long, it was difficult for Arlo to establish his own singing credentials. Yet Arlo overcame this pressure, and moved past the pure folk, leftist-political vernacular of "Alice's Restaurant," to do the rock-flavored "City of New Orleans" (a Top 20 hit in 1972). Later, he became even more eclectic, by combining ragtime, Irish reel, country, gospel, and pop/blues on his LP, *Last of the Brooklyn Cowboys* (1973). Having already enlarged the boundaries of his father's folk tradition, he could turn political again, as was strikingly evident in his savage attack on Richard Nixon in "Presidential Rag." Yet most of his subsequent writing has a decidedly spiritual, confessional quality. In two albums, *Amigo* and *Outlasting the Blues,* he confronts the possibility of inheriting his father's disease, but these musings are more than a mature, lyrical reflection on death. They're a symbolic leave-taking, an assertion of Arlo's own individuality apart from his father's fame.

It was, however, a costly evolution. Arlo is no longer the free spirit, dedicated to making music for its own artistic sake. Unlike his father, who was ever wary of the System's corruptions, Arlo has become less critical of the Establishment, and is hoping to join the corporate structure by financing a deal to take over a group of Massachusetts TV stations. Angrily insisting that the music industry "has made it impossible for me to get my work to the public," he feels such "media participation" will assure him more air time, and "a chance to revolutionize the system from within." To assure the requisite licensing, though, Arlo has already agreed to be the model citizen. Now living in Washington, Massachusetts, not far from the scene of his past "crimes" in Stockbridge, he's active in community affairs, and performs as the bubbly grand marshal of the local Fourth of July picnic. While dismissing these activities as playing the game, Arlo recently joined a group of other businessmen for lunch at the Reagan White House.

"I'll admit it, I'm a nasty conservative. I like what America stands for, we just have to be concerned with making this country better," exalts Guthrie, relaxing in the living room of his modest mountaintop house. Exhausted after cleaning a recent accumulation of snow from his driveway, he takes a hearty sip of coffee before adding, "Maybe I'll be remembered as a revolutionary. But that would be a shame. I just pointed out, through humor, the absurdity of a myopic society. That sounds hard, yet there's more than one way to be an American.

"The toughest moment of my life was when they were inducting me and they wouldn't believe I was a sincere patriot. That pissed me off. I didn't want anyone telling me 'Love it or leave it'. I don't want the Left or the Right deciding how I should lead my life. I'm involved on the political level because I want to make those decisions. Everyone has the responsibility to do something for America. I like being here, that's why I was opposed to Vietnam; I thought the war, and people anesthetized from doing anything, were hurting us."

Despite the emotion in Guthrie's voice, this patriotic paean seems strangely out of character. For in the late 1960s, Arlo was the consummate flower child, from his symbolically rebellious, shoulder-length hair, to the defiant strains of his tunes. He's now espousing a "rugged individualism," akin to his father's own wanderings through the train yards and dust bowls of Depression America. But these beliefs, even if they celebrate a certain "freedom," are only a faint echo of his former battle cries. In "Coming into Los Angeles," Guthrie gives dope smugglers a rousing fight song, while "Alice's Restaurant" mocks the social order so blatantly, it's an anthem for anarchism.

The Arlo of these latter songs is the kid the Left loved in the 1960s, and that persona is far more familiar than his new incarnation. Perhaps Guthrie's politics have changed as a result of some Freudian revolt against his father, his recent musical failures or maybe it's just a reflection of our me-oriented society. Arlo now has a wife and four children to support, and the financial benefits from a TV station or two would be a hedge on their future security.

But whatever the reason, this thrust for middle-class respectability is still surprising. Even as a child, growing up in Brooklyn's famed Coney Island, Arlo was an outsider, a loner who frequently drifted between mischief and all-out rebellion. Or as a child psychiatrist succinctly put it, he was "strange."

"I guess I had gotten into some kind of trouble at school, and, in looking for an excuse to get rid of me, this shrink told my mother, 'He's acting very strange, but after meeting you, it's understandable,' " laughs Arlo, remembering how his mother had to interrupt her work with the Martha Graham Dance Company to bail him out at school. "I was absolutely opposed to everything that went on at school. It perpetuated an insanity. I think of school as learning to do things you don't like, things that are against the better aspects of human nature."

A different sort of education was provided at home. Though Woody spent most of the early 1950s in a hospital, the Guthrie living room was a meeting place for the stars of the folk circuit. Whenever Pete Seeger, Leadbelly, or Ramblin' Jack Elliott came to visit, they showed the young Arlo how to pick their guitars, and by the sixth grade, he combined this talent with a budding virtuosity on the piano.

Realizing he could play both instruments "faster and cleaner" than his teachers, Arlo started to go dancing with girls, and inevitably discovered the Everly Brothers. "They were it, for dancing slow and being close to girls. The Everlys were something," Guthrie says, blushing boyishly. "Their album was the first one I ever bought. I still have it.

Those were the songs I first started to play. The harmonies were great, real simple."

Arlo became dependent on the guitar the way most boys need a baseball glove. It gave him status. Unable to compete with his peers on the athletic field, yet wanting to be accepted by girls, he was constantly entertaining people. At camp, on vacation trips, wherever he went, Arlo took along his guitar, and "could always be counted on to liven up things."

But admitting, "I could still be a real pain in the ass," Arlo got into enough trouble on the streets to be sent away to a Stockbridge, Massachusetts, boarding school. That experience was supposed to give him new self-discipline. Though, as Arlo admits, "Just the reverse happened. There were a lot of weird kids there, enough of us to convince the rest of the population that we were having a lot more fun. The seeds for the '65 riots at Berkeley were planted in my class. We changed the course of history."

Only fourteen at the time, Arlo again ignored his schoolbooks in favor of more esoteric pleasures. It was 1961 and he began to wear his hair longer, and to be swept up by the growing tide of social protest. He attended civil rights and "Ban the Bomb" demonstrations.

"I went to Washington a great number of times. I was very concerned, and because I was Woody's kid, I was always next to Martin Luther King or other personalities," remembers Arlo, as his eyes sparkle with pride.

While such activism seems far behind him today, after pausing to get a second cup of coffee, he humorously continues, "These demonstrations were a lot more important than my studying chemistry, besides, my political convictions were all in place." He laughs. "Seeger or Ochs usually took care of me, they made sure I wasn't stepped on. I think Dylan had to watch over me at the Newport Folk Festival in '61. I don't think he ever talked to me, he just pointed me out, 'Here's Woody's kid.' I grew up knowing all these people as caretakers."

In the early 1960s, Arlo used these contacts to make the Greenwich Village scene. His interest in the rising folk movement had become such an obsession, he remembers feeling, "You had to be overwhelmed by the power of what was happening. So much was going on. I was hanging out with Ramblin' Jack, living at [Phil] Ochs's house, I just knew all these people. I had the thing scoped out. I knew where Dylan was, and while I wasn't too impressed with his personality, I knew he was important.

"There were also a lot of old blues people around, Mississippi John Hurt, [John] Sebastian, the Fugs were starting up. I knew all of them. I just went from place to place, knowing I could pick up ten dollars for playing. One of the nicest nights in my life was when I played with Hurt and Sebastian at the Gaslight. Hurt suggested it, I did some pickin', and just loved it."

His face glowing, Arlo sighs contentedly. He then adds, "Boy, did I love it. I knew the old guys, they were Dad's friends. I could go in any club, it didn't matter if I was underage . . . I wasn't an outsider, I wasn't alone any more. I had found a niche."

Acceding to his mother's wishes, however, he went to music school, to "the only place that would have me," Rocky Mountain College in Billings, Montana. Six weeks after arriving there, he heard Dylan's "Positively 4th Street." Blown away by the song, he said to himself, "Wow, things are really happening," and quickly returned to the East Coast.

The war in Vietnam was heating up at this time (1965–66), and losing a college deferment was risky business. But Arlo didn't care. He wanted to make music. And besides, he felt the war was wrong. It didn't matter that the draft board was pursuing him. It was time to take a stand.

In an "unofficial" Stockbridge garbage dump.

"It seemed like a logical place to put it, there was a lot of other garbage around," explains Arlo, ingenuously describing how the remains of his Thanksgiving dinner led to a forbidden field—and a heap of glory. "I didn't have any choice. The town dump was closed, and I wanted to help my friends, whom I was having dinner with. Well, as you know, I was arrested, fined. The judge in the case *was* really blind; everything was so funny, I started to sing about it."

The comic relief of "Alice's Restaurant" made it a hippie-era theme song. Unlike the strident calls from the barricades, or the shrill demands of certain war protestors, "Alice" had a sweet, nonintimidating flavor. It questioned Authority, but Arlo's gentle, lulling voice gave the fifteen-minute tune universal appeal.

"Once the song came out in '67, the girls went crazy, they chased me down the street, and attacked me on the stage," chuckles Arlo, who at thirty-nine, has gained even more sex appeal, as his long hair is now handsomely flecked with gray.

"I liked that kind of attention, who wouldn't? The only thing I wasn't comfortable with was the hype. It seemed dishonest. So I toured a lot, I wanted to get away from the dishonesty.

"Then, the movie came out in '69, and it seemed as if the whole world was after me. There was no way to get away from it. I got married, but I didn't think my being a celebrity was good for kids, so I bought this place. I don't get bothered too much up here.

"As for the movie, I have mixed feelings about it. Only some parts of it were true. They fictionalized real people . . . but I wasn't an actor, they wanted me to be someone I wasn't. There were a lot of things in the film that betrayed people. One scene leads you to believe that I'm having intimate relations with Alice . . . that kind of thing disrupted all our lives. As a movie, I love it, but to have made it, I'm sorry.

"The movie, though . . ."

Before Arlo can talk about the film's impact, the front door slams open, and a parka is heaved onto a living-room coat rack. Arlo's fourteen-year-old son, Abe, is back from school.

"How did it go today?" shouts Arlo.

Hurrying into the kitchen to get a snack, the teenager smiles shyly, pats his father on the back, and without saying a word, runs out the door.

"He has a studio above the garage," explains Arlo, shaking his head. "He's talking about being a drummer.

"But what was I saying about the movie? Oh yeah, in the general sense it was helpful, it showed people the system was idiotic, that they could be against the authorities . . . and maybe it even gave people the guts to challenge two presidents. There was a loss of fear, *that* was the impact of the movie."

After snickering, "Warner Brothers made a fortune off it," he talks about his being "a new marketable product," and the "great commercialization of rock" after Woodstock.

"Once that film was successsful, the Establishment realized there was an audience out there they could market to. People realized you could sell soap if you just called it natural.

"I never wrote 'Alice's Restaurant' to make money, but in three days Woodstock changed the American perception of who we were. We weren't just a few crazies, but everyone's kids. That event changed everyone's life . . . and I became a product . . . I made a fortune, and spent it as quickly as I made it."

The early seventies were indeed a fun time for Arlo. After Woodstock and "Alice's Restaurant" certified his leftist credentials, he toured extensively, both abroad and on American college campuses. He also made it to the Top 20 with "City of New Orleans" in 1972. But as Arlo admits, the success of that song almost eluded him.

"Steve [Goodman] wanted to play it for me in a bar in Chicago, but I really didn't want to hear what he had written," says Arlo. "I was tired, or something. I just wasn't interested. But he was so persistent, I said 'Okay, kid, I'll listen if you buy me a beer.' I'm glad he did."

Subsequently, Arlo wrote most of his own material, and while his LPs were usually hailed by the critics, their sales were very disappointing. This hasn't dampened Arlo's spirits. Insisting "My best songs are still in front of me," he defends such albums as *Hobo's Lullaby* (1972), *Arlo Guthrie* (1974), *Amigo* (1976), then chides record companies for "not knowing how to market my stuff."

"I feel like a farmer who has a product no one knows what to call. So it can't go up on a shelf in the supermarket for people to see. I'm interested in communicating, but I can't get my message out there right now. Record companies don't look at the value of music, they're only interested in making money, in 'hot' records, then it's good-bye . . . the only way to change this marketing approach is to own the suckers. What I want to do is to establish my credentials, for I feel my ideas are of value, artistic and economic. It's worth a shot."

While Arlo pursues this dream of owning a few TV stations, he's a fixture on the international touring circuit. He'd rather recapture his American audience, but extended tours in Italy, Scandinavia, and other parts of Europe are a "decent income," and he still gets to do occasional benefits with Seeger. These engagements are enjoyable, and help satisfy his yearnings to "experiment with new ideas, new directions in my music."

But Arlo has different priorities today. Married sixteen years, to "a woman [Jackie] who's just as crazy as I am," he has four kids to take care of, and that gets most of his attention.

"There's nothing more rewarding than raising a bunch of kids in the country, but I need all the energy I can get," says Arlo, grinning broadly, after one of his three daughters comes home from school, and mischievously dips a cracker into a pot of simmering chili.

"Hey, get out of that," shouts Arlo. "Mom's been making that for dinner. Go do your homework."

Instead of listening to him, the little girl picks up a jigsaw-puzzle box and runs off to her room with it. One of the family dogs also scampers through the house, adding to the general tumult, but Arlo isn't perturbed. He lights a cigarette, and, smiling as sweetly as he did in the

1960s, says, "Some of my music setbacks have been painful, but my wife and I think that having a family is far more important than fame or anything else. Money's helpful, but you got to remember that working is like a kid's game. You should just play at it. You have to remember that you must go home and have dinner with someone you care about. Family makes life interesting, worthwhile.

"You gotta make time for your family life. You have to dedicate most of your energies to it. A wife and kids is what life's all about. For the truth is, we're all gonna die. And your family, or what you have going with your wife and kids, is the only significant thing a person really has."

Since these musings are punctuated by the loud arrival of more children and dogs, Arlo can't be asked the inevitable question: *Is he worried about inheriting his father's dread disease?* There's just too much life around him to probe such a delicate matter. He might be haunted by such a possibility, but as he frolics with one of his daughters on the couch, such a question would be grossly out of place.

Besides, it's better to see him laughing and smiling. We remember him for his boyishness, that aura of innocence which symbolized the 1960s. So why dampen his spirits? Or darken the mood? Sadly, too much about him has already changed.

Don McLean
It Certainly Wasn't Apple, Blueberry, or Peach

No one was smiling in 1971. America was bleeding. Our soul had been ravaged, and angry, warring voices echoed across the land.

Vietnam had done this to us. By this time, the war seemed never ending, a permanent sadness in our midst, that foreclosed any hope, any purpose, any reason to go on.

As the daily casualty reports mounted sickeningly, the headlines kept repeating themselves.

The deadly seventies began with Kent State. The war came home to us then, as four students lost their lives on an Ohio hill. While this fanned the flame of revolt—over one hundred universities were closed down in a sympathetic show of bereavement—the military high command wasn't impressed. The word "escalation" took on new meaning—"incursions" into Cambodia and Laos, "blockbuster" air bombs from "Stratofortresses," and by February of '71 a confession. Lieutenant William L. Calley, Jr., had directed the mass execution of twenty-two South Vietnamese civilians in an irrigation ditch at My Lai.

The litany of crimes went on and on. The Pentagon Papers underscored the sad fact. But we didn't need reports, Dr. Daniel Ellsberg, policy study groups, think tanks, or even Walter Cronkite to tell us what was happening. Our national nightmare was all too close. Like Calley, we were now mired in death.

Seeing the American Dream explode in the rice paddies of Vietnam, Don McLean felt the war was "ripping away at our souls . . . ruining what had been special about us." This "loss of spirit" theme weighed on him for years. It was expressed in "Orphans of Wealth," and then, in "Tapestry," with its cries against greed and ecological disaster. But by the spring of 1971, as the news from Vietnam grew progressively worse (casualty totals were mounting to new yearly highs), McLean felt even more betrayed by America.

In what can only be described as an apocalyptic vision, McLean had "one of those rare moments, when everything is connected . . . everything makes sense." Seeing the links between "the death of our spirit and the death of God," he took this idea to its inevitable conclusion, and saw Satan's role in yet another death, that of music.

"It was an idea that had to be stated," says McLean, with a passion that evoked the temper of those terrible times in America. "It didn't matter if I was branded a pariah in the business, the idea had to be expressed."

And so it was. While visiting a friend in Philadelphia, he sat in the living room, and in a matter of hours, his flagging spirits gave birth to an American classic. He wrote "American Pie."

Though McLean warned people against interpreting the song, its acid lyrics clearly sounded a dirge for sixties optimism. The imagery, replete with devils, court jesters, and sacrificial fires, had a mystifying, metaphysical bent. But the bottom line of this poem was clear: America had gone astray, and would pay for its sins. Because of its mad adventurism abroad, the country's soul had sickened and died. And in this milieu, where hope and idealism gave way to bullets and bloodlusts, music lost its meaning, its redemptive power.

The song was an instant sensation. It sold over 75,000 copies a week for several months, and quickly hit the top of the charts (since 1971, over 3½ million copies of the single have been bought, while album sales total close to 2 million). Mirroring this climb, McLean suddenly became "a hot property." He was a wandering troubadour at the time, singing in the Massachusetts school system to supplement his often irregular income. But now, the outspoken antiwar activist, who has raised money for ecological causes along with Pete Seeger on the Hudson River sloop *Clearwater,* was in demand. Griffin, Carson, Cavett, Carnegie Hall, London's Royal Albert Hall, they all wanted him. And for a long-haired, twenty-six-year-old folk singer, who simply wanted "to make Americans think about what was happening to their country," the notoriety was a terrific adjustment.

"My life was no longer mine; my agent—and everyone else—was

calling the shots," remembers McLean, while strolling through the woods that surround his small yet comfortable house in upstate New York. Visited during a lull in his extensive touring schedule, one that has him playing over two hundred engagements a year between Australia and Europe, he seems to welcome this rare opportunity to relax, to look proudly at a pair of prized horses in a nearby corral, and to talk about the past. "In those days, I didn't have the kind of time to be here, or the time for horses. Other people were telling me where to go, what to do, I didn't have any control over my life. Things had gone from being simple, from my living in a lean-to in the Berkshires to my being a big business in Hollywood.

"Geez, it was heavy. There was tremendous pressure for me to tour, produce new records, do TV. I did it. On the road 250 to 275 nights a year, I went into overdrive, and for a while there, I was really spinning my wheels. I was suddenly a rich man, but things got so heavy, I had to do some soul searching. That big prize I was always going after didn't look all that big anymore."

There were also other pressures, as McLean's prophecy came true with a vengeance. He was viewed as a "reactionary heretic" by the music press, and they crucified him at every possible opportunity. Besides criticizing his albums and concerts, these rock writers constantly questioned the imagery of "American Pie." Who was the "jester," or "Jack Flash"? These kinds of questions, which inevitably raised doubts about his loyalties to rock 'n' roll, dogged him. His critics had been weaned on Presley and the Everlys, and since they felt his lyrics signaled a death knell for rock 'n' roll (even though McLean dedicated the album to Buddy Holly), this Judas had to suffer. For years, the critics made his life miserable.

Despite his dark message, McLean wasn't a traitor. He has always been a faithful follower of the music, especially during his childhood. Then, an asthmatic condition kept him out of school for two to three months a year, and since this meant a lot of time alone at home, he turned to records. Little Richard, the Everlys, Bo Diddley, Elvis; these men became his companions. Because of his health problems, he couldn't travel down to the Brooklyn Fox from New Rochelle, New York, like the rest of his friends. But he still showed his loyalty to the "King" by playing "Don't Be Cruel," or "Love Me Tender" a hundred times a day, and suffering the consequences for it.

"My parents would come totally apart, they couldn't stand the noise, and they'd let me know it," says McLean, with a big, crescent-shaped smile. "I guess they figured out I was seriously into the stuff . . . and once my father realized I wanted to be a musician I think he would've preferred my hanging myself."

Ignoring his parents' protests, the thirteen-year-old McLean started to play the acoustic guitar, and joined a rock 'n' roll band. Playing local record hops made him "feel important," but since the frail teenager began to think "it was a drag carrying that heavy shit around," his interests changed. "I didn't throw out my rock 'n' roll records, I just listened to them half of the time." He wanted to play solo, and that urge led him to a new group of heroes, folk people like Josh White, and the Weavers.

In 1960, about a year after this switch, McLean's father died. The fifteen-year-old was now called upon to take care of his mother, and while he remembers this as "a sad, terrible time," the period was also liberating. No longer criticized at home, he could concentrate on his music; and as McLean more cheerfully adds, "I haven't come up for air since."

This enthusiasm was fueled by Jim Croce. The two singers met at Villanova University, after McLean bowed to his mother's wishes and continued his schooling. Except for an interest in theology, he didn't pay much attention to his studies.

"He didn't teach me that much, we came at the music from very different directions. But he was the big man on campus, he had his own radio show. I was a basket case in college, it was very hard for me. But knowing him made everything palatable. He was constantly reassuring me . . . and after a while I could say, 'Brother, I've been made for this, I gotta go for it.' "

Enlivened by this memory, McLean drops a seltzer bottle he's been carrying, and runs after his dog, Bonz. The terrier, perhaps used to his master's games, scampers back and forth along the tree-lined trail. Though forty-one, and a bit paunchy, McLean is ready for the challenge. In a few moments he catches up with the dog, and gives him a loving pat on the head.

"Whew, that's tough work," exclaims McLean, the sweat dripping from his forehead. "I guess I'm getting old."

Chuckling, he returns to where the seltzer bottle was dropped, and takes a hefty swig. With the bottle still poised near his lips, he chortles, "Maybe we should get back to the past, it's a whole lot easier."

It seems that way now. After fifty worldwide platinum records, he came back onto the charts as recently as 1981 with "Crying" (number five), and is still playing to large audiences.

But much to his dismay, moving from Villanova to the folk circuit wasn't all that easy in the mid-1960s. Abruptly leaving school after only six months, he soon realized "the folk thing just wasn't happening." Except for a few dates at Philadelphia's Main Point, and the Bitter End in New York, there were so few opportunities for him, he made another rash decision in 1965. He returned to Iona College, to study philosophy and graduated in 1968.

Up until this point, he had always said, "I wouldn't care if I had to live in the woods somewhere without a nickel, just as long as I could make music." And upon graduation, that's exactly what happened. A New York State agency hired him to play a series of summer concerts in parks, Hudson River towns, and remote wilderness areas.

Through this job, he became friendly with the father of the folkies, Pete Seeger. The noted political activist was doing concerts in the Catskills for various ecological causes, and invited McLean to join him. Recalling, "This was a turning point for me," McLean had to write several new songs for his growing audience. And by the end of the summer, he had enough material to issue his first album, *Tapestry*, in 1970.

Though *Tapestry* didn't sell that well, it got such favorable reviews, McLean was soon opening for the "heaviest and loudest acts around"— performers like Blood, Sweat and Tears, and Steppenwolf. He was now part of the music establishment. The William Morris Agency signed him, and he made enough money to buy some land in upstate New York. The house came later.

As McLean wistfully says, "This was the greatest period in my life. Later on, all the questions about 'American Pie' were a drag. But then, things were relaxed. I could focus on my playing, the writing, and growing as a musician. I had time for real things."

"American Pie" changed that. It made him a public figure, subject to the caprices of the market place. He could be "the new force in popular music" one year, a nonentity the next. It all depended on how he played the game; on his willingness to sacrifice himself for fame and riches. And for a self-described "loner," who stubbornly held on to his iconoclastic beliefs, this was a frightening new departure, one that eventually robbed him of his spirit.

" 'American Pie' became my hook that everything revolved around, and, God, was I skewered with it," relates McLean, halting on the path to lean against a tree. His tanned face mirroring both anger and pain, he caustically continues, "It was like being an ex-Beatle, people wouldn't question Paul McCartney about anything else. 'American Pie,' 'American Pie' . . . it was horrible . . . every time I'd have another record I'd be asked, 'But is it as big as "American Pie"?' It was a draining, totally annoying experience."

"People just went ape shit over it, they had to have everything interpreted. That was the least interesting part of it. I wanted to keep the mystery and when I wouldn't answer I was pictured as a spoiler, the person who was out to kill rock 'n' roll. Damn, was that heavy. I was in such a bind."

"I got so frustrated, I'd tell people I wasn't going to sing the song anymore. But did I learn a lesson in show business, whew! Was it horrible! I did this show in Saratoga Springs in '73, and when it was over I told some friends 'that's it for "American Pie," I'm not going to do it again!' Well, some AP person overheard that, and it went over the wire services. It was completely false, I didn't mean it. But people picked up on it, and for a long time people wouldn't come to see me—that was it —my career was really hurt."

Ironically, "American Pie" now drove McLean to Europe. Here, he could escape from his inquisitors, without any perceptible drop in income. For "Vincent," his tribute to artist Vincent Van Gogh (on the *American Pie* album), had already propelled him to the top of the European charts. The press also treated him as a returning hero, and when remembering that, McLean gets noticeably irritated. Wincing, he defensively says, "unless you host 'The Tonight Show' you don't get the big crowds in this country. Maybe that'll change in the future, with a new record I'm going to release *The Best of Don McLean*. But I've always had greater strength in Europe and Australia. I don't know why, I'm just eternally grateful."

Spending most of his time abroad during this period (1972–77), McLean fared badly in America. His albums, particularly *Playin' Favorites* (done in a country/bluegrass style with mandolinist Frank Wakefield, on United Artists) and Arista's *Prime Time* (which even McLean calls "weird") didn't sell very well, and by 1978, he was looking around for a new record company. Arista picked him up for *Chain Lightning* (1980), but McLean's covers of Gene Vincent's "Lotta Lovin'," Buddy Holly's "It Doesn't Matter Anymore," and Roy Orbison's "Crying" got little air play. As of 1980, McLean was admittedly, a dead issue.

Strangely, though, "Crying" suddenly started to attract attention in

Holland over a year later. DJs there got hundreds of requests for it, and the song soon climbed to the top of the Dutch charts. This sparked a similar surge of interest in England, and by 1982, "Crying" brought McLean back home. Once again he broke into the American Top 10 (number five).

"My whole career has been a fluke," says McLean, a smile returning to his face. "Every few years something pops out. What's going to happen next, who knows. I'm going to try to get my songwriting career together. I have some plans for beyond '85, there's a whole lot of music I want to explore."

"But whatever happens, I've had my dreams come true. I've put out eleven albums, and best of all, a lot of these songs have been adopted by people. They're handed down to their children. I got a lot of flak for 'American Pie,' but people have chosen it as their anthem. It doesn't matter if people called me a reactionary thirteen years ago. It's a great song, people cherish it."

Turning around now to walk back to the house, McLean stops to stare at his two horses. He talks about their Arabian lineage for a moment, and then, echoing the mood of the sixties, he forcefully concludes, "Yeah, that song makes me happy, but America's still on life-support systems. There's no commitment to anything. My generation's in power now, but they're only giving lip service to the old ideals . . . and the music, it has such a terrifying, fascistic edge. It's just riffs, something to watch fashion by. Maybe we can right ourselves out of this wicked turn, but now, I sometimes feel like a silent screen star. The music just doesn't seem important anymore."

Joe McDonald of Country Joe and the Fish
Woodstock Is but a Distant Memory

As thousands of people frolicked in the mud, high on love or other intoxicants, the Woodstock crowd was swept into the revolution.

"Give me an 'F,' " bellowed a long-haired zealot, shaking a clenched fist, and moving frenetically around the stage.

Evoking the spirit of a Bible Belt revival meeting, the cry was greeted with a deafening roar, a thunderclap of "F's" that seemed to sway nearby trees.

"Give me a 'U,' " he exhorted, charged with the collective energy of his troops.

Expecting a more innocent "I," the crowd was instantly electrified. Boys with beads around their necks, girls stripped to their waists, smiled, and happily obeyed their leader. The revolution was on.

Over 400,000 youths were ready for another command. Peace and love would be the battle cry, but first, the freckle-faced cheerleader on the stage cleared his throat and asked for a "C."

The din was terrific. When Joe asked for a "K," the assemblage seemed to summon all its strength; this scream had a deeper more cathartic effect. Unlike the other, more cheerful roars, it was a wail, reflecting the discontent that had been sowed through the 1960s, from the end of Camelot, through the blood-soaked years of Vietnam and urban unrest. The blast, therefore, was felt far beyond the boundaries of

Max Yasgur's farm. Rumbling across the countryside, all the way to Washington, it even made the Nixon White House tremble.

Appropriately, this rebellious cheer was led by someone named after Joseph Stalin, the long-time Berkeley radical Country Joe McDonald. The son of socialist parents, Joe saw his father blacklisted during the 1950s McCarthy hysteria, and he was a natural for the barricades. Nurtured on the protest sounds of Pete Seeger and Woody Guthrie, he felt it was his mission to expand the consciousness of the counterculture, and to change the world through rock 'n' roll. Together with the Fish, a collection of similarly minded musicians, Joe went on the offensive at antiwar teach-ins, where he began his effective attack on the LBJ presidency. Though this targeted him for various FBI/IRS investigations, Joe and the Fish kept flailing away at the Establishment with satire and sometimes savage profanity. This, in effect, made them the Left's musical arm, the group that would eventually be credited for enlarging the contours of political music. For, as Joe says, "We were out there, we were unafraid to martyr ourselves."

And yet, Joe's battle cry at Woodstock can only be called a historical accident.

Many of the greats: Joan Baez, the Who, Joe Cocker, and the Grateful Dead, had already performed, and because of threatening weather conditions, electric groups couldn't play. The crowd was growing restless. To keep the show going, the festival's promoters had to get someone on stage quickly. But who? Fearing a downpour, many of the performers had helicptered back to New York.

Fortunately, the emcee saw Joe in the audience. Rushing over, he asked, "Can you help me out? We really need someone to play!"

Joe was initially reluctant. The Fish had already performed, and their contract didn't call for any encores. But the emcee pleaded with him, and as Joe recalls, "Since I knew the guy, I finally said okay. The only problem was I didn't have a guitar. I left it somewhere when I went off to watch the show."

Chuckling, Joe moves to a shadier seat on his Berkeley patio and continues, "I thought that would put off the guy, but he comes back with this Yamaha he borrowed from a stagehand. I told him I couldn't play it because I didn't have a strap. He then went and got a piece of rope for it. Nothing was going to stop him. I didn't even have a pick, so I wound up using a matchbook cover."

Though admitting, "I didn't really know why I should play, no one was paying much attention by this time anyway." Joe went backstage and asked his business partner if he should try the cheer. Only a few months earlier, at a Central Park concert, he had replaced the original F-I-S-H cry with a spicier version and was banned from all future park festivals. After jokingly asking, "Do you think I can get amnesty after fifteen years?" Joe and his partner agreed that he should do it. "It didn't seem to make much difference; no one was listening. But it's strange, doing the cheer that afternoon really launched me on my solo career."

That *is* ironic.

While Woodstock represents a coming together, that fateful time when music united a divided country, Joe was already set on a more singular journey. Unlike thousands of people around him, who were basking in communal love, Joe felt far less kinship toward the Fish, and wanted to make it on his own. The group had been a family, often rehearsing ten to fourteen hours a day. But Joe saw the band falling apart, the victim of too many concerts, and too many newspaper stories. As he puts it, "There was just too much too soon. We were this hippie band, flying all over the place, and it just got to be too crazy." So after realizing that the Woodstock film would widen his own appeal, he felt he had acquired sufficient reputation to travel around the world, with or without a band.

That might sound harsh, or even calculating. Revolutionary heroes are supposed to be more principled, more loyal to their brothers, but by 1969, Joe was also distancing himself from the Movement. His old, "up against the wall" fervor was dying. Strongly disagreeing with the use of confrontational politics at the 1968 Democratic Convention, he stayed away from Chicago and insisted, "The most important thing to me was to get a new culture. And the only way to get that was through rock 'n' roll, not through politics."

As Joe had foreseen, Chicago was a bummer. The violence horrified him. Angered both by the police and by Jerry Rubin's Yippies, he could only find one middle ground; he turned inward. With the coming of Nixon, that passage was accelerated. "When I saw Tricky Dickie flashing the V-sign, and using the language we invented in the sixties, I knew politics was just a bunch of illusions and rhetoric, both on the Left and the Right. I guess I gave up some of my dreams of what life could be. It was my childhood's end."

It's a mournful lament, one that is shared by many members of the Woodstock Generation. A time gone awry, good people left confused, in search of a cause. Joe was luckier than most. By the time he got to Woodstock he had exchanged his hippie beads for credit cards, and was making nearly eighty thousand dollars a year on the psychedelic circuit. But his leftist commitments ran deep, and to see the revolution awash in violence plainly hurt. It upset him so much, in fact, that his emotionally charged cheer becomes understandable. Though he had admittedly left the Movement, he still felt the need to vent his bitterness. The cheer was his irreverent farewell to the sixties.

Adrift politically, and estranged from the Fish, Joe went abroad. Still a crusader, he put together the All-Star Band, a group of instrument-playing women, and did three European tours a year. The money was good, and Joe enjoyed having an international audience. Even more important, though, these wanderings allowed him to cool out, to recuperate from the sensory overload of the frenetic American rock scene.

Fame wasn't all cash, and LSD; life with the Fish was a grind. The group had done three albums *(Electric Music for the Mind and Body, I-Feel-Like-I'm-Fixin'-to-Die,* and *Together)* in a year and a half, which exhausted them. Not only did they have to promote these albums, but the Fish were also groundbreakers, who took a strange, irreverent message into the heart of middle America, a land where hippies and freaks weren't always welcomed.

"It wasn't easy being at the forefront of the counterculture," recalls the forty-four-year-old Country Joe, straightening in his deck chair, to emphasize the point. Echoing those sixties battles, his voice is deeper than before, and falters. The wrinkles on his freckled, suddenly flushed face also deepen, for this type of reminiscing is painfully tiring. Long-suppressed emotions are released, and that inevitably opens old wounds.

"You have to remember, it was a very tense time in America. There was this thing going on called 'Let's end the war in Vietnam,' and the Fish were in the front of that movement. That might have made us popular in the Bay Area, but once we got away from here, things got very questionable. People were always trying to beat us up, they cursed us, made threats—we had a lot of problems. In the mid-sixties, it just wasn't fashionable for us to be into drugs and against the war. There was tension all the time."

Along with these frontal assaults, the group was further weakened by internal conflicts. None of the members were ready for success, and when they were pressed to be public personalities instead of hippies, quarreling was inevitable. They'd fight over what engagement to accept, money, travel arrangements, and eventually the philosophical or artistic direction of the group. This ate away at friendships. By 1969, the ties that had been formed between Joe, drummer Bruce Barthol, guitarist Chicken Hirsch, and bass player Barry Melton were destroyed. Once again the Fish were a few years ahead of their time, as they said good-bye to Woodstock and walked into the "me" generation.

"The success ruined everything; it destroyed the personal relationship of the group," Joe admits, turning away to hide the hurt. Gazing at his backyard garden, he falls silent for several moments and then says, "The group was just a hobby, a just-for-fun kind of musical group. We didn't want to be too successful. The fame separated people who wanted to be professional musicians, and it did it in an abrupt and rude way. There were arguments and disagreements that have only recently been settled. The wounds have healed.

"I stayed in there and made records, that kept me alive. But the group just burned itself out. We couldn't handle the craziness. All of a sudden we were in Manhattan making a record, then we were in London, then we were in Chicago, then it was Hawaii. There were good times too. It was a great era. But not to be out there like we were. We traveled a million miles, more miles than we thought we'd travel in our lives. And we made more money than we dreamed we'd ever make in our entire lives. That's what I mean by burnout.

"There were members of the band that just said I'm not traveling anymore; I'm not going to Chicago this week or next. We'd have arguments over that, yet we had to go, we had to make more money, and pay the bills. This stuff is supposed to happen to rock groups in ten years. But it happened to us in two years. It was really hard, really hard. We were just swept away."

Amid this "craziness," Joe tried to have a normal social life. He returned from England, and got married for the second time. Afraid of repeating mistakes of the past, he stayed at home more, and led an instant middle-class existence, complete with a baby and swimming pool.

To support this life-style, Joe did occasional concerts during the early seventies, and concentrated on soundtracks for films. Working with Chilean leftists in 1972, he helped produce the political documentary *Què Hacer.* Then, because of his popularity in Scandinavia, he was asked to work on the film version of Henry Miller's *Quiet Days in Clichy.* That led to his joining Jane Fonda and Donald Sutherland, in their *Free/Fuck the Army Revue,* and, more recently, he scored *The Secret Agent,* a documentary about Agent Orange.

While these films were artistically satisfying, Joe didn't make much money from them. His debts started mounting, and, remarried for the second time by 1976, he was forced to return to the European concert circuit. With his new Save the Whale band, he again hopscotched from one place to another, often performing for months at a time. That frenzied pace still characterizes his life, and Joe has gotten to enjoy it, but, at that time, he had little choice. He had gotten married for the third time, but his third wife eventually divorced him, and the alimony payments were a tremendous burden.

Now married for the fourth time, Joe rather reluctantly admits, "I used to be more neurotic than I am now. Maybe it's been difficult to find the right person because I've felt bigger than life. That's the nature of this business. It gives you a false sense of your importance. You come home and think someone's going to ask for your autograph at the dinner table. Until now I never felt safe at home. Whoever you're married to has to be able to see you as a person, not as a star. If that's not so, a lot of problems arise. A lot of problems.

"Now, I'm not blowing myself out of proportion. If you're constantly being told that you're great, and you're getting a lot of money, and everything is easy, you can go on believing you're great and wonderful. There were times I thought I was invincible. And that I would change the world *forever.* I certainly don't feel that way anymore. We have power as individuals, but I'm reluctant to take the spotlight like I did before. Then I could tell people they should take drugs or they shouldn't join the Army. I just can't do that anymore. I'm getting older, and I'm supposed to have some sense by now."

After attributing these changes to "a little more humility," Joe talks about his new fathering and husbanding priorities. He now has two more children, and that prompts him to remember his own father, whom he praises for "hanging in there, even at the worst of times."

A union organizer in the 1950s, Joe's father lost several jobs at the height of the Red Scare. The McCarthy-led witch hunt meant severe financial adjustments for the family, and the elder McDonald eventually had to sell chickens to support his wife and child. Yet he didn't waver. Despite FBI subpoenas, and various investigations, he remained loyal to his political beliefs, and accepted, as Joe says, his lot as an outcast.

Joe, too, has apparently been blacklisted. He says he can't find work in this country, and has to remain in exile in Europe because of his sixties activism.

But that's where the similarities end, and why the praise for his father has a hollow ring. Though working to "save the seals," and on the behalf of Vietnam vets, Joe hasn't hung in there. His political beliefs have drastically changed.

While insisting, "I still believe in peace and love," he calls his music of the sixties "a passing radical phase," and says, "It was crazy to think that wars were won or lost in the streets. I was at the Save the Seals demonstration recently, and there are people there who'd do anything for the cause. Well, I just have to temper that, and tell them to think about what they're doing, think of the repercussions. For me to be a crusader today, I'd have to ignore the responsibilities I have . . . and be like Timothy Leary, espousing all kinds of weirdness."

Then in classic eighties terms, he adds, "I wouldn't lead an F-I-S-H cheer against [Ronald] Reagan. The F-I-S-H cheer works against me at certain times. I'm not willing to say whether I will or will not lead it, you know, it depends on the deal. If someone makes a deal with me not to do it for so much money, then I won't. Besides, I don't feel Reagan is responsible for everything that's happening."

That does sound reasonable and more mature. The single-devil theory of the sixties which exposed LBJ and Nixon to savage personal attacks was often cruel and irrational. But there are too many contradictions here. On the one hand, Joe wants to be remembered for leading the charge against those men, as he poignantly says, "The Fish were really out there; we invented a new psychedelic sound, real cultural lyrics. We were a hundred percent counterculture. We took more acid than the Grateful Dead . . . and really worked hard for the Left."

Yet, when discussing his latest album, *Peace on Earth,* a self-described collection of "very unradical" love songs, Joe longingly says, "I really hope to break into the mainstream . . ."

And that's a far cry from the F-I-S-H cheer at Woodstock.

Chubby Checker
Twisting in the Wind

The self-proclaimed "Albert Einstein of rock 'n' roll" is burning. He's smoking with so much rage, being near him in his manager's New York office is suffocating.

"Do you know I'm as important to rock 'n' roll as Edison was to the electric light bulb? Do you know that? Do you?"

"The most important thing that ever happened with rock 'n' roll is that people were able to dance to it. Who made that possible? Who? It happened because of me. Does anybody give a shit? Society doesn't care."

This is the only part of that outburst that can be repeated. The rest of Chubby Checker's words are an obscene torrent.

His tirade, though, is understandable. It's born out of a deep discontent, a feeling that white America overlooks the black man and his accomplishments. Chubby won't talk about this. In fact, Mr. Twist is so distressed by the way the rock press has ignored him, he refuses to discuss his past, or anything else. When Checker is urged to reconsider, his chubby cheeks swell with anger, and he blisteringly fumes, "Just put my picture in the book, and tell people to shove it."

Chubby deserves a far better remembrance. He did make America dance.

A product of the Philadelphia ghetto, Ernest Evans came North from South Carolina to pluck chickens in a poultry shop. Hoping to supplement his income, he did Fats Domino imitations in local clubs, and was eventually steered to Cameo-Parkway records by Frankie Avalon. Nothing came of that for a while, and like another Philadelphia

dreamer, Rocky Balboa, Evans had to keep plugging along. That is
until Dick Clark needed a Christmas gift. The famed "American Bandstand" leader came to Cameo-Parkway with his wife, looking to cut a
record that could be sent to his friends as a present. As Clark's book
The First 25 Years of Rock & Roll relates, they were so delighted with
Evans's imitations of Domino, Clark's wife Bobbie compared him to the
noted Fat Man, and hence the name, Chubby Checker.

About six months later, in the summer of 1960, Clark also discovered
that the kids on his show were wild about a new Hank Ballard song,
"The Twist." He then convinced Cameo-Parkway to do another version
of the song, and since an exact imitation was agreed upon, Clark knew
just the right person to do it.

But not even Clark, the all-time wizard of spotting rock 'n' roll
trends, could have predicted what would happen next.

Once Chubby debuted "The Twist"—the "dirty dance," that inspired
people to shake their pelvises as never before—on "American Bandstand," it became *the* national craze.

Everyone did it, from the Kennedys and jet-setters to teenagers and
little old ladies. Twistin' was easy, as simple as "putting out a cigarette
with both feet," the nineteen-year old Checker explained. Unimpressed,
many Southern states (and foreign countries) banned the dance, calling
it "lewd" and a threat to our young people. "But this only spurred the
phenomenon. People defiantly kept shaking, and in a matter of months,
over 40 million "Twist" records were sold.

America was clearly "twist crazy." Twist-related products became
the rage. There were "twist"-ed cigars, fringed clothing designed for
"twisters," Barbie dolls dressed to do the twist, and one enterprising
manufacturer who came up with a "twistfurter"—the promoters boldly
suggested, "The twist has now danced its way onto the dinner table."

Chubby, unfortunately, didn't profit that much. As he told a reporter
later on, "Then I watched those kids dancing what I had started. I felt I
had built a rocket ship, sent it to the moon, and I forgot to get on."

But "twisting" was only the first step in the dancing revolution.

Over the next few years, Chubby did the "Pony," the "Hucklebuck,"
"the Fly," and that chiropractor's delight, the "Limbo Rock" (in case
you have forgotten, a bar was placed between two poles, and gradually
lowered, as people sensually slithered under it). The songs that accompanied these strange dances all charted in the Top 10. It was an amazing
run. By 1963, Chubby had sold over 70 million singles, 30 million albums, and along with making two dreadful twist movies *(Twist Around*

the Clock and *Don't Knock the Twist),* he married Holland's former Miss World, Rina Lodders.

Not much was heard from Chubby after that. While other groups scored with the Frug, the Watusi, and the Jerk, he left Cameo-Parkway in 1963, and didn't do another album until 1982, when MCA came out with *The Change Has Come.* One cut, "Harder Than Diamond," got a fair amount of air play, while other songs on his "comeback" LP were also praised by the rock press. But feeling that MCA didn't do enough to promote the LP, Checker left the company, and returned to the cabaret/Kiwanis Club circuit, where he's been a mainstay for over two decades.

At these engagements—and there are over two hundred of them a year—Chubby, now forty-five, is still a fast-stepping, passionate performer. Though he is down in weight, from 250 to 190, his deep-barreled voice hasn't lost any of its power over the years. Spiritedly, he delights each crowd with the "Pony," the "Hucklebuck," a medley of classic rock oldies, from "Good Golly, Miss Molly" to "Tutti-Frutti," and of course, a few "twisters."

Since this usually sets off a wave of dancing, it's understandable why Checker calls himself an "Einstein." Once people hear him, they move parts of their body that haven't stirred in twenty-five years.

And while this won't get him onto that long-departed rocket ship, Chubby should take heart. We all know he discovered the secrets of dance-floor propulsion.

Barbara Lee of the Chiffons

Her Next Stop, St. Elsewhere

"Mike, get that blood sample to the lab, quick. They're waitin' for it, so don't mess around!"

Never taking her eyes off a computer terminal, the Bronx, New York, hospital dispatcher ignores a grunt from the messenger, and continues to peck away at the keyboard.

As her fingers sweep across the keys like a high-tech Liberace, more orders are issued, while such heady terms as "serology," "cytology," and "bacteriology" dance upon the screen. There's no letup. The lights keep flashing. "BC 6857 in room 385, Bone Marrow." "Pick up XK 112 at endocrinology." "Dialysis for 236807 in ICU."

For the untutored eye, at seven in the morning, this is too much to comprehend. In fact, only the complaints of the khaki-clad messengers in the back of the room are intelligible. Not yet in tune with the dispatcher, they chat among themselves, thumb through newspapers, chug coffee, and squawk repeatedly.

But Barbara Lee has always had a commanding voice. The Chiffons' most acclaimed singer, she just has to belt out an order, and the sleepy-eyed men in the Transportation Unit snap to attention. The moaning stops, and another test tube, or tissue sample is on its way.

"I'm happy working here; not only am I helping people, but I have a secure job," says Barbara, after directing the men to their appointed rounds. Lee and the Chiffons were the leader of the pack that gave us such goodies as "He's So Fine," "Sweet Talkin' Guy," and "One Fine Day." She looks out of place now in this small, drab room. Here, instead of spotlights there are only responsibilities, the never-ending kind that rarely nets a performer any applause.

Barbara is used to that. Since the early sixties, the Chiffons have sold over 20 million records—and yet, she and her three song-sisters have only received a token percentage of the royalties. Her writers, producers, and record companies made the big money. But like a host of other big names from this era, Barbara made the mistake of signing various contracts without expert legal advice. Only sixteen at the time of her first record deal in 1960, she didn't know, or care, about the meaning of "residuals" or "exclusive rights." The Bronx-raised teenager only wanted to be a star. So today, Barbara is just one more music veteran who has to console herself with gold-record plaques, and a few happy memories.

"I know things could've been different. I know we could've been really big," muses Barbara, in a remarkably controlled, unemotional voice. One might think these thoughts of the old days would bring back the finger-popping, hell-raising Barbara, the "Queen" who really smoked, the one with the beehive hairdo and Cleopatra eyeliner. But instead, she softly sighs, "What can you do? The past is the past, and there's nothing you can do about it. Sometimes the past brings me a little sadness, but, for the most part, the girls don't even talk about these things anymore."

Content to "think about the hits we did have," and to do an occasional East Coast show (usually at small clubs, company parties, and community organization benefits), she's reluctant to talk about her past "business mistakes." Only after a great deal of prodding does she finally admit, "It used to hurt a lot, we'd hear our voices on a record or in a movie, and we knew we weren't getting anything for it. That had to hurt . . . bad. When we started to speak up, we got cut off. None of the record companies would touch us. Not for years. But what can I say? That's the past. We only wanted to work. Our only regret is that we weren't more business-wise. We were too busy thinking of other things, bein' 'stars' and all that. Those record companies knew that; they took advantage of a lot of young people back then."

Now, the Chiffons are not just singing about "sweet-talkin' guys," they're fighting back. They've sued one of their former record companies, and have also taken legal action against a few of the members of the Tokens, the group that made "The Lion Sleeps Tonight" famous in 1961. Some members of the group later worked as their producers. Sighing when she starts to talk about these lawsuits, Barbara says, "We don't want any trouble, we only want what's rightfully ours. When we first signed those contracts we were told we'd get royalties for as long as the records sold. We were young and poor, so we believed that, but we haven't received anything for years. We're talking about a decent amount of money here, enough to keep me from working."

Her voice reduced to a whisper, Barbara looks down at the floor, around the room, and then at her watch. The messengers will soon stream back into the room, so our conversation will be put on hold for a while. But before readying herself for another bout with the computer, and the men, she mournfully adds, "You know, my father always told me the entertainment business was a lousy one. That I should really look out for myself. I guess I should've listened to him, instead of getting hooked on the glamour."

Barbara was first bewitched by those charms in junior high school, when she and two other Chiffons, Judy Craig and Patricia Bennett, did talent shows at Bronx community centers. The girls didn't always win, because they often had to compete against another local group, the Ronettes. These hand-jiving, leg-jerking battles were so intense, Barbara sometimes felt she didn't have the right "do wop" to make it. But visions of rock's high temples, the Brooklyn Fox and the Paramount, kept her going. Sitting in class, she'd have these fantasies in which her dream "intro" always sounded the same note: "Here's Barbara Lee, the Bronx's brightest new star."

Barbara got a taste of real success in 1960, after she met songwriter/ manager Ron Mack. He brought Sylvia Peterson into the group, and together they had a small hit with "Tonight's the Night." Not much happened after that. The Chiffons rarely left the Bronx during the next few years, and Barbara became a telephone operator. The only songs she heard were those of her girl-group rivals, the Crystals, the Shirelles, and the Ronettes.

That all changed in 1962. Mack wrote "He's So Fine" for the group, and they did a demo early that year. Initially, none of them thought much about it. As Barbara recalls, "We just forgot about the demo; nothing was happening with it. Besides, we were too busy working, doing other things, to really care all that much." But Mack had given the song to Hank Medress, who in turn sold it to Laurie Records, and by September of '62, the song was on the radio. "I'll never forget it, a friend called to give me the news," coos Barbara, remembering that she quickly turned on a radio to hear herself. "I had given up hope, but there I was, singing 'He's So Fine.' It was so exciting."

And dizzying. Within two months, Barbara was thrust into the limelight, as the song soared to number one. She and the Chiffons were now asked to countless record hops, and they joined other legendary performers, like Anthony and the Imperials, Dionne Warwick, the Dovells, and the Marvelettes on traveling road shows. All of their dreams were coming true, yet, in the flush of teenage success, scant attention was being paid to business matters, least of all to their contracts.

"We were young, poor, and understanding those contracts wasn't easy," explains Barbara, who couldn't sign anything at the time because of her age, and was thus forced to rely on her mother's judgment. "We were so ecstatic, we would've taken anything. The money we were getting was more than we got from our regular jobs, so none of us complained. The singing made us happy."

Later in 1963, the Chiffons went on to record "One Fine Day," which eventually peaked at number five. Being "good, quiet black girls," they didn't complain when producers changed their name to the Four Pennies and had them record two more songs that year, "My Block" and "When the Boy's Happy." As Barbara relates, "There was some money rolling in by this time, so we didn't want to question anything. The producers felt those two songs weren't what people expected from the Chiffons, and we didn't argue. Not about anything."

But the road shows, when the Chiffons traveled by bus with the greats of rock 'n' roll, eventually changed that.

The Chiffons gained a great deal of knowledge on these long jaunts. Able to talk candidly with their heroes, they heard how other performers had fought for better contracts, and as Barbara puts it, "We were shocked that we were getting so little, and that you could *do* something about it. We really had our heads turned."

They soon hired a new manager, and challenged their 1965 royalty statements from Laurie Records. That led to a legal settlement the following year, but it was a hollow victory. No one would record them, and over the next two years, they were rarely asked to perform. Barbara insists they were blackballed. And, while that's conjectural, one thing is sure. The Chiffons' career came to a quiet halt.

"We never found out what the companies were saying, but they probably saw us as uppity troublemakers," says Barbara, sounding far more defiant now. Dressed in a plain purple suit, the forty-two-year-old singer stands up for a moment to straighten her skirt. Assured that her clothes aren't getting wrinkled, she praises a nearby supervisor for giving her this extra time off. The sweet talking then stops, as she adopts a more fiery tune. "After a while we realized that companies didn't want four black girls to be too smart, especially in business matters. They wanted to keep us in our place."

Strapped for money, and not wanting to return to their old jobs, the Chiffons went back to Laurie in 1968. They took with them, "My Sweet Lord." The song was later made popular by George Harrison, and would spark a lawsuit against him by Laurie Records. The melodies are similar to those of "He's So Fine." It was established in 1976 that the former Beatle had "unknowingly" plagiarized the 1963 hit. But, in the meantime, "My Sweet Lord" wasn't the Chiffons' salvation. The song went nowhere, and Barbara had to get a job selling wigs.

Quickly adjusting to this new life-style, Barbara proudly recalls that she became the store's best saleswoman, and enjoyed "people looking in all the time, or asking for autographs." Chuckling while saying this, Barbara again disregards the bad times; the early 1970s, when she was having marital problems, and desperately needed this job to support herself and three children. Money was a constant problem then. There was little in the way of royalties, and the group's future prospects looked dim. Two of the girls left for other careers, and the newly constituted group only got occasional weekend gigs. The Chiffons were finished. They would never regain their former prominence. Barbara knew that, and wisely looked ahead.

In 1975, she left the wig business for a better-paying job at Montefiore Hospital in the Bronx. Initially assigned to clerical duties, she took several computer courses, hoping that would lead to "a little security in my life for a change." It did. She's been the hospital's chief dispatcher for nearly nine years.

It's a demanding position. Besides monitoring the flow of all laboratory samples, she's responsible for getting patients to clinics and operating rooms. Timing is clearly essential. Blood and urine samples can't get lost, nor can people be delayed. Vital tests must conform to a specific schedule, and that often forces Barbara to get tough on her fourteen messengers. The short, soft-spoken dispatcher doesn't seem right for the part, but Barbara keeps delivering, even though she has a host of other problems.

"Those lawsuits keep you busy, but I want the best for my children," says Barbara, her face etched with worry. "Who knows how things are going to turn out? I can't follow all the legal moves. I only know that I want my three girls to get a good education. The benefits are good here, the hospital has a good pension plan, but those royalties could help a lot."

Forcing herself to smile, Barbara insists sardonically that these constant legal battles have made the Chiffons "very business-wise." "We're looking at every scrap of paper these days," she continues, in a strong, forceful voice, "and there's nothing getting past us." The Chiffons did a two-week tour of England a few years ago, and they've recently crisscrossed Texas. "When we go on the road these days, we approve everything, and I mean everything."

Despite this new toughness, those recent tours still delight and disarm her. Recalling the crowds, and the rave reviews the group played to, Barbara is again the sentimentalist, the teenaged girl with sparkling brown eyes. Her voice choked with pride, she touchingly says, "We're still working, so they must remember us. I don't think I ever want to stop performing. It's so exciting to see people on the road. The cheers get into an entertainer's blood, and never leave it. Those cheers . . ."

She's interrupted by a group of returning messengers. They tease her for taking a long break, and jokingly ask for equal time. Quickly dismissing their requests with a shrug and a menacing glare, she finally says, "The cheers are great, but I get a lot more satisfaction from my daughter Danielle. She plays my 45s every day. That's quite a feeling."

Jan Berry of Jan and Dean

Wipe Out at Dead Man's Curve

The words from "Dead Man's Curve" were an evil prophecy, a dark voice from a Stephen King book. But like Frankenstein, they took on a life of their own, and mercilessly ravaged their creator.

Obscured by the gleaming California sun, that terrible curse went unrecognized in 1964. The accident was still two years away. "Dead Man's Curve" was just another "surfing song," an ode to wild beach parties, Sandra Dee look-alikes, and souped-up Corvettes. In this carefree speed-crazy world, there was nothing frightening about roaring engines, or squealing brakes. These were the sounds of good times in the early sixties, the *Vroom*-charged beat that took millions to the beach, to Surf City U.S.A. That's where the fun really started. Only you had to get there first, over the hills, and past "Dead Man's Curve" at 70 MPH, one arm nestled around a girlfriend. It would be an unforgettable joyride to the bikini-filled beaches.

"Dead Man's Curve" had a flip side. It was a notorious real-life bend in Beverly Hills, dangerously close to being a pure right angle. Too many drivers were unable to negotiate the turn, and would slide into the oncoming lanes. The screech was horrible, the accidents one long "Wipe Out." Surfboards came tumbling off car roofs, while the smell of gasoline and things burning hung in the air. As cars slowly inched past these wrecks, girls turned away in fright, hoping their Johnny Be-

Goods would comfort them, with "Don't worry, I'm in control." They were, at that moment. Yet there was always the next time.

Jan Berry rode past these horrors nearly every day. A medical student at UCLA, even at the height of such Jan and Dean successes as "Surf City" and "The Little Old Lady from Pasadena," he had to take this route to get to school. Invariably, an accident delayed him. Upset by the blood and gore, he'd get out of his own new Corvette to help the victims. This made him respect the curve, while others taunted it, gunning their engines. Feeling "spiritually moved" to steer people away from it, he collaborated with friend Roger Christian, and immortalized the treacherous bend in song. Sadly, however, now he's a monument to his own message.

Partially paralyzed, reduced to garbled mumbling, his brain severely damaged, Jan bears the scars of taking on the curve in 1966 and losing. Since that terrible April accident, which sent Jan into a coma for eight weeks, dozens of rumors have circulated. The world first thought that he had been drinking or was high on drugs. Other accounts pictured him leaving a draft board in a rage, after he was supposedly denied a deferment. It was also said that three people died in the mishap. These stories are now dismissed by Jan and his father (sitting close by, he often speaks for Jan or prods his memory) with either a laugh or a shrug. They don't feel longer disavowals are necessary. But there's no denying Jan's enfeebled condition, his blank stares, and incoherent mutterings. This is the "new" Jan, the shell that painfully scratches away at the piano for hours, to write a few notes. The older, more creative one was destroyed long ago.

Why didn't Jan pay attention to his own lyrics? Was "Dead Man's Curve" some evil incantation, a prophecy that had to end in self-destruction?

This search for answers is a painful process. It means watching Jan struggle, like someone in a straitjacket twisting to get free. His bonds are a short-circuited brain and there are too many dead ends. Memory is now haphazard, so Jan gets tangled up. While talking about one set of events, he drifts off, lost in a babble of other experiences. The return trip is then a traumatic one. He must be prodded continually. That too is an ordeal. It exhausts the interviewer, while Jan, in his desperation to make sense, grimaces with every thought. He gallantly persists, but eventually the agony is just too much. Again he must retreat to a different world.

Perhaps those dark, empty meanderings force him to look for easy answers. But whatever the reason, when talking about the accident, Jan attributes his fate to the mystical workings of the supernatural. Remarkably free of any bitterness, he insists "Dead Man's Curve" was a portent of the crash, a miraculous omen of things to come. This cheerful acceptance of the mishap might sound macabre. Yet it might also be founded on a great leap of faith. For Jan frequently talks about miracles, and only a belief in divine intervention would justify his calling "Dead Man's Curve" his favorite song.

"There's a really nice omen in 'Dead Man's Curve.' The story of my accident is in that song," says Jan, munching on a Snickers bar in the living room of his parents' Los Angeles home. Keeping the bag of candy close to him, he surreptitiously dips his hand into it every few minutes and smiles. A few minutes earlier he was reluctant to leave the piano, to sit for the interview. But now he seems pleased, chewing away at his piece of chocolate-covered heaven.

"I believe in a philosophy of miracles," continues Jan, his slurred speech but a faint echo of the voice that once launched millions of surfboards. "They do happen. They are great. There's a miracle everyday. There's an omen in everyone's life."

Unable to clarify his use of the word "nice," except to say the accident was predetermined, Jan bravely tries to remember the events leading up to the crash. One suffers along with him, as he gropes for words. But after a while, this attempt must be abandoned. Since he can give us only a portion of the story, his father has to fill in the blanks.

On that fateful day, Jan left his home in the hills of Santa Monica around noon, for a business appointment in Beverly Hills. Late for his meeting with a record-company official, he rounded the bend near Sunset and Whittier at about fifty miles an hour. Unfortunately, there was a gardener's truck parked alongside the curb, and because of the oncoming traffic, passing the vehicle on the left was impossible. Jan now made his terrible mistake. Going too fast to brake, he decided to pass the truck on the right. If not for a high curb, this maneuver might have worked. But the Corvette careened off the walkway, and plowed into the back of the truck. The impact rumpled the car like a paper bag. And in the hail of flying glass, Jan's promising career came to an end.

"I can only remember the hospital bed, and the movie projector my producer [Lou Adler] brought over," says Jan, managing a slight smile. "We'd play Laurel and Hardy films, I liked that. Other musicians would come by, and we'd have a good time watching those guys."

Jan pauses for a moment. When asked about Dean, his face brightens a bit, and he says, "Now, it's completely different. I love Dean 'cause in my mind he's better. I can accept more things. He's been a good friend to me recently. We've done a couple of gigs, and in the future they'll be a lot more. That's good."

Before the accident, there was a stronger bond between the two boys. Jan and Dean were America's surfboard darlings. Mirroring the good times of the golden beaches of California, in their blond crewcuts and innocent faces, they inspired a certain vision—of cruising in a Sting Ray down to Surf City, when the girls outnumbered the boys two to one.

High school classmates, they first played together in Jan's garage. Other aspiring rock 'n' rollers, like Sandy Nelson (Teen Beat) and the Beach Boys' Bruce Johnston, would frequently join them; and as Jan now recalls, "The noise would drive my mother nuts." But the beat went on, even after Dean had to join the National Guard. Together with another school friend, Arnie Ginsberg, Jan got his first taste of success with "Jennie Lee" (number eight).

Calling themselves the Barons, Jan and Arnie were suddenly BBOC, the big boys on campus who had to fend off girls and singing engagements. Jan enjoyed the attention. Wearing his Barons jacket at lunchtime, he'd act like a DJ, throwing discs on a record player for impromptu hops. The girls loved these performances, but keeping his cool, Jan wasn't sidetracked by this new notoriety. He still wanted to go to medical school.

Realizing a singing career was a precarious, often frustrating pursuit, Jan saw the importance of having "a second career, something to fall back on." Understandably, then, he didn't quarrel with Arnie's decision to forego the rock world for a law degree. The split did cause some immediate consternation. A few proms were already booked, and Jan didn't want to break any hearts. But, luckily, "America's sweet-sixteeners found an ally in Uncle Sam—Dean Torrence was released from the military. And the two eighteen-year-olds went back to the garage.

In 1959, they began their long stay on the charts with "Baby Talk." While the song climbed to number ten, Dean went to USC to study graphic design (his album covers later won several awards), and Jan had such a terrific magnetism in the lab, "the other students would stop their own work to watch him," recalls William Berry, staring proudly at his son. "The professors really felt he was a bright student. He had to be. Even while he was touring, he'd be studying and dissecting mice on planes."

Jan was also writing songs. The chief lyricist for the duo, he mixed a wide range of vocal overdubs with strong-sounding guitars, and often employed talented studio musicians, like Glen Campbell and Leon Russell. This equation became synonymous with lighthearted summer fun. Typified by such hits as "Surf City" (number one in 1963), "Drag City" (number ten in 1964), and "The Little Old Lady . . ." (number three in 1964). The music was a constant beach party. There were so many images of bronzed beauties in bikinis frolicking in the surf, the lyrics can be reduced to one bottom line. They were rock's version of a Coppertone ad.

Appropriately enough, in 1964, Jan scored the soundtrack for Fabian's beach movie *Ride the Wild Surf.* Jokingly, Jan says he would have liked a starring role in the movie; but he had to settle for guest appearances on various TV shows. On these less than memorable occasions, he'd exchange a few witty lines with such hosts as Dean Martin and Jack Benny, then get embroiled in some ridiculous Laurel and Hardy takeoff with Torrence (who usually brought along a surfboard, just in case a wave appeared).

Anything went in those halcyon days. Stunned by the John Kennedy assassination, the country wanted to forget. It was time to have fun, fun, fun. And that made Jan and Dean the perfect escape.

"The early sixties were a beautiful time for rock 'n' roll," Jan exclaims, speaking in a surprisingly authoritative tone. Showing no signs of being aphasic, he playfully juts out his chest to flaunt a "Spring Break" T-shirt, then continues, "The music was great then, and I was a teenage hero. I wasn't sure if rock 'n' roll would last, but it did. Rock 'n' roll, and what we did was very important. People got a lift from us. I liked that. It was hard to have a private life, studying took a lot of time. But that was okay. It's better to be pushed by girls than to be forgotten."

The fame also brought him a luxurious Bel Air home, the means to throw extravagant parties, and, of course, gleaming sports cars. A self-described normal, All-American boy, Jan certainly liked this life in the fast lane. But unlike other overnight Hollywood celebrities, he wasn't spoiled by the attention. He remained the innocent, wholesome medical student, who took his surfboard on cross-country plane trips, and clowned in hotel lobbies. He clearly didn't take his fame too seriously. And while that is commendable in this age of pampered, over-glamorized stars, Jan made one mistake. Ever boyish and unsuspecting, he didn't take "Dead Man's Curve" seriously enough.

The accident meant a different life-style, a nightmarish one, based on total helplessness. When Jan awoke from the coma, he couldn't talk, his entire right side was paralyzed, and he was unable to read or write. In effect, he was an infant—and most harrowing of all, doctors said he wouldn't improve. They believed that Jan would never talk or walk again.

Mournfully recalling those days in a wheelchair, when he couldn't remember a single lyric from any of his songs, Jan poignantly says, "I was no one. My brain was pretty well shot. I had to relearn things, like reading and writing. It was hard. Just thinking about it makes my head hurt."

Jan leans back on the sofa. Speaking has been difficult. At times he's reduced to stammering, and at others he can't find any words to express a thought. His face mirrors this struggle; it's frozen in pain. But after closing his eyes, seemingly to gather some hidden strength, he does go on. "The hesitating is hard. I don't want to do it. I want things to be like they used to be, before the accident. I want to speak clearly, without hesitation. That's too frustrating."

Jan has still come a long way. After several operations, speech rehabilitation, and incalculable pain (not to mention the great expense) from seventeen years of physical therapy, he's performing again. The old beat isn't there. And the Berrys' finances have suffered with every disappointing "medical breakthrough." But Jan *is* on the road back. Even if there are detours, like bouts with depression, he's still in there fighting, intent on writing another chart-making song.

"My hope now is to be active, to do concerts, and to write some good songs," says Jan, forty-five, trying to sound optimistic about his life. "At times, I'm a frustrated person, and I'll drink to forget. I wish I could be back in the old days. I know I'm not the same, and I won't have the same accomplishments. But that's the way it is. I cry sometimes, and ask, 'Why me?' But I've gotten back to reality, and today I feel it's a good life. I'm trying to get better."

New developments in microelectronic surgery might ease that recovery. Mr. Berry has recently consulted specialists in the field, and the family is confident that such an operation would restore the movement to Jan's right side. Now, only the funds for the surgery have to be found. Most of Jan's assets are gone. His old home had to be sold, and while he's retained a few investments, selling 20 million records is basically history. Royalties don't amount to much anymore, yet, his father optimistically says, "Jan's progress has been an inspiration to thousands of handicapped people. And well it should be. He's come so far. Don't worry, we're not going to let him down. Not after all he's done. Somehow we'll find the money."

The prospects are gloomier for Jan's future relationship with Dean. The two men have been performing together; at various festivals and amusement parks, and they sang the national anthem at the 1984 Rose Bowl game. But tensions still exist as a legacy of bad feelings. While Jan speaks lovingly of Dean, and has purportedly tempered his feelings about his infrequent hospital visits, the "desertion" issue won't go away, not as long as Dean performs with Mike Love of the Beach Boys. Anything but a full partnership smacks of betrayal.

The Berrys feel they've been burned before. Particularly galling to them is the TV movie version of "Dead Man's Curve," the 1979 CBS Special that Dean helped produce. Calling the film a gross distortion, Mr. Berry feels Jan was characterized as an arrogant, self-serving singing star and that some people profited from this distortion. "There's no doubt about that. Somehow, a lot of shots favorable to Jan were deleted."

Meanwhile, Jan has quietly retreated to a safer world. Feeling the movie is "over with, and dead in the past," he's back at the piano, pencil in hand.

"I really have to finish this song, I don't have time for the past," says Jan, eyeing several blank music sheets in front of him. "It's a nice song; it's called 'Almost In Love.' I'm going to send it to KLRA, to my friend over there. I think people are going to like it."

Distracted by the roar of a plane, Jan looks wistfully out a window, at the dancing ocean in the distance. Through the late afternoon haze, the waves have a coppery glow. They seem tarnished in a way, but Jan still smiles, and says, "Yeah, I'm a good song writer. I've written some important music. I was a star. I don't know if that would be true today, but I want people to remember what I wrote. Jan and Dean had a special beat. Just like the duo, that sound is lasting. I hope it's forever."

Al Kooper of Blood, Sweat and Tears

Meaner than Rambo, He's the Soda Shop Kid

Remember Marlon Brando in *The Wild One?*

Or James Dean, as that troubled youth in *Rebel Without a Cause?*

Angry, confused, and usually brooding, they personified fifties alienation, the generation that Paul Goodman talked about in *Growing Up Absurd.*

Well, they were only movie characters, but on New York streets there was real action. JDs, or juvenile delinquents, in black leather jackets and duck's-ass hairdos, roamed city neighborhoods and ruled by switchblade. These young lords terrorized shopkeepers, stole cars, went on death-defying joyrides, and took advantage of many a young lass. Simply stated, they were trouble. The mean and menacing kind.

In Queens, the brass-knuckling was especially violent. Here, in an otherwise quiet, predominantly middle-class borough, numerous gangs competed for the same turf. The Savage Disciples. The 59th Street Rangers. The Bayside Blades. They were all tough. Real tough. But when the fists stopped flying, and the hubcaps were counted, there was one unquestioned victor—the Cavaliers. And their leader was none other than the baddest of the bad, Big Al Kooper.

No one messed with *him.* Not if they had any sense. The guy who would later play with Dylan, write "This Diamond Ring," form Blood,

Sweat and Tears, and discover Lynyrd Skynyrd, was the twelve-year-old scourge of his community. He played the good little boy at home, but he had only to walk down the street—after changing into his Brando gear in a friend's garage—and panic-stricken neighbors would immediately get the message. With Kooper around, anything was possible.

People had reason to worry. Young Al was tormented. He'd sit at the local soda shop, and halfheartedly run his spoon through the whipped cream. Nothing made him happy, not even the cherry. Dark, Hamlet-like thoughts were always spinning through his head.

"What am I going to do with my life?" the youngster pondered, twirling his spoon with a dexterity that would later lead him to the keyboard. "Which is it gonna be, my switchblade, my brass knuckles or rock 'n' roll music."

The other Cavaliers sat nearby, hoping to influence his mighty struggle. They pulled at his sleeve, frantically urging him to think about Studebakers and all the chrome they could steal.

But another force was at work. It made Al's leg shake, his heart quiver. Deep inside, all the way to his groin, the sounds triggered an explosive rush.

E-L-V-I-S! The giant with gyrating hips knocked Al off his soda-shop stool. All shook up, he couldn't think straight.

Would Al stay with the Cavaliers, and pull more hubcap capers, or would he surrender to this "hunchin' and ajackin'," and play rock 'n' roll?

This existential quandary was eventually resolved. Al succumbed to the material. With his father offering to buy him a Sears, Roebuck Silvertone guitar, he switched allegiances to the Aristocats, thrilled at the prospect of wearing their embossed satin jacket. According to Al, "They were a lively, pretty decent band, and besides, it made my father happy. He thought I'd stay out of jail."

But even in 1957, at the tender age of thirteen, Kooper wasn't about to be reformed. A product of street wars, he came to the music through subterranean channels and was still bent toward the rebellious. This would eventually make him rock's quintessential bad boy, a distinction he still flaunts with unabashed pride.

In Polygram's New York office, while shaking off the effects of a night on the town, he pointedly says, "As a kid I had a lot of hard-core friends. They were all headed toward jail, and if I didn't play music I probably would've had a life of crime too. But then again, maybe I didn't escape it. Isn't rock 'n' roll a life of crime?"

At least for Al it was. For he quickly established himself as an outlaw; a free spirit who went through bands the way George Steinbrenner goes through managers.

With the Aristocats for less than a year, he revved up his Silvertone, and joined a new group on the block, the Royal Teens. They hadn't done "Short Shorts" yet; their piano player, Bob Gaudio (who would also lead the Four Seasons to fame), would write this novelty song a year later. But the group did present a singular opportunity: Al could be his crazy, wacked-out self.

"When we'd go to Chicago, Boston, Minneapolis, I'd never tell my parents; they thought I was with a friend," confesses the bleary-eyed Kooper, falling back on a couch to sip a much-needed cup of coffee. It's nearly noon, but he finds speaking difficult. Only after a long pause does he add, "Even if I had to lie to my parents to do it, I wanted to be a star. I was obsessed.

"Elvis did that to me. I always loved music, but he centered it for me. He grabbed me by the throat, and drove me crazy. I just had to be playing.

"This lying caught up with me many times, but the really classical moment was the time I got home from an upstate [New York] gig at six in the morning. While I was getting out of a cab, dressed in an iridescent blue jacket, my father was walking out of the house in his suit. He gave me this look that said I was fuckin' useless, that there was no hope for me. I was a little scared. Once again, I had blown it. I guess they were worried about all the sleazy people in the business, and later about the drugs." He laughs. "Eventually their fears were confirmed."

For two years the Royal Teens were an on-again, off-again thing. Then Al made his big move. Instead of attending high school classes, he'd hang out in front of Broadway's famous Brill Building, and do studio piano work. Eventually, he met his "godfather."

Aaron Schroeder, who had written songs for Elvis, adopted him. Besides encouraging Al to write, he took him around Tin Pan Alley, and introduced him to other budding stars. On several occasions, Al was even asked to play talent scout at Schroeder's auditions. One incident still stands out.

"I was blown away," Al shouts, remembering the time Gene Pitney played for Schroeder. "This guy was something! He was like Elvis! Was he good! So Aaron signed him as a writer, and as it turned out, I got to play on some of his demos. 'Rubber Ball,' 'He's a Rebel,' 'Hello Mary Lou,' I'm on all of those. He was really nice to me. When he got successful he was one of the few people to record my songs. It's too bad he dried up. Maybe he was hurt by the environment."

The "sleazy" milieu still terrified his parents. Though Al protested, they made him finish high school, and insisted on his going to college (the University of Bridgeport in 1961). Afraid of "causing a war in the house," Al grudgingly acceded to their wishes. But once again he was an outsider, the self-termed "bastard child" who didn't fit in.

The curriculum was his major problem. He wasn't a jazz or classical pianist, yet the school only offered theory and composition. Uninspired by the teachers, he got bored, and returned often to the Brill Building. Schroeder and others gave him ghost-writing assignments at one hundred dollars apiece, and by 1962, he decided to make this a full-time pursuit.

While Al's shocked parents "went fuckin' mental," he convinced two Brill occupants to give him some office space, and began to write in earnest. One of his first products was a black version of "This Diamond Ring." The song was meant for the Drifters, and while Al is hazy about how the tune got recorded by Gary Lewis and the Playboys in California, he does say, "Seeing the song make it was a great feeling. It knocked '[You've Lost] That Lovin' Feelin' ' by the Righteous Brothers out of number one. It was the most exciting thing that ever happened to me. You couldn't turn on a radio without hearing it."

Even more important, the hit gave Al credibility. His parents quieted down; Schroeder gave him more money for songs; and indicative of his new stature in the industry, Al started playing the bar mitzvah circuit with Paul Simon. They were quite a duo. With Al on lead guitar, and Simon doing twist songs, it's understandable why they didn't get much work. There were so many lulls that they often went down to the Village. It was on one of these jaunts that Al discovered a new patron saint.

"We saw this guy playing an electric guitar, I think he was doing 'Baby, Let Me Follow You Down,' and Paul asked me, 'Well, what do you think?' " recounts Kooper, a hint of emotion creeping into his hoarse voice. "I wasn't all that impressed at first, but then I got it. Something basic and pleasant was happening, and it was transferable to rock 'n' roll. From then on I was a Dylan freak."

Taking this admiration to an extreme, Kooper changed his name to Al Casey and went folk. Predictably, the metamorphosis caused an instant stir. Kooper lived up to his already earned ballsy reputation by showcasing a song about Kitty Genovese, the woman who was murdered in Queens while thirty-eight people sat idly by. Radio stations picked up on it, as did the press, and, amid the uproar, Al almost got killed in a Queens club. But on a more positive note, he used the headlines as his calling card, and wangled a meeting with Tom Wilson, who was then producing Dylan.

Musically, that confab was truly historical. It resulted in Kooper's playing the organ on Dylan's 1965 breakthrough hit, "Like a Rolling Stone," backing "the Master" at the 1965 Newport Folk Festival, and establishing a friendship that matured through other collaborative efforts, like *Highway 61 Revisited, Blonde on Blonde,* and *New Morning.* He also met Mike Bloomfield at the recording sessions.

When talking about his relationship with Dylan, Kooper sounds like an awestruck little boy who's dressed for the Sunday school choir and genuflecting before some holy apparition.

"Dylan was like a god to me," sighs Kooper, his face ablaze with new color. "You don't realize it at the time, it's good that you don't, it would mess you up. But I was doing classics with him back then . . . and I'll admit, by *Blonde on Blonde,* it was impossible for me to think that I was just playing music. It sounds weird, but I felt we were doing something a lot greater than that."

Turning his attention to the Newport Festival, where the newly amplified Dylan enraged folk purists, Kooper continues, " 'Like a Rolling Stone' was about to come out, and Bob wanted to duplicate the record at the festival. So he asked Bloomfield and me to play with him, and I said to myself, 'Oh, wow, I'm his keyboard player . . .' Our personal relationship was just starting, and while I was a little intimidated at first, as time went by I felt established myself, that maybe, just maybe, there was stuff I could teach him."

This note of humility is disconcerting, for it runs counter to the Kooper legend. According to people in the business, he's supposed to be a cross between Simon Legree and Billy Martin; a boastful, self-centered man who's always having problems with fellow band members. But that provocative side of him is hardly in evidence this particular afternoon. Besides being the gracious host, with a ready supply of Danish and coffee, he talks candidly about his "past mistakes," and is surprisingly apologetic. Admitting "I wasn't a very nice person, I was rude to people," he says at one point, "I was clinically insane, but I'm much more in control now."

Perhaps.

For the moment, it's impossible to explore that point. Still numb from the night before, he stretches out on the couch, and mumbles, "We're going to have to finish this some other time, I'm just too tired right now."

Two months later, in Kooper's Hollywood office, he finally picks up on his post-Newport beat—joining the Blues Project, that folk and country-blues sextet put together by Tom Wilson, and occasionally serving as a backup band for Chuck Berry. Al only stayed with them for about a year and a half, but the association was significant. Though opposed by founder Danny Kalb, Al started to experiment with songs that required horns, as well as with an enlarged rock format that included elements of jazz, blues, and classical music.

This brassy-sounding rhythm-and-blues would eventually be harnessed by Blood, Sweat and Tears, but it remained only a vision for several months. First, Kooper had a nervous breakdown.

"I couldn't do my songs, not with Kalb, and to show you how crazy I really got, I went to California to recuperate," mutters Kooper good-naturedly. "Something had snapped in my head. I think I was catatonic for several days in some Oakland crash pad. I was under a lot of pressure to make a living, I was married . . . and yet I knew I was out of the band. I must've cried for days.

"I finally went to L.A. and played at Monterey (the Pop Festival). I could see there was an 'underground music' coming together, and working there must've channeled my insanity, because I didn't know what I was doing up on stage . . . I saw one face out in the audience, Otis Redding, and he seemed to be saying 'What the fuck is that guy doing?' . . . but I still had this dream, a dream of Blood, Sweat and Tears."

That became a reality in 1968 when he returned to New York, to do a benefit with Steve Katz, a former member of the Blues Project, at the *Café au Go Go*. Al was set to leave for England after the show, but he couldn't raise the airfare. He was forced to look around the city for some horn players. "I put an ad in the paper, and, while a lot of heroin addicts and bookworms applied, we finally had ourselves a band."

Columbia Records quickly signed them to a contract and Kooper celebrated by giving up marijuana, but there were problems right from the start. Disputing Al's contention that "democracy leads to disaster," the other members wanted to share the decision-making with him. When he resisted, a rival faction formed consisting of Katz, Jerry Weiss and Bob Colomby. While they all tried to patch up their differences at "rock therapy" sessions, Al was told to get lost after producing the highly successful album *Child Is Father to the Man.*

"It doesn't hurt now," insists the forty-two-year-old Kooper, looking like the consummate A & R man, behind a desk cluttered with albums and tapes. "Things worked out okay, they burningly wanted to be famous, and I was just thinking about making a musical statement. Maybe they weren't pleased with that, but I didn't get mad, I just got even."

His revenge didn't begin and end with Blood, Sweat and Tears. That would have been far too easy. Out for bigger game, Al vented his frustrations on the entire industry. He became a staff producer at CBS.

After sweet-talking Clive Davis into giving him the job, Al decided "It was time to do the Bloomfield thing." He got his guitar-playing friend into a studio to jam with him, and, about twelve hours later, CBS had the first side of *Super Session.* Since the often erratic Bloomfield was at the top of his form, Kooper still derives a great deal of satisfaction from the album. He laughingly admits his own singing "was some of the worst stuff I ever recorded," but quickly adds "To me, it was Mike's best playing. I'm proud of that. But the guy just went nuts after that. It was his insomnia, or junkiness, I don't know what . . . he just split for San Francisco. I already had the studio booked for another day, and luckily, Stephen Stills just showed up . . . that became the album's second side. The beauty and the magic of it all is that no one had a stake in it. We were just three guys, who had all been kicked out of bands, and none of us had anything to prove . . . we just went into a room to play music."

About this time, Al found a new specialty. Having to concentrate on his A & R duties, he spent less time playing, and began a five-year period of "tucking bands into bed at night" for CBS and MCA. Imagining Al as a chaperone might seem strange, even shocking, but this was the music business, and Al's new duties did pay off, especially for MCA.

In 1972, Kooper discovered Lynyrd Skynyrd. He spotted them in a small Atlanta bar, while on a Badfinger tour, and went on to produce their first three albums—*Pronounced Leh-Nerd Skin-Nerd,* the 1974 platinum; *Second Helping,* and *Nuthin' Fancy.* The group eventually became the most adored southern rock band since the Allman Brothers; a distinction which prompts Kooper to say, "Not too many people give me the credit for finding them, but that doesn't matter, not at all. I know what I did."

This caustic, raspy-edged remark belies one of Kooper's three absolutes in life: "Things change." The other two maxims are: "Sex rules the world," and "A cowboy hat blows off in a stiff wind." He's still an outspoken, bad-assed iconoclast, despite the "mellowing" that's come with raising a teenage son. With such altruistic statements as "I can help groups avoid the mistakes I made," Kooper continues to mock the system—and to curry its favor. He stands apart, decrying the "commercialization" and "crassness" of the industry. Yet, at the same time, there's still a need to prove that he belongs in the business. These contradictory impulses gnaw at him, so the tortured, Brandoesque anger of his youth continues to surface.

"I don't care how I'm viewed by history, or what people think of my contributions," storms Kooper, bolting up in his chair. "I don't have a press agent . . . my only interest is in setting the record straight . . .

"This job, that's what's important. In the sixties, rock artists didn't go to work for the enemy. The Beatles, and all of us, had lofty ideals. But the commercialization came out of the closet. It's one of my tasks to humanize the company, because it can be an important avenue of expression for an artist. I can help others make it. How many rock 'n' roll people do that, huh?

"That's where it's at. I don't need to make an album every year anymore. It's much more gratifying to find some kid in a bar, steer him in the right direction, and get him to number one. I don't even have to enjoy his music. I just want them to believe in themselves, to have that passion. I've always been impressed by *that.*"

This is the new Al Kooper, the one dedicated to his fledgling rockers. But the old one isn't dead yet, not by a long shot.

"Look," Kooper says, with a devilish chuckle, "get the story straight, but don't forget what I want written on my tombstone. It has to be something silly, like 'Turn me on dead man,' or maybe, 'Now I can finally get some sleep.' "

Tommy James of Tommy James and the Shondells

It Played in Peoria Until . . .

Everything was chewy-chewy, sweet-n-bubble-gummy.

Life couldn't have been better in 1966, even as the carnage in Vietnam began to filter home to us via TV.

Everyone was doing the "Hanky Panky."

It didn't matter that the song's lyrics were repetitive, inane, of no social value, and, worst of all, starting a trend that would pave America with sticky, bubbly, air-headed sounds.

This was escape music. You could drink beer to this kind of stuff, without thinking about anything. Unlike the psychedelia of the Doors or Cream, or the surrealistic Airplane, there was nothing heavy or freaky about this sound. Its straightforward cadence urged blue-collar Middle Americans to have a good time—and, in appreciation, Everyman found a new hero, one of their own sons, Tommy James.

"My songs had an elementary style to them because we were seeing enough heartaches on TV, I didn't want to add any more," says James happily, explaining how he became the voice of the blue-collar rock 'n' roller. "I just wanted to do fun music. There was a complex simplicity to it, that I felt would stand the test of time. But back then there was a disdain for it, people didn't take you seriously if you weren't writing political music about Vietnam. I didn't care. My thing was fun, helping folks enjoy themselves. My stuff did that, and I'm convinced it's still influencing people. That makes me feel like the lone survivor of a plane crash."

Tommy had a legendary talent. He could turn bubble gum into gold. Along with his backup group, the Shondells, he minted fourteen gold singles in five years, most notably, "I Think We're Alone Now," "Mony, Mony," "Crystal Blue Persuasion," and "Crimson and Clover" (the latter sold over six million copies).

This hit parade really began for Tommy at age thirteen. He put together an early version of the Shondells' record "Hanky Panky," and while the song wouldn't be discovered until 1966 (Tommy likes to joke, "I'm one of the few five-year overnight successes in the business), the wait was well worth it. Over the course of his career, James sold over 35 million records.

But the gold, and all the pressures that went with it, were also blinding. Feeling "confused, burnt-out . . . with no more worlds left to conquer," Tommy looked for something that would fuel his creative fire. While still appearing squeaky clean to his blue-collar followers, he turned to drugs. He likes to dismiss the severity of this amphetamine habit, saying "It never interfered with my work." Yet the truth is more distressing. Tommy collapsed on a Montgomery, Alabama, stage in 1970, and nearly died from an overdose.

It was his own Armageddon. He'd had to retire to an upstate New York farm and be nursed back to health. Though he came back to record "Draggin' the Line," a number four hit in 1971, the 1970s were the dark ages for him. Off the charts until 1980 ("Three Times in Love" made it to number nineteen), it was only recently that he came out of seclusion to pursue an acting career.

"My acting's not a big deal, I have nothing to prove anymore," insists Tommy, leaning over a cup of coffee in a New York restaurant. Speaking slowly and methodically, to emphasize the new balance in his life, he smoothes his flowing golden hair, and continues, "Once you hear the cheers, they can be intoxicating; you can need them like any other kind of addiction. But all that's an illusion. Needing mass approval becomes vulgar after a while, it loses its meaning. You have to think in lifetime terms about what's really important. If you don't, you can really lose yourself."

Despite this calm, well-reasoned attitude, James is a disquieting figure to be with. He seems cheerful enough, talking about movie ambitions, and the hopes he has for his teenaged son. But when the conversation drifts back to the past, to his string of hits, he only inspires sadness.

Tommy James was on *such* a roll, that for him to be merely surviving now is pitiful, even tragic. There was reason to expect a whole lot more.

James seemed fated to be one of rock's biggest stars. After he recorded "Hanky Panky" in 1960, and went back to playing fifteen-dollar-a-night gigs in Niles, Michigan, for five years, a DJ in Pittsburgh accidentally found a copy of the record in a storage bin. Once he played it, the phone lines never stopped ringing. While Tommy had long forgotten the record, he was suddenly a local celebrity.

"When this guy called me and asked me to come to Pittsburgh, I thought it was a friend of mine playing a joke," recounts Tommy, grinning broadly. "He kept telling me that my record was number one, that someone had bootlegged eighty thousand copies of it into town, but I didn't believe him. How could I? It had been five years since I'd done 'Hanky Panky,' and to tell you the truth, I didn't think I had much of a future."

Calling this turn of fate "a Cinderella story," Tommy was persuaded to go to Pittsburgh, and, with a new group of Shondells, did a series of shows for three thousand dollars a night. Within four months, the group's renown spread to New York. Roulette Records decided to buy the rights to "Hanky Panky," so at age eighteen, Tommy found himself in New York, on the way to everything a singer always dreams of, but also frightened to death.

Now he was competing with "the real heavies in the business," and as Tommy admits after a long, thoughtful puff of a cigarette, "It was just too much for a young kid. Everything happened so fast, I was absolutely spellbound. I had just gotten married, and I also had to keep my career going by writing, arranging, and producing new records."

Remembering these pressures, Tommy laughs ruefully. "The whole thing, even with a number one record, gave me two feelings: I was out of my element, and yet, I also had a great sense of adventure. Boy, this made for some kind of schizophrenia, that took years to sort out."

The confusion would eventually lead to drugs, and a high-wire balancing act between success and self-destruction. But in the meantime, the popularity of his next record, "I Think We're Alone Now" (number three in 1967), a song about tormented teenagers, was a double-edged sword. While reviewers couldn't dismiss him anymore as a flash in the pan, their new scrutiny was highly critical. They sneered at his "plastic, superficial" lyrics, dubbing him the "bubble-gum kid." Tommy insists, "This didn't bother me." And that's probably true. For in 1967, Tommy had a host of more serious problems.

Each new success meant added responsibilities at Roulette. They gave him a freer hand in the producing and promoting of his records, but this took so much time, he was rarely at home. Ultimately his marriage fell apart, and once alone in New York, the twenty-year-old was vulnerable to the business's most unscrupulous characters.

"When you're new on the streets you're immediately surrounded by all the worst people," says Tommy, lamenting the mistakes that cost him millions of dollars. "They're waiting for you—you don't know who your true friends are—and while I was growing at Roulette, I didn't recognize the hazards of the business, not yet."

His face pales, and, drawing a cape more tightly over his shoulders, he again stammers, "I was a terrible businessman. I don't know what I lost, maybe seven figures a few times over. I'm just fortunate that I kept on having the hits to recover from those losses. Thankfully I had God watching over me. I saw so many artists who, by the time they understood the business, were out of it, totally devastated and destroyed. It's one of the great tragedies of our profession."

Tommy risked such a fate in 1968, when he took the biggest gamble of his career.

Tired of the music he'd been doing, he decided to abandon "bubble gum" for a psychedelic sound. His backers warned him against this, saying it would be a betrayal of his blue-collar audience. But Tommy was so impressed with the advent of space-age synthesizers, he "pounced the hell out of these new toys" to give sugary vocals a high-tech flavor on his milestone album, *Crimson and Clover.*

By far, the title song was his most spectacular—and controversial—recording. Its allusions to sex and drugs, caused it to be banned on numerous radio stations. Yet it kept him competitive with the increasingly popular acid sound of the late 1960s, and he proudly says of this self-produced work, "I knew I was going to sink or swim with that song. I saw major changes coming in the industry, and I really felt I was taken more seriously after I did it. I started to paint pictures with my music—I made sounds wiggle. As an artist, *Crimson and Clover* means the most to me."

Netting five gold singles off that 1969 album, Tommy saw himself as "a recording artist," instead of "a simple performer." Various people asked him to do production work, including Beatles McCartney and Lennon, who had recently formed Apple. Not wanting "to go backwards," he rejected demos that the two Beatles wanted him to record—

and even turned down a chance to play Woodstock, a refusal he now calls "a very foolish mistake."

So much was going on, Tommy felt increasingly independent, and pointedly asked the Shondells, "Where do we go from here?" Realizing there wasn't much left for them to accomplish, he decided to go it alone. But the breakup soon unnerved him. On his own for the first time in years, Tommy became terribly frightened. Unable to handle the pressures of being "a one-man show at Roulette," he started to rely on amphetamines, because "there just weren't enough hours in the day to do my work."

This period in his life, when uppers and downers tortured him, is hazy. After his brush with death in Alabama, Tommy went into isolation, and won't talk about those painful days, except to say, "I needed a rest." In fact, the subject makes him wince, and his usually clear, azure eyes turn weary. Evidently, these memories of the early seventies are still terribly upsetting. He lost his drive and passion back then, the forces that helped him create, and for an artist consumed with his craft, that was a fate worse than death. It left him with nothing.

Except for writing two songs in 1970–71, he remained inactive for five years. He didn't leave his farm until 1976, when he did *In Touch* for Fantasy. Yet it was admittedly a halfhearted effort, and feeling "the seventies didn't make any sense to me," he again retreated to his upstate New York home.

Four more years passed.

Then, in 1980, having had a "born again" experience, Tommy finally felt ready to give song writing another try. Putting himself on the line again wasn't easy. Among his insecurities, was a fear that he'd still be viewed as a druggie, and, also, the 1980s with its punk trends and rock videos, were a far cry from James's "bubble gum" hits. But, as Tommy cheerfully says, "I sensed if I was ever going to recapture that spark, I had to do it then. I saw a rekindling of interest in my music. Entire excerpts from my songs were in Billy Idol's stuff, Joan Jett, Lene Lovich—basically what they're doing is 'bubble gum' with synthesizers. It's not new. I was seeing the music come full circle, so I had to get back into it."

Once near death in his own solitary hell, Tommy returned to record another Top 20 hit "Three Times in Love. Delighted to see "girls and their mothers screaming" over his music, he got a new satisfaction from performing, and confidently branched out into other areas of the entertainment business.

Along with acting, which he sees as "far more dimensional than a twelve-inch piece of plastic," Tommy wants to direct motion pictures, and to open up his own music-publishing company. His goal here is not to make money. For despite all his past mistakes, he's still living luxuriously with his third wife in a spacious New Jersey home.

So what's propelling this drive to be creative? If it's not money, or a need for cheering crowds, why's he struggling to notch new successes?

"Everything now is dedicated to my son," explains Tommy, his face flushed with enthusiasm. "He wants to be a drummer, but I want him to have some kind of family business to fall back on, some insurance.

"I know how horrible this business can be. It can destroy everything inside you. Let me tell you, that fire I had got very, very dim. Things were so bad, my story could've ended at any point. But now I'm going after these new goals, reaching out for the challenges in front of me. I'm not doing it so much for myself. No, that's not it, I want to show my son I'm stronger than ever."

Fabian
Of Playgirl Centerfolds, Tombstones, and Shattered Mirrors

"Oooooooooh!"

"What a face, what hair, what . . ."

In pre-Pill America, this blissful reverie was usually interrupted by:

"Suzie, hurry-up. Stop your dilly-dallying, and get ready for bed," yelled by the typical American mother, at the foot of the staircase. "I'll be up there in a minute to tuck you in."

While Mom trotted off to watch the last few minutes of "The Honeymooners," little Suzie put on her flannel pajamas, and did as she was told—with one exception. Once in bed she'd reach under the covers and again look at her latest copy of *Teen* magazine. She knew the older kids were reading something called *Peyton Place,* and talking about S-E-X, but this didn't bother her. Not now. As she hurriedly flipped the pages, past pictures of Elvis, Bobby Rydell, and Frankie Avalon, only one thought consumed her: *Him.* Mr. Peachy Perfect.

Her pulse was racing now, and when she finally reached page thirty-seven, a soft cooing sound again rolled off her lips, "Oooooooooh!"

There he was, her smiling, dimple-cheeked Adonis. Even here, on these black-and-white pages, his sandy hair had a golden hue. Each strand was carefully arranged to form a slight "V" in the front, and there was just the hint of a wave. Equally striking, his blue eyes glowed with boyish innocence—and something mysterious.

She couldn't describe this other quality, not at her tender age. But lying there, her mind awhirl, she thought, "Oh, he's so wonderful. If I could only see him in person . . . get his autograph . . . be close to him . . ."

That was Fabian Anthony Forte's effect on millions of young girls. He was the Crown Prince of beauty, the Face that inspired countless riots in theaters and fan clubs, that adorned look-alike dolls—and, for mothers, inspired a wave of fear. To them, he was a threat, the embodiment of S-E-X, a boy who could unleash a torrent of "unnatural" feelings in their youngsters. And yet, when these women tidied up their daughters' rooms and came across one of his photos, a certain response was inevitable. They'd giggle childishly, and utter a long, deep sigh.

"Fabe's" good looks *were* overpowering. They dazzled us, and made him an overnight, sixteen-year-old sensation, despite his lack of original material and his imitation of Presley's "Turn Me Loose," "Tiger," and "Hound Dog Man." Somehow, these 1959 tunes crashed the Top 10. But the real artistry—and sadness—is the styling of Fabian's public persona. It was Madison Avenue, par excellence. The people behind "Fabe" shaped, packaged, and marketed an image, specifically aimed at a ten- to twenty-year-old audience. Intent on selling him like a bar of acne soap, they sacrificed his evolution as a singer for a quick payday. As a result, Fabian's personal needs were ignored, and he became a prisoner of his own image.

"I was molded, manufactured to fit a certain ideal, and I'll probably wind up with a plastic tombstone," complains Fabian, angrily recalling how he lost control of his life. Though still handsome and wrinkle-free, his sun-bronzed face is a mask of rage, as he quickly adds, "I was in the claws of people who didn't give a flying fuck about me. They thought the image sold and never took the person into consideration. I understand the image thing, but the personal manipulation—they controlled what I did, who I dated, what I said. That makes me angry. I had to be a pretty face, and that's all, just a pretty face."

Dealing with far more than the discontent of a fallen rock star, Fabian's mind was plagued for years by a terrible anger—an anger that finally exploded, even after a long period of psychotherapy. He tangled with policemen, assaulted his former wife and mother-in-law, and, after receiving a two-year suspended sentence, attacked a Las Vegas district attorney. "Defeated" and near bankruptcy by the mid 1970s, Fabian had to grasp at straws. Cracking under the strain of overdue alimony and child-support payments, he sang in places where "they used the dressing room for customer toilets." Most troubling to Fabian, perhaps, he posed nude for *Playgirl* magazine.

Fabian apologetically says, "I made lots of mistakes, *lots* of them, but I thought these things would help my career." His anguish only leaves us wondering what went wrong. Why did success turn so sour? In 1959–60 Fabian was a budding superstar, a bonafide rival of Elvis's. He commanded movie roles and was being groomed by Jimmy Stewart, among others, for future greatness. But only a few years later, almost as quickly as he rose to prominence, the twenty-year-old Fabian was essentially finished. The movie studios were offering him only "psychopathic killer" roles in grade-D movies—he's still trying to figure out the plot of one of these epics, *Dr. Goldfoot and the Lovebombs*. But, worst of all, there were no more record deals. His money was gone, and he was left with only a half-paid XKE coupe and a taste for alcohol.

Why?

Well, for one thing, "Fabe's" image was a problem. It surrounded him with a certain aura, one that was progressively out of tune with the times.

But this could have been overcome, if not for his Achilles' heel. Fabian wasn't a rock 'n' roll star in the truest sense of the term. Unlike thousands of teenagers who sharpened their singing on street corners during the 1950s, he didn't have a passion for the music. Reluctantly entering the business only to support his mother, he never hungered for the proverbial golden ring. An expert marketing plan led to success, but lacking commitment, he didn't have the resolve to get through the bad times. And that deficiency ultimately proved devastating.

Talking about the past is difficult for him. We sit in his manager's Los Angeles office, while he nervously tugs at a pair of neatly pressed tennis shorts (he's an avid racquetball player) and goes through a pack of cigarettes. His temper frequently flares. He is especially riled by his treatment at the hands of "serious" rock 'n' roll magazines. He vehemently curses them, sparing no four-letter expletive.

"It hurts, it fucking hurts to be thought of as some fluke in a pompadour," he says, as his eyes take on a cold, menacing look.

He's not the only one in pain. It's distressing to watch him—even frightening—for the office seems uncomfortably small.

"I don't know what people want from me. I've had some monster hits," he continues, still upset. "But, shit, from day one I knew I was being overlooked. I knew I wasn't getting credit. Wherever I went I was received like the Beatles. But I never got any recognition. Even Al Capp, the cartoonist, put me down. The records were selling, the times were good, and I couldn't get zip.

"I was plastic—manufactured—to these fucking people, these so-called 'experts.' I was always traveling in someone else's footsteps. There was nothing I could do about it. I understand that to them I wasn't a writer, I was a molded figure, kind of a phony."

His voice cools, he looks forlornly at his thighs. "Well, I've rationalized it over the years and I feel I was more than that."

Now, at forty-three, Fabian has found solace through therapy. Psychological counseling has helped him establish closer relations with his family and given him a better perspective on the past. But, most important, after wrestling with painful insecurities for years, he's finally realized the critical role he played in supporting his family.

Even as an adolescent growing up in a lower-middle-class neighborhood in South Philadelphia, Fabian had to have an afterschool job. His father was a policeman, but his civil servant's salary wasn't enough to keep the family out of debt. The ten-year-old Fabian, known only as Tony then, worked as a janitor's assistant. It was dirty, disgusting work, and he still remembers, "I hated it. The roaches would run up my sleeves."

When Fabian turned fourteen, though, things got worse. His father had a severe heart attack. While he would eventually recuperate, he couldn't work for months and, at that time, policemen didn't get any disability insurance. "We were really hurting," recalls Fabian, who went to work for a pharmacist. "With all the bills and everything, we didn't know what was going to happen. My brothers and I tried to help, but it just wasn't enough. It was a scary time."

One day he was sitting in front of the house, crying. A passerby came up to him, and, as Fabian tells it, asked "Have you ever thought of being a rock 'n' roll singer?" Annoyed by the man's question, Fabian quickly shot back, "Don't bother me. Get the hell out of here."

Undaunted, the stranger asked a neighbor to intercede and a formal meeting between Fabian and Robert Marcucci, the same marketing wizard who had brought Frankie Avalon to prominence, was finally arranged.

"I only wanted to make some money," says Fabian, summarizing their first meeting. "I liked rock 'n' roll, but I was only in it for my family and the money. With my father sick and all that, the overriding need was cash . . . and this seemed the best way to get it."

Fabian was immediately treated to an Elvis-style image. His hair was greased, sculptured, and puffed into a giant wave. Wing-shirt collars were turned up to hug his baby-faced cheeks. A little make-up was applied. And, in less than two years, "Fabe" had teenage girls swooning. In quick succession he placed three songs on the charts in 1959, "Turn Me Loose" (number nine), "Tiger" (number three) and the title track from the movie "Hound Dog Man" (number nine). The film, which marked his acting debut, was about a boy and his dog—and, as Fabian jokingly reminds us, "I played the boy."

Other roles were a bit more auspicious. By this time he was living in Hollywood and cavorting with the stars. His next appearance was in Blake Edwards's mindless farce *High Time,* alongside Bing Crosby and Tuesday Weld. Portraying a college student predictably fixated on campus panty raids, he flip-flopped from one prank to another, and finally had a torrid love affair with Weld. Seen as the heir apparent to the Great Seducer himself, Rudolph Valentino, Fabian secured a similar part in *North to Alaska,* an equally forgettable film about the wild Yukon gold rush which starred John Wayne. Those were rock-em, sock-em days, and, in keeping with the wild West spirit, Fabian dodged assorted left hooks to go after a few blondes. Numerous champagne bottles were uncorked in this pursuit, but, alas, early sixties morality won out yet again, as the virginal-looking seventeen-year-old came up empty.

Fabian missed the chance to sing the title song, since that honor went to Johnny Horton, and the snub underscored his declining musical prospects. He wasn't miffed, however. He was too busy doing three other films, two with Jimmy Stewart, and one, *Dear Brigitte,* with Ms. Bardot herself. All in all, he was leading a typically crazy Hollywood life. Admitting "I had an image to keep up," Fabian often skipped film school classes, despite Stewart's scoldings, and "went overboard with my new freedom." Living away from home for the first time, he partied constantly, got drunk, and tooled around in his Jaguar. Not one for concentrating on the road ahead, he didn't see the future closing in on him.

And close in it did, like a vise, tight and merciless.

Hollywood has a vicious curse: typecasting. One never escapes it. Once a psychopathic killer, always a crazy-eyed, blood-curdling murderer. Fabian foolishly played that role in an episode of Robert Altman's 1962 TV series, "Bus Stop," entitled *A Lion Walks Among Us,* and continued to bludgeon young starlets for the next four years. Usually pictured as a Dr. Jekyll-and-Mr. Hyde type, he became synonymous with evil, a younger version of Vincent Price. In the process, as he frankly admits, "I lost all my credibility. It eventually became impossible for me to find any work."

Married, with two kids, and still supporting his parents, Fabian couldn't cope with the financial pressures. His drinking got worse, as did his frame of mind. "I went into therapy, but the clinic had no idea what to do with me. They had never dealt with a rock 'n' roll star . . . and didn't know what the hell was happening to me. They gave me Librium, and said things would be fine. Pills, that was their answer. Later on, I talked with some good people. They helped. But then, no one asked me to change, no one."

Laughing sardonically, the image of one of the macabre figures he used to play, Fabian quickly adds, "I was hurting inside; I didn't know where the hell I was going. I smashed up a few cars, got into fights . . . I was terribly angry. Everything around me—my marriage, my friendships—everything was falling apart.

"I missed the singing. I wanted to perform again. That's what it was. I wanted to get out on the road again—do a few big rooms—the thought of it really excited me."

In 1969, "Fabe" did just that. He put a band together and played Harrah's Club in Reno. Surrounded by a bevy of beautiful girls in "Elvis outfits," he tried to recapture his old magic with little success. The audience didn't boo him. People just looked on grimly, saddened by what had happened to him.

Still hopeful of landing a record deal, Fabian tried a different route for a few years; the small backwater clubs, places like the Golden Banana. Dubbing this particular Kentucky cafe "a dirty toilet," he angrily says, "I did a good show there. I gave it everything I had. But when I went to get paid the guy said I wasn't worth the money. I went after him, and before I knew it, the cops were all over me, clubbing me with their nightsticks. I was lucky to get out of there with my life."

Skidding toward oblivion, Fabian clutched at one more straw—a *Playgirl* centerfold. Believing the publicity would give him a much needed boost, he didn't accept any money for the stunt, and still insists, "I told them I'd do it for free, but, in return, they had to promise me they wouldn't show my genitalia. That contract mysteriously disappeared. What could I do? I knew it was a mistake the minute I saw the thing being sold in a brown paper sleeve. I could barely live with myself."

Instead of helping his career, the photospread ignited such a furor, Fabian was forced into seclusion. Shocked and confused, he didn't perform again until 1981, nearly six years later. When he did resurface, another ugly incident provoked an even greater crisis.

Over dinner with his estranged wife and her mother, a heated argument about child custody developed and he viciously punched each of them. He notes now, "but for the grace of God, it could've been a Marvin Gaye scene." Fabian was arrested and subsequently placed on probation for two years.

But, incredibly, that wasn't the end of his problems. During that two-year-period, his wild temper again got the better of him. In 1982, Fabian was puffing a cigarette in the nonsmoking section of a plane traveling from Reno, Nevada to L.A., when a passenger abusively shouted, "Hey faggot, put that damn cigarette out." Fabian obeyed by sticking the lighted ash right into the man's chest. The man turned out to be no ordinary passenger but the Las Vegas District Attorney. Again Fabian was jailed, and only a quick bit of sweet-talking saved him from another court hearing.

Since then, his energies have been applied more constructively, and he insists, "My temper is getting a lot better." Recently remarried, he feels his new wife has "played a major part in helping me." His optimism has been fueled also by a revived interest in film-making. Anxious to make a documentary, he now sees himself as "a good detail man, someone who knows how to direct." While conceding that his old image might hinder him in Hollywood, he's still confident about convincing a producer, or even a network to trust him.

"I have a lot of hard work ahead of me, but I know I'm gonna make it this time," says Fabian with assurance. "I'm still saddled with that fifties image, so I'm never going to get a great role unless I produce it myself. I will; I'm sure of it. Cher Bono gives me that confidence. She was a freak, too, a manufactured person, and look how far she's come. I already have a few projects in mind. One of them is bound to happen."

In the meantime, he occasionally performs, and has become a rock-revival show promoter. At these events, he's the old "Fabe," replete with "letterman" cardigan, penny loafers, and well-oiled hair. "Turn Me Loose" is sung with a more bluesy edge, but that can be forgiven—it's a long-delayed *rite* of passage.

"I went from an adolescent to an adult overnight. That's why I made so many mistakes. I never had a chance to look at things, to understand what was going on. At fourteen I was supporting a family, and before I knew it, I had two kids (a boy now sixteen, a girl fourteen) and my career was over. Not once did I have to make a decision. I was just led

from one thing to another. For sixteen years I lived that way, supporting my family, and never growing up."

Exhausted by these memories, Fabian leans back in his chair and
sighs. His voice is noticeably strained. As he takes a long puff of a
cigarette, he blurts out, "I knew I shouldn't have done this interview;
it's too painful."

But in a few moments, he says, "I could never talk about these things
with my mother, rest her soul. If I had, I would've apologized to her for
not explaining how I was, that I was too young to know what I was
doing in Hollywood, and all that. I'm talking to my father now, and
maybe that'll help. But the main thing is not to repeat the old mistakes.
I'm keeping the lines of communication open with my children. They're
slowly finding out who I was . . . and I hope the three of us can bury
that old plastic image once and for all."

Doug Ingle of the Iron Butterfly

There's No Taming His Paint Brush

And a mountain boy, wild and savage, shall lead them . . . unto the Garden, the pretty and bounteous Garden of Eden.

It was indeed ironic.

At the height of the flower-power movement, when America's children were parading with garlands in their hair, a violent, quick-tempered *enfant terrible* rose from the fire. As a youth he had broken a young girl's collarbone with his fists, but in 1968, Doug Ingle was suddenly a hero of the counterculture, the "genius" behind "In-A-Gadda-Da-Vida."

That odyssey was an epochal one. For Ingle's song revolutionized rock 'n' roll. It was harder-edged and more haunting than most hippie-era mainstays. The seventeen-minute song, mixing the melodic with the tribal beat of a pulsating guitar, mirrored the confusion of a swirling, mind-blasting LSD trip—a trip Ingle was on when he wrote it. It sold over three million copies in 1968–69 alone and acid rock gained new credibility. The "freaks" had been given an anthem; background music for getting high. As a result, the broadcasting establishment buckled. FM radio stations had to adapt their schedules in order to play the song in its entirety. This change later became known as "progressive" programming, and while the scraggly-bearded, wild-haired Ingle says, "I wasn't trying to break new ground," the self-described social misfit will always be remembered as a pioneer. As their lead vocalist, he made Iron Butterfly soar to new heights, and willingly or not, we were forced to go with them.

"A lot of people see these Christian messages in it, but, shit, I see it more as an expression of the times, an echoing of our desire to slow down, and to return to the bush," Ingle says of "In-A-Gadda-Da-Vida," quickly adding that the song has sold over 12 million copies.

Taking a hearty gulp of beer after noting this remarkable statistic, Ingle flops back on a couch in his manager's Van Nuys, California, office, and props both feet up on a table. His movements have a certain coarseness, and wearing tattered jeans, a faded T-shirt and sunglasses, he looks like an outsider, an angry outsider.

"The song was a vehicle to intensify my growth process, it justified what I'd been doing, and that I didn't have to answer to anyone," Ingle says, his gravelly voice strident. "I know the establishment wasn't for me, I had already succeeded at being a nonconformist. So I didn't care how my community viewed me, or the song. The song was my standing up, my being me . . . *vida* in Spanish means life, and that's what it's all about, a theme of exploration, a search for new horizons."

Often couching his views in broad metaphysical pronouncements, Ingle will drift away from the topic at hand, and talk incomprehensibly about hallucinogens, the "surge in Eastern theology," tribal communes, and other sixties phenomena. Yet when he focuses on his own strivings, and "lust to make a statement," he's a far more understandable—and sympathetic—figure.

"We'd been opening for the Doors and Jefferson Airplane at the Galaxy [in Hollywood], and we were breaking records there. They were lining up around the block for us. It was great. But even though I didn't have any master plan, or big goals, I wanted us to be more than a house band. I saw us making a statement, coming up with a new definition of extrasensory perception.

"Well, one night, while I was working on some conceptual patterns, I really got plastered. [Ron] Bushy [the Butterfly's drummer] came home, and asked me if I'd been working. I could barely talk, but in slurred speech I was telling him, 'Yeah, yeah, in a Garden of Eden, in a Garden of Eden.'"

Mimicking a drunk, Ingle relives the scene, slurring each syllable of the song's title, and then continues, "We almost got into a fight over it. I wasn't trying to get into anything religious, but Ron kept talking about Christianity, Christianity, and pushing these buttons in me. Finally I passed out. He confronts me the next morning, and he keeps telling me 'I like it, I like it,' so the title just stuck."

As a conceptual pattern for the late 1960s, the Garden of Eden was an apt choice. This *was* the era of flower power. The counterculture, in protesting against the war machine and computerized society, cried out for a beatific "return to nature." Innocence *could* be regained, for paradise now came to mean life on a commune, perhaps amid geodesic domes and acres of alfalfa sprouts.

There's only one discordant note here. While Ingle's "garden" metaphor suited these rebellious times, the "greening of America" was also a peaceful stirring—and that's completely out of harmony with his violent life.

As a youngster in Evergreen, Colorado, he didn't conform to the normal standards of society. Instead, seeing himself as "a wild savage," he roamed the hills, stalking small animals, and thirsting for adventure. This trail led to his temporary expulsion from elementary school, which in turn, further estranged him from his surroundings. A vindictive rage began to well up in the eight-year-old, for as Ingle now recalls, "When things went wrong, I'd get even, without even thinking about it."

To illustrate the point, Ingle chillingly explains why he flunked out of the first grade. Not knowing how to write, Ingle had looked at a little girl's paper, and she foolishly told the teacher he was cheating. Exposed, he got teased by his classmates, and as Ingle casually puts it, "This really got me cued up." He eventually caught the girl in the playground, jumped on her, and broke her collarbone.

Most people wouldn't admit to such aberrant behavior, but Ingle doesn't seem troubled by it. His manner is quite relaxed. He simply adds as a footnote, "I was very wild," and goes on to talk about his early distaste for the establishment, including the sales post his father held at an aluminum company. "My dad was always telling me the early bird catches the worm. Well I never liked worms. I don't know what would've happened if I was a more cooperative person, but I wanted to do things my way."

This rebelliousness was later expressed in his music. After moving to San Diego, the sixteen-year-old formed a band called the Pages. It was 1961, and the group, which included three future members of the Butterfly, became a favorite at local teen clubs.

"Even in those days we were taking the norm and stretching it," says Ingle, his face finally showing a hint of emotion. "I felt alive then, I was standing up and being counted. I was intrigued by the search for a new sound . . . no matter what it cost."

A few years later, upon the invitation of "some flower child," Ingle went to Los Angeles, met the owner of the rock club Bido Lito's and the Pages soon had a steady gig. As Ingle recounts, "I wanted to be heavier, more physical . . . plus there was a mystique of the melodic," so he felt obligated to make some changes. Along with picking up a few new musicians, he renamed the band, and by 1966, the Iron Butterfly was ready to fly.

Though they were an immediate hit at Bido Lito's and the Galaxy, their backstage maneuverings were as fractious as a political debate. The basic dispute was over leadership. Ingle saw himself as the group's main conceptualist, while guitarist Danny Weis wanted the Butterfly to follow his own musical direction. Factions sprang up, and by 1968, Weis and bass player Jerry Penrod split to form Rhinoceros. Vocalist Darryl DeLoach left to open a restaurant in San Diego, and in their place, Eric Braunn and Lee Dorman joined the band. While this shuffling solidified Ingle's rule, he would soon face new challenges.

Atlantic Records initially pressed him to do a shorter version of "In-A-Gadda-Da-Vida." They wanted to get more tunes on the album, which a 17½-minute song prevented. The group sided with Ingle during this battle, and he fondly remembers their support, "We won out because of our oneness, we felt it was our ground, and we collectively stood together."

It was 1968 and the group was riding high. "In-A-Gadda-Da-Vida" 's success (eighty-one weeks in the Top 10) brought them scores of engagements, and these shows were quintessential sixties psychedelia. Crazy-quilt blobs of color were projected onto a screen, to help the audience take a magical LSD trip to the subconscious. The band timed the brightest patterns to the highest notes, and in further celebration of this cerebral journey, a mock altar was set up on the stage, complete with burning pyres. Ingle directed this entire show, and at its loud conclusion, he led the group into "a crash mode," signaling that the "quest for truth" had been successful.

It was an impressive display, but by 1970, something else was also exploding—the band members' egos. The unity they had achieved during the Atlantic clash now dissolved, and once again a power struggle erupted, between Ingle and a Braunn-led faction. Only this time, the battle was far more savage than the Weis affair. And much more destructive.

"I felt restricted. I wanted to travel faster, but Eric was like an anchor to me," says Ingle sharply, clutching his beer can more tightly, and scowling. "He was seventeen, eighteen, I was going on twenty-two, twenty-three, it was difficult for me, I wanted to pursue my leanings without slowing down. My necessity is to pursue with a free hand, but I felt imprisoned at the time. We had this heavy metal image and I personally wanted to get into some softer ballads. But Eric and I, we were both playing to different drummers."

Their feud, which resembled a Machiavellian drama, lasted for about a year. There were plots, subplots, ugly exchanges on stage, and as Ingle admits, "we were fighting more than we were playing." He finally prevailed, and Braunn was ousted. But these skirmishes sapped the group of its strength, and less than a year after Braunn's departure, the Butterfly disbanded.

Ingle, attributing the group's demise to "the less hopeful, post-Woodstock times," became a house painter in Portland, Oregon. Meeting "regular people for a change, instead of those backstage types," and feeling "a connection with the working masses," Ingle enjoyed this lifestyle for thirteen years. He still played the guitar on weekends, at local "cherry pie" festivals. But paint brushes provided more satisfaction. As Ingle immodestly explains, "those brushes used to dance, and spit fire."

Today, though, the forty-one-year-old Ingle has other visions. "The surge of computer technology has spawned a new desire to get back to the bush," he insists and he's back in the studio, with a reformed Butterfly. Using that old name has already caused problems. Braunn and Ron Bushy feel they own the rights to the Butterfly tag, and have threatened him with lawsuits. When asked to respond, Ingle is surprisingly restrained. He smiles, albeit weakly, and states his willingness to negotiate the issue.

If these talks occur, and indeed bear fruit, the Butterfly could again offer an inspiring metaphor. They would have outstripped Adam, and returned to the garden.

But overcoming the past won't be easy. For beyond "In-A-Gadda-Da-Vida," the group's only legacy is acrimony. As Ingle pointedly says, only moments after priding himself on his new maturity, "I have every moral right to call my group 'my group,' and to use the name I want."

Eric Braunn of the Iron Butterfly

Still Angry After All These Years

Listening to Eric Braunn condemn Doug Ingle is a very trying experience. It's always painful to hear how a friendship went astray and turned to hate, but, in this case, Braunn's outbursts are especially unsettling. They echo the passing of the sixties, the death of a certain spirit—and are consequently a cause for grief.

"Yeah, I respected Doug's craft in the beginning, we shared a lot at first, but he got caught up in the ego thing, the star syndrome, and believed he was some type of god," rails Braunn, sitting in his cluttered, dimly lit Los Angeles apartment. Album jackets and guitars are strewn about the place, next to dozens of half-finished, ragged-edged song sheets. These things are a reminder of Braunn's Butterfly days, his song writing and guitar playing. But the disarray also signals a struggle, Braunn's attempt at a comeback, and his simultaneous imprisonment in the past.

"Doug got so far from reality, he thought everything was his doing; the song, the crowds, the money, everything," continues Braunn, his words hissing like an overheated steam kettle. "He treated the rest of us like we didn't exist, like we were crap. How do you think that felt? I don't even want to think about it. He took the fun out of everything. He was this, he was that . . .

"It got to the point that I didn't even want to be around him. He was always talking about 'In-A-Gadda-Da-Vida,' what he'd done. But that's the biggest joke of all. He wrote the original lyrics, and the melody, but that's only two to three minutes' worth of stuff. We all worked hard on that song, and put so much into it . . . it's ridiculous that he gets all the credit, and all the money for it. Does he care that I worked on that song for weeks? The African wildlife stuff is mine. Shit! There's been no split. I haven't seen any money in years."

Braunn didn't care about money initially, nor did the rest of the Butterfly. At most clubs, they played four sets a night for about fifty dollars a week. Yet, there were no complaints. Only the music mattered. No one's ego was inflated, and there was a sense of purpose. Everyone was working together, in a spirit of mutual respect. As Braunn concedes, "They [the band] were a great opportunity. There was a strength there. Bushy was a talent, and Doug, he had a great voice, he could really sing."

Then came success. "In-A-Gadda-Da-Vida" made millions. According to Braunn, royalties from these sales reached a peak in 1970, when the band made close to $3 million. That meant lots of wild parties, big houses, cars, women, everything rock 'n' roll dreams are made of.

There was only one problem. Amid all this high living, no one bothered to file a tax statement. Braunn admittedly shares the responsibility for this lapse, but he also suggests, without naming names, that "there were lots of shady dealings going on.

"Something wasn't right. I don't know what it was, but the IRS really picked us apart. They attached all our incomes. Our properties went into default and we all lost our ass.

"To the IRS, I guess, we were just a bunch of rock 'n' roll hippies. I personally lost over three million dollars in assets, and when the case finally ended, the band was totally broke. They were supposed to pay me twenty thousand dollars for leaving, but to this day, I haven't gotten a penny."

Braunn's memories aren't all bad. After being ousted from the Butterfly he went on to form Flintwhistle with Bushy, and also discovered one of the 1970's biggest draws, the heavy-metal Black Oak Arkansas band.

He's now hoping to put his own group together, and most days are spent in front of a piano, writing new material. This work usually excites him. He'll confidently wave recently made demos before guests, and talk about meetings with producers. Then, his smiling, barely stubbled face, still framed by a Beatle-bowl haircut, has a true boyish sparkle. The glow is infectious, and his saying "I'm going to make it" sounds believable.

But even if Braunn does put his devils to rest, and overcomes the past to notch new successes, the struggle has already taken a toll. In place of his old innocence and joy, there's a cynicism, a weighty lament that questions the very essence of rock 'n' roll stardom.

"So many performers are like Ingle. They get swept away by their image, and really start believing in it. They actually see themselves as gods. How can they not? There are fifty thousand people screaming out there, jumping up and down, and that person *is* a god to them. He knows that. But you have to know you're a human being too. Otherwise, the success just isn't worth it. You lose all the potential for reality and joy in your life."

Phoebe Snow
Tender Mercies

It was called the "Big Crackup."

The pressures of "overnight success" were purportedly too much for her. People said she'd gone crazy, and mercilessly mocked her. Once heralded as the "greatest voice of her generation," she was now labeled a "weirdo," who believed in UFOs, and extraterrestrial beings. She had fueled this gossip by admitting to an "encounter of the second kind." So the talk about her missing engagements, taking drugs and fighting with company officials mushroomed, spelling doom for her once promising career.

Amid these rumors, one tragic fact about Phoebe Snow was overlooked—that nightmarish, all-consuming aspect of her life which made hit records and public acclaim seem trivial. In 1976, she gave birth to a severely brain-damaged child, an ineducable daughter named Valerie who after years of therapy can barely walk or talk.

Overcoming her shock and confusion, Phoebe became a profile in courage through this ordeal. More than just a dutiful mother, she's given her daughter an inordinate amount of love, as if kisses and hugs would cure the child's infirmities. While Valerie's little grunts, and pitiful attempts at moving have a numbing, overwhelming effect on visitors, Phoebe tirelessly remains by the little girl's side. In her role as a self-described "safety net" Phoebe is a constant source of maternal comfort. She doesn't get any help from Valerie's father, who left her several years ago. So Phoebe hangs in there alone, determined to prove the doctors wrong—doctors who said Valerie was doomed to be a "total vegetable" —and determined to be a survivor herself.

In the late 1970s, after the success of "Poetry Man" was eclipsed by
Valerie's brain operations and anguished cries, Phoebe was devastated.
Her early albums (especially *It Looks Like Snow)* had a certain
strength, a thumping, bluesy growl. As these deeply emotional works
hit the charts, critics marveled at her voice, its extraordinary high
range, and raw "gutsiness." But with Valerie confined to a bed for three
years, Phoebe lost that energy in a sea of despair. Hearing only a
drumroll of pessimistic medical reports, she was hardly interested in
making music. Now, poetry men with lilting melodies were replaced by
ghoulish specters in white uniforms. And in her jangled, disordered
mind—there was only one way to escape these terrors—suicide.

"Once I woke up to the realities of the situation, I knew my world
was shattering," says Snow, while frolicking with Valerie on the floor of
their Fort Lee, New Jersey, apartment. Both of them are swatting at a
balloon, desperately trying to keep it aloft. But when it finally lands out
of reach, the chubby, brown-haired child loses interest in the game, and
crawls toward her therapeutic exercise bar. This show of determination
makes Phoebe smile, and for a moment she's decidedly upbeat. "Now
Val has a lot of mobility, she's doing great. There's been so much improvement . . ." But after her voice trails off, she sighs, "When everyone was predicting the worst, I was totally distraught. I don't know
why I didn't commit suicide, everything was so bad. I kept wondering,
how am I going to get out of this one; how am I going to extricate
myself. It was rock-bottom time. I just gave up on myself, emotionally
and professionally."

Phoebe clears her throat, then continues, "I couldn't communicate
these feelings to anyone. And I also felt that they [record company
execs] were not in a position to be supportive of me in this matter
anyway. It was their job to sell records. I was a commodity they were
selling. So part of me was very protective and private, like a mother
lion, about the situation. I didn't want to share it with anybody, so I
had a great deal of trouble communicating to people exactly what was
happening in my life. A part of me was destroyed, shocked, overwhelmed. I wanted a lot of pats on the back, I wanted to be comforted,
I wanted to be told 'Hey Phoebe, you're incredible, you're strong. Hey,
I'm Mr. Record Company executive, and I'm behind you all the way,
and we'll throw you as many parties as we can, and tell you we love you
everyday.'

"But that's not their job. This is a business relationship, and business
and personal, you don't mix. Being emotionally distraught, I'd go so far

as to say I was emotionally unstable at that time, but none of that occurred to me then. I was constantly going through depressions. It started to affect my health; I was sick all the time, and I lost the ability to communicate to people what I was really feeling. Hey, I'm freaking out because my daughter's brain-damaged. I'm freaking out because I'm a single parent; my husband and I separated and ultimately got divorced a year after Valerie was born.

"I was angry that I didn't get more support from my family. I went through a great period of animosity and anger. But look here, it's a very difficult thing, I can't blame anyone for bailing out. At this point, I expect it of people, not because they're weak, or they're shitty, or they're less than human, or whatever criticism you want to lay on them. It's because it hurts, it's painful. There are times *I* want to run away, and go through all kinds of changes. But I wouldn't wish it on someone I hated. Because it's that painful."

In 1979–80, however, after several albums had bombed, Phoebe wasn't so reasonable or forgiving. Confronted with a never-ending stream of medical bills, and the nerve-wracking pressures of establishing a home-therapy program ("Valerie belonged with me, I couldn't bear the thought of her being institutionalized"), Phoebe pressed CBS Records for more help. Expecting them to be "humanitarians," even though her promised album was several months late, she upped her salary demands, believing she should have been treated like a bigger star. It wasn't apparent to her that she was being irrational. Alone, desperate, and feeling Valerie was "half alive, half gone," Phoebe "dumped everything into CBS's lap," insisting that they get her through the crisis—or else.

"I was whacked out of my skull, absolutely insane," concedes Snow, admitting CBS wanted to keep her on their label, but that she "stupidly" walked out. "Here I was carrying my burden alone, I said to myself, 'gotta work, gotta work, single parent, gotta make a living.' I had a home-therapy program going on in my house that was run by a bunch of volunteers. My home was like Grand Central Station; it was a zoo. I didn't want to put Valerie in a school, so here I was, fighting to keep my daughter alive. I was fighting to keep the therapy program going, too. My only thoughts were that I had to be bigger, I had to command more salary . . . and I was like 'Come on CBS, you can do this for me.'

"I had to have this for my daughter's survival. I had to have that paycheck coming in. So I went up to the big guys at CBS and said

'Look here, I need you to pay more attention to me, and you're not [sticking her tongue out] nyeh, nyeh, so I'm leaving,' and that's what I did. I left, and I've regretted that ever since. That's when my career started to really go in the toilet . . . and they kept looking at me with this meaningful expression, like 'Are you sure?' I'm going, 'Yes, I'm sure.' I wasn't sure of my own name and address at that point.

"I was gone, totally crazy because I would not put my daughter anywhere but in my home. That's where I felt she belonged, and I felt it was up to me to keep the situation going. I wanted more—now, better, bigger, and it just doesn't come that way. That's not how a career process works. They couldn't pull a rabbit out of a hat, and that's what I was asking them to do. And when it didn't happen fast enough, and when it wasn't wonderful right away, I left. A big mistake. And that's when my career started to skid. I have to apologize to CBS. I'm sorry I was nuts in 1979. I'm very sorry for what I did."

After talking about the four "terrible" albums she did for CBS ("I was just in it for the money . . . creatively, I wasn't there"), Phoebe moves over to the exercise bar and encourages Valerie to do a few more routines.

"Come on, keep going. Bring your hand over, that's it, grab onto it," exhorts Phoebe, standing under a stationary, horizontally positioned ladder, as her daughter desperately tries to move from one rung to another. "One more, one more . . . just stretch your arm out, come on."

Once the ten-year-old progresses to the next bar, Phoebe's dark brown eyes turn watery, and she claps in approval.

It's a touching scene, one filled with love and courage. There's hope here, an undying faith in miracles. Maybe Valerie will be able to walk, perhaps she will learn a few rudimentary skills and finally begin to talk.

Maybe. Tragically, even her mere survival is very iffy.

The only certainty is that Valerie will never experience the joys Phoebe savored as a child. Unlike her mother, who was nurtured on the strains of Bartok and Beethoven, Valerie won't be taking piano or clarinet lessons. Snow's own father was a music teacher, and she was playing both those instruments by age nine. The little girl will not come to appreciate her mother's "patron saints," Benny Goodman and Billie Holiday, nor will she travel to Greenwich Village from the wilds of New Jersey, with "a ratty old" guitar case in hand, to play at the Bitter End or Gaslight. While these wanderings were often traumatic for Phoebe ("I was a fat, curly-haired teenager growing up in the Twiggy era"), Valerie will never take such evolutionary journeys. Her world is too shadowy, too circumscribed for adventures.

When Valerie's future is discussed, Phoebe's face darkens, the glow in her eyes disappears. She understands all too well that her daughter's prospects are limited. But each of Valerie's movements, however slight or awkward, gives her a little more hope. Phoebe can't despair, not now. For the child's sake, she has to remain optimistic.

"Here was a little girl whose life was doomed from the start, and here she is thriving," says Snow, sitting down on a couch between some toys. "No, she won't ever be normal, she'll never be perfect. But neither will you. She's lived till now, and that's far beyond the doctors' best prognoses. She's living a delightful existence, she's a happy little girl.

"And if she can live through all she's been through, there's great hope for humanity. We can certainly go past our own obstacles. My kid's a living example for anyone who has to overcome hardships. *She's* setting an example. There's reason for faith."

Phoebe seems to be engaged in a dialogue with herself at this point. Preparing for those dark moments that lie ahead, she's giving herself a pep talk, a rallying cry that she will rely upon to summon strength. She desperately needs a mental edge. Without seeing, or accentuating, the positives in her life, she could hit rock bottom again—as she did in the early 1980s, after CBS failed to meet her contract demands.

"I lost touch with myself, I gave up, and I started putting on a lot of weight, and I mean a lot," says Phoebe, grimacing. "I felt like the walking wounded. I was emotionally adrift, anyone could do what they wanted with me. I had bottomed out. I'd been ripped off, and people could finagle their way into my life. They had a patsy in me; I was emotionally and physically unable to fight back. It was the final stages of the drowning-man syndrome.

"I didn't have any identity, any self-image, and to this day I don't have a good self-image. You have to realize, I went from being a child straight into the music business. I was a child with a hit record, then a child with a handicapped daughter. Finally, I've been able to see some facets of who I am. I've grown up a little. Even if my daughter dies, or my new boyfriend leaves, I still have me. In that, there's hope."

Besides losing forty pounds since that "godawful time," Phoebe's now convinced that the "timelessness" of her music can lead to another recording deal. That's not to say that all of her old insecurities have disappeared. They're still very much in evidence, as she belittles her "experiments" with an acoustic guitar ("this high-tech stuff won't be accepted by the industry"), and laughs nervously about a recent appearance on ABC's "20/20."

During that show Phoebe was asked if she were a junkie—the implication was that her purported drug habit affected Valerie's fetal development. While denying this suggestion, Phoebe pales when the subject is discussed, and her voice has a distinct hollowness.

"I've heard all sorts of stories—I was supposed to be dead; I heard I was an alcoholic; God knows what else." Phoebe bristles and shifts in her seat. She's on the defensive and nearly screams, "Was I a junkie?"

That question is left unanswered. But judging from the strained look in Phoebe's eyes, she's suffering from another syndrome—the overwhelming guilt that links her with all mothers of handicapped children.

To relieve some of this pain, Phoebe has put Valerie's story to music. Reaching deep inside herself to understand "the meaning of these past few years," she's written a sensitive ballad, "Stand Your Ground," that urges Valerie to persevere. Indifferent to the song's commercial prospects, she's gone public to give people an "inspirational message," to convince them that handicaps can be overcome.

"Symbolically, Valerie is telling people they can make it. Why is she here? What's the point of her life? She's done so much with so little, and that can be a focus for people, it can help them reach goals they once thought were impossible.

"Because of Valerie I'm not worried anymore about being a success. I'm not concerned about my comeback. The thought, 'What if I don't make it?' never crosses my mind. I've already accomplished so much, it doesn't matter if I have success singing. It would be a personal triumph if I could win some award, and be able to hand it to my daughter . . . but the music, the sheer joy of performing is my motivating force and the reason any of us should remain in this business. Fame is nice, but I don't need it; I'm stronger now. I'm not ecstatic, I still have my doubts and insecurities, but I'm content. I'm a survivor, too, even if I do get down, but I can wait to see what happens next. I can live through the next day, or wait for tomorrow."

By this time, Valerie has snuggled next to Phoebe on the sofa. After they exchange a few kisses, Valerie crawls off to get a toy, while Phoebe turns on the stereo, and looks fondly at her daughter. "People say she doesn't belong—but we're going to prove them wrong. We sure will. She's gonna stand her ground. She'll make it on her own—She'll stand her ground."

Felix Cavaliere of the Young Rascals

The Long Winter of Discontent

There used to be a lot of good, good lovin' between them.

The [Young] Rascals were so close, people thought they were four brothers—or at least our answer to the Beatles. For they were on their own magical mystery tour, with such jazzy, rousing hits as "People Got to Be Free," "A Beautiful Morning," "Groovin' " and of course, "Good Lovin'."

Then they got too big and famous, and everything fell apart.

Managerial problems, ego battles, hassles with record companies, drugs, women—all this contributed to the group's downfall.

But as Felix Cavaliere, their chief songwriter and vocalist bitterly suggests, the Rascals' demise is more the stuff of a scandalous Tommy Thompson novel; lost dreams, innocence adrift in a sea of greed and orgies, power plays, and savage personality clashes that scarred and bankrupted the group's soul.

"We had so much camaraderie, we were having so much fun, we didn't see what was happening to us," cries Cavaliere, his dark, bearded face reddening with despair. Wincing, as if talking about the death of a loved one, he shuffles past an impressive array of oriental antiques in his living room. Finally plopping down on a sofa, he shakes his head disgustedly, and insists, "We could've been a household word, we could've done so much. We had the world by the tail; we were so damn hot it was insane . . . there was no reality whatsoever. I felt like I was an astronaut.

"We were going so high up we lost all control. Everything was happening too quickly. The notoriety overcomes you, the money, the wild parties, the women, the kids screaming, the constant pressure to produce . . . stardom sweeps you up, and changes you . . . None of us dreamed we were going to get so big. Remember, in two years [1966–68], we had nine Top 20 hits . . . that was unbelievable, but it ruined us . . . all of a sudden we're in L.A., around people who've been stars for years, and if you're not a strong human being you never come back. They're space cadets out there, and you get sucked into it . . .

"Instead of candy, people gave us LSD, drugs, you name it. We had a harem, orgies in the back seats of cars . . . it was sickening, at least for me . . . I was very disillusioned. There's a falseness about being a hot artist . . . being on top is very precarious. I got confused and started to question things . . . the other guys didn't want things to change, they saw the money coming in, so the fighting got very stupid, very vicious. A lot of resentment surfaced. We split into cliques, and fighting just got to be too much, too, too much . . . The tragedy of the Rascals is that we lost our dream, we were a very special group, and we blew it . . . we had a dream there . . . and we'll never regain a tenth of that."

While Cavaliere is still mourning that loss, the Rascals' influence lives on. They crossed the color line, and flavored pop music with a distinct R & B sound. The group was also a political trailblazer. They wouldn't perform unless black acts were included on the bill, and while this predictably caused them a lot of trouble in the South, several clubs and arenas were ultimately integrated.

These accomplishments prompt flashbacks for Cavaliere, and when talking about them, he drifts between pride, rage, and sadness. Entombed by "what might have been," he derives limited satisfaction from his family, his lush Connecticut surroundings, and recent attempts to get back into the business. He's tried to find some solace in Eastern mysticism, and judging by the numerous portraits of the Swami Satchinanda in his house, that faith is still strong. But even this guru has failed him in a way, for there's a void in Cavaliere's life. He grew up with a dream, a consuming passion to be respected as a musician, and only wound up with a few years of glory. That need to be acknowledged couldn't have been fulfilled. There was promise for so much more.

As a youngster, growing up in New Rochelle, New York, Cavaliere was forced by his mother to take classical piano lessons, and by age twelve he was winning contests at Carnegie Hall. Even then he fell into a "trance" when writing lyrics, and felt a need "to create my own stuff."

His father didn't understand this musical absorption. A traditional Italian of the old school, he wanted Felix to follow his own footsteps, and become a dentist. Meanwhile, Mrs. Cavaliere encouraged her son's musical interests, but she died in 1956 when Felix was only fourteen. He was quickly ordered not to play rock 'n' roll in the house.

"Blown away by Ray Charles, Jerry Lee Lewis, and Fats Domino," Cavaliere didn't give in. He surreptitiously joined a high school band, and was constantly going "to the wrong side of town" to hear people like the Clovers (they had a 1959 hit with "Love Potion No. 9") and the Drifters.

When remembering these early jaunts to ghetto clubs, Felix finally perks up, and breaking into a smile, says, "One time I freaked out. I saw a Hammond organ for the first time, and it popped my head off. That's what the Rascals were all about, that organ, sax, drums . . ."

Stirred by the sound in these forbidden haunts, Cavaliere openly rebelled against his father by becoming "blacker and blacker." Besides forming his own band, the integrated Stereos, he slicked back his hair, wore a black leather jacket, and hung out with such songwriters like Neil Diamond and Carole King, in the beatnik coffeehouses of Greenwich Village.

Each downtown trip heightened his father's anxiety, and finally, the eighteen-year-old was sent to Syracuse University. This pre-med training was meant to turn Felix away from music, or, as he good-naturedly quips, "My father thought it would end this rock 'n' roll foolishness, and put some sense into my head." But freed of all restraints, Felix sang in enough black clubs to earn the nickname "Ray Charles." In 1963, he met "Mr. Twist," Joey Dee.

"This was the turning point for me," says Felix, as his wife brings a tray of tea and cookies into the room. After exchanging smiles with her, Cavaliere again turns grim. Recounting how his introduction to Dee eventually led to his joining David Brigati and the other Starlighters on a European tour, he bristles, "Joey got all the attention, 80 percent of the take and I felt I was working in toilets. He was very intelligent in picking his players, but I'd been a small-time *star,* and now I was only a sideman. The whole thing was very discouraging, I lost all my confidence.

"The only good thing going on was playing with the Beatles. We'd turn up in the same small clubs in Hamburg and Sweden, and seeing the hysteria they caused, you could tell there was something happening. I could see the beginning of a revolution."

Still there was the discouragement of his career "coming to a grinding halt." He turned to drugs, and was soon overcome by marijuana, pills and hash. A woman, with whom he had two children, restored some of his confidence, but he continued to play with Dee until 1965.

That's when he met Eddie Brigati, David's brother, who was singing regularly at the Choo Choo Club in New Jersey. Felix went there one night with another Starlighter, Gene Cornish. After the three did a few numbers together, Felix was so impressed by the audience's reaction, he sensed that "This was something special we had to take advantage of.

"The rebel was rising up in me, and I told them, 'Look, we really did it right, so why not start our own group? We were great out there, our music went POW!' "

The others agreed, and after Felix secured the services of long-time friend Dino Danelli, Them, as the Rascals were initially called, came into being. For months, they appeared at the Choo Choo Club. Then they hooked up with Soupy Sales at the Barge (a discothèque in East Hampton, Long Island), and their whole act changed.

"We were still doing funky versions of Beatles tunes, but we wanted to attract more attention," recounts Felix cheerfully. "Dino got us out of our suits and ties, and we started wearing these ridiculous knickers. That's when Soupy said, 'I'd like to call you the Little Bastards.' We couldn't do that, so he called us the Little Rascals."

It was Big Break time. Since Cavaliere's group was filling the Barge, record people inevitably came to see them. An RCA representative, various agents, and even Phil Spector offered them contracts. But Sid Bernstein, the impresario of the Beatles' upcoming Shea Stadium concert, talked the sweetest. He became their manager, and in August 1965, the scoreboard lights at Shea flashed, "The Rascals are here."

They certainly were. Aided by that appearance, Bernstein ignited a bidding war among the major record companies, that eventually led to a deal with Atlantic. This brought them "some decent money," but Cavaliere bitterly fumes, "The first thing Sid did for us was the last. So many bad moves were made, we were run like a little candy store. It was ridiculous. I don't really blame him; we saw what was going on, yet we were schmucks; we let them happen.

"Right away Sid called us, and said we can't use just the name 'Rascals,' then without our knowledge, he put in the 'Young.' I hated that name.

"We were also losing control over what we recorded . . . but did Eddie or Dino care? Shit! They'd been poor all their lives, so the only important thing to them was the money. I was always the bad guy, the guy making waves."

Despite this turmoil, the Rascals spun off a string of hits. First there was "Good Lovin'," their remake of the Olympics' 1965 song, which soared to number one by May 1966. Then "I've Been Lonely Too Long," written by Cavaliere, and "You Better Run," which was co-authored with Brigati, came next. Both songs hit the Top 20, but by 1967 they had abandoned their spirited, black R & B sound and adopted a lighter, more carefree style for the song "A Girl Like You" and their album *Groovin'*. The album's title song, about a lazy Sunday afternoon, was one of the year's top sellers.

Most of these songs had an airy, whimsical quality. Felix's singing and organ playing were decidedly upbeat. But, by 1967, the "screwing around" and the LSD parties had soured him—and in turning to the Swami Satchinanda for spiritual help, his songs became progressively more serious and introspective.

The Rascals, in turn, became more hip. They dropped the "Young" from their name, stopped wearing Edwardian knickers, and moved from poignant ballads like "How Can I Be Sure?" to the psychedelic-edged "It's Wonderful."

This effort to keep up with the times kept their streak of hits alive for a while, but when record sales started to drop at the beginning of 1968, they were ill-equipped to deal with adversity. Their chemistry, the bond that keeps groups together, had already been destroyed by years of fighting. The group went on for a few more years, and even scored with two more smash hits, "A Beautiful Morning," and "People Got to Be Free," yet, as Cavaliere mournfully suggests, the feuding got so bad, these 1968 successes had little meaning.

"The gulf between us was so wide; there was really a break-up," says the forty-four-year-old Cavaliere, leaving his seat to walk out a rear door that leads to acres of wooded land. Once outside, he ignores the icy winds blowing off a nearby lake, and heads toward a cliff edged with huge boulders. On the way, he gruffly continues, "The other guys always resented my leadership role, but when I got close to the Swami, they thought I was insane. That's when the fighting got out of hand. They thought I was deserting them, and viciously went on the attack.

"The group was coming apart at the seams . . . everyone was panicking . . . especially when I went off to Mexico with the Swami for a while. But the big mistake was Bernstein's letting them into the decision-making process. They had no training for that, and a manager should have kept them in their place. We were a democracy, vetoing things we never should have. I wanted to open up new territories, like South America and Japan, but they always said no. I can understand their frustrations, too. I was often headstrong and cut out some of their songs, but they put me against the wall."

Feeling trapped and increasingly frustrated by "bad business decisions," Cavaliere insists, "I had to save myself, so I got tighter and tighter with the Swami. He was like the perfect father for me; he never put me down. We had such a rapport, and, unlike the other people I was meeting, he never asked for any money. I never had any warmth from my father, so maybe he was the replacement. I loved him; he's a good, intelligent, sensible human being.

"If not for him, we would have never done '[It's a] Beautiful Morning'. I was ready to give it all up, but he told me it was my obligation to the kids to spread joy and happiness. So the group stayed together . . . but there was no spirit left. It was long gone."

The Rascals still had enough energy to do their memorable swan song, "People Got to Be Free," a lively retort to a racist incident at a Fort Pierce, Florida, concert. The song stayed on the charts for months (number one for five weeks) in 1968–69, and has since sold over four million copies.

They adopted a jazz motif next, incorporating free-flowing instrumentals from people like Ron Carter and Hubert Laws, and their audience deserted them. Albums such as *See* and *Search and Nearness* were commercial disasters. The magical mystery tour was now over. In 1970, on the eve of signing a new deal with Columbia, Eddie Brigati left the group.

"I couldn't believe he'd do that to me," says Felix, shaking his head in disgust. "I took him in and inspired him to be a lyricist. We were like this [he touches his thumb with his forefinger]. For him to turn on me like that . . . it still hurts. I'm extremely pissed off by the whole thing. I was treated like a greedy S.O.B., but that's bullshit. I always put the group first. In those days, I turned down a lot of money, many times, by refusing to do solo ventures."

After Gene Cornish left in 1971, Felix and Dino kept the group alive by bringing in three new musicians. This allowed them to do two more albums for Columbia, but, in reality, the Rascals had already died. It only became official in the summer of 1972.

While the other Rascals joined different groups, Cavaliere retreated to his Connecticut home. After two solo albums, he shied away from the business for several years, until Laura Nyro asked him to produce *Season of Light.*

Admittedly, the mid-1970s were tormenting for Cavaliere. None of these musical efforts recaptured the magic of the Rascals, and this preyed on him. Besides struggling financially and emotionally, he felt like "an outcast in the industry"; someone who couldn't relate "to the mass of Wall Streeters that came into the business after Woodstock."

Many of these corporate types have pressured him to put the Rascals back together, floating rumors about their revival; and on several occasions, the group has even talked about a string of concerts. While Cavaliere could certainly use the money, each meeting has only strengthened his conviction that such a reunion would be wrong. He sees it as "a ripoff of the public," and even more pointedly says, "It would be a disaster to get together again, a smear on the Rascals' good name."

Gritting his teeth in disgust, Cavaliere hops off a boulder on which he's been sitting, and continues talking while pacing around, "Look, we're just not one big happy family anymore, so the right reasons for a reunion aren't there. Why kid ourselves? It's no good. It's a sellout if I do it. I don't want people to see what they're really like. I don't want the public to see what the others have become. The most important thing to me is not the money, but keeping a little of our magic—the illusion—intact."

Hoping to create "new works of art that will also dazzle people," Cavaliere is writing the musical score for a Joseph Papp play, *Five Guys Named Mo,* and producing records for a few Connecticut rock groups. This latter endeavor brings him into contact with record-industry people, whom he still distrusts. Felix angrily complains, "The business is so damn political, I can't cope with it at times," but he's still devoted to helping "kids" avoid the "mistakes" he's made.

"I've gotten beaten up. Your feelings can really be bruised by how the business is run today. There are a lot of slimy people around; they're so commercial-minded. But my religion has kept me sane, and I'm getting a lot of happiness from guiding these groups. The Rascals never got much help; that's why we didn't reach our full potential. Yet the past doesn't have to repeat itself. I know I can be of value to these kids. They don't have to go through the crap we did."

These biting remarks belie Cavaliere's assertion that "there's no sadness in my life," and hint at a deep inner torment. Despite living comfortably in a beautifully furnished house that resounds with the happy laughter of two young children, he's still burdened by the past. "There's some life in the old man yet," he'll happily chirp when talking about his new interests, yet the conversation always drifts back to the Rascals, especially to their unfulfilled promise, and then his lingering regrets become all too clear.

"I'm happy that the Rascals will be remembered by their songs. We're still played. Unlike the Doors, who've made a conscious effort to stay alive, no one's pushing our songs, and I'm proud of that. That lasting recognition is something I always wanted, even when I first started to play the piano as a young kid.

"But it's a shame; that moment we had on the stage was so short . . ." Smacking his palms together to illustrate the brevity of that moment, Cavaliere falls silent for a while. His face etched with regret, he finally sighs, "It was so short, it was so damn short."

Delaney Bramlett of Delaney and Bonnie

It Must Have Been Quite a Night!

It was a whirlwind romance, the wild, passionate variety, that Hollywood directors might cast with Sam Shepard and Cher in the starring roles.

Boy meets girl. He feels "an instant buzz." She is enraptured. One week later, in 1967, after an exhausting burst of passion, the two aspiring rock stars are married.

In time, Eric Clapton, George Harrison, Leon Russell, and a host of other legends fell under this couple's seductive spell. Joining the pair to form a musical caravan, they all partied together, cut albums, staged unannounced shows with John Lennon's Plastic Ono Band, and roamed the world in search of the next high. These forays led to 750,000-dollar record deals for the two "love children," and, quite predictably, they blew all the money the minute they got it. These were the free-wheeling sixties, and, like many people, they thought the magic-carpet rides would last forever.

But something happened.

Like most frenzied romances, this one went haywire. It exploded into a nightmare that sent the young couple—Delaney and Bonnie—reeling. Their souring passions meant more than a fiery separation; it was the end of the starship, the loss of a promising career. No matter who was at fault, or why it happened, two lives were suddenly wrecked. Instead of the glitter, the beautiful-people parties, and rousing, countrified rock, there were only angry recriminations and deep despair. Two children, Suzanne and Bekka, were scarred by this mess. They survived, but their parents' strained voices, edged sharply with bitterness, tell a difficult story. An ugly, hellish one.

"We had it all, we were on top of the world, the money was rushing in, and then, in a flash, Bonnie's craziness destroyed it; everything was lost." Delaney Bramlett grabs two pails of oats out of the stable to feed the horses on his Rock 'n' Roll Ranch. Paying little attention to the packs of barking dogs surrounding him, or to the scorching San Fernando Valley sun, he hooks the pails onto a corral fence, then mournfully continues, "Everything, we had everything; mansions, diamond rings all over our fingers, mink coats, two incredibly beautiful daughters, and what did she do, she threw it all away. I know the life was hard, playing together all the time meant we had no freedom, we didn't have any privacy from each other, but I never saw anything like her. She was so changeable, she'd get so mad, so damn crazy. That was worse than hell for me. There was no place to hide."

Sighing loudly above the squawks of a chicken running madly through the yard, Delaney grits his teeth. He is clearly disturbed by the memories of these tempestuous confrontations. He lovingly pets one of his mares as the animal dips her head into the oats. This brings a slight smile to his round, full-bearded face. But once the horse moves away, bad memories intrude again, forcing his heavy-set body to shudder.

"Oh, she could be such sugar and syrup, you wouldn't believe it. That sweetness was intoxicating; it was a turn-on that helped get Clapton, Harrison, all of them to play with us. Plus she had so much energy. That's why everyone wanted to jam with us; she was such a force. I remember George Harrison seeing us at a small place up in North Hollywood, and telling her, 'You gotta get out of here; you both deserve so much better.'

"We had such a great sound back then, all the record companies thought we were black. No wonder we were making it . . . we had so much going for us. Clapton, Harrison, they loved us. But what did Bonnie do? The booze, drugs, these things ruin people's lives. I did immoderate things, too, but with her it got out of hand. She'd later say things to the kids which were unbearable—the language—I couldn't take it.

"A big part of me was glad when she cut out, even if it did mean the end of everything. I was just sick and tired of all the crap. It would've meant a lot—a lot of money—if she had stuck around, and honored our contract. At the time [1972], we still owed Columbia one more record, but Bonnie, she didn't give a shit. She said the one album we had already done was all they were going to get. She just got on a plane, went to St. Louis, and that was it. Some people are still suing me on account of that fucked-up move."

Delaney's voice bristles with anger. Bonnie's departure not only left him holding the bag, or, in this instance, the diapers of two baby girls. It also forced him to give up his career. Someone had to take care of the kids. And, while this task ultimately became a joy for him—he now calls his two teenaged daughters, "the greatest source of happiness a man could possibly have"—fatherhood was only a burden back then. Parenting meant an ignominious retreat from the limelight to a more mundane world of PTA bakeoffs and Sunday school sings. In this setting, he was no longer "sitting pretty . . . like a king on a throne." Instead, he had to ponder the future and the past—why "everything I had striven to create was suddenly destroyed."

Raised on a Mississippi farm, Delaney realized as a teenager that music would be an escape from the tedium of growing cotton. Strapping a guitar over his shoulder, he'd hitchhike to Memphis for talent shows, excited by the prospect of "seeing a different world, turning people on, and maybe winding up like Carl Perkins, or even Elvis." Those desires continued through high school, and propelled the seventeen-year-old to form his own band after he joined the Navy in 1956. From playing in service clubs, he graduated to the "big time," four-dollar-a-night gigs in Los Angeles, which almost brought his budding career to an abrupt end.

"We played joints like the Saddle Club in L.A., where even the performers had to throw beer bottles, or punch their way onto the stage," laughs Delaney, more relaxed now after feeding all the animals. "It didn't matter how tough or weird the place was; I was desperate for the work. I'd even guarantee club owners that I'd pack their places. And let me tell you, I did!

"I'd do Little Richard solos, stuff from other black artists. Eventually Ben Weisman (the writer of several Elvis Presley hits) saw me, and liked my voice. He asked me to do demos for Elvis, who was the type of guy, if he heard the demo and didn't like one note, the song was finished. So I'd have to imitate Elvis, for fifteen dollars a song, and hope the studio people would call me back. I'm sure Elvis didn't even know my name."

Delaney made important contacts, however, that led to his joining the Champs, the West Coast group of session men who sold more than six million copies of "Tequila." Regulars at the famed Palomino Club in Los Angeles, they'd often jam with other southwestern musicians like Leon Russell and J. J. Cale, the two country boys who would introduce Delaney to producer Jack Good.

"ABC wanted to do a live TV show, 'Shindig,' and Good asked me if I was interested in heading it (1965). I wouldn't know what to call the music we did; it was this crazy blend of country, funk rock, a little R & B, but the Shindogs were put together, and the show ran for over two and a half years.

"Basically, the Shindogs were clones of everybody; the Beatles one day, the Stones the next. We did a whole tour once with acts like Billy Preston, Glen Campbell, Rosey Grier, and it was fun. Besides being recognized everywhere I went, I was suddenly making great money, something like fifteen hundred dollars a week."

Delaney would still moonlight at times, and one night while playing at the Carolina Lanes, a Los Angeles bowling alley, he got to talking with Bonnie Lynn O'Farrell. Though they quarreled right from the start—she didn't want to open for the Shindogs, and tried to change the format—Delaney was immediately struck by her "raw gutsiness."

"BAM! She just hit me over the head, and turned everything inside me upside down," remembers Delaney, still shaking his head in bewilderment. "I don't know what it was—maybe it was her chemistry—I just don't know. I didn't have any intention at all of getting married, it was just one of those things. Before I knew it, there we were, staring at four walls, and realizing we were living in an apartment in the Valley, as Mr. and Mrs. Delaney Bramlett. God . . ."

Besides setting off these emotional shockwaves, Bonnie also spelled doom for the Shindogs. Even though she joined the group for a while as its soulful lead singer, Delaney quickly felt that her energy was being wasted on "the boring Top 40 stuff" the band was playing at the time. Bedazzled by the effect she had on crowds and convinced by her arguments for "doing something original, as well as outrageous," he pulled the plug on the Shindogs. And, with "a little help from my friends . . ." the party began. Wherever Delaney and Bonnie appeared, old buddies like Russell or Cale would drop by to play a few licks. Although their first two albums generated little interest, the single "Long Time Comin'" hit the number-one slot on the R & B charts, an occurrence which induced Eric Clapton to come see them. The guitarist's short-lived group, Blind Faith, was about to begin its 1969 tour of the United States, and he asked the couple to be the opening act. After this rollicking jaunt across America (Bonnie likes to boast that she gave Eric his haircuts in their van), the entire entourage went to England.

And that was where the fun really began.

John Lennon. Dave Mason. Ringo. Jimmy Page. George Harrison. They all joined Delaney and Bonnie on various stages. Clapton certainly attracted some of these stellar musicians, but the young couple also had a magnetism, an enticing allure, and the famous wanted to share in their good times.

"I'm sure we transmitted these positive feelings—an energy—we had to. When I got to London I felt I was on top of the world," recounts Delaney, after leaving the corral for the comfort of his cluttered living room. Surrounded by guitars, stacks of sheet music, and empty beer cans, he enthusiastically confides, "Playing with Page, Clapton . . . all that was satisfying. But more importantly, I could hear our music growing. That was the satisfaction. I felt good on stage. I didn't find true happiness until I settled down and bought this place, but it was gratifying to be appreciated by other musicians. Duane Allman gave me his favorite guitar three weeks before he died. The Beatles watched us at the Albert Hall [in London]. John Hammond gave me a guitar, and Jimi Hendrix said our music was 'spiritual.' I kinda liked that. It made me feel good inside."

After Blind Faith dissolved, Eric Clapton toured Europe as a sideman with the couple (resulting in the album *On Tour),* and they were eventually joined by George Harrison. In addition to performing, Bonnie was taking care of two infants, a fact that prompts Delaney to reason, "I really think the pressure of all the traveling got to be too much. After a while, we wanted to hide from crowds. She couldn't handle what was going on. I remember this guy in Boston; he broke through the guards and dropped his pants in front of us, right when Bonnie was singing. She got mad at me for not beating him up. We'd have some real good fights, shouting, throwing things . . ."

The details of their final spat are a bit obscure. Delaney says he doesn't know why Bonnie finally split or is perhaps reluctant to talk about it [she adds only, "The marriage wasn't fun anymore"]. But, in any case, Delaney was suddenly faced with a new gig, fatherhood, in the most pressurized sense of the word.

While having the presence of mind to buy a ranch, to get the kids away from "the drug-crazy world of Hollywood," he confesses, "I was a very miserable man. I didn't know what I was doing; the breakup was very hard on me. It was just the trauma of her leaving. She was someone I loved. I had her kids. I had to feel something, no matter what had gone down. I had fun with that woman, at dinner, in bed, whatever. All of a sudden she's not there, it doesn't matter how bad things are. It's crushing.

"After the breakup I didn't do anything for six months. I wanted to be alone. I guess it was my period of recuperation. I had to get my head straight again. I wrote a theme song for a Stockard Channing TV show, but, for the most part, I had to get away, especially from the drug scene, which seems to thrive because artists suffer at the hands of record companies.

"This period was plenty tough. I had everyone helping with my daughters—my mother, girlfriends—I think I did a pretty good job, though. They're just good kids, real ladies." Suzanne is nineteen, and Bekka, who purportedly 'sings like a mockingbird,' is seventeen.

Once the divorce became final in 1974, the trauma of this new life-style eased somewhat. Gradually feeling more self-confident, as a result of a new faith in God, Delaney began to write again, concentrating mainly on gospel songs. Another "try at the golden ring" didn't interest him, as his enthusiasm for "the commercial end of the business had definitely waned." Yet, at different times during the mid to late seventies, needing to take a break from the tedium of household chores, he put together new bands, like Blue Diamond, and Delaney Bramlett and Friends.

Today, even though the forty-seven-year-old Delaney is intent on reviving his career by getting a record deal, he's still the dutiful father. Not wanting to "lose my perspective on what's really important," he spends lots of time on the ranch with his teenagers, riding horses with them, helping them take care of the house, and involving the girls in business matters. Intensely proud of both daughters, he'll offer long, loving accounts of their most mundane exploits. These feelings are so powerful, in fact, that he's ignored his "better judgment . . . about how corrupt the business is," and allowed Bekka to join him on stage.

"She's great. We're doing small clubs in the area, and I hope this teaches her what to watch out for. She really sings from the heart," Delaney gets up, and walks into the kitchen to ask his mother when Bekka is due home from school.

Upon returning, he cheerfully adds "I want you to meet her, she's a beauty," and then, in a far more restrained manner, discusses his own future.

"I want to have a new group, I want to get a record out. I'm ready for this now. But I don't want to beat my brains out. I still want to ride my horses and play with the kids. If I don't make it back, I can handle it. I just want to try it again. If you try something real hard, and it doesn't work out, there's no reason to feel ashamed, or to view yourself as a failure. You just have to know that you did your best, and then forget about it. I know it's not the sixties; I don't have any great delusions. But I also know I'm a better artist these days.

"And that's saying a lot. If not for my marital problems, I would've been gigantic. That doesn't cause me sadness anymore, but I had a real honesty in my music. Those songs were from the heart. I want people to know me for those things. I always tried to be a decent person. I wasn't out there to scam people.

"I think our friends, Eric, Lennon, Duane [Allman] knew that. The honesty brought us together, why there was a real affection between us. I definitely felt that when John [Lennon] called us up at Clapton's house, and asked if we'd all be in the Plastic Ono Band. He was a 'good ole boy.' He really liked rock 'n' roll. He used to kid around about Paul and his 'muzak.' For us he had a different tag. Always funnin' around, he'd call us Bonnie and Clyde."

Looking genuinely bereaved, Delaney sits quietly on the couch for a few moments, until a banging door breaks the silence.

"Hey, Bekka, is that you?" calls Delaney. "Come on in here, and tell these people about your singing."

A few minutes later, a tall girl with long blond hair enters the living room, still holding her schoolbooks. After kissing her beaming father and saying hello, she takes a few flyers out of a notebook, distributes them, and in a forceful tone that conjures up images of Bonnie, insists, "you better come down to the Palomino Club next Monday, it's going to be a real fun time. I expect you to be there."

Bonnie Bramlett of Delaney and Bonnie

But Oh What a Morning!

Time hasn't been kind to Bonnie Bramlett.

Despite makeup, wrinkles are visible around her eyes. She looks tired.

In her heyday, she was a wild, "mean mama," whom you didn't mess with. Elvis Costello found that out—the hard way. After he said some rather unflattering things about Ray Charles, Bonnie bloodied him, and threw the New Wave hero off a stage.

Now Bonnie is but a shadow of her former self. A "reformed" gospel singer these past few years, she's lost most of her old fire. Speaking disjointedly, and in a voice laden with strain, she seems confused, tormented, and often refuses to talk about certain matters, most particularly, her children. Like a schoolgirl, she'll giggle nervously when describing escapades with Eric Clapton, other old friends, or her celebrated antics on the road. But even these accounts have a desperate, frenetic quality. Bonnie is obsessed with them. Unable to crack the pop charts for years, she needs the past, and the glories that went with it. They are her only salvation.

This sad picture emerges in a Hollywood restaurant, as Bonnie sits next to her new boyfriend, coquettishly playing with a sleeve of her *Flashdance*-styled sweatshirt. Sipping a cocktail after a late-afternoon session in a recording studio, she's now hoping to combine gospel sing-

ing with a TV video, or even a movie role. But before elaborating on
these plans, she leans back in the booth, and smiles wistfully.

"As a kid I'd do these make-believe shows in the living room, and
pretend to be Pearl Bailey," says Bonnie, recalling her "real nice, loving" home in Alton, Illinois. The daughter of a steelworker, she was
eventually encouraged to sing at church, where people treated her as a
"queen bee."

"Everyone was always telling me I had a great voice. My uncle—he
was very musical—and I saw Mahalia Jackson, she did a spiritual number and the chills ran through my blood.

"But I wanted to be a gymnast. Unfortunately, I got tall very quickly.
I hated that. I didn't want to hear I could be a model. My mother
would always tell me, 'Don't worry, you have long legs; the boys will
love you.' But I wanted something more than that. I just didn't know
what it was."

Once Little Milton, a celebrated blues artist, came to town, her future
became a lot clearer. Swept away by one of his performances at a
YWCA show, the thirteen-year-old started to lie about her age to get
singing gigs. As these engagements multiplied over the next few years,
the inevitable happened. Tiring of Smalltown U.S.A., she hungered for
bigger and brighter lights.

And this is where her life took its first wild turn. She ran away from
home.

"I went to Hollywood to be a star, to make it, and in a flash, I felt as
free as a bird." Bonnie seems to still savor that burst into the unknown.
"I was in Holllyywooood (exaggerating the pronunciation to underscore
her delight). I was in the middle of things; the place was like a Disney-
land to me. I was having fun."

After trying an hors d'oeuvre and taking a long sip of her cocktail,
Bonnie clears her throat, and offers an assessment of her journey that
could easily serve as an epitaph for the 1960s: "I went from motorcycles
to flowers."

This heady transformation also had a down side. She had to stomp
around Hollywood for a number of years, unrecognized and unre-
warded. In the mid-sixties, after singing the blues in dozens of no-name
clubs, she finally hooked up with Ike and Tina Turner—and appeared
in their revue as a blackfaced Ikette.

Unfulfilled by her anonymous choir-girl role, she went solo again,
returning to the sleaze circuit of honky-tonk bars, blues clubs, and
bowling alleys in Los Angeles. Here, every artist was struggling to stay

alive. The competition didn't allow for niceties. A performer had to scratch and claw for every last minute on a show, even if it meant clashing with your future husband.

"He got me really mad," says Bonnie, in a soft, muffled voice, that belies the emotion of her first encounter with Delaney. "The Shindogs, as I understood it, were supposed to be my backup band. They were good, sure . . . but they didn't know I was."

The vacant look on her face disappears, and for a brief moment the old intensity flares.

"After they heard me, they gave in and said they'd back me. But I said 'No way, you lost your chance. You'll have to follow me.' "

Somehow, this exchange led to instant romance. Unwilling to elaborate on events that evening, Bonnie only says, "I guess we connected. It [getting married] seemed like the thing to do. That's showbiz."

Speaking mechanically again, Bonnie quickly adds, "The marriage wasn't fun. We were put in some form of competition. It was just too much, too soon. But it got too late to do anything about it.

"We were together twenty-four hours a day, doing everything together. That's too much pressure.

"People wanted us to fit a certain stereotype. After I had the kids, I know they wanted me to be in gingham dresses."

Fortified by another sip of her drink, Bonnie poignantly continues, "Let me tell you, I was confused after we broke up, but I was also relieved. I didn't know what to do. I'll always want to make it in the business, but I'll never want to do it behind a lie. You just can't cheat at solitaire.

"I always knew we were going to get to the top; the notoriety we achieved didn't surprise me. But Delaney wanted me to be humble. He was going to be the energy, the power. I had to know my part. That was hard on me, it was asking too much."

These feelings could certainly undermine a marriage, and, apparently, led to Bonnie's sudden decision to leave Delaney at an airport.

But even before this departure, sensing she was a mere appendage of her husband, Bonnie looked elsewhere for satisfaction. Rebelling, she developed strong friendships with members of their entourage, getting especially close to Eric Clapton, Duane Allman, and George Harrison.

Grinning broadly when recalling these relationships, she proudly says, "I seem to be blessed; I've always been surrounded by great people. They've wanted to share with me. In the sixties everyone loved everyone. I've been overwhelmed by everyone being so gentle and sensitive, but they love me because I can sing good. That's how we got so close.

"I can express things to people that they wouldn't pick up otherwise. They trust me. Why, I knew the Allmans when they were the Allman Joys. There was a bond between us, a type of spiritual feeling that also existed between me and Eric [Clapton], and George [Harrison].

"I love Eric, he was a doll, a real human being, gentle and sensitive. I don't want to say too much—those are personal things—But he's a fair person, him and George both. We were stunned when they chose to play with us; they were big stars. But they were also musicians. That created a bond, we had a special type of communication.

"That's why Eric allowed me to give him his haircuts, he trusted me. I didn't cut off too much—a man really trusts you when he lets you give him haircuts. I even gave Greg Allman a haircut."

History, however, is not made by giving haircuts. Wanting to "do something the world would remember," Bonnie stopped living "the great lie," and fled from Delaney (according to him, she also abandoned her children) for a new promised land. Leaving rock 'n' roll by the late seventies, after a short stint with Stephen Stills and the band Enemies (formed by Three Dog Night's Danny Hutton), she returned to her origins, gospel singing.

"I got the opportunity to cut a gospel album, so I took some time off from rock 'n' roll to do it. But when the Christian music industry expected me to reject rock, I refused, and instead integrated the two into a gospel rock 'n' roll record. When they heard it, they refused to promote it, and it became a 'top secret' album. Gospel means the truth and everything on that record is true. It blesses my soul. It's good to me. If my singing blesses other people's souls that's great. But my albums, like *Step by Step* (on the Christian label Refuge), aren't meant to beat anyone over the head with the Bible. It's the funkiest gospel you've ever heard. People bounce when they hear it."

That uninhibited, untamed "creature" has apparently been left in the studio. For in the restaurant, there's a lamblike, beseeching quality to her. Instead of a "world be damned" attitude, that once cut her off from family obligations and other commitments, the forty-one-year-old singer seems to be crying out for understanding, if not sympathy. This is a vulnerable Bonnie Bramlett, one that's human.

"I like people to like me . . . I hope I can express things to them that they wouldn't pick up otherwise. I need that kind of satisfaction; all entertainers do. We're all egomaniacs; we crave input, encouragement. We have to have people applauding us. It's impossible for me to be in an audience watching.

"To be able to express your innermost feelings up there on stage, that's what it's all about. It's a need you have to act on, it's a release. I have to be up there. I don't really know why. I just have to.

To satisfy these cravings, Bonnie has traveled a lonely road. Still a "flower child" in many respects, she has no home, except for a room in a friend's house. This might change if she can indeed get into movies, or do videos ("I want to feel my sweat when I perform"). But in the meantime, she's alone, estranged from her family, and in a far different place than her old friends. She's only comforted by the past, memories like playing Carnegie Hall—and by the legacy she left her daughter Bekka.

"I'm glad she wants to be a singer; I think she's got my genes," muses Bonnie, smiling slightly. "She's got my DNA, my thoughts, my memories. It's tough in the beginning; you're too insecure, you're trying to find yourself. You can't handle certain responsibilities. But she's quite a kid. She's my baby."

Janis Ian

Billie Holiday Should Have Invested in Real Estate

"The IRS . . . the IRS . . . the IRS . . ."

The initials raced maddeningly through her head. It was her only thought; the nightmare was coming true.

"Pay up, you owe four hundred thousand dollars in back taxes, four hundred thousand," bellowed the husky, gravel-voiced Internal Revenue agent. Staring at her coldly, he had a sadistic glint in his eyes. And as the four-foot-ten seventeen-year-old turned away in horror, a chill ran down her spine.

"We've gone through all the royalty statements, the concert receipts, the checks; you either pay, or . . ."

These words floated by her. Too dizzy to hear them, she looked blankly at the piles of papers, overwhelmed by her mounting fears.

"What am I going to do, I can't raise that kind of money?" said the panic-stricken teenager, popularly known as Janis Ian. "Nothing can save me. Jail, that's where I'm going. They're going to send me to prison. I can't believe it . . . me, in a prison cell."

Ian didn't wind up in San Quentin or Leavenworth. The IRS wasn't *that* cruel.

But she was presented with a hefty tax bill in 1968—a debt that weighed upon her for the next nine years. During that traumatic period she had to change her entire life-style. She teetered near bankruptcy. A romance fell apart. And most agonizing of all, the pressures made writing extremely difficult. Billed as a "female Dylan" at the age of fifteen, she couldn't regain the magic of her most notable success, "Society's Child," and was cruelly dismissed as a flash in the pan.

Ian did come back. After wrestling with all sorts of inner conflicts and demons, she fulfilled some of her earlier promise with "Jesse," "At Seventeen," and "Watercolors." Though these songs have a brooding, "relentless sob" quality, and reflect a vulnerability that kept her from becoming a full-fledged star, they at least showed she wasn't a fluke. In 1975 alone, Ian sold over four million dollars' worth of records, and won a Grammy award as the best female vocalist.

The Janis Ian story, however, is a depressing one. For it goes beyond the mere chronicling of one single life, to probe the fragile, often bitter-sweet nature of success. Through her tale we experience the joy of being a commercial phenomenon at fifteen as well as the anguish. And since she was a romantic, highly sensitive poet, better versed in Dylan Thomas than in business practices, the disappointments were inevitably overwhelming.

"Once I became quote 'a success,' it got too crazy, too many people wanted too much, I felt I'd been sucked dry," complains Ian, sitting by a piano in the living room of her Los Angeles home. Wearing a tightly fitting denim jumpsuit that's provocatively unbuttoned at her chest, she reaches for a cigarette, and asks a maid to prepare a pot of tea. Then in a quavering voice, she continues, "I knew I couldn't be a serious writer if I was famous. So I wanted out. I got away from everything: friends, problems, hurts, even from my Janis Ian persona. I didn't want to be a Barbra Streisand, a Bowie, or a Dylan. That kind of life robs you of too much. I always get out when I'm close to the top. I could've had the world, but I wanted to have a successful life instead of a successful career."

Married to a foreign businessman, whom she lovingly describes as a "Renaissance man" with "an aristocratic" family history, she seems to have found a measure of happiness. No longer plagued by financial worries, she also praises her husband Tino for giving her "the security and encouragement to continue writing." Paraphrasing one of Voltaire's famous lines, Ian adds, "Because of Tino's support I've been able to cultivate my garden, that's the greatest thing a person can do. I have a new interest in life." Such optimism has prompted thoughts about writing a Broadway musical, and of a possible collaboration with Chick Corea. She discusses each of these fantasies with unbounded enthusiasm. And as her dimpled, full cheeks turn red, a visitor is left with an unmistakable impression: this is the Janis Ian of the 1960s, the saucy, bubbly, pint-sized idealist who once touched people's hearts.

It's upsetting, therefore, to see that she's still tormented by the past. Despite her protestations to the contrary, it's quickly apparent that her tax battles are not ancient history. She tries to discuss these devastating events in a clipped, staccato manner, but eventually, her voice cracks, rent by pain. How else could she react? In 1967 her world collapsed. Besides the financial devastation, she was thrown into an existential void, an abyss where her self-worth was destroyed.

"Writers go through many deaths of the soul, they expend so much energy in just staying alive," murmurs the thirty-five-year-old Ian, talking of how she was forced to redefine herself. "There was a lot of peeling off, not layering on . . . that's the true way to learn. I was suddenly asked to grow up. Being a star at fifteen I was protected from a lot, not that there were bad people around me. There was just a huge dichotomy between my writing and being . . . I was very confused, especially when I was met by a cold, hard flush of reality . . .

"There's no preparation for this business [the music world]. You can't train to be famous. The fame thing is nice, but there's a lot of pressure. People kept things from me for my own good—like business matters. My first lawyer thought I'd be a one-hit wonder, so he did a contract reflecting that (he opted for bigger cash advances instead of higher royalty percentages). I couldn't sign the contract anyway . . . since I was under eighteen everything had to go through a surrogate's court. In theory a judge watched over the monies, and I got an allowance, but it was so corrupt. I didn't get any financial advice . . . I wound up giving most of the money to friends, to charities, I bought guitars . . . I didn't even have my receipts or commissions when the tax thing came up."

Such innocence—or naïveté—is understandable. Practical, everyday concerns never mattered much to Ian. Even as a child, she was the quintessential free-spirited poet, too wrapped up in intellectual affairs to care about the mundane.

"I think I was born a poet . . . it's a wisdom and I think I have it," says Ian, who gravitated to poetry after playing Mozart piano sonatas at the age of five (1956). "Poets are not just people who write, they're people of the heart. Especially Dylan Thomas. He expresses so many feelings through beautiful words . . . I still go to him . . . He wanders a lot, but he's a master."

Inspired by him, Ian wrote her first song at twelve ("Hair's Spun

Gold"), and was soon neglecting her schoolwork to sing in Greenwich Village hootenannies. Escorted to them by her "very untypical" parents, she started to meet other folk artists, like Eric Andersen, Phil Ochs, and Buffy St. Marie. Older and more established, they didn't accept her at first. To them, she was "the little kid on the block."

But then the "Queen" intervened. And everything started to sound like a fairy tale.

"No one knew what to do with me, not until [Joan] Baez gave me the stamp of approval," recalls Ian, grinning broadly. Assuming a yoga-style lotus position on the piano bench, she goes on to explain, "Once Joan said I was okay, it didn't matter anymore that I couldn't hang out, or go drinking with them. I became family . . . gee, Joan was always great to me. She's terrific."

Once Ian was ushered into this world, she became a true child of the sixties, rebelliously dropping out of high school during her junior year. Ignoring the pleas of a guidance counselor, she decided "it was time to define myself by myself," even if that meant "driving my parents crazy."

While those counseling sessions failed to sway her, they were still productive. For she sat in the waiting room, and wrote the lyrics to "Society's Child," the autobiographical song about her interracial romance. Though banned from scores of radio stations, that controversial work was one of 1967's biggest hits (in the Top 10 for several months). It not only made the fifteen-year-old Ian a celebrity but also a soul sister to thousands of young women; a muse that dreamily moved them.

As Ian suggests, though, this type of reverence can also be a pressure, and a "breeding ground" for a host of serious misunderstandings. "Fame is not a reality of life, it's just a persona, or false shell. I'm famous when I work, but then I go home, and I'm not famous. The perks of fame are nice. But that's very separate from what you give to an audience or from being a writer.

"And when you're so special to people, there's a need in them to believe in certain things, even if they're far from reality. When I had my tax problems, and hit my slump, people couldn't accept the fact that a seventeen-year-old had had enough and walked away. It was easier for them to believe that I was crazy, or drugged out . . ."

One can speculate as to what happened first, Ian's disenchantment with the business, or her tax problems. But in either case, she wound up in Los Angeles, broke, with "no prospects."

To occupy herself, Ian studied the banjo, orchestration, and got healthy at a local gym. Contrary to rumors, and some written accounts, she insists, "My moving to L.A. had nothing to do with any man, or romance. I know what's been written, but I was never married.

"There was just a rebelliousness in the air, and I wanted to be part of it. I did what I wanted to do . . . I made lots of friends, and eventually [1973], I wanted to record again. I started missing it."

So after three years of inactivity, she did *Stars,* the album that featured the now legendary "Jesse" (a smash hit for Roberta Flack). Ebulliently describing that song as "a turning point," Ian plays a few bars on her piano, then exclaims, " 'Jesse' was a song that changed my writing forever . . . I knew I was hitting it, not blowing it. A song like that comes to you in a flash. You have to get past a certain point which could still make you blow it . . . then you get beyond it, and couple the inspiration with writing. This doesn't happen too often . . .

"After *Stars* I wanted to do a lot of recording. There are certain songs, like 'Jesse,' which you don't feel comfortable with until you record them yourself . . . It was a big compliment that Roberta did it, but I felt I could do it better. I've always wanted other people to record my songs. My ideal is for them to get famous, so I can stay at home and write."

Like her beloved poets, she then probed the inner recesses of her soul, coming up with another autobiographical "document," *Between the Lines* (1975). An intensely personal work (which included such tender songs as "Watercolors" and "At Seventeen"), this album couldn't be sung by anyone but her. So Ian gave up her privacy and returned to the studio.

"That album was an exhilarating experience, those songs changed people's lives," coos Ian, blushing with pride, as she demurely sips her tea. "People know my name from '. . . Seventeen,' that song's special, you only get one of those once in a while. Anyone could have written it, though . . . it's about growing up, the transitions or passages we all go through. So I think I tapped into humanity with it, the song makes that journey so personal . . . it can really silence audiences, and that's magic, wonderful magic."

After calling the album "a monster hit," Ian turns more sullen. As evidenced by the widening frown on her face, the success of *Between the Lines* also meant more conflicts and compromises. For suddenly, she was a public personality again, forced to contend with a variety of pressures. While it was heady stuff to be singing on college campuses— often on the same bill with Billy Joel or Bruce Springsteen—the constant traveling was hardly glamorous. Her days were punctuated by endless newspaper interviews, long, tiring bus rides, and lonely nights in hotel rooms. But even more troubling, fame posed the Great Dilemma. Should she commit herself to this type of life-style? Or was her blossoming romance with Tino more important?

This tormenting quandary wasn't resolved until 1978. Ian then decided to tie the knot and, ever the romantic, gave up most of her touring. Apparently, Ian has no regrets over these decisions, for she passionately declares, "My life is totally balanced now between being a wife and a writer. I do get nuts at times . . . and I still cry and get angry easy. But I'm saving most of my energies for my work and love life. I don't need Madison Square Garden or Carnegie Hall . . . I have my writing and it's getting stronger. I want to be a great writer, I'm about 20 percent there, maybe even 40 percent once in a while. It comes in time. You can't push, you can only work at it. Tolstoy said a writer has to lead a day-to-day life, it's the only way to stay human and to remain in touch with yourself."

Eyeing her most recent compositions, which are strewn haphazardly atop the piano, Ian then talks about other writers, and their effect on her. "You can do what Dylan did to be great, you can take a lot of drugs. I've been thinking a lot lately about this impulse; I don't want greatness that badly. Just look at the casualty list of the 1960s . . . I always resented Hendrix's dying. I could've bashed his head in. We lost a prince, he should've been born in 1500, he could've been a sultan or Othello. His playing was touched by something . . . the night I heard he died I was with B. B. King, and B.B. just played real blues, as blues was defined. We were too choked up to speak, so the music was Jimi's eulogy.

"Music is great that way. It's the invisible art. You can freeze-frame movies, look at a ballet, but music, it's either on the ear or not. There's no way to stop it, real music transcends time and cultures. I'd really like to go back to the Greeks and see how they did their scales . . . [laughing for a moment] when I grow up I want to be an orchestra. I'd like to play universal songs, melodies that affect the world. [She now turns bitter again.] Anyway, that's what Jimi did, he had that kind of worldly impact. His death was stupid, it was a dumb-ass loss . . . the same with Joplin, there she goes and blows everything . . . what a fucking shame . . ."

Still outraged and confused by these deaths, Ian winces, and hurls a few more obscenities.

While it's distressing to see her react this way, her outburst is understandable. Hendrix and Joplin were some of her heroes, fellow artists who inspired her "to reach for greatness." Their deaths, however, meant more than the loss of two friends. For Ian, these "tragedies" represent the passing of an era, a symbolic end to the "truth and optimism" of the 1960s.

"In the sixties we painted such bright colors; there was great hope, everyone felt we could really change things," says Ian, her face still lined with pain. "That's what the sixties were all about, reality and truth. The songs were meant to convey that joyousness. Music is much more important than politics—it changes people, it gives them heroes."

Reminded that she too was adulated, Ian modestly stares at a painting for a few moments. Her eyes look less troubled now. And while it seems strained at first, a smile creeps back onto her face.

"I haven't thought much about my role in the sixties, I don't really want to. I just hope I created a little patch of truth. That was my obligation as a writer. You have to be truthful to yourself, so maybe people have seen that, maybe they can still respond to it . . . I think they can. I'm not cynical or depressed. People might not see that in my work, but I have a lot of hope. My songs are feeling, open, brutal, stripped-down feelings. The assumption is that I'm in pain. I am in pain, but I'm also in joy. I'm in terror, fear, but also in all the other emotions I can grab.

"People also said Billie Holiday's songs were too depressing. But do you know what?" Ian's voice borders on anger, and the question seems directed more at her critics, than toward her guests. "It's like that great lady said, 'These people just aren't listening hard enough.'"

Peter Asher of Peter and Gordon

The Spiderman's Million Dollar Web

James Taylor and Linda Ronstadt don't have to worry. The music business's barracudas won't ever get near them, not with Spiderman on their side. The guardian of all that's moral and right is consumed with their well-being. It's his passion, it keeps him so busy he doesn't have time to talk to his wife.

It's a bit nerve-wracking, therefore, to enter his private domain. He's constantly interrupted by a fleet of secretaries, scampering madly through the labyrinthine Los Angeles offices. Their hushed tones indicate they're carrying Top Secret messages from the White House, and the looks they give outsiders could turn even Superman to jelly. *Pure ice.* But maybe that's to be expected. Once someone is celebrated as a genius, the *wunderkind* of Hollywood, the stardust persona is all important, real communication is no longer necessary.

"You've got twenty minutes," the cold, steely voice comes from a chair next to a seven-foot-high poster of Spiderman, affectionately autographed by the great man himself, Stan Lee.

What's one to do? How can the British Invasion, the glorious sixties, and the Taylor-Ronstadt connection be discussed in twenty minutes?

Indifferent to such concerns, the red-haired, freckle-faced figure sitting close to Spiderman keeps his head buried in a stack of contracts. Decisions must be made, dozens of them, quickly. Suddenly, this isn't the time for interviews, for reminiscing about the past. Urgent telephone calls have come through. Linda is having problems on her tour with Nelson Riddle, and poor James, he's still wrestling with writer's block. They must be coddled, encouraged, assured everything's okay. That's a vital aspect of managing/producing these megabuck properties, but Peter Asher isn't daunted. He's always ready to climb walls, untangle emotional cobwebs, or tackle adversity for his prized clients.

"Representing Linda and James is a full-time commitment, a passion of mine, that's why I don't take on too many other people," affirms Asher, who first got an intimate look at the music business in 1964, when he soared to the top of the charts with Gordon Waller and "World Without Love." Subsequently a producer at Apple Records and the creative genius behind such blockbuster hits as "Blue Bayou," "You're No Good," "You've Got a Friend," and "Handy Man," he's become a star himself because of his fanatic attention to details. He was *Rolling Stone*'s Producer of the Year in 1977. Linda and James might be able to choose a favorite brand of chocolate-chip cookies, but when it comes to anything else, like making record deals or approving song ideas, their man in Los Angeles calls all the shots.

"When we came over to the U.S. in '64 to do 'World Without Love,' the road trips were a nightmare of inefficiency and confusion. Our manager was never around, and there were times we didn't even get a chance to sing. The whole thing was crazy. No one cared about the performers. You should've seen the old bus we had to travel in . . . it was sheer chaos. And that doesn't happen if a manager is thoroughly involved, totally committed to his clients. A sensitive writer like James should be able to do his music in peace. He shouldn't have to worry about the corporate nonsense or anything else." Creating this tranquil environment for his superstars is a twenty-four-hour-a-day obsession for Asher. Professing "a great love" for both Linda and James, he's unable to trust anyone "to look after them the way I can," and consequently delegates few responsibilities to subordinates. This constantly keeps him in the recording studio, or on the road, so he has limited time for simple pleasures. Driven to be an even greater success, he doesn't seem saddened by this loss. Not initially. But his reserved, mechanical self eventually breaks down. After expressing desires to spend more time with his wife and newborn daughter, he says in a lowered voice, "it's a tough business, a very tough business . . . it takes a lot out of you."

As Asher has discovered, the business can also destroy friendships. Most poignantly, his relationship with Waller.

In the early sixties, his former partner introduced him to the music of Elvis and the Everlys, and to the revolutionary movement of Little Richard's shimmying hips. Gordon would climb over a spiked wall at an exclusive London boarding school so the two boys could play local clubs together, and was a source of comfort when Peter's dad, a very proper British doctor, complained about his son's rising rock 'n' roll fever.

By 1963, Peter got to know Paul McCartney through his sister Jane, who was dating the Beatle. When he came to the house, the conversation naturally focused on music. Paul had written "World Without Love," but since no one wanted to record it, he finally gave the song to Peter. Within days, Peter and Gordon cut the single, and it became the biggest seller they ever had. It was a number one hit in Britain and led them to "The Ed Sullivan Show" and a Top 10 entry in the U.S. charts.

Touring with the Shirelles and Wilson Pickett was fun for a while. Peter liked the star treatment, the screaming crowds, and the hordes of young girls who ran after him. The twenty-year-old's only complaint was, "Once they caught up with you they could only drool. They didn't know what to do."

As the tour got progressively more disorganized, Peter's disillusionment increased. Raised in a home where everything had "a certain consistency," he couldn't cope with the scheduling snafus that often meant limited playing time. Even before the tour, he preferred the tranquil atmosphere of the recording studio, so when the duo broke up in 1968 after a string of moderate successes, "Nobody I Know," "True Love Ways," "Lady Godiva" Peter was hardly upset. His future, working in a studio, was far more important.

After producing the single "And the Sun Will Shine" for ex-Mannfred Mann singer Paul Jones, he accepted an offer from Paul McCartney to become a talent scout for Apple. Only a few days after accepting the post, he got a telephone call from James Taylor. Still unknown, the singer wanted Asher to listen to one of his tapes. The two men soon got together, and by December 1968, Apple released Taylor's debut solo album, which featured such songs as "Knocking 'round the Zoo," "Something in the Way She Moves," and the still popular "Carolina on My Mind."

Asher got a heady rush from producing the album. But the internal squabbles at Apple disgusted him. He saw board meetings as "a clash of competing egos," and since each of the Beatles wanted to sign different artists, his decision-making powers were severely limited.

"Those meetings were like a war, and I couldn't figure out who I had to answer to," says the forty-two-year-old Asher calmly, even though his nerves back then were admittedly "frayed." "There was no organization whatsoever, I didn't know who I was supposed to sign, who they were signing . . . the whole thing was a disaster."

With Apple's finances also in disarray, the Beatles brought in former Rolling Stones manager Allen Klein to save them from bankruptcy. The sweet-talking, ever-hustling Klein had pulled off a coup, renegotiating the Stones' contract with Decca to the tune of a $1.25 million advance. Lennon was particularly impressed by this, but Klein's business tactics (which would eventually lead to an ugly housecleaning at Apple, and a wider rift between Paul and John) nauseated Asher. He soon quit the sinking company, and took Taylor with him.

Opening an office in Los Angeles, Asher quickly got Warner Records to cut Taylor's eventual bestseller *Sweet Baby James.* The success of that album led to other projects; Asher co-managed Cat Stevens for a short time, did production work for Tony Joe White (a country-rock star who once toured with Creedence Clearwater), and managed James's sister Kate. When she gave up recording in 1973, Asher felt he had enough time to help Linda Ronstadt complete her *Don't Cry Now* album—and thus began one of the longest, most successful "marriages" in the industry.

As she told *Rolling Stone* a few years ago, "Peter's real out front with people . . . [He] gets into every facet of the record so that it's always a team effort . . . He keeps a very journalistic tone so nobody has to feel personally rejected if an idea is rejected . . . His enthusiasm [for the recording process] is real contagious, so he explains stuff to me. As I start to understand how things work, it makes it easier for me to communicate what I'm trying to say . . . He's never gonna run any little nasty games on you, I never have the feeling that he's trying to flesh out his frail identity by everybody else's . . . Peter is a producer."

Preoccupied with an emergency at one of Ronstadt's tour sites, Asher takes yet another phone call before saying, "My manager made a lot of mistakes back in the sixties, that's why Peter and Gordon never became really big. The guy was too spread out, with old-time comics and stage stars. But I'm not going to repeat those mistakes. I've helped Roger Waters [Pink Floyd] a bit, but it's basically just Linda and James. They're getting my full attention."

The strength of Asher's commitment isn't evident in his voice. It's characteristically dry and unemotional. On the office walls, though, there are more dramatic reminders of his involvement: a *Time* magazine cover photo of Ronstadt and Taylor, a dozen platinum records, and innumerable framed newspaper stories about his celebrated clients.

"Since I had people cheering for me, I don't need to live vicariously through James and Linda . . . that helps me make the right kinds of moves. My ego isn't involved here; I think too much of both of them.

"James has been worried lately about his writing, but I'm not concerned. He's gonna come back; he's put together some really good songs.

"As for Linda, she'll still be a star thirty years from now. I don't know what I'll be doing then. I don't think in those terms. But she can go on and on . . ."

Asher smiles ever so slightly and again burrows his head in a stack of papers. It's his polite way of concluding the interview.

But, before getting up to take a call in an adjoining office, he hastily adds, "I love both of them. I'd be very sad if they didn't feel the same way."

The Chambers Brothers
The Many Faces of Slavery

Their time certainly came. And just at the right moment.

Across the country, ghettoes were exploding. Watts. Detroit. Chicago. Newark. From one firestorm to another, violence was tearing the races apart. Peaceful voices like Martin Luther King's were being extinguished, while angry Black Power extremists chanting "Burn, Baby, Burn," seared our consciousness. This aspect of the late 1960s was indeed an ugly one—filled with gross human-rights violations, and equally repugnant Molotov cocktails.

In the midst of this strife, the Chambers Brothers burst upon the scene. Racially integrated and chiming the "Time Has Come Today" for a new, more peaceful world, they offered America a hopeful sign, evidence that the races could unite in friendship.

They were "family," four blacks and a white; and mirroring that combination, they synthesized a new musical formula: psychedelic gospel. As echoed in their eleven-minute-long 1968 hit, "Time Has Come Today," this meant an amalgam of rock 'n' roll guitar playing and the spirited group vocals of the black church. The resulting pop/rock/soul fusion had universal appeal and was vastly different from Motown, or the other soul variations that characterized the 1950s and 1960s. Consequently, the brothers were pioneers, the spiritual forerunners for such hybrids as the Commodores, the Fifth Dimension, and Sly and the Family Stone.

The four black members of the group were especially inspiring—they overcame. Lester, George, Willie, and Joseph Chambers all grew up in Mississippi, on a small farm tended by their sharecropping parents.

There were nine other children in the family, and the term "abject poverty" barely describes their plight. Crowded into a three-room wooden shack, they often went without shoes, clothes, and food. As Lester relates, "We couldn't have been any poorer, we were always being hungry, hungry, and more hungry."

They still labored in the fields, incessantly. There were a few animals to take care of, and, of course, the cotton had to be picked. Sharecroppers were virtual serfs, with the South's Jim Crow laws assuring their continued feudal existence. Against this backdrop of ever-mounting debts, the Chamberses didn't have the time—or the freedom—for amusements. And so the family's only relief came from religion, or the singing they did while working.

"Singing was the only thing we had, those spiritual hymns gave us the energy to keep bending our backs and dragging the sack," recounts Lester Chambers, evoking images of a loathsome time in our nation's past. Relaxing in his dank, sparsely furnished New York apartment, between fruitless attempts to secure a few bookings, he somberly continues, "They called that work sharecropping, but we knew we were slaves. There was no going out of our surroundings, or past a certain borderline. If we did, there'd be no more Chambers brothers. So the singing was our only release. It freed us from the heat, the dead still air, and the very long days. I remember those days, they were very painful. I just couldn't understand why we weren't allowed to do so many things."

Gospel singing was a natural outlet for these miseries, so the family packed into a small truck and drove about twenty miles to sing at the Mount Calvary Baptist Church.

At these foot-thumping, hand-waving meetings, the family could dream about freedom—or the opportunities their father, George Chambers, Sr., envisioned in the Promised Land out west in Los Angeles. He continually encouraged his brood to think of a brighter future, and one night in 1953, the family decided it was time to act. Risking their lives, they surreptitiously left the farm, and fled to California.

Adjusting to city life was initially difficult. The brothers were used to trees, rivers, and to getting their hands dirty in the soil. While the work was grueling, their crops were a source of satisfaction. In Los Angeles, their creativity languished. Feeling estranged at school and in their new neighborhood, they didn't have many avenues for self-expression. So they turned, as always, to religion. The church was the one constant in their lives, the place where they could sing their hymns, and find quick acceptance. It was security, so the boys eagerly attended nightly services, and soon formed their own gospel group, the Mount Calvary Junior Singers.

Their singing was immediately popular. Besides appearing at their own church, they were asked to sing at other congregations, and neighborhood social functions. Eventually, the demand for their services was so great, they had to charter buses for long-distance trips throughout California. Lester and Joseph were only in their midteens at this time, but they enjoyed being celebrities on the evangelical circuit, for as Lester says, "The attention we got was so different than our life in Mississippi. We would pack those churches, and I guess that made a lasting impression on me. I like making people happy."

This innocent, fun-filled period lasted about three years. During that time, the boys either finished high school or got jobs, and the family bought a bigger house. Then, around 1959, success brought its inevitable complications. Other gospel groups viewed the brothers as "big stars," and jealously complained to the organization that supervised church shows, the Inter-Denominational Singers Alliance. For reasons that are still unclear to the brothers, that body barred them from performing in churches. Suddenly, they were cut off from their natural audience, and had to endure months of painful inactivity.

"We didn't know what to do, quit, or come up with some different kind of act that really wasn't us," recalls George Chambers, who at fifty-four is the family's elder spokesman. George Sr. died five years ago at age ninety-eight. Joining Joseph and Willie at their mother's Los Angeles home George ignores a dozen screaming children running through the house and calmly says, "Getting kicked out of the alliance confused me so much, I didn't see much of a future for us. I never liked the traveling anyway, so I was ready to give up the singing. But, like always, our dad kept encouraging us and kept talking about giving it another try. That was great! It kept us at it. But we still didn't know where to go, where to play."

Out of this indecision came the Great Leap—they left the land of hallelujahs for that sinner's paradise Hollywood and its untamed, ungodly Sunset Strip.

Here, among late 1950s beats and bikers, the emphasis was on a new nonconformity. In the spirit of their patron saint, the quintessential rebel James Dean, the cool crowd awoke from the drowse of the Eisenhower years and rocked the night away. Hipsters partied, smoked dope, drank, and slept with people on a casual basis. There were no rules, no boundaries. It was time to enjoy life, and in the frenzy, old idols like the Beaver, Annette Funicello, and Lucille Ball gave way to sex symbols such as Elvis Presley, Brigitte Bardot, and Jayne Mansfield.

Up and down the strip, in the Insomniac, the Troubadour, and other coffeehouses, the music was also changing. Where it was headed was still a mystery, for Pete Seeger could play a set and be followed by Glen Campbell. But this shapelessness was ideal for experimentation. Unlike today, club owners weren't hooked into particular sounds. They were looking for lively new acts that would make people start "shakin'," even if that meant oddities like four young blacks playing a funky brand of gospel.

"I wasn't too crazy about going to Hollywood, but I must admit, the idea worked," says George, smiling. "We got a chance at the Ashgrove [another club on the Strip], on the same show with Lightnin' Hopkins, and things really broke for us. We were soon getting calls from the other coffeehouses. It was funny, since we were mixing up the gospel with rhythm and blues, no one knew what to call us . . . But that didn't matter. The crowds came, they certainly did . . . and that justified our father's faith in us."

The brothers were now a "happening." And mirroring this new success, their life-styles quickly changed. By 1961, they bought their own house, and started to hang out with Joan Baez, Sonny and Cher, Pete Seeger, and the Smothers brothers. That fraternity was more than a symbolic crossing of the color line. Quite significantly, it led to vital connections in the industry, modifications in their music, and the sustenance an entertainer can get only from his or her peers.

As Lester poignantly remembers, "We needed those friends, we were in a strange world, and they gave us support. Don't get me wrong, we had fun too, lots of it. The brothers had the first rock 'n' roll house in L.A., and we had some big parties. Did we party! We were like one big pack, and because of that tightness there was communication. We learned about the business, what to watch out for, and when we made mistakes, we could count on them to cheer us up."

Alone in New York, Lester doesn't have much of a support system these days. Intent on cracking the big time again, he's left his family behind in California, and has thrown himself into a very competitive scene. Up against younger, fresher-sounding performers, he is accepting dates at the city's smallest clubs, even if that means playing for twenty minutes at three in the morning. Understandably, his bloodshot eyes have an emotionally spent look, which makes him seem a lot older than forty-six. And yet the past isn't weighing on him. Though old friends have long disappeared from the city's folk clubs, he's comforted by his memories, and is confident about the future.

"I'm sure I'm going to make it back, 'cause the one thing I got from Baez and all those people was a belief in myself. Just being with good people back then gave the brothers strength.

"We knew we had something, and we were able to share that feeling with audiences. I still feel that way. I don't think that belief will ever die."

Back in 1962–63 the brothers needed all the confidence they could muster. While still on the Strip, they lacked a definite musical style, and weren't even sure if George would continue playing with them. The brothers now joke about his indecisiveness, but, at the time, George was clearly troubled by the group's change in direction. He argued against their drifting into rhythm and blues. It was a horrifying signal to him. It meant a progression that would inevitably lead them to rock 'n' roll.

"I wasn't against the group being successful, but I hated the screaming associated with rock, and didn't want any part of it," admits George, raising his own voice to compete with a crying child. "I wasn't a rock 'n' roll person. The music, the scene, all that was too crazy. I saw us headed in that direction, and I didn't feel it was us. I certainly wasn't going to give up my wife and kids to be a rock 'n' roll star."

These misgivings were exacerbated by the times. In the early sixties rock 'n' roll was in limbo. While a few performers like Little Richard and James Brown continued to attract frenzied crowds, the payola scandals of 1959, the subsequent firings of several well-known DJs (Alan Freed, in particular), and the riots after concerts had cast a shadow over the music. There was a demand for a different sound, one that matched the spirit of Camelot. In essence, our heightened social consciousness needed music with a message. Folk singers came back into vogue. They had a raspier, funkier edge. They got the "in" club bookings, while still-unamplified rockers waited . . . and waited . . . for someone to turn on the electricity.

In the meantime, the brothers settled their identity crisis. Prodded by his mother, George forgot about going to automotive school, and renewed his commitment to the group. They, in turn, began echoing the popular beat and were restyled as a funky folk quartet. Following Bob

Dylan's lead, they journeyed to New York in 1964 and played coffee-houses like the Café au Go-Go, in search of a new audience.

The revolution was already on in these small clubs. Much to the chagrin of his most avid admirers, Dylan had been experimenting with an electric guitar. He would soon play this instrument at the Newport Folk Festival in July 1965, and change the entire face of rock 'n' roll. But even earlier, the shock waves of this departure were being felt.

Groups had to change their acts, in accord with this new rock beat. For the brothers, this meant some new amps and adding a white drummer, Brian Keenan.

They met him quite accidentally, through Dylan. Bob was having a romantic affair with Joan Baez in '65, and since the brothers were on friendly terms with her, they often accompanied the pair to New York clubs. One night, at a place called Ondine's, Dylan asked them to jam with him—and as George dramatically says, "the Chambers brothers then became *the Chambers Brothers.*

"Dylan borrowed this drummer from the house band, and all of us just speeded up the tunes we'd been doing. We knew right then Brian was right for us. He was the missing ingredient."

Keenan's addition was immediately hailed in folk-rock circles. Both Dylan and Baez praised the move, and this connection soon proved crucial to the Brothers' career. They were invited to Newport.

"Newport was the most phenomenal thing that ever happened," says Lester, his eyes suddenly sparkling. "Our sound, it just went over, right away. We were the first electric band on stage, and that got the whole crowd excited. They all came forward to dance. I'll never forget it, we played some blues, some Chuck Berry stuff, and when it was over, we wound up with a couple of years' worth of bookings. We didn't have to go back home and say we were hungry."

The brothers didn't have to go naked anymore, either. Once they signed for a year's stay at the Unicorn, a Boston rock club, George turned haberdasher, and outfitted the entire clan. Still delighted by the incident, he cheerfully recalls, "We went into this men's clothing store, and the salesman sort of hinted we couldn't afford to be in there. He wasn't going to show us the suits. I didn't say a word. I just went over to another salesman, and started flashing some money. I wound up buying twelve hundred dollars' worth of clothes. Then, on the way out, I gave our salesman a fifty-dollar tip. I'll never forget the other guy's face. He couldn't believe it."

Newport also meant other rewards. The brothers cut a few albums, and intermittently appeared at New York's Apollo Theater, the Electric Circus, and the Fillmore. Even more impressive, they continued to play at the Unicorn for nearly two more years. That certainly gave them some security, yet the brothers wanted a lot more—namely national prominence and the big bucks. As of early 1968, their time still hadn't come.

At least, not yet, but . . .

The brothers were living in Connecticut then. They had a modest house, and sounds reverberated through the rooms. One afternoon Willie Chambers was downstairs, strumming his guitar, while Joe was on the floor above, working on some new lyrics. As Willie enthusiastically recalls, "Joe came bounding down the stairs, and asked me what I was doing. I told him I was just fooling around with a little tune, but he kept smiling, and all of a sudden we were singing his lyrics. We played them again that night, and you should've seen our brothers' faces. They were amazed, just plain amazed . . . but I'll tell you, everything about 'Time Has Come Today' amazed me, it was . . ." He stops, smiles broadly, and shakes his head.

A zany, self-described "free spirit," who loves to play pinball machines, and go for thirty-mile bike rides, Willie suddenly pauses, to give George a playful slap in the ribs. Instead of retaliating, George looks affectionately at his forty-eight-year-old brother, and then smiles at Joe, who's sitting on the living-room floor a few feet away.

"Come on, Willie, are you going to finish that story or not?" George asks good-naturedly.

Mischievously, Willie doesn't say anything for a moment. But never one to disappoint an audience, he finally says, "Well, everyone loved the song. How couldn't you? It was terrific, we knew that right away. I knew that night it was going to take off.

"A few weeks later we played it in New York at some club, and people responded. They could let go with it, we could all scream with it, go crazy together. That was the thing about our audience, they came to be free. We relaxed people. It's a complete satisfaction to know we achieved such positive results, the music was total communication."

"Time Has Come Today" had another stirring side—it made the brothers rich and famous. They were now celebrities who didn't work for less than $60,000 a night. This new money bought them a fourteen-room mansion in Connecticut, complete with a swimming pool, a recording studio, and butlers. And when they weren't partying there, or in New York discos with the Beautiful People, they were flying around

the globe. At their peak, from 1968 to 1970, they repeatedly appeared in
Europe, and did two world tours. Columbia Records ballyhooed each of
these trips. In company press releases the brothers were called "the
country's hottest artists." And so it went. The brothers were on top. For
now.

Thanks to hindsight, the brothers insist they never thought the cheers
would last forever. But perhaps we should take them at their word, for
amid the glitz and glamour, they were always aware of a lurking
shadow. They were black, and no one would ever let them forget it.

"Countless times, high-class white people who had never been in a
room with blacks would observe us, and say, 'You're real gentlemen,
you act so different than I thought you would,'" rails George, the
bitterness crisp in his voice. "We couldn't believe it; these people were
startled by the way we'd act. Here we were, singing about love and
peace . . . or how the time had come for that, and these folks thought
we'd come out of the jungle. The whole thing was very sad."

The brothers were also a unique phenomenon at Columbia, to put it
mildly. Until 1968–69, the biggest stars on the label were Paul Revere,
Moby Grape, and the Byrds. The company had already had problems
with Aretha Franklin, another outspoken black artist. So imagine the
scene at corporate headquarters in those racially tormented times, when
four tall black men, outfitted in outlandish clothes, arrived to press their
cause. Trouble was inevitable.

"Columbia loved our selling records, but by 1969, after a few tours or
so, we started speaking up for ourselves, and that scared the shit out of
them," flares Joe, breaking his previous restraint to hurl a stream of
invectives at the "white establishment." At forty-three, he's the youn-
gest—and most outspoken—male in the family. His brothers jokingly
call him "the baby," but they now show their respect by slapping his
hand, high-five style, while chorusing "That's the truth, that's the
truth."

Emboldened by these shouts, Joe continues, "The whole industry
didn't know what to do with us. We came through the back door unexpectedly, and no one was prepared for us. We wanted to remain true to
ourselves, but every time we talked to record people, they'd tell us we
had to play more rhythm and blues, wear the same suits, dance on
stage, wear white gloves. It was unbelievable. We were misfits to them.
No way were they going to have four blacks and a white out there,

singing about love, peace, and happiness. We would've been too great a threat to all those white kids who loved rock 'n' roll."

Taking a far less angry stance, Lester blames success for the group's eventual collapse. While insisting "None of us got lazy, or stopped struggling for everything we got," he does say, "We got into this terrible rut. We became too dependent on 'Time.' We didn't take our success, or the future for granted, we knew there were too many forces aligned against us. But we just did that song too much. We couldn't break away from it, and come up with new material. We got boring, there was no spark . . . when you're not doing anything exciting, the singing gets to be a job. After a while, we didn't know whose fault this was, the record companies or ourselves. We started causing problems, antagonizing people. The whole thing became a lot less fun."

Whatever the reason for the group's demise, Kent State was their death knell. The violence there led to other campus disturbances, and, in the ensuing backlash, school entertainment budgets were severely slashed. Since the "peace and love" brothers were especially dependent on these audiences, George admits, "we were soon behind the eight ball. We'd been making close to $1 million in bookings at universities. But when Kent State blew, all those funds were zapped away from us. We had had it."

Once other engagements fell through, Columbia lost all interest in them. Though the company released two more albums, *Chambers Brothers Live at Fillmore East* (1970) and *A New Generation* (1971), they hardly promoted them. Agreeing with Joe that "the rug was being pulled out from under us," the group quarreled with Columbia, club owners, their management people, and finally started to argue among themselves. In 1972, Keenan left the group, while the others, according to Lester, "got so frustrated with everything slipping away, we blamed each other, and our minds got poisoned."

The group stumbled through the next few years, somehow managing to put out *Unbonded* for Atco. But by 1975, their time ran out. Amid more harsh words, they disbanded. Lester left to play with James Cotton, and after several aborted attempts to patch things up, George finally went to automotive school.

"The whole period was very painful, we couldn't even sit down to talk for five minutes," says George, sadly shaking his head. "I just couldn't handle it; for the first time we weren't getting along. There was no communication. Not only wasn't there any brotherly love, but to make things worse, there was no money. We had been keeping things going just to pay our taxes, and to keep our name out there. But finally, with no real current product, we couldn't kid ourselves anymore, we had to go on."

This has been difficult. Except for George, none of the brothers was prepared for the "real" world. Lacking basic job skills, they struggled to find work. And when these attempts failed, their dreams of "coming back" got the better of them. They've tried to recapture the magic repeatedly since the late 1970s—with only mixed results.

While they did a gospel album with Maria Muldaur in 1980, and a TV commercial for Levi's jeans in 1982, their comeback hopes seem to be nothing more than fantasies. There have been few club bookings, and even less interest in recording circles. That lack of success hasn't discouraged the brothers, nor has it sparked a new flurry of acrimony. The family seems tighter than ever.

But there are still conflicts that bode ill for the group's revival. Despite Willie's writing "hundreds of songs a month" (his bike trips are often inspiring), and Joe's saying, "I'm sure my time will come again" (he's now laying floors in new houses), George doesn't see much of a future for the group, and has little interest in performing again. Much like Lester, he wants to establish his own identity, one that isn't based on "Time Has Come Today." Content to be "one of the top mechanics in L.A.," he poignantly says, "Oh sure, they'll be times I'll drop a flywheel on my hand, and the first thing that runs through mind is 'Wow, I can't play.' I'll kick the tools around, and really get angry at what I'm doing. But the way the music scene is going, I'm glad I'm out of it . . . very glad."

Pausing, George looks at his seventy-five-year-old mother, Victoria, in the kitchen, grins proudly, and continues, "It's great to be back with my family. I hated the road. But please, don't get me wrong. I don't have any regrets. The Chambers Brothers were a very important part of all the changes that went down. We opened doors for other black acts, the guys who came after us didn't have to go through the same shit.

"Now I see these rock shows on TV, and every time they skip right over us. We're never given credit for affecting people's lives. This hurts me, but . . ."

His voice mellows and he quickly adds, "I'll never forget this one concert we did in South Carolina. Everyone in this place was either drunk, or from the [Ku Klux] Klan. When we decided to bring these five black kids in there to watch us, I thought it was the end of us. I really thought the crowd was going to tie us to a tree.

"Well, a few years later we got this telephone call from a guy who said he wanted to do a movie about the Chambers Brothers. We set up a meeting, and he turned out to be one of those Klansmen. The music had taken effect on him. Later on, he told me, 'The music you guys did changed my whole life.' "

Roger McGuinn of the Byrds

Finding Answers at 40,000 Feet

Intoxicated by the supercharged tempos, Lenny Bruce, Jane Fonda, and the other hipsters in the Hollywood club were much too high to see the future. Yet the use of pulsating, highly amplified guitars was decidedly revolutionary in 1964, and a portent of a bold new era, the Psychedelic Age.

Part of the crowd at Ciro's might have suspected the old limits were being tested, stretched, and redrawn. The music was definitely different, an acoustic sound that could only be described as folk rock. But amid the tumult, with strains of Dylan's "Mr. Tambourine Man" crashing overhead, no one realized that the group on stage would soon mount a challenge to the Beatles, influence Dylan to go electric, and help crystallize a new phenomenon—the LSD trip.

That is the Byrds' legacy. The five-man group was always splitting up, reforming, or barely surviving under the strain of countless ego battles. With such disparate temperaments as Roger McGuinn, David Crosby, and Chris Hillman in the Los Angeles–based band, this internecine strife was almost predictable. Each member of the Byrds had his own musical philosophy and a different perspective on the group's future direction. But during those rare lulls in the fighting, they changed the American music/social scene with their strong use of acoustics, and highly controversial "drug" tunes, "Mr. Tambourine Man" (1965) and the single many radio stations banned, "Eight Miles High" (1966).

In fact, this latter song, which was influenced by John Coltrane's saxophone playing and Indian ragas, became an anthem for hippies. These flower children were eager to explore, to reach new levels of consciousness, so the chaotic, wandering melodies of "Eight Miles High," reflecting McGuinn and Crosby's fascination with outer space, encouraged more than an LSD experience. Stirred by McGuinn's ringing twelve-string lead guitar, youngsters took off on a voyage of self-discovery.

"We were clearly saying something that these hipsters or hippies could grab onto, that gave them a fresh, more daring outlook," muses the blond, blue-eyed McGuinn, after getting out of his VW camper to stroll along the beach in Morro Bay, California. "These underground types were our people, they were the first ones to respond to us. And when we started to get high, to make drugs a philosophy of life, they naturally came along with us.

"The Byrds were always hired to play at Jane Fonda's parties and for Sean Connery, Marlon Brando. I was blown away by that, the success was kind of a shock. I didn't talk much with these people, and I'll never forget, while we were playing at Brando's house, he started to come on to my wife."

For the soft-spoken, well-educated McGuinn, this "fantasy trip" into a world of Porsches and amphetamines was a difficult adjustment. Raised in more refined circles on Chicago's near North Side, he received a classical education at a fancy prep school, and was strictly "a low-key, studious type" at the folk-oriented Old Town School of Music. Here he met guitarist Bob Gibson, who was appearing regularly in many of the city's renowned folk/jazz clubs. McGuinn began to hang out with him, and one night in 1958 at the Gate of Horn, the Limeliters asked the sixteen-year-old to play banjo with them.

About four months later, after a brief stint with this group, McGuinn got a solo gig in a Los Angeles club. While working there, he was introduced to fellow guitarist David Crosby, a member of Les Baxter's Balladeers. Viewing Crosby as "a kindred spirit, who I could really talk to," Roger drove to San Francisco with him, in hope of playing some North Beach coffeehouses. During this period he was Jim McGuinn; he would change his name in 1968, after embarking on a solo career.

Still a relatively innocent teenager, McGuinn had his eyes opened a bit on that Ken Keseyian fling. But the wild partying was suddenly interrupted when Roger got a call from a friend of Chad Mitchell's. He wanted McGuinn to fly East, to join Mitchell's trio for a Greenwich Village engagement. The offer was financially appealing. And of course, there were visions of breaking into the big leagues. So Roger packed up his guitar, unaware that he was heading for a gig that would last over two years.

"The money was great, it gave me a lot of freedom, but I was a little frustrated by the experience," concedes McGuinn, following the progress of a lone wind-surfer in the distance. After remarking "I love this place, I stopped here for lunch and never left," he turns more somber. "I'd been a folk artist, and I lost that purity playing with Chad. Everything was too commercial, it began to prey on my mind after a while. I felt I was bastardizing my art."

Because of these misgivings, McGuinn left Chad Mitchell to sing harmonies and play acoustic guitar behind "Mr. Mack the Knife," Bobby Darin. Aside from the slick Sinatra routines, this was more than just another commercial venture. Darin's "Splish Splash" was bonafide rock 'n' roll. As noted by *Rolling Stone* critics John Swenson and Dave Marsh, Darin influenced Dion, Frankie Avalon, the Rascals—and would have a vital impact on McGuinn's evolution as a rock guitarist during the year and a half he stayed with Darin.

"The time I spent with Bobby was the most educational experience of my career," says McGuinn reverently. "Bobby was a real pro. People I met later on in rock 'n' roll were for the most part unprofessional. But he was old school, he taught me what the business was all about, how to get ahead. Basically, he taught me how to be a real performer."

When heart trouble forced Darin to give up performing, he opened a New York music publishing company, and hired McGuinn as a writer. For a few months in 1963, Roger gratefully sat in a Brill Building office, composing songs. At the same time, though, folk music was again commanding SRO crowds in Greenwich Village. Young artists like John Sebastian; Bob Dylan; and Peter, Paul, and Mary had infused the genre with new energy. And hoping to share in the excitement, McGuinn left Darin to work with Judy Collins on her third album, *Judy Collins #3*. "The move had to be made," says Roger, "I felt confined in a tiny office, while folk was becoming a genuine happening. It wasn't underground anymore. There was a new spirit. It was a warm time, people's places were opening up, there was a feeling of communion. No one cared if they'd get a record contract. It felt like love."

Joyously believing "a new age was dawning," that would offer "limitless possibilities," McGuinn returned to the land of opportunity, California. Starting out at the Troubadour, a Los Angeles club, he soon met the Byrds' future tambourine player, Gene Clark. They agreed to work together, but since someone else was needed for harmonies, their act didn't get off the ground. Not until McGuinn was reunited with Crosby.

"It was a miracle, he just walked in the door (of the Troubadour) one day," recalls McGuinn excitedly, forgetting the relationship deteriorated into ugly name-calling and near-physical confrontations. "Everything happened so wondrously, it seemed as if we were destined to be together. No one got frustrated, not even when our first demo was a disaster. We were sure everything was going to work out okay. . . ."

McGuinn's voice trails off for a moment. It's unclear if those past skirmishes still bother him, or if he's simply engrossed by the windsurfer's sudden fall. In any case, he soon continues, "David was a real force back then. He had so much enthusiasm . . . through his connections, we were able to record at a studio for free. Then he got us to Jim Dickson (the group's eventual producer, who knew Dylan), and as you know, that's how we really took off—Dylan let us record 'Mr. Tambourine Man.' Before we knew what was happening, we were very hot, [laughing now] 'L.A.'s answer to the Beatles' (a phrase coined by Dickson and former Beatle PR man Derek Taylor). Unfortunately, some of us believed those press releases . . . perceptions changed, egos took over."

As McGuinn disgustedly suggests, Crosby challenged his leadership of the Byrds as soon as "Mr. Tambourine Man" became a number one hit in 1965. The most business-wise member of the group, Roger had been making the financial decisions. And now that the group was commanding five thousand dollars a night, instead of a few hundred, he felt "It was no time for a democracy, someone had to take charge." But Crosby, according to McGuinn, wanted an equal voice in policy matters. The two men naturally clashed. Factions also formed, and as tensions rose, the strife sapped the Byrds' creative power.

"Some scenes in the studio were very ugly, we were searching for material at times and this led to terrible fights," admits McGuinn, disconsolately. "Things wound up okay, we got 'Turn, Turn, Turn' out there [1966]. But the rub between me and David, that I guess *always* existed, got more strained. Our differences infected the group . . . that hurt us terribly. Instead of overcoming our internal problems like the Stones did, we drifted further and further apart. We really weren't a group after a while. We just went into the studio together."

With McGuinn and Crosby coming close to exchanging blows, Clark got so disgruntled that he left the group in March, 1966. He'd been the Byrds' principal songwriter, so his departure caused immediate havoc. The group had to be reconstituted; Hillman became the lead vocal, while McGuinn and Crosby did most of the song writing.

While the truce between these two talents was extremely fragile, it somehow lasted for several months. During this period, McGuinn dipped more into jazz, saying he "liked its free-flowing quality," while Crosby was also experimenting with scales, and the use of various instruments. The result of their explorations was *Fifth Dimension,* the "psychedelic" opus that rallied the subterranean drug culture with "Eight Miles High."

"Even though I got into drugs real bad later on, pills, percodan, speed, coke—'Eight Miles High' got a very bad rap; it wasn't meant to be a drug song," says the forty-four-year-old McGuinn, after finding a place on the beach to sit. "Because the song had the word 'high' in it Crosby always said it was druggie. I disagreed. Gene [Clark] and I had worked on the lyrics before he left, and it was simply about flying, other realms, self-discovery. We were into LSD, the counterculture thing, but there are only slight innuendoes in the song, there's no heavy drug message."

Apparently, trying to be even more convincing, McGuinn recites the lyrics of the song. Before finishing this exercise, he's sufficiently convinced to bitterly add, "Soon after the song was released, we arrived in England, and did the press tear us apart! What crap! They went all out to destroy our image, so we wouldn't be seen as the counterinvasion to the Beatles. The whole thing was very upsetting. I'll admit, we couldn't hold up on stage, we were much better in the studio. But the press knocked everything about us. We were just victims of an early witchhunt."

Though the controversy spread to the United States, as dozens of radio stations banned the song, the publicity guaranteed its commercial success. "Eight Miles High" took on a certain mystique. People had to know what the fuss was all about, and in the process, the single went to number twelve on the charts.

Another type of censorship had a far more devastating impact on the group.

In early 1967, Crosby wanted to record a song about two women, a man, and their *ménage à trois* relationship. He met immediate resistance from McGuinn, who had begun to study Zen Buddhism, and felt "the song wasn't only poorly conceived, it was blatantly immoral." Stung by the rebuke, Crosby became abusive, calling McGuinn "mindless," "a stupid ———," and ridiculing his music. Tempers even flared on stage, as the two men had several angry exchanges in front of audiences. Finally, in October, McGuinn and Hillman had had enough. Staging their own version of a palace coup, they told Crosby to get lost.

"He had to go, there was no other way, he was destroying the group, and we let him know it," fumes McGuinn, his voice rising sharply, unsoftened by the passage of time. "It was a little hard to do, the guy was one of us, we had all struggled together. But it was like a marriage gone sour, you had to free yourself before it ruined you. There was too much bad blood . . . he was impossible, just impossible to deal with. We offered him a fifty-thousand-dollar settlement, it was worth it . . . and he said, 'Come on guys, let's patch things up, we make good music together.' I was so disgusted I said, 'Yeah, but we can make better music without you.' "

Caustically, McGuinn adds that Crosby bought a luxurious cabin cruiser with the money. "He did okay, I even think we did him a favor. Soon thereafter he was with [Stephen] Stills and [Graham] Nash. He'd been hanging out with Stills long before we broke up. So it was just on to another group, bigger money, more success."

Though McGuinn is convinced the Byrds had to split up, he's still nagged by dark, depressing thoughts. The Byrds fell into mediocrity after Crosby left, and all attempts to reclaim their past glories failed. McGuinn admits as much, for in a saddened, near bitter voice he says, "We were even less of a group after David left, our spirit was totally gone. We used to be a club, a street gang with lots of energy. We cared about the music, the [creative] process inspired us . . . but with David gone, the whole thing was just for the money."

In the wake of Crosby's departure, the Byrds also adopted a different sound. Influenced by a new addition, singer-songwriter Gram Parsons, they did a "country-rock" album, *Sweetheart of the Rodeo.* The work was more than a commercial disaster. It was seen as "redneck music" by their admirers, according to McGuinn. "Our fans felt we were traitors, who had sold out, and since the true country people always believed we were Communists, you can understand why the album flopped."

Predictably, Parsons soon left, in October, 1968 to be exact, and after Hillman joined him to form the Flying Burrito Brothers (with Chris Ethridge), McGuinn put a new Byrds lineup together (Clarence White,

John York, and Gene Parsons). "The whole thing was a mistake, I should've gone solo right then," asserts McGuinn, alluding to the group's inability to score a commercial hit over the next four years. The Byrds did do the soundtrack for the Peter Fonda–Dennis Hopper film *Easy Rider.* But since members were constantly leaving or feuding among themselves, McGuinn became increasingly disgusted and disbanded the group in 1973.

"There was no integrity left, it would've been wrong to continue. Everything we did was some sort of compromise. Besides feeling we were taking advantage of our fans, I felt I had to start my solo career. It's hard to establish your own identity, so the quicker I got on to that the better. I just didn't want to kill what the Byrds stood for . . . I had to drop it, start something new . . . that was the only way to keep the nice memories intact."

Except for another artistic/commercial disaster—a Byrds reunion album in 1973—McGuinn returned to places like the Troubadour, hoping to launch his second career. Then, in 1975, he hooked up with Dylan's version of a wandering minstrel show, the Rolling Thunder Revue. Describing this two-year odyssey as "the best time of my life," Roger wistfully adds, "There was so much love between everyone on the caravan, I wish it was still going on.

"Really, it was like the early days in Greenwich Village, there was such a camaraderie between people. Dylan, Baez, Joni Mitchell, Arlo Guthrie, Willie Nelson, Allen Ginsberg, David Allan Coe, we had such good feelings toward one another, we were so tight knit . . . Everything about it was fun.

"We'd either turn up in a small town, surprise people, or call up a radio station and say Dylan would be playing somewhere a few days later. It was like living in a Fellini movie, it was so bizarre and colorful. Dylan wanted it to be picaresque. Sam Shepherd was around for a while, doing his initial work on [the film] *Renaldo and Clara* . . . there was just so much going on. And Dylan footed the entire bill! It was his attempt to get back into time, and it succeeded. The tour was even an improvement on it. What a time we had. It was the perfect punctuation to the end of the sixties."

Lamentably, that age of innocence had long ended for McGuinn. And while the Revue was certainly a madcap adventure, rich with tender memories, it was also a dangerous flight into fantasy. For the tour kept him from confronting a deadly serious problem, his ever-mounting dependence on cocaine.

Like others hooked on the stuff, McGuinn paid a severe price for the powdery high. His habit financially devastated him. Tormented, he became listless, undisciplined, and was often unable to work. Ultimately, his first marriage fell apart. He realized drugs were a curse, and could see that his life was enveloped by "a giant black cloud." But there was no getting out from under it. He was paralyzed.

Except for the size of his doses, nothing changed until 1977. McGuinn then had a "born-again" experience. "Once Elvis died I had a spiritual awakening. I said 'wow,' the speed and downers had killed him, and would do the same thing to me. This shook me up. I sobered up enough to realize Jesus was the messiah, that he was using Elvis's death to tell me something.

"Ever since then I've had no desire to get high. I've gone through a thorough cleansing. Now I don't know what I liked about it. Maybe there was a peer pressure to use it, people hung out with you because of it. And for a while I thought my world would come to an end without drugs. But I have more control over my craft now, my music is definitely better. It has to be; I feel freer. Drugs were an albatross for me, I was always uptight on them."

Bolstered by a new self-confidence, McGuinn "experimented" with various musical combinations over the next few years. He first put together the band Thunderbyrd, to do an album of the same name. While the work got decent reviews, it didn't sell. So the inevitable happened. On a Canadian tour, Thunderbyrd opened for Eric Clapton, and McGuinn again jammed with Hillman and Clark. That led to their reuniting for two more albums, the commercial hit "Don't You Write Her Off," and ten months of touring in 1979–80.

Now McGuinn insists, "I have no intention of getting back together with them again. I really feel inside that I have to preserve and pursue a solo career. I probably could do better financially if I was with them. But I enjoy the freedom of being alone, I like what I'm doing with my acoustic guitar. I can express myself like never before."

Speaking slowly to emphasize each thought, McGuinn stands up, walks a few yards, then points at a fishing boat entering the picturesque harbor. In support of his being "a changed man," with "a whole new set of priorities," he earnestly says, "I don't need anything besides this. I'm very content these days. It's like the 1950s all over again, living in a place like this.

"I'm probably happier now than I've ever been. Inner peace supersedes my drive for success and money. All that is just gravy. It's enough for me to be playing, folk, country, rock, whatever, and to be traveling with my wife [Camilia]. It's a taboo in the business to take your wife along, but we get along great. We have a good time, and she's quite a road manager."

Muffling a chuckle, McGuinn again looks out at the ocean. Yet this time the view doesn't seem to please him, for his face has turned pale.

"With all these good things going on, I don't think much about the past, or of the Byrds. But I do think about David, I love him more than ever. He's so vulnerable now, so in need of help from those rotten drugs, I have to be concerned. I don't know what I can do for him. I can only pray for him. Maybe he has to reach bottom before he comes up. Who knows? I just pray he can make it back. We all need him and his talents so much."

Donovan Leitch
Surviving the Seasons of the Witch

In a world hardened by terrorism, threats of nuclear disaster, and Big Brother machinations, the sensitive artist could easily feel dwarfed. Why shouldn't he despair? In the face of such potential destruction, aren't beautiful "paintings" superfluous? What influence could they possibly have on the world's seemingly bleak landscape?

Despite the cynicism that abounds, Donovan Leitch refuses to be intimidated. Believing that art still has a role in changing people's lives, the Scottish-born minstrel continues to sing surrealistic ballads and love songs. The mellow flower-power period may be over, but Donovan, who was once likened to the pre-electric Dylan, has restyled such folk-rock tunes as "Atlantis," "Lalena," "Barabajagal," and "Mellow Yellow"— he remains the Sunshine Superman.

"It isn't the sixties anymore, yet I'm still writing about peace, I'm still painting musical pictures that will help people reach their inner selves," says Donovan, in a familiar, gentle voice. Hoping to launch a U.S. comeback, after years of living in obscurity, he's left his rural English cottage to do a string of dates in America. While relaxing in a New York hotel, a few hours before a Carnegie Hall engagement, he's boyishly ebullient. "The sixties were such a great event. There were peace movements, discoveries of the self through drugs and meditation, and an urge to sensitize the male. All of these events have happened; they developed throughout the seventies and eighties, so I'm still writing about these subjects. I believe, as Dylan does, that ideas change the world. So while it's shocking to me, there's still a need to paint pictures through lyrics about peace, love—relationships between men and women are still out of kilter."

Affairs of the heart are crucial to this ever-smiling, sweet-tempered troubadour. He's a true love-child, who constantly talks about his own wife, Linda, a former mate of Stone Brian Jones. She's Donovan's source of inspiration, the woman he's depended upon through the lean 1970s and 1980s. She's now credited for putting him on the charts, and, as he affectionately says, "Every love song that I wrote during the period '65–'69 was in a way a longing for Linda (they didn't get married until 1970). She appears in so many songs, 'Catch the Wind,' 'Sunshine Superman,' 'Legend of a Girl Child Linda,' 'Turquoise' . . . All of those tunes made me a success." And while these remarks bring a sparkle to Donovan's grayish-green eyes, the forty-year-old balladeer falls curiously silent for a moment. He also knows that Linda has pulled him through innumerable seasons of the witch.

On top of the musical world for five years, the naïve-sounding Donovan went the way of other innocents in the seventies. As the Vietnam War escalated into Cambodia, and assassinations numbed the national consciousness, people weren't interested in dreamy, rainbow-tinted lyrics. It was a blood-soaked era, marked by marauding protesters and police; it wasn't a time for smoking bananas (the theme of "Mellow Yellow"). Ever the romantic, Donovan couldn't adjust to these realities —or to the post-Woodstock commercialization of the industry. So like other mystics, the twenty-four-year-old retreated in 1970 to safer, less nightmarish surroundings.

"The sixties were a party, a dream. We were discovering. We kept pushing the barriers to extremes, and that brought super success for socially concerned artists," says Donovan, who's grown gray and lined since that "wondrously exuberant" time. "So many young people were released, there was such a lowering of the spirit, but as you know, this movement has its own sundown. The new music of the early '70s challenged this breaking down of the barriers. It became clear that the party was over in the '70s. We didn't sleep on the floor anymore, and the radical element asked, 'Am I going to continue to be radical, or should I be conservative and look after my own house?' The '60s were very much out, there was a great closing down, an inner restriction. The generation went into itself.

"I continued to live my ideals, but in obscurity. I continued with Linda . . . I followed many of my contemporaries and withdrew to places in Ireland, Scotland, California. I continued my beliefs, but like many artists who had been popular, I had to deal with the aftermath of success in the early seventies, which meant many lawsuits and business problems, dealing with record companies and managers . . . While I was sorting this out, a realistic music movement came in rather than a romantic one."

The strain in his voice heightening, Donovan takes a sip of a Heineken, then continues, "We believed in the dream, we believed in the events [concerts, happenings, records, etc.] we were doing. But on the other side was the reality, everything was a business, and you couldn't walk three feet off the ground anymore. All the artists had to come to terms with this. We wound up with all these financial problems, we had to work them through, and many couldn't deal with it, some died . . .

"It was essential for me to drop out in the early '70s, because I had never grown up. There were many things I hadn't done offstage that a young man usually does, because everything I had done at age eighteen was either photographed, promoted, or recorded. Basically, I wanted to have a family, to draw, to try a bit of film music. Or to try a different sound that is not quite what you call Donovan. To continue in the seventies as Donovan was very difficult, because when success comes, certain images are indelible. The indelible image of the flower power, the indelible image of the folk-rock star associated with Peter, Paul and Mary, Dylan, Pete Seeger, these images became solid—so everyone knows me as a certain figure, and one had to try to break that mold. I took time out because I couldn't play the game anymore of being continually asked to do another 'Mellow Yellow' or 'Sunshine Superman.' "

That adjustment took nearly a decade. With Linda's support, he finally accepted his place in rock culture. "I see myself as an interpreter of a generation." And he has even gone on to write children's stories, music for films, and a play about the lives of three women married to rock stars. That play, *Lives of the Wives,* and a yet unnamed album, illustrate the "new" Donovan, the artist content with his rock legacy. And yet, they also give us a look at a man in transition, at a sensitive, uncompromising soul, who's still searching for self-fulfillment.

This introspective journey began in Glasgow in 1963, as Donovan left home to attend art school in a small town outside London. Not wanting to work on a lathe like his father, he was far more interested in the masters of French Impressionism. Envisioning himself as a painter, "in the most romantic sense of the word," he pictured a life of seclusion, "living by the sea with seagulls flying overhead, with a girlfriend in a rollneck sweater . . . intent on investigating nature." At this time, rock 'n' roll didn't stir him. The music wasn't cerebral enough to meet his intellectual demands. Instead of hanging out in raucous pop clubs, he adopted a more bohemian life-style, frequenting coffeehouses and folk-jazz clubs. It was here, in these caldrons of sixties free-thinking, that his views about art radically changed.

Discussing this alchemy with an infectious enthusiasm, he announces, "My original idea was to be a traditional sort of painter, the kind that's attached to a studio. That was romantic to me, but I also got into the pop arts, for what I really wanted to do was to promote ideas, rather than pictures. Andy Warhol was working away with images he hadn't even created. The impact, that's what was exciting me. Peter Blake and David Hockney were early British pop artists. But quite frankly, if only two artists out of the entire British art system made any money, or had any impact, it seemed as if the days of having a studio and being a painter were an aristocratic luxury. Or else it was a poor man's decision to live in poverty and obscurity. So, in a way, I chose to embrace the performance arts, while bringing with me a very traditional viewpoint of nature. I added mystical ideas. I hoped to promote this as a popular, highly visual event. So, as a painter, I could never be anymore. I wanted to make radical pictures on an audio canvas."

Performance art was already stretching rock's parameters in England. The Who's Peter Townshend, for example, with his penchant for smashing guitars on stage, certainly created a visual experience, as did Mick Jagger with his outrageous antics. But when Donovan first discarded his paint brush for a guitar, he wasn't very threatening. Wearing a floppy denim cap, *à la* Dylan, he debuted in folk clubs, singing ballads that evolved from his Celtic background. Tunes like "Catch the Wind," and "Colours," celebrated "the beauty of nature" and brought him his first taste of stardom—an appearance on the British TV show "Ready Steady Go" in 1965.

Only later, with the full dawning of the Psychedelic Age, did Donovan seem more shocking. Abandoning his Dylan image for flowing robes and sandals, he adopted a decidedly effeminate pose. His softly sung lyrics, now steeped in full-blown mysticism, were a perfect accompaniment to drugs. The repetitive rhythms of "Sunshine Superman" and "Mellow Yellow" rang like mantras for young hippies. Donovan was thus hailed as their guru, a Herman Hesse-like figure who led them down meditational paths. But being on the cutting edge of a new social order also has drawbacks, namely a vulnerability that exposes an artist to torrents of abuse.

"I've always felt that music was a meditational tool . . . because I could drop people's consciousness into themselves," says Donovan, who followed the Maharishi Mahesh Yogi to India in 1967. "Music in spiritual matters has been important throughout the ages, the depths of music are a religion really. But this message, coupled with performance art, had a quite shocking effect on the masses. As long as it was a minority bohemian event, these ideas were quite normal within the in-crowd. When these ideas were projected into pop records, and became popular, there was an obvious refusal to believe it. Everybody was in bobby sox, and curled-up hair, the boys all had short hair, and nobody got high, or understood their inner selves. The press, or the masses reacted against these ideas, they had to protect themselves . . .

"We were upsetting people, we were getting up their noses, no doubt. That was the power of the radical event, what we were saying wasn't quite accepted, and it was quite scary to the establishment. But the establishment rapidly became the youth. And they were ready to understand something new."

Still, Donovan encountered problems, as he introduced "other colors, other layers" to his work. "By the time of 'Sunshine Superman' (1966), I had started to dress myself in the image of my songs, and then I became a pictorial event. Through colors and costumes, I projected the song's lyrics, very much the way Boy George shocks today. Many people thought I was homosexual, 'cause I thought a man could be beautiful, and I sang that a man could be sensitive. In its day, this view was looked upon in the same way that Boy George is today. The androgynous visual he projects—I projected an androgynous visual in my lyrics. Brian Jones projected that same image in his early costuming; a sensitized female man. If there was shock, that was okay. It was much better to work on a shock value, and to project an idea.

"I'll give you an image. I was working in a college town, maybe somewhere in Ohio, in '68 or thereabouts, and I was walking through a corridor that led off a football field to the stage. The corridor was lined with young men still in their football, gladiator clothes, walking very slowly with helmets under their arms like figures from *The Right Stuff.* They are the males of their day in America. Meanwhile, all the females, their girlfriends, are screaming and crowding into the gymnasium, waiting for this phenomenon called Donovan. And I walk along the corridor, with my flowers and entourage, and coming towards me is the image of male America, *big boys*. As they walk by me, their mouths fall open.

"And as my mouth fell open, I realized here was the conflict—I was presenting a feminine male that had nothing to do with homosexuality. I was a straight man in the normal sense, but I was projecting a feminine side which was very outrageous, a side that was accepted mainly by women. They were looking for a feminized male, and the men were looking for a male-fem in themselves. We know where that crossed, and the problem it presented, because the conflict hasn't been resolved yet."

Donovan thrived on raising people's consciousness. Though the sixties remain a "blur" to him, "one big party of fast and furious events," he felt he was promoting ideas that were changing—and radicalizing—history. "The period was exciting because you could introduce new ideas to people, and get a response. I could say what I wanted. That you could manipulate success to present these ideas was wonderful. It was the only time in the whole century that you could actually push an idea on a mass-produced album—and the record companies would go for it. They didn't know what the bloody words were about. So you were actually radicalizing the entertainment industry, while you were entertaining."

The impish smile on Donovan's face is a reminder that he did all this in his early twenties. While he barely understood "this crazy-paced life," that was "based on the unreality of such temporary events," his message did come across. There's no question about that. Between 1966 and 1970, Donovan's "romantic mysticism" dominated the charts. It didn't matter if the lyrics were syrupy, or cryptic, tunes like "Hurdy Gurdy Man," "Atlantis," "Barabajagal," and "Jennifer Juniper" showed the flower-power movement was flourishing. And that Donovan the Love Child was one of the Woodstock Generation's most influential voices.

"I couldn't really assess the impact I was having, everything was moving so fast back then," notes Donovan, after ordering another beer. "It was always on to the next album, the next concert . . . the only substantial, firmly rooted thing in my life was Linda. If you ask any musician how he's doing, the only essential he can relate to is his relationship to a woman, because everything else is so transitory. You live amid extremes; you get ostracized, or you get put in a position where you're not real. Whether a musician is talking about a new tour, or a new record, it's really all based on whether you are enjoying it. Is it fun, do you have somebody that at the right time can turn to you and say the right thing. And you would know it was honest.

"Too many women with men in this business come into it too late, and they're a little bit amazed. Often it's only a roadie who can speak to a musician, he's the one that has to speak sense, and he can say 'You're over the top man, you're quite over the top here . . .' cause this business has extremes, and you can be expanded and supported, and the fire can be fanned so much you can over indulge, as you know, in many ways with drugs and drink . . . an artist can wind up with all sorts of people around him. But in the event that you need the real relationship, and it's a woman, it's important that the woman knows what's going on in this business. Linda does, and that's allowed us to protect ourselves. We've looked after ourselves more than most friends of mine.

"Not too many people have a relationship like mine. I've felt supported by Linda. We're more like true friends. We have a very strange relationship compared to others . . . There seem to be peaks of passion, excitement, and also times of separation, then there's children and lots of contact, and more solitary times. But the basic thing is that Linda chose to move with me, whereas most women would remain in the mansion, and the artist would create his relationships, and she would create hers, so, slowly they'd drift apart. It's very sad. The relationship gets farther and farther apart. Whereas Linda and I, through the sixties and postsuccess, chose to move together. We've done it together, we do it together, and still it's okay. It's nice."

That bond had to be strong. The 1970s weren't a time for psychedelic mellowness. As love-ins and transcendental odysseys faded from the scene, time dissipated our collective consciousness. People became more insulated, protective of themselves. Optimism was dead. And so the music became harder-edged, more frenzied, and jarring to the spirit.

Donovan was consequently *passé*. While continuing to make albums, he grudgingly realized that no one was listening. "In the sixties I had been pushing the barriers, but once those events I wanted to create were accepted, the masses asked, 'What do you have for us now?' What I'd been doing was no longer radical; it had already become part of the culture. So my big problem then was, could I break through more barriers? After a while I realized that I had already set my path, I soothed more than I agitated. And, as the seventies went on, the questions got deeper and deeper, as did the collective depression."

Bolstered by Linda, and the warmth of their family (two daughters, Astrella and Oriole, and Brian Jones's son, Julian), he was never overwhelmed by these problems. Watching the "dream," or "party" come to an end was certainly painful. His mental energies were still invested in the Cause. And, as he admits, the seventies demanded musical adjustments. But feeling "My life was more than hit singles," he began to explore new avenues of self-expression.

"I didn't appear on too many charts, that's for sure, but I did continue to work, to branch out in different directions," says Donovan, speaking in a mild, even-tempered manner. "It became clear to me that I was a writer, or interpreter of ideas, and that I'd been accepted not just as a chart artist, but that I was also part of the culture. My songs had entered people's lives, and had meant so much to them. So I kept on recording; I wrote children's songs; I even acted in a few movies *(If It's Tuesday This Must Be Belgium),* and did the soundtracks for some films (most notably, Franco Zeffirelli's *Brother Sun, Sister Moon).*

"Isolating myself wasn't the answer, music was my business. I toured sporadically, you'd see me, then you wouldn't. I was trying to come to terms with what the business was. Early success is very difficult for an artist because you haven't fully developed. It took me from '70 to '75 to sort all this out. I saw then that the music I wanted to do was once again new, that I didn't have to compete with the punk or the New Wave. Most importantly, I realized that if I wanted to continue to make popular music, I'd have to treat it as a business. I couldn't continually make another record deal, so I stopped making those deals. I stopped getting involved in those large events, the management deals, the *déjà vu* events; the manager, record deal, a tour, the manager, record deal, a tour."

Speaking more rapidly, he excitedly discusses how he escaped from that "trap." "I broke that pattern by becoming my own company, I'm my own writer, and I'm developing my own works. I'm really seeing it as a business that originates from me, rather than a business I join. That was a lot more healthy for me, because I needed the freedom. I didn't want to record just some danceable singles—I wanted to develop ideas, and make social comments."

Donovan has been pursuing these goals in earnest since the late seventies, writing children's poetry, working on theatrical musicals, and, by composing "Peace," a song for protestors in Communist-dominated Czechoslovakia. As emphasized in "Slow Down World" (besides being a 1976 release, Donovan says "It's a cause as I am"), he wanted people to look at themselves, to develop their inner consciousness, so "they could really see the beauties of life around them." Though this message sounds drug-influenced, Donovan renounced the use of hallucinogens and marijuana in the late sixties, insisting, "drugs never produced poetry, I already understood the inner life of nature."

Along with his revived interest in American touring, Donovan is now focusing on bringing *Lives of the Wives,* a musical about three "sisters of rock 'n' roll," women who lived in the shadows of celebrated musicians to either a British or U.S. theater. Drawing on Linda's relationship with Jones, and her connection to other rock wives, the play is essentially a tribute to these women. It's recently been staged in a small Los Angeles theater, and, while talking about his more ambitious plans for the show (an album, and video production), Donovan turns poetic. "In the *Lives of the Wives* of the gods—talk about rock 'n' roll royalty, these pretend princesses with their country houses and their joints with tea—in the *Lives of the Wives* of the gods there is sadness and suicide sometimes. All their dreams have come true, but their man's in another clime . . . It's up, it's fun, it's jazzy, more than rock, but it has its tragedy, there is a death. Of course, there are many deaths. There are three kinds of women in this piece, and I'm investigating the situation through the eyes of a central character who is Linda."

If this play leads to a video single, Donovan's U.S. touring plans will surely be bolstered. After a seven-year absence from the American scene, he needs the publicity attendant on an MTV spot, for many fans have been wondering if he's still alive.

Even more significantly, however, a video deal would signal the fulfillment of a dream. Ever since art school, he's been hoping to "paint radical pictures." And a film clip that explores the less glamorous aspects of a rock 'n' roll relationship would be a break with the usual pap.

"The traditional painter has now moved into video and video music is the culmination of putting popular art before the people," notes Donovan, as a road crew member walks into the room from an adjoining suite. After being reminded that he's due at a sound check, Donovan chuckles, "I haven't played Carnegie Hall in years. I'm going to do my best not to be late."

There's a nervous edge to his voice, as he reaches for a pack of cigarettes. Instead of lighting one, he looks around the elegantly furnished room and smiles. Clearly proud that he's back in the limelight, even if it's only for a night, he says, "I just hope I don't disappoint anyone tonight . . . it's great to be back in New York.

"But as I was saying, doing a video would be keenly satisfying. On one side of my father's bookcase was Marx and Lenin, while on the other, Byron, Shakespeare, and Shelley. So between these two influences at home, and what I wanted to do with my life, I think I've hit a happy medium, promoting those ideas, and getting involved in the pictorial arts, rather than being a straight painter with paint and brush. Late in life, I'm the painter I always wanted to be, but in video, or in images, or in musicals. So yeah, the painter I wanted to be, I became."

Far from disappointing anyone, Donovan took his Carnegie Hall audience back to the sixties, to that heady time of tie-dyed shirts and V-shaped peace signs. Magically, through his lilting ballads, these images came alive for the crowd, even though most of the people in attendance were mere toddlers back then. Donovan's new admirers were so swept away, they threw flowers onto the stage, and surged forward to blow loving kisses at him.

Everyone roared after "Season of the Witch," which prompted Donovan to talk about Janis, Jimi, John Lennon, and other heroes who have "passed away." Dedicating the entire evening to them, he then sang his most haunting love song, "Lalena." This prompted a teenager to run down the aisle to give Donovan a small teddy bear. After thanking her, he put the toy on a table next to him, and grinned. It was a tender smile, filled with love.

And during the ensuing hush, a picture was painted. Everyone knew that Donovan's gentility would withstand the passage of time.

Dave Clark of the Dave Clark Five
From Soccer Fields to Xanadu

Upon entering the plushly furnished penthouse situated high above the smart shops of Mayfair, one is immediately aware that the 1960s rock scene has been forgotten.

There are no platinum records on the wall. Group photographs aren't displayed. Nor are there any mementos of worldwide jaunts or appearances on "The Ed Sullivan Show." In fact, the minimalist decor is only softened by a quietly burning fireplace, rows of leather-bound books, and a framed invitation to Buckingham Palace for the wedding of Prince Charles and Lady Diana from Queen Elizabeth.

This is clearly a rarefied world, one that suggests great wealth. And while rock 'n' roll isn't the language here, visits from Arabian sheiks and other high-powered financiers do revolve around music. These investors are looking for a "sure thing"—another box-office hit like *A Chorus Line* or *La Cage aux Folles*—and they come calling on Dave Clark to find it.

One of the leaders of the British Invasion, Clark has become a Citizen Kane of the music business. Pocketing millions of dollars from his Dave Clark Five hits, due to recording contracts which were specifically structured to give him complete control of the "masters," or the original tapes, he's now producing a Broadway musical extravaganza tentatively called *Time.* Along with writing the score for the show, he's releasing an accompanying album in conjunction with Capitol, and is negotiating a movie deal with several Hollywood moguls.

All of these efforts are based on a "terrific gamble." *Time* has to be a smash. Otherwise, the four years he's spent on the project could be viewed as a "woeful waste of time." Clark recognizes this potential for disaster, and understands that his reputation in the music community would be severely damaged by a flop. But the former drummer, who had notions of becoming a pro soccer player before scoring with such classics as "Glad All Over," and "Bits and Pieces," is a scrappy, hard-driving individualist. He felt it was time to make an artistic statement, even if it meant certain risks, like falling flat on his face.

"Doing a show like this has always intrigued me, so I'm ready for whatever happens . . . if you want to do the exceptional in life, you just can't rock along and play everything safe," observes Clark, his blackened right eye a visible reminder that he pays more than lip service to this ideal. The injury, incurred in a recent soccer scrimmage, is a testament to his "taking the good with the bad," and in this same, combative spirit he continues, "I'm not worried about failing, or losing money. If I didn't feel good about this show I wouldn't have spent all these years working on it. I remember when I made my first record ('A Session with the Dave Clark Five'), everyone thought I was crazy to be the artist and the producer. Then, when it was a success, everybody patted me on the back. Well, that shows you got to do what you think is right.

"This show could be the biggest disaster ever. But, in our business, you have to go with a gut feeling. I believe *Time* will be a big success. If it isn't, then as long as I've written and produced the show the way I wanted, I have no excuses. Of course I'll be very upset, but then you get on to the next thing. Too many people live in the past, and you can't do that. I don't go on TV talk shows or do too many interviews because I don't want to talk about the past. I'm interested in today, tomorrow, next week, next year. The past is great but I don't want to live there.

"It's like Muhammad Ali. He was a great champion. But he always had to have one more fight. When we had our last million selling record, I thought we should quit while we were ahead. Now I'm just thankful that being successful in the sixties has given me the independence and freedom of choice to do things I really enjoy."

As Clark suggests, his life hasn't always been this blessed. Growing up on the outskirts of London, in a working-class section of Tottenham, he wrestled with poverty throughout his adolescence. Both of his parents worked; Clark's father was a postal employee and his mother a teacher. The family struggled to pay the rent—and that didn't allow for too many luxuries. When Dave wanted soccer shoes or other paraphernalia, he had to raise the money himself. This meant a lot of odd jobs, and eventually led to the formation of the DC5.

In 1962, the twenty-year-old Clark was invited to Holland for a soccer match, along with other members of his Southgrove Youth Club team. But, like Clark, most of the squad were of working-class origins and didn't have money for the trip. However, a few of his teammates did have musical talent: Denis Payton was an experienced saxophonist; Rick Huxley and Lenny Davidson were guitarists; and Mike Smith played the piano in local pubs.

Ignoring his own lack of playing ability, Clark came up with an idea: Why not form a band and play around town to raise funds for the trip? Though the scheme was quickly approved by his four teammates, the group was still incomplete. They needed a drummer. So Clark bowed to necessity and bought a secondhand set of drums for twenty dollars at a Salvation Army outlet. Plunging into a new world of Chuck Berry, Elvis, and Little Richard, he practiced incessantly for a month. A rock 'n' roll career was still the farthest thing from his mind, but he enjoyed "the challenge of mastering a new skill"—and that was the DC5's eventual ticket to places far beyond Holland.

This was immediately evident after the boys returned home from their victorious soccer match. While on the verge of disbanding (Clark was more interested in scoring goals than hits), they got a phone call from a Buckingham Palace official. After explaining that one of their business cards had turned up in his office, he asked them to play at a staff party. Unable to ignore such a regal request, the guys persuaded Dave to load his drums onto a subway train, and to meet them at the palace gate. The courtly surroundings must have made a powerful impression, for there was no more talk of quitting—at least not for the next six years.

Their next show at the Palace, however, a command performance for the Queen in 1965, was still a long way off. First they had to perfect their act, and, in the early part of 1963, that meant doing club dates only on weekends, when they wouldn't conflict with regular jobs. Money was still a problem. Clark was against the group's turning professional, feeling "My playing was never a monetary thing. If you do things right, they pay off in the long run. If you go in for the kill to start with, then you're dead." So despite their getting a long-term gig at the Tottenham

Ballroom (the DC5's loud, crashing drum motif came to be known as the "Tottenham Sound," and was often compared to the softer, more melodic "Liverpool" beat), the group didn't have the cash to rent a recording studio.

That is, not until Dave played "demolition derby." Risking life and limb, he got hired as a stunt car driver in a movie and took on brick walls for about a hundred pounds (around two hundred fifty dollars) a pop. It was jarring, mind-boggling work. But after a week of headaches, enough cars had been destroyed to get the boys into a studio to do a cover of the Contours' 1962 hit "Do You Love Me?" which was written by Berry Gordy.

Having outwitted death, Dave wasn't discouraged when the British-based Tremeloes used that song to score their own hit. Shrugging off the "theft," as "one of those things," he used the recording to secure a contract with EMI Records—a deal which quickly led to the making of "Glad All Over."

That tune not only became a runaway hit, it also bumped the Beatles from the top spot on the charts for the first time in nearly a year and convinced Clark to turn professional.

"I knew we could sustain ourselves, that we had staying power," recalls Clark, in a dry, even voice. Showing little excitement over the rush of events in 1963, he sits calmly on the edge of a couch, ignoring a ringing phone and the spectacular view of London's East End. "When two of our songs made it to number one, that showed me we were for real. The problem with most people is that they believe their own publicity. They fall into a trap, they just want to hear the good things. Well, with me, I never saw myself as a star . . . I only felt as good as my next record, so, I always felt our careers could end tomorrow."

Those insecurities dogged Clark throughout his career. They partially explain his reluctance to turn professional and his abrupt decision to disband the group in 1968. But even Clark was optimistic in 1964. "All of a sudden everything seemed possible, it looked as if a new age was dawning." Along with a number one song, he had destiny on his side in the person of Ed Sullivan.

At that time, the famed dour emcee was enamored of British rock groups. He had piled up Nielsen points with the Beatles' appearance, and was eager to bring other bands onto his weekly TV "shooooe." His talent scouts heard about the DC5's triumphant touring of American military bases in England and contacted Clark. Characteristically, Dave was initially reluctant to make the big trip.

"I never wanted to go to America; I'd been playing these bases, where it seemed like everyone was drunk, so I thought America would also be the pits," explains the forty-four-year-old Clark, his eyes suddenly twinkling with delight. "I said no to Sullivan at first, but then I was told that they'd pay for all the air fares, hotels, and ten thousand dollars. It seemed like a lot of money for a weekend, so we went. We did three songs on the show, and it was wonderful . . . the power of this man. And at the end of the show he announced that we'd be on the following week.

"We couldn't, because we were supposed to be back in London. I told him we were sorry, but we just couldn't do it. He told me to come up to his office, and said, 'I just told 70 million Americans you'll be back on.' Well, to cut a long story short, we found a way. We cooled off in Jamaica for four days, came back the following week, and when we landed at Kennedy Airport, there were thirty thousand American kids there. The rest is history. We got five records into the charts at once. That was the power of this man. He was responsible for the success of the 'British Invasion.' "

Over the course of the next few years, the DC5 would appear on the show sixteen more times—and sell over 50 million records in the United States alone. Mainly because of Sullivan, they became the Beatles' chief rivals, especially in 1964–65, when they logged four Top 5 hits, "Can't You See That She's Mine," "Bits and Pieces," "Because," and "Catch Us If You Can."

While Clark modestly refrains from explaining this popularity, he does say, "The reason the English groups hit off was that we were the first generation that didn't actually get drafted. Up until three years before, you were automatically drafted at eighteen, so our freedom of expression wasn't knocked out of us, there could be a freethinking, free-spirited DC5, Beatles, or Stones.

"And of course, we weren't manufactured, that's why we were so successful in the States. Every fifties rock star who did interviews made certain everything was perfect. They were told what to say, what not to say, and they were manufactured to a certain degree because America is the greatest country in the world at commercializing. And then, when the English groups appeared, people asked them questions, and they answered them honestly. Or said what they felt. It shocked Americans, and they loved it."

Though quick to pity those who "remain trapped in the past," Clark leans back on the sofa, luxuriating in his memories. "It's nice to look back, I look at the sixties with great affection. There was such hope, you didn't care where the pound or the dollar was. We didn't worry about inflation or unemployment. Anything was possible, and that was wonderful.

"You got a buzz from what was going on. When you went out on the stage, with fifty thousand people screaming, or whatever, you'd put your arms out and the roar was unbelievable . . . it was like being heavyweight champ of the world.

"Unfortunately, too many groups couldn't get past that, those cheers became too important. And when you become desperate that way, you forget about being good, you only listen to the bullshit. But before things became routine for me I got the most wonderful feelings from performing, the crowds, even the hellos from doormen were exhilarating. It was an electrifying time—it was fun."

On the strength of Denis Payton's resounding saxophone (the DC5 was one of the few groups to employ a sax in the mid-sixties), and Clark's thumping compositions, the fun lasted until 1967. There were numerous international tours, SRO performances in 100,000-seat stadiums, and millions of records sold. As Clark says, "Performing with the DC5 was never work; it was love, because I enjoyed making music."

Before the joy of playing could go stale, Dave left the group. Albums like *5 By 5* and *Everybody Knows* were still dominating the charts in 1968, but the minting of gold records lost most of its luster. Needing to "come back to earth after these crazy DC5 days," he enrolled in London's Central School of Film and Drama, to prepare for a career in the theater.

"I basically needed to understand people better. To be a good producer or director you've got to understand other people's insecurities and especially performers', because they're very insecure. That's why they're brilliant, you see, that's why a great performer is great, because they never know whether they're actually going to be good or not. They always have this fear that they're going to fail, and I think this gives them an edge, an extra push.

"Where I've been very lucky is that I've been on both sides, I know how far to push somebody to get a good performance, and when to stop. Because you can destroy people if you go too far. You can only get this [sense] by having been an actor or performer . . . the greatest film directors for me are the directors who've been actors, like John Schlesinger and Arthur Penn. They're great directors because they know how to excite and push people, how to challenge them, how to make them look inside themselves. That's why they get great performances."

When Clark speaks so admiringly of these men it becomes clear why the DC5's attempts at regrouping were doomed to failure. Even though they hit the revival circuit at odd times in the seventies, playing the old songs wasn't a challenge for him. No longer exhilarating, the touring became a tiresome routine. Paling next to the satisfactions of drama school, it didn't push him to plumb any new depths of self-discovery, or provide that buzz of creativity. Even the 1978 success of *25 Thumping Great Hits,* a collection of past favorites, failed to ignite that missing spark. Clark longed for something more, a sense of artistic achievement —and having the financial security to be selective in his pursuits, he spent most of the 1970s looking for that one special project.

Since that search has consumed him, Clark has had little contact with his friends from the DC5. Nor has he shown much interest in raising a family, or even in getting married. A bachelor, he lives on a country estate outside London, and cheerfully says, "I love my freedom too much to change. I like to take off when I want to. Maybe the right person hasn't come along, but there are too many other things in my life right now."

That essentially means *Time.* After seven years of looking for "just the right material, something very original," he plans to spend the next five years making the musical a worldwide phenomenon. This is the "challenge" he's been desperately thirsting for. The enterprise that will perhaps bring him the plaudits usually reserved for Stephen Sondheim, Joseph Papp, or Michael Bennett.

"I know this show is *right,* it's something I've always wanted to do," Clark says fervently. "It's a concept album with a lot of big international names involved. Then there'll be the stage production in London, and we'll go to Broadway, Los Angeles, other European countries, Paris, Germany, Australia, places like that, and then we'll go on to the movie. If it takes off as planned, it will be the next five years blocked out. I'm sure it'll take off, I just know it."

If *Time* doesn't take off, Clark will lose millions of dollars. His ego will also be jarred, but it won't be a devastating blow. For unlike most artists, he's been steeled on a soccer field. He can even take a shot to the groin and still come back. And besides, one failure won't destroy what he's already accomplished.

"I have a certain freedom, while in the past I didn't. I only do the things I enjoy. This might sound schmaltzy, but I was brought up in a working-class background where you're broke at the end of the week, or your family doesn't know where their next penny is coming from. That gave me a set of values in life, I appreciate my traveling around the world, the money I've made, all the success and respect I've gotten. For a poor kid I haven't done too bad."

Clark now smiles triumphantly. And as he looks around at his expensively furnished penthouse, that swollen right eye doesn't look so mean. It becomes a badge, proof-positive that he's ready for another challenge.

Mickey Dolenz
of the Monkees
Did Groucho, Harpo, or Chico
Ever Study Physics?

They were the Marx Brothers of rock 'n' roll, four skillfully packaged "crazies" who became heartthrobs for millions of teenaged American girls.

Every week in 1966, on their nationally aired TV show, Mike Nesmith, Peter Tork, Davy Jones, and Mickey Dolenz would cavort in front of us, staging romps that saw them portraying anything from fish or chickens to corrupt dictators, Frankenstein, and madcap adventurers. None of the boys was extremely talented, at least not in a musical sense. Mickey and Davy had been child actors who knew nothing about playing instruments, while Mike and Peter had been going nowhere with nameless coffeehouse bands. Until the Monkees had a nasty confrontation with the show's producers, the boys were only allowed to lip-synch on the show—and it was evident to most observers that the Monkees were simply cashing in on the success of the Beatles.

But the group can't be dismissed as a mere commercial rip-off. The Monkees, with their long line of hits, such as "I'm a Believer," "Pleasant Valley Sunday," and "Last Train to Clarksville," gave adolescents too young for the Beatles their first taste of rock 'n' roll, and, as Dolenz astutely suggests, "We didn't have much effect on the development or evolution of the music, but we had a tremendous impact on the marketplace. If anything, we were probably the originators of the music video; we'll go down in history as innovating that visual form.

"In the 1960s we opened up a massive new audience for rock 'n' roll, which was the underteens, the teenie-weenie boppers. At that time, they had been totally neglected. They'd never been considered, and many of them didn't understand or have any interest in the Beatles. Our fans were the younger brothers and sisters of Beatle fans who didn't want the same music their older siblings liked. They could respond to our zany style of comedy. Usually kids started buying records at thirteen, fourteen, fifteen, and we kind of broadened that age down to nine, ten, eleven, so that definitely had historical import. We were good-time slapstick artists. There was nothing heavy about us, and that gave kids a new fascination with the music."

So despite the banality of their songs, the Monkees became one of the 1960s' most important cultural artifacts. Besides their TV show, which was deliberately styled after *A Hard Day's Night* by producers Bob Rafelson (later of *Five Easy Pieces* fame), Bert Schneider, and Colgems' boss, Don Kirshner, the group had Monkees comic books, a series of look-alike toys and a line of clothing. They were the inspiration for a Saturday-morning cartoon show. Their TV show helped sell records, and, from 1966 to 1968, they had seven Top 5 hits. Kirshner had a stable of writers including Neil Sedaka, Carole King, and Neil Diamond to turn out new songs. There was no stopping them. Everything they did meant millions of dollars, and as the boys implanted themselves on the national consciousness, the rock world learned a vital lesson; that relatively new medium, TV, had enough power to make anyone a star, even a circus boy, without musical talent, who had only chased after elephants.

The son of a British dramatic actor, Dolenz had his own TV series, "Circus Boy," at the age of ten. For three years he palled around with an elephant named Bimbo, and thought it was quite natural to "follow in my father's footsteps."

He continued to get small parts through his teenage years, while attending school in Los Angeles. Acting wasn't that important to him then; he had a great fascination with the sciences, and was studying to be an architect.

"I loved acting, but since I'd been doing it all my life, and since I had some success, I didn't have the same kind of manic drive and ambition others might have," confides Dolenz, while preparing lunch in his suburban London home. Today he is forced to fend for himself, while his wife recuperates from giving birth to the couple's third daughter. Mickey delights in *haute cuisine*. Smiling, he delicately unwraps a frozen chicken Kiev dinner, complete with vegetables and rice, and pops it into an oven. Once satisfied that lunch will be a success, the slightly balding forty-one-year-old continues, "I really wasn't pursuing my acting career at the time. I'd go on interviews once in a while, yet I was fascinated with designing, working with architectural drawings. I've always been manual in all my hobbies. I love electronics. I've had a laser for a while. Right now I'm going for a degree in physics at a university here in London."

Before Dolenz could become another Frank Lloyd Wright, his agent spotted an ad in the *Hollywood Reporter* (September 1965), which called for "four insane boys, aged 17 to 21," to be in a TV series about a rock 'n' roll group. Mickey, then the lead singer of a nightclub band, the Missing Links, forgot about returning to school, and jumped at the chance of having another national TV show. He'd eventually see his frenetic, highly pressured days with the Monkees as being "thrown onto a ship of fools." But at the time he was still a self-described innocent, who only saw a great deal of potential in the show, and didn't care "what slice of the cake" he got.

"Given a neutral environment I wouldn't have chosen a theatrical career. I had already experienced a fair amount of success," says Dolenz, the group's frequent lead singer and drummer, sipping a cup of tea in between bites of chicken. Sitting in the sun-drenched, glass-paned conservatory at the rear of his modest house, he's momentarily disturbed by the wails of his newborn baby, Georgia Rose, but quickly adds, "I was interested in more pragmatic things back then; I really wanted to try my hand at designing, yet a series on national TV was a major thing. It couldn't be passed up. I might've been young and naïve, but even then I knew the TV show was an opportunity to break into an industry that was, notoriously, a closed shop, a power structure that was quite a little Mafia. If you didn't go up the ropes there wasn't a chance in hell you'd get anything in Hollywood. So here come the Monkees and, in effect, they bypass that whole mechanism overnight. I saw the possibilities from the beginning. A group like the Monkees didn't need the record companies, the radio stations, because they came in with a full-blown nationwide TV show that pushed the records for a half hour every Monday night."

Musical talent, therefore, wasn't necessary. Rafelson and Schneider simply needed "four crazies" who looked good on stage, or could bedevil audiences into thinking that they were watching an Americanized version of the Beatles. Such aspiring artists as Danny Hutton (Three Dog Night) and Stephen Stills were rejected by the two producers, and instead they chose Davy Jones, a Paul McCartney type who had starred in the Broadway musical *Oliver;* Peter Tork, a folksinger who drifted around Greenwich Village after flunking out of college; and Mike Nesmith, a session musician-cum-writer for the Stone Poneys. They were an unlikely group. As Dolenz admits, they didn't have much in common, and were ill prepared to rival real musical "heavies"—Dolenz didn't even know what "the charts" meant. Yet Rafelson and Schneider dressed them in tight-fitting Nehru jackets, complemented their Beatle-styled haircuts with music lessons, and turned to hit-maker Kirshner for some "bubble gum" magic.

The Colgems' impresario didn't disappoint them. Besides commissioning Ellie Greenwich, Carole King, and Jeff Barry to write Monkees songs, he secured the Candy Store Prophets for backup work, and, by 1966, the group scored three Top 20 gold singles off their debut album: "I'm a Believer," "Last Train to Clarksville," and "Stepping Stone."

Since the entire Monkee operation was so slick and unabashedly conceived to manufacture hits, the group quickly came under fire from the rock press. The boys were denounced as frauds, two-bit actors charading as musicians. Their songs were mocked. Even though the group could be viewed as a fabrication, a way to make a quick killing for their backers (companies like Screen Gems and RCA were also reaping profits from the Monkees' success), some of the criticism was plainly unwarranted. Though the Monkees lip-synched on their TV show, they did their own singing on the albums and eventually learned to play their instruments. And they did sell records. Millions of them.

"I couldn't have cared less what the press said, or if I sang or not," insists the unshaven Dolenz, after telling the housekeeper in strident tones to keep the children quiet. "I was an actor. I wasn't a rock 'n' roll musician, or singer. I was an actor playing the part of one, and I trusted the judgment of the producers, maybe in my naïvete. But let's face it, the proof is in the pudding. We were very successful. Though Mike and Peter weren't happy, and eventually insisted on playing their instruments in everything we did, I was pretty happy-go-lucky about it."

"I must admit, though, after a while I did get fed up with magazines and newspapers criticizing us for being a fabrication. It was ridiculous, they said we were manufactured, yet no one is ever concerned that Leonard Nimoy wasn't really a Vulcan. And that's exactly the comparison. We were a TV show about a rock 'n' roll group, like "Bonanza" was a TV show about a bunch of guys living on a ranch. I always found it curious that no one ever criticizes actors who don't do their own stunts. I still find it a bit annoying, but, in actuality, the press never influenced the people that mattered to the Monkees. We still became one of the most successful acts of the 1960s. All these little people in the music industry got pissed off. Yet nothing they did, all the criticism they could muster, made a hill of beans of difference. I had three hits on the charts, and didn't even know what the charts were, or what *Cashbox* or *Billboard* were all about."

Still, as Dolenz suggests, there were grumblings. Though the group continued to reach the Top 10 in 1967, with such songs as "A Little Bit Me, A Little Bit You," and "Pleasant Valley Sunday," Nesmith got increasingly annoyed by the media criticism. He threatened to quit if the Monkees weren't allowed to play their instruments on all future records, and told *Look* magazine, "There comes a time when you have to draw the line as a man. We're being passed off as something we're not." The media knew about the group's backup musicians, but Kirshner still tried to keep this a secret from the fans.

After a few months of bitter wrangling, Nesmith got his way. Starting with the album *Headquarters,* the group did their own music. This made each of the boys happy, at least temporarily, and they buoyantly prepared for the American segment of their international tour. Before the Monkees were turned loose on U.S. audiences, Dolenz spotted the still-unknown Jimi Hendrix in a London club, and persuaded him to be the opening act on this tour. Dolenz may have had an eye for talent, but Monkees fans weren't so impressed. Unhappy with Hendrix's feverish, psychedelic style of playing, they mercilessly booed him off the stage, and he was quickly forced to leave the tour.

Once the Monkees returned to the studio for the 1967 TV season, there were other problems. The grind of rehearsing for a show every week, which meant the constant producing of new songs, began to exhaust them. Peter and Mike started to talk about leaving the show, and even Mickey questioned the value of their nonstop schedule. "Sometimes we had to pump out three, four songs a week to keep up with the demand, and this was extremely daunting. It was the first time a group of young boys faced such pressure. We had to record at night, do gigs on the weekends, rehearse the show during the week. It was terribly draining."

Some of the jokes, or "romps" on the show also got tired and stale.

NBC saw the ratings plummet, and, in late 1968, the show was canceled. Putting on a brave face—or unwilling to face reality—Mickey, Mike, and Davy decided to go ahead with plans for another world tour. But Peter, feeling he could be more creative on his own, left the group, and that was essentially the end of the Monkees' two-year fling with greatness. But, as Mickey points out, the group is still with us, winning the affection of youngsters around the world thanks to TV reruns.

"At the time we all felt we could go out and make it on our own, and be just as successful as we'd been with the Monkees," says Dolenz, a note of irritation creeping into his voice. Remembering that Peter wasn't satisfied with the group's "creative evolution," he shakes his head disgustedly, and bristles, "But all those thoughts were utter nonsense. We would've been well advised to stick together for another two or three years so that we could've kept going at a successful level. As it was, we quit at our peak, and while some people say that's not such a bad thing, I have some doubts about how we played it."

Though Dolenz goes on to insist, "I wasn't depressed by these events; intuitively I knew every up had a down," it's apparent that the group's premature demise still annoys him. The lines under his eyes deepen when he talks about the breakup, and, sounding both regretful and angry, he says, "I was kinda prepared to go on, I had had success before, and knew what the downside was all about. But we should've kept it going for a few more years, it was too abrupt. We still had a lot left; we were still wanted out there. The kids loved us . . . there was no real reason to pull the plug then."

The breakup didn't cause financial problems for Dolenz. Unlike two members of the group, whom he refuses to name, Mickey was never "foolish enough to trust a manager," and had wisely given his paychecks to his mother to invest in property. So even though "the Monkees never made the money you would think we made, the producers and film company people got the biggest slice of the cake," Dolenz retired to his Laurel Canyon house in the Hollywood hills, and did "nothing" for the next five years.

"The Monkees were such a debilitating experience, I just partied, bought a laser, and went hang gliding," says Dolenz, proudly pointing to a twenty-four-inch scar on his right arm, a souvenir of a hang-gliding mishap. "During the Monkees we never had a chance to have a good time, it was just constant work. Not only were we recording, but we also were doing concerts and filming a TV show twelve hours a day. It really burned us out. I don't know if we could've gone on much longer, it would've killed us. We needed time to recover. Laurel Canyon was amazing, libidinous. We never got that involved in drugs, the producers had protected or isolated us from that kind of stuff, but things really got crazy after the show stopped."

During the mid-1970s, the Monkees, in various hybrid forms, regrouped. Mickey occasionally played with Peter and Davy in West Coast nightclubs, or only a pair of them would appear. According to Dolenz, they got "very good money" for these mid-1970s engagements, because "people were just crazy to hear our old songs."

But Nesmith never got involved in these efforts, choosing instead to establish himself as a country music artist (he now refuses to talk about the Monkees), and the reformed group wound up in Reno or Las Vegas casinos, opening for stars like Olivia Newton-John.

By 1976, having gotten "tired of singing Monkees' songs for the four hundredth time," Dolenz decided to return to television. He had produced a few commercials under Rafelson's tutelage in the late 1960s and he had directed the documentary *Shark Hunt*. He also appeared with Miss "Deep Throat" herself in *Linda Lovelace for President*. Dolenz used his entertainment world contacts to become a full-time producer/director.

"I remember just when the whole thing soured," notes Dolenz, in a flat, even voice. "We got this gig in Harrah's in Reno, and I should've been excited. This was a lot better than a lot of the places we were playing. But I'll never forget, I was reading Bertrand Russell's *History of Western Philosophy* backstage, and when I went out to perform, I noticed that all the people I was singing to were all drunks, hookers, and losers. I couldn't figure out why they were such a nasty audience. Not until this guy there told me that all the winners were still at the tables. It's true, there were these horrible people, just looking up, and going [wincing, and in a hoarse, raspy voice, Dolenz tries to imitate some of the 'low-lifers' he met] 'Make me laugh, you asshole, entertain me.' It just went real sour at that moment. I started to make plans to move on to greener pastures."

After returning to London in 1978 to costar with Davy Jones in a play called *The Mermaid,* he was hired by the British Broadcasting Company to direct the drama *Story Without a Hero*. Noting "This show won such excellent reviews, I haven't looked back since then," the budding director went on to do a TV series about a robot, "Metal Mickey" ("a cross between 'Mork and Mindy' and 'Bewitched' "), dozens of commercials, two short films *(The Box* was done in collaboration with two

Monty Python actors), and the highly acclaimed British TV series "Luna" (a science-fiction adventure comedy about a little girl living in the twenty-first century). In 1983, he directed a musical, *Bugsy Malone,* which ran in a central London theater for over a year, and he is currently working with Nesmith (now a rock-video maker in California) on a TV series destined for one of the major U.S. networks.

When describing these shows, Dolenz quickly credits the Monkees with "launching me on the road to success." While joking "Our popularity was such a fast, overnight kind of thing I don't know if I had a good time, people only tell me I enjoyed myself," he feels his Monkees' experience gave him valuable insights into the TV industry and a solid base for a future career. "Without the Monkees, none of my recent projects would've been possible," says Dolenz. "A lot of ideas for all kinds of shows came out of those crazy TV episodes and my involvement with various people; for that I'll always be grateful."

A force in British television, Dolenz has reason to be cheery. Money isn't a problem (the Monkee TV reruns are also a decent source of income) and, since TV people are constantly offering him work, he's avoided the plight of many ex-rock stars. He hasn't had to take out his old Nehru jacket and resurrect Monkee tunes in endless one-night stands.

Yet Dolenz also seems troubled. He describes some of his projects in a listless, unemotional monotone, as if they were keeping him from more fulfilling pursuits. Finally, when pressed about his lack of enthusiasm, he admits to "a need to change directions at this point. I'm at a crossroads; I want to explore several options. I'm getting itchy for something else."

Still in doubt about what a career change might mean, he thoughtfully closes his eyes for a few moments, and, as the strain of this midlife quandary edges onto his face, Dolenz adds, "I've had a very successful career. I'm not bored, not exactly. I don't have to go out and slop my guts every day to make a living, but along with that comes indecision and frustration. I don't want to waste my time, yet I don't want to do things that are wasteful. I might want to do more writing. I've just finished a short story, and I'm about to begin a screenplay. And as I said, I'm getting a degree in physics. I've always been intrigued by the sciences, and I might also want to study philosophy."

He laughs nervously. But before he has time to continue, a baby's crying in an upstairs bedroom interrupts these lofty thoughts.

"You're going to have to excuse me," stammers Dolenz, "I have to go change a diaper."

Peter Tork of the Monkees

No One's Laughing, Not Anymore

"Three hots and a cot."

It's not much, three meals and some sort of shelter. Only a Bowery bum or a defeated character out of Kerouac would find contentment in such lowly pleasures.

Ever since Peter Tork left the Monkees in 1968, he's stumbled so badly, "three hots and a cot" evoke visions of grandeur for him. He hasn't had security or any peace of mind these past seventeen years. Instead, an idealism admittedly out of touch with the reality of the times has forced him to roam around the country in a trailer, in search of an audience for old Monkee tunes. Along the way he's gone through three marriages, been forced to wash dishes for fifty dollars a week, played for several nameless bands, and dealt with a severe case of alcohol addiction. He now insists, "I've found a new core, a framework that I'm reaffirming, reestablishing everyday." But, true to his tortured, hippielike existence, Tork admits, "I'm not concerned with externals, things are going to work out . . . I'm just not sure what I want to do when I grow up."

The sadness of this type of life-style is starkly apparent when one meets Tork. While the other Monkees have grown up and gone on to successful careers in other fields, he's been reduced to living with a girlfriend in a cramped New York City apartment where he spends most of his time curled up in an armchair, idly strumming a battered guitar. He hopes the phone will ring, because fantasies about playing Monkees songs in local clubs, or doing another tour, preoccupy him. It seldom does, though, so he has to wage yet another fight. He can't give in to impulses which would again turn free days into drinking orgies.

"Even when the Monkees were at their height, there was a feeling of emptiness inside me, a corelessness, that manifested itself in drug and alcohol abuse," complains the forty-four-year-old Tork. In the mid-1960s, the Monkees' bass player was described as the group's "comic genius." He had perfected his art in Greenwich Village clubs, masquerading in ridiculous Shakespearean outfits as the "Court Jester," much to the delight of friends Richard Pryor, John Sebastian, and Stephen Stills. Stills was the first person to tell Peter about the upcoming TV show. Now, those royal rags have been replaced by a threadbare sweater, a faded red Duofold undershirt, and tattered jeans. Tork's wan smile has also lost its magic, and he plaintively says, "All my life I've felt a sense of dislocation, dispossession—dissynchronous with my surroundings. I've never had a central purpose, but the drinking made the rootlessness, the frameworklessness worse. It was a disease, a compulsiveness that I had to overcome before I could find out who I was. Drugs and alcohol shut down concerns about corelessness. The human machine is under pressure to grow, but as long as you stave off those demands with chemicals, the pressure builds up. There are terrible biophysical side effects; the despair of not knowing myself, of not being able to grow.

"That's not to say I didn't have a wonderful high time with the Monkees. We were swinging along in a wonderful way. We'd hang out together and took heart in each other's projects. I really enjoyed being with Mickey. We laughed a lot together, and I shared a great deal of communion with Davy; he's a person of great depth. All the guys chipped in two bucks each and bought me a watch when I left. It's inscribed 'from the guys at work.' But I'm keeping hold of my core now —the emptiness has begun to fade—and I still have a lot of my idealism. I just don't know how rooted it is in reality. There are a lot of things out there that I'd love to fix, but I don't know if they're within my range, so part of my recovery is knowing what I'm capable of doing. There's no reason to add to my discomfort."

In his usual convoluted manner of speaking, Tork is obliquely referring to how idealism led to his leaving the Monkees, and to years of problems. By 1968, Tork felt the group wasn't living up to its creative potential. He constantly urged the other members to demand more control over the production process, and to focus on live performances. Tork and Mike Nesmith had led an earlier fight with the producers, which he says "steered the group away from making Tab Hunter kind of records; we were finally allowed to express our musical talents." But his latter "idealistic quest" to change the group's image failed. Content with their commercial brand of music, and the marketing apparatus that was behind it, the other members distanced themselves from Tork's acid-induced visions. This left him little choice. Determined to express himself, he had to split.

Only after the repeated failures of such groups as Peter Tork's New Monks, the Aquarian Age Choir, Peter Tork and/or Release, and living off friends' charity has he realized, "At the time I thought I was quitting because I couldn't convince anyone of my ideals. Now I see that as immature, shortsighted, and selfish. Because I see that I only had the right to ask for personal participation in the projects. That had been granted, but it wasn't enough for me, I wanted everyone to want what I wanted. That was insane. Now that I'm recovering it's important for me to see that my mistakes led me down the primrose path."

Insisting that a new set of values has given him a better "fix on life," Tork attributes this optimism to his finding some mystical "source," or a "contextual framework that's so endlessly mysterious, it can't really be named."

But Peter's new seriousness goes only so far. When pressed about future plans, he's still the court jester.

"Maybe I'll teach at a children's school, or a place for freethinking people. Who knows? I'm at home in front of TV cameras, so maybe I'll run a late-night movie show for some local TV station in Dubuque, Iowa or something. Maybe I'll get a cable TV show. Maybe I'll be a resident philosopher on somebody *else's* cable TV show or someone else's network show. Or maybe I'll be the George Burns of rock 'n' roll. Who knows?"

Richie Havens
A Brain Surgeon as World Leader

For some people, the dream never dies.

Through the fire and ashes, they keep holding on, believing in the impossible. No amount of killing or destruction can dissuade them. No injustice or senseless act of terror can weaken their resolve. They're vulnerable because of their faith. The "real" world often mocks them as strange, foolish romantics—and when this ridicule becomes intolerable, exile is the only escape.

Still, the dream doesn't fade. To the contrary, it only grows stronger, more palpable, for rock's "ambassador of goodwill," Richie Havens.

Visions of peace, love, brotherhood, those same emotions that gave birth to Woodstock and an ensuing generation, still inspire and sustain him. Convinced the world can be "a place where people meet on common ground," Havens insists it's his "cosmic duty" to crusade against nuclear weapons, international hunger, and "to bring down the false boundaries" between nations. This is admittedly a lonely mission. Since social-protest songs are no longer fashionable in the recording industry, the frustrated Havens often escapes to Italy. He spends five to seven months there annually while the rest of his time is divided between other European countries and New York. The constant traveling is exhausting, but still viewing brotherhood as "crucial to world survival," he's not about to slow down.

"All people are basically the same, we all sleep, eat, drink, work for a living, so that's why I'm still out there, we have to come together," says Havens, forty-five, leaning on an Arabic staff, and looking like a latter-day Moses in his flowing, brightly colored cape. Unable to relax, he stands in the middle of his manager's New York office, and continues his fervent plea for world fellowship.

"I'm part of everyone on this planet. I just don't live in Italy or New York, and I'm not just an American. My destiny is tied up with the rest of the world's . . . and even in this period of punk or heavy-metallists, people have to discover their common bonds, they have to see that governments want to keep us apart. I can point them in this direction, I can help them understand that we face the same problems of pollution and atomic weapons. We can only guarantee our mutual survival by communicating with one another . . . and that's the whole point of my music and my work with young people, we have to connect spiritually."

Havens experienced that kind of "fusion" in 1969, on a hillside in upstate New York. In contrast to the loneliness of his youth, when he sang in the street "just to be part of something," Havens was no longer the "alien," excluded from the mainstream because of his skin color. Instead, the thousands of youngsters at that Woodstock gathering made him feel "part of a cosmic whole"; they lifted him "to the top of the mountain," and affirmed the worth of his long struggle to be heard.

"Up until Woodstock, I hadn't seen America, there was no unity, and my singing was only a scream, a cry against the polarization," says Havens, in a soft, melodic voice that's characteristically free of any anger. Smiling beatifically, as if this early suffering had indeed prepared him for a higher calling, he moves around the room with grace. The rows of African beads around his neck tinkle with every stride. And as he emphasizes various points with a wave of his cane, the strapping, heavy-bearded Havens has a mesmerizing effect on visitors. The authority in his voice is so clear, it seems as though he's still speaking from that mountaintop.

"I realized early on, even as a teenager in Brooklyn, that rock 'n' roll was for social purposes. It was the only outlet I had, and the only avenue the white kids had to protest against their condition, to fight the system, our parents, and to express ourselves. That's when there was a common ground in the music, but by the time I was fifteen or sixteen [1956–57], I saw the United States wasn't united. I was living in a country that was supposed to be a conglomeration of everyone, and I found that wasn't true. It was a false image.

"When I realized that these dichotomies also existed in Brooklyn, my 'world community' where every nationality lived, I left school at sixteen, and traveled around the city. Greenwich Village was that universal place I lost in Brooklyn. Thinking people were there, folks who had found a clarity, beatniks. To me, their poetry was a real universal, a natural expression. So I discovered folk music . . . it too was a mental expression . . . it meant something . . . and I eventually bought a guitar."

The "innocence" of the early sixties sparks a glow on his mocha-colored face. Eyeing the rings on each of his fingers, he begins to describe the journey that eventually led to Woodstock.

"I didn't make up my mind to be a singer, it just happened. I sang for fun in the Village, did some hootenannies, and I just liked the sensation of making people smile. I never wanted to be a star, being a star means the business made you, not that you made yourself.

"This guy, though, Jacob Solomon, Magic Jack as we called him, told me that when I was on stage singing, my music was so intense, people didn't get a chance to come down from one song to the next. They sort of phased out, but Jack said I had to talk between songs, that I had to let them out of the heaviness. Well, this helped, it gave me a new camaraderie with the audience . . . and he became my manager [Solomon also managed Janis Ian].

"We had a lot of rough times in the beginning [1963], most nights I was lucky to make five, ten dollars. Yet he still kept trying to get me and Janis started . . . I had faith in him . . . and he eventually took me to Jerry Schoenbaum, who created the Verve label. They couldn't find a sound to put around me, so I wound up doing something with a jazz guitarist, a bar mitzvah bass player, and a classical pianist [the 1967 album was *Mixed Bag*]. I felt terribly privileged. I never thought I was going to do more than those Village clubs. I wasn't looking to make it. As far as I was concerned, songs like 'Morning, Morning,' 'I Can't Make It Anymore,' were a new beginning, I was just starting now. I was conscious of what I was trying to do, I knew what the larger picture was."

After falling silent for a moment to listen to music playing in an adjoining room, Havens cheerfully adds, "Once the record caught on in the spring of '68, I started playing at every university in America. That was a communication time for me. Magic Jack had opened me up to talking, and I saw that audiences just wanted to talk. In the sixties people were more open, they wanted to learn. I absolutely feel I changed people's consciousness, something was happening between audiences and performers. The world was changing and people were being awakened by attitudes that had never touched them before.

"It didn't matter if my songs or remarks were controversial. We were revealing ourselves to each other when talking about drugs, politics, religion. There were no rules governing these exchanges. During the sixties you could discover things about yourself and others, it was a renaissance for experimentation, and I was confirmed in my understanding that the culture was changing. I saw people change right in front of musicians.

"That's what Woodstock was all about. It was the pinnacle of social change, the inevitable result of that communication process. The people there discovered that differences didn't exist between whites and blacks. That was the beginning of the real America. For me to be on stage and see the diversity of people all mixed together and clapping—wow! We were all being moved by the same force. A black could say, 'Look, here's a white guy appreciating the same thing I do . . .' We were affirming our humanity on that New York farm.

"What was supposed to be a concert turned out to be a cosmic event. Why? Woodstock was basically about affirmative action. It confirmed our numbers, for we knew now that if a million people made it to the event, there were at least five million who didn't. People who were opposed to the government, or to the restrictions of their parents, became comrades-in-arms. We said to the world the love-peace vibe was real, that the killing of people in Vietnam or the South wasn't real. But the best thing about the event was its effect on parents. It forced them to reassess their children, they had to recognize that their kids had changed because of this new fraternity. It was very subtle, but Woodstock led to the greening of America all over again. Then it *was* the country of the free and the brave."

In the wake of that "great social upheaval," Havens's life was also transformed. He had won respectable reviews at earlier jazz and pop festivals, but Woodstock secured his standing with young people. They could be whipped into a frenzy by the Who, Jimi Hendrix, and the more "physical" stars in attendance, yet Havens moved the crowd in a different way, as borne out by his haunting rendition of "Freedom" (thousands sat entranced during its performance). He was seen as an inspirational force, a prophet of the new order, and, in keeping with this lofty status, weighty responsibilities were thrust upon him.

"One just couldn't sit back and bask in the glow of a single triumph," says Havens somberly. "There was suffering throughout the world. Everyone has a government, and government is a problem everywhere. So after Woodstock I made yearly trips to Europe. Kids there had to be talked to. I didn't view this as an entertainment thing. They needed a message of hope. They had to storm the palace the same way we went after Nixon."

As Havens recognizes, however, Woodstock also sent a signal to the recording industry. For company officials were also adept at counting bodies. They too were impressed with the huge crowds, and realized there was a tremendous untapped market for the music. Accordingly, rock couldn't be limited to small theaters and cabarets anymore. It had grown into a full-blown phenomenon, and as Havens laments, the revolutionary aspects of the "Aquarian Age" were quickly dwarfed by a wave of commercialism.

"After Woodstock, record execs were only interested in numbers, sales figures . . . so artists like myself, Country Joe, David Bromberg, who depended on intimate contact with audiences, on sharing information with them, were cut off. We belonged to the people, but we were denied access to them because we weren't very commercial," says Havens, overlooking his Top 20 hit "Here Comes the Sun" (1971).

In response to his being "shut out," Havens moved from one record company to another. But since albums like *Mixed Bag II* failed to get any promotion, he goes on to say, "I didn't have any visibility because I wasn't allowed to have any. When I went to a place like Michigan, instead of playing in theaters, I had to go to universities. This hurt me monetarily and emotionally. I wasn't destroyed, thankfully; I had built up enough of a cushion. But I couldn't be part of the big festivals. People were always telling me I wasn't a rock 'n' roll singer, but I eventually realized that America wasn't the entire world. I decided to go where the majority was anyway, and where I had no problems."

Havens's feelings of estrangement led him to Europe. There, he was assured a hero's welcome, for the *Woodstock* movie was still playing to large, enthusiastic audiences. He thus became a fixture on the European touring circuit in the mid seventies. And during those rare lulls in a schedule that often had him traveling for four to six months at a time, he'd vacation in Italy, usually near Naples. This city holds a special fascination for him, since he describes it as "a meeting ground for dozens of different cultures." Having discovered his "Arabic and African roots" amid that mix of nationalities, Havens now credits Naples for reshaping his music, and often fantasizes about living there all year round.

"I've found a musical sophistication in Italy that far surpasses what we know in America," says Havens, who's currently producing a group of young Neapolitan musicians (their band is called Popularia). "People have a basic musical understanding there, the environment is far more realistic and open for an artist. There's real music in Italy, while in the United States synthesizers have replaced real instruments. There's melodies there, you have to remember that fifties and sixties rock 'n' roll was an Italian melody—Dion, Connie Francis, [Paul] Anka, the Four Seasons."

Convinced that people want to hear those melodies again, Havens has recently brought Popularia to America for a cross-country tour. An album partially funded by the Italian government is now in the works. And Havens is already writing songs for the group's follow-up effort.

As for his own singing career, he still visits American campuses, and gives concerts to raise money for the crusade against world hunger. In 1984, he released *Common Ground,* which has received several favorable reviews. Featuring songs like "Things Must Change" and "Lay Ye Down Boys," the album has that inimitable anti-war ring of the 1960s. For nearly every song is dedicated to global unity—and to that kind of world where love replaces the need for weapons.

Clearly proud of this message, Havens insists, "We're right back in the 1960s, I can influence a whole new generation of kids. They might not be the activists of the past, but that kind of consciousness can be stimulated. There are a lot of kids out there who are just discovering rock 'n' roll, and, once again, the music can be used to unlock secrets. It can foster ideas that the governments don't want these people to have . . . and I can help lead them to these truths."

After talking about his own four daughters' prospects of surviving the Nuclear Age, he tries to lighten the mood.

"You won't believe it, but as a kid I didn't care much about music. I only wanted to be a brain surgeon."

Shaking his head in mock disbelief, he laughs heartily. But after letting a few moments pass, he confidently adds, "You know, that dream actually came true. In a way, I did become a brain surgeon, only instead of a knife, I use my music to get into people's heads."

Bo Diddley

Say Hello to Memphis Minnie for Me

"He-e-y-y-y Bo Didd-ley!"

"Yeahhh, sing it . . . !"

"Come on . . . Heeyyy Bo . . . Didd-ley!"

The SRO crowd in New York's Bottom Line Café is on its feet, stomping and yelling to the *chink-a-chink-a-chink, a chink-chink* beat of the Legend's music. Screaming themselves hoarse, these worshippers have turned the place into a rocking Bible Belt gospel house. This is their tribute. They know how important this man is—Diddley has influenced everyone from the Stones to Springsteen with his whipping, hell-fired blues. So the roars continue, through such groundbreakers as "Mona," "Say Man," and the steamy, sex-charged "Who Do You Love?"

"Do it, Bo!" cries a young woman, leaping onto a table, and clapping her hands.

The Legend smiles, and, when others take up the chant, he quiets the crowd with an operatic parody of an Italian love song.

Besides spurring another round of cheers, this mocking impersonation prompts a burst of laughter. An admitted ham, Diddley then closes the set with "You Can't Judge a Book by the Cover," and an explanation.

"You lovely people might be wondering why my name is flashing across this guitar," says Diddley, looking at the miniaturized electric "message board" that is wired into the face of his guitar. "Well, it's been awfully hard for me to get my name up in lights, so I decided to do it myself."

Though Diddley has been overlooked by many rock historians, his dressing room seems like the Vatican at Eastertime. It's filled with well-wishers who each get a bearhug, and a hearty, "How ya doing, man?" A few of these old cronies stay for drinks, and are introduced to the Legend's "hope for the future," his twenty-eight-year-old lead guitarist, Nancy Luca.

"My wife can't understand my taking an interest in her, but I want to help young artists get started," says the fifty-eight-year-old Diddley. "Her being a girl, and me being a man with a family, somehow or another your family doesn't understand. I've wanted to help young people for a real long time; I don't want them to run into the problems I have, but I'm finding myself running into a few obstacles. It's a funky business. Man, you got a wife who says she doesn't mind, but you find out she does mind. I love my wife, but it's a matter of getting ahead and making a few extra bucks to better your condition."

Dressed in a tight-fitting orange bell-bottomed jumpsuit, the 220-pound Diddley wipes the sweat off his rose-tinted glasses, and continues, "This is America. I saw this girl and saw dollar bills, so I took it upon myself to get her career going. Some people in Canada loved the tape we did. The single's called 'I Wanna Do It.' "

To the delight of his guests, the Legend starts to sing.

"I wanna do it, I wanna do it with you. The girl wanna do it, she want to do it with you. The girl knows how to do it . . . dah-de-dah.

"It's jumping music. It's what I call blood-shaking music. I wrote it with her help. We're talking with these Canadian folks about a video, maybe a few other things. It's worth the family problems. You have to prove that you're not out there bullshitting. You're strictly business. It's hard for a woman to understand that. But being in the business I'm in, if I'm going to mess around, I could mess around right around the corner by the house. My aim is not to be looking for a woman. That's bullshit. I'm out for dollar bills. I'm looking for something else to have going when I get to the point where I don't want to jump on stage no more. That day's gotta come; the day I might wanna, but I can't. It's not coming soon, I might make it to eighty, ninety, still jumping and doing my thing, but don't forget, I'm human too."

That basic truth is hard to accept. Rock 'n' roll without the Legend would not be rock 'n' roll. Ever since the early 1950s, he's been thumping out "hambone," the syncopated beat that bridged blues with rock. Nicknamed "Bo Diddley" after an African musical instrument, Ellas Bates McDaniel should thus be called "one of the founding fathers." For in the pre-Elvis era, his cracking and popping rhythms bordered on heresy. To put it bluntly, this was "nigger" music that never made it to the white radio stations.

The adopted son of Mississippi sharecroppers, Bo was used to discrimination. After playing the guitar on Chicago ghetto streets for nickels and dimes, he literally fought his way to the top the hard way. A Golden Gloves boxer, he scored a few impressive KOs before leaving the arena for a nether world of tough, mob-controlled nightclubs. By 1955, he joined fellow "great" Chuck Berry at Checker records, and like a host of other black artists, lost the rights to his music to fast-talking producers.

Diddley is now suing various companies to recoup thousands of dollars in lost royalties. It's unclear if he'll emerge victorious, but on one point there's no argument: his collective body of work has been an encyclopedia for a glittering array of performers. Decidedly indebted to him, the blues-oriented Animals paid homage in their "Story of Bo Diddley." The Legend's songs have frequently turned up on albums by the Stones, the Doors, and the Yardbirds.

In spite of this legacy, Diddley is still scrambling for "dollar bills" (after one of the Bottom Line shows, he lacked the cab fare to get back to his hotel). In a less "funky" world, he wouldn't be doing over two hundred dates a year, or be leaving his Gainesville, Florida home for the rigors of endless touring. He's a national treasure, a charter member of rock's Hall of Fame, and he shouldn't have to be grappling with "tired, aching bones" to prove it.

And yet, Bo's far from discouraged. Buoyed by his new "youth-saving" mission, he's "itchin' to take on all kinds of projects." Especially those "people-saving things" that will help repay an old debt.

"When I first got to Chicago [at age seven in 1935] I saw this violin in church, and the folks there took up a collection and bought me one," recalls Diddley, as he sips a Grand Marnier with a Heineken chaser. "It cost twenty-nine dollars, and Dr. Frederick, the great Professor O. W. Frederick of the Ebenezer Baptist Church, gave me lessons. I've been trying to find him; I think he's dead. I owe everything to that man. He took me—I was a little hard-headed boy running around Chicago—and if it hadn't been for him, there's no telling where I'd be. He trained me without charging me one quarter. I can't forget that. Things were so bad in those days. I was hung up in that dude [the church] so much, I almost slept in there.

"I know what hard times is, I know what it means to be without. That's why I want to help people today, why I want to put something back . . . There was no work in those days, only relief, or welfare, and music helped me make some money. It made me who I am now. By playing on the streets, I learned; it was experience. I learned how to work an audience. Because of music, I didn't have to know what poverty was, I was happy, I was eating everyday.

"Don't get me wrong, I did my dirt. We were all bothered by the Man back then. But those black cats on the [police] force, man, they were rough, they beat your head right in. I was glad for a white dude to arrest me, 'cause all he was gonna say was, 'Get in the wagon, boy.' And that was great. I didn't care nobody calling me 'boy.' Because I *was* a male. That word 'boy' don't mean shit to me. But these dudes would call you something else. And usually the first word was, they'd call you motherfucker right quick. And then if you said something about it—upside your head. You see, they wanted to whup somebody. But you know what, they cleaned up a lot of neighborhoods. They *cleaned* it. You were the rug and they were the vacuum cleaner."

One of the Legend's listeners pops out of his seat, and yells, "Ain't that the truth, brother." In a moment, everyone is laughing uproariously, and exchanging "give-me-five" handshakes.

Nearly falling out of his own chair, Diddley reaches toward one of the "brothers," with his big, heavy palms outstretched for "a little skin."

"You watched your ass in those days," cackles Diddley, his whole body shaking, as he launches into another story. "You didn't monkey around because they had some bad dudes in my neighborhood, called the King Cole Trio and Two Gun Pete. These men were nuts, they hung around the 708 Club where I first started playing. Got old enough to work in this club and Pete come in there, beat on the door one night, and said, 'Come here boy, let me see some ID, go in your pocket slow. They called him Two Gun Pete but he actually had three. Had a .32 back in a holster in the middle of his back, and one on each side of his body. If you took them two, you ain't done nothing, for this man would shoot you, real quick, *guaranteed*. Then there was Indian Joe; he used to throw bombs in store windows. Thank God I'm alive today. These guys protected that club, that's where I played opposite Guitar Red and Memphis Minnie. She sang a song called 'You Are One Dirty Rat' [snapping his fingers, he starts to sing], 'some day I'll find your trail, de-de-de-dedah-dadah, and when I do, I'm gonna hide my shoe under your shirt tail.' "

Slapping his thighs, and pounding out the beat with his left foot, Diddley again bursts into hysterics. His deep bronze face is now covered with perspiration, prompting him to take off his large, black cowboy hat. But he quickly continues, "A lot of great people played there. When I was there, I was known as the Hipsters, or the Langley Avenue Jivecats. I had two guys playing with me, Jerome [Arnold] and Roosevelt Jackson. Roosevelt played the washtub, that was our bass fiddle, and I had a little raggedy *gee-tar*. Those days were great. We had a system. We used to have thirty-nine places, and we'd get a dollar from everyplace we stopped. But we'd end up with more than a dollar, you understand me, we'd look into the hat, shake it, and put it back down there and say, 'One dime one more show.' We'd play a couple numbers, and get ready to walk out the door, the cats would say, 'Hey, hey, wait a minute, play that song you all always play, kid. So we'd put that hat back down there, and say, 'Feed the kitty, feed the kitty.' For kids, sixteen, seventeen, eighteen years old to go to school with fifteen to twenty dollars in your pocket, we was rich. *We was rich!*"

After perfecting his act in such hot spots as the Blue Note, the Rum Buggy, and the Sawdust Trail ("The sawdust was so thick you didn't know what you were stepping in"), Bo married his first wife, an eighteen-year-old who obviously had different taste in music, for one day she smashed his now characteristic rectangular guitar with a Pepsi bottle.

"Me and my old lady really got into it, whoa, did we ever," moans Diddley, "I don't like Pepsi today, 'cause it beat up my *gee-tar*. My [foster] mother came home, and I was sitting on the sidewalk, crying. My mother says, 'What's wrong with you?' I says 'You better go up there and get her, because I'm gonna choke her.' My mother said, 'Don't you put your hands on that girl.' I said, 'Well, how about throwing her out the window or something, anything.' My mother kept telling me 'Don't you touch that girl.' Here I had to pay rent, I have no *gee-tar*, no amplifier, and she said, 'Good for you. You ought to get a real job.' I said, 'I am working,' and what does she say? Just like a lotta folks who didn't like the guitar, she says, 'For the devil.' "

In 1955, Bo overcame these obstacles and went to work for Checker records as a backup musician on several Chuck Berry tunes (including "Memphis" and "Sweet Little Rock 'n' Roller"). Diddley supplemented his income for a while by operating an elevator in an auto-parts factory, but by the end of the year he had his first R & B hit, "Bo Diddley." As was customary in racially divided America, that song didn't make it to the white-dominated pop charts. This latter province, which assured commercial rewards, was reserved for the likes of Pat Boone and Brenda Lee. So the spinning of legends, at least for blacks, was all the more difficult.

Still bothered by that "racial crap," Bo angrily raises his voice, to give his listeners a lesson in rock 'n' roll history. "All these music books are bullshit, plain bullshit; there's enough credit going to the Caucasian musicians without excluding the blacks and what they did. People are given credit who weren't even involved in rock 'n' roll. It's a racial thing, pure and simple. I was very much excluded, because I was the first son of a bitch out there in the first place, the very first, number one. But I just started to say that, because no one else was going to say it. Lotsa kids out here don't even know I exist. They look up and the first thing they see is Elvis Presley. The music didn't start with him, he only started six, seven, eight months down the line. The boat was already in the water when he jumped on board."

Struggling to make a living, Bo wasn't so outspoken in the late 1950s. Along with a band that included his half-sister "the Duchess," and maracas shaker Jerome Green, he hustled between one-nighters, thinking this was the way to the Promised Land.

Bo's patience finally paid off in 1959. "Say Man," his biggest-selling single, hit both charts, and gave him long-sought respectability in rock circles. Now other artists started to listen to his frenzied "hambone" beat. For these driving, highly amplified rhythms weren't endemic to the white man's world. Angry and explosive, Bo's tunes were shaped by a far more tortured experience, his many years of frustration.

But recognition caused more problems that still provoke Bo's fury.

"Yeah, I started a new type of music, you hear my little thing all the time, that goes chonk-chonk, chonk-chonk, chonk-chonk-chonk, chonk-chonk," says Bo bitterly. "But other people ripped it off so much, I quit hollerin' about it. There's nothing I can do legally; they can get away with using phrases of a song, or twelve bars. But if I used stuff like that, I would acknowledge that I got this from such and such person, and they don't, this is what bothers me. I don't steal nothin' from nobody.

"People that produce the groups don't acknowledge nothin'. They took my stuff. They know they did. That's the hurtin' thing. I don't mind these cats copying me. That's great. I got something they want. I'm the leader. But don't exclude me, and say I had nothin' to do with it. That's the part that hurts."

So a soul-splitting conflict arose, that would torment Diddley for years. On the one hand, he was an integral part of the rock world, the inspirational founding father whose riffs were freely mimicked, but on the other, he was the despised alien, our invisible brother who felt the cruelest stings of racism.

To make matters even worse, Diddley was also a victim of changing musical styles. Once the British Invasion gave way to the mellower sounds of Donovan and the Spoonful, or to the Dylan-led folk renaissance, Bo was *passé.* This wasn't a time for demonic-edged tunes, so he tried to stay current with more upbeat motifs, like his foray into surfing music *(Surfin' with Bo Diddley* and *Beach Party,* in 1963–64).

"They were pretty bad; that stuff wasn't the real me," says the Legend, nearly whispering, "I hated those surfin' albums, to me that stuff sucked. I never wanted to do it. 'Hey Bo Diddley,' that's me, that's what I'm all about. Look, I came along with this rhythm shit, ching-a-ching-a-ching, ching-ching, it sounded like twelve instruments. A locomotive is the way people described it. It was frightening. Kids started buying the records, and parents were so freaked out, they broke the records. So forget that surfin' crap, or some of that other nonsense *(Bo Diddley Is a Gunslinger,* and *Have Guitar Will Travel).* I'm the sucker who opened the door, and everyone ran through it. I'm the damn doorman."

The Rolling Stones recognized this. They made the Legend one of their opening acts on a few international tours. But essentially, Bo was out of vogue from the mid-1960s to the late 1970s. Except for occasional appearances in small American blues clubs, he was restricted to the European circuit. In countries like England and France, however, Bo's legacy found new currency. He wasn't a forgotten man abroad. And feeling legitimized, he could "dream again." All kinds of "damn things" were suddenly possible.

"You'll be surprised what I'm fixin' to do," says Diddley, who toured with the Clash in 1979, and then appeared alongside Eddie Murphy in *Trading Places* (1983). "I'm gonna show people the other side of Bo Diddley. Why am I gonna do this? Do you like broken records, go *nyeh, nyeh, nyeh, nyeh?* Wouldn't that drive you crazy? Well, I feel the same way. I have a lot of other talents, and maybe some people out there might like it. I don't want to go down in history as just a chink-a-chink-a-chink, a chink-chink, because that's the way everyone describes me. They have no idea about my potential or anything that goes on in my head. You'll see what I can do, you'll see. You're not supposed to leap out of your category, your slot, to something else, but I'm going to fool a lot of people. You'll see."

After hinting that he would like to own a dance hall, Diddley gives Nancy Luca a warm smile and says, "I want to team up with this young lady. I think we can do it together. I know we can make great music. I want those greens."

A few of the brothers add a loud "Amen," but there's no pumping of the flesh or belly-laughing. Everyone realizes the future will be difficult for Bo, that several obstacles complicate his making a comeback at age fifty-eight.

The Legend knows this too. Sitting quietly for a moment, he looks uncharacteristically grim and withdrawn. Suddenly, he seems tired, the dragged-out victim of too many encores.

But he's also a real pro. On several levels, the show will go on. So he dabs a little makeup onto his face, signaling that the "old locomotive" is ready for more bravura performances.

"I'm not making the money that I should be making, or that I want to make," says the Legend somberly. "But I'm happy. My day is just about fixed to come. In my lifeline I have a freaky belief that what I'm doing wasn't meant for me to do until now, like helping this young lady. I believe that somehow or another I've reached the point where it's time for me to do somethin' with someone else—to help *them* get started. I'm not worried about my family problems, or anythin' else. Helping the young is just somethin' I've got to do."

Alice Cooper

If Alice Doesn't Live Here, Who Does?

Blame the nightmare on Count Dracula, *The Creature from the Black Lagoon,* and on Jack the Ripper's deadly knife thrusts.

The exploits of these villains were so stunning, so grotesquely hypnotic, that two personalities clashed in the style of Dr. Jekyll and Mr. Hyde. It was an unholy chemistry, doomed to wreak chaos. One side of this new persona was the All-American boy next door, as innocent as *Leave It to Beaver*'s Eddie Haskell. Symbolic of Dullsville, U.S.A., he evoked his own terrors. But the other combatant in this psychological tug-of-war was even more loathsome. For this figure was a modern-day incarnation of the Marquis de Sade.

Eventually, all that is evil won out, the real-life Vincent Furnier gave way to a devilish stage presence, Alice Cooper. Dramatizing anything that was gross and perverted—bestiality, necrophilia, sado-masochism, infanticide—he dangled a boa constrictor around his neck, wore fangs, and appeared against a backdrop of guillotines, bloodied dolls, and disfigured mannequins. As a child, Vincent adored horror movies—Bela Lugosi fascinated him—and by 1972, these images of wanton destruction were resurrected. Freed from the crypt, the beast trampled on all that society held sacred, parental authority figures, government leaders, sexual mores, religion. Similar to Lenny Bruce, Alice Cooper became the messiah of a new libertinism, or, as he hauntingly chuckles, "the *National Enquirer* of rock."

Cooper's androgynous appearance and simulated sex orgies may have scandalized the rock world, and they assuredly horrified parents, but by

1975, his *danse macabre* was *not* an act. Not anymore. By drinking two
quarts of Seagram's V.O. daily, Furnier actually became Alice C. He
lost sight of his true self. For years, the "violent, insane, distorted" edge
to his psyche dominated him. He was a man possessed, transformed,
like the mother-possessed Anthony Perkins in *Psycho.* Vincent/Alice
was so detached from reality, the character switch became permanent,
and his original identity was all but forgotten.

Playing fiendish, hide-and-seek games with one's self demands an
exorbitant amount of energy. Cooper stretched his mind and body to
the breaking point, and he was eventually confined to a psychiatric
institute ("It was just like *One Flew Over the Cuckoo's Nest*") for alco-
hol-rehabilitation treatment. That experience was another sojourn in
hell.

Yet Furnier has emerged from the wreckage to regain control of himself—and Alice. The two of them are now co-existing, or "living more
in balance with each other," according to Vincent. And now that a 1985
"comeback" tour has wrought its predictable madness, Alice has shown
himself to be as immutable as Boris Karloff and Lugosi. Once again,
we've been assaulted with the "Thing" that wouldn't die.

No wonder Vincent, or Alice, laughs devilishly. The critics in 1972–
73 said this strange "shock-rock" figure wouldn't last, that it was too
"hard" for a world dominated by mellow Woodstock sounds. Cooper
not only fooled them, but his deafening, unsettling perverseness, his
stage act, ushered in a whole new era of rock theatrics. Cannibalizing
the guerrilla street theater of the 1960s, each Cooper show whipped
crowds into a savage hysteria, a catharsis to exorcise their darkest emotions. In time, these "trips to Hades" permeated the rock scene, influencing groups like Kiss, Led Zeppelin, Devo, and more currently, Van
Halen, Twisted Sister, and Mötley Crüe. Cooper can now be viewed as
the original punker, the force that plunged rock into upheaval.

Why did the Woodstock Era end? Cooper didn't bring about this
revolution by himself. America was experiencing its own catharsis during the bombing of Southeast Asia and the Watergate horror show.
Perhaps he only tapped into the Satanic, the ugliness that was first
unleashed by Altamont, but he did give the grotesque a new acceptabil-
ity. He was the apostle of a new musical order. How did he gain such
currency? What was ripe among us for him to become rock's Prince of
Darkness? That story is called the Revenge of Alice Cooper.

Evangelism wasn't a strange departure for this budding rock legend. Though Vincent Furnier was the All-American boy, with an interest in sports and fast cars, his background is steeped in fire and brimstone. Both his father and grandfather were revivalist-style preachers. To them, the Apocalypse was always upon us, and sinners would have to purge themselves, through emotionally wrenching displays of repentance. The church was another type of theater, where allegories of rebirth and damnation constantly played.

These weren't the only blood-curdling images bombarding Furnier. The youngster loved horror movies. All through his impressionable adolescence (despite rumors of his being reincarnated from a witch, he was born in Detroit in 1948), Vincent huddled next to his sister as Godzilla gored another victim.

"I don't think I ever grew out of my horror-movie phase; I was diabolical even as a kid," confesses Cooper, dressed completely in black and standing in front of a living-room wall lined with over six hundred Grade B movie cassettes. These remarks are an understatement, for his thirty-seventh-floor totally glassed-in Chicago lakefront apartment is a rogue's gallery that would even give Alfred Hitchcock pause. Besides a framed silver dagger that was allegedly used by Jack the Ripper, and a stuffed raven perched above a signed photo of Edgar Allan Poe, there are dozens of framed or encased autographs on the walls. The signatures of Lon Chaney, Oscar Wilde, Boris Karloff, and Harry Houdini are only a few of Cooper's acquisitions (there are about two hundred more "bad guys" in this collection). In the middle of the room, there is a six-foot-long ebony coffin. It's Cooper's "altarpiece," for inside it, caressed by red velvet, an autographed photo of Bela Lugosi lies in state.

"I especially liked Dwight Faye, the guy who ate spiders and rats in Dracula movies; he was an unsung hero," Cooper continues, after offering his guests a more conventional lunch. It's a bit unnerving to see him playing the quintessential host. One has been warned about entering his lair, yet instead of encountering Alice, that menacing stage ogre, visitors find the private Cooper to be cordial, easygoing, and boyishly enthusiastic.

"Mummies, crazed werewolf stories, the 'Twilight Zone,' the worst movies imaginable, I loved all this stuff . . . *The Creature from the Black Lagoon,* now that was a classy movie. I think that's the first film that forced me to leave the theater. I had to run out; that was a pretty good creature!"

Ghoulishly, these phantoms preyed on the youngster's mind. By the time Furnier was sixteen, he had moved to Phoenix and become a high school track star. But there was no escaping his childhood "friends," or his love of the shocking.

"I was a big Elvis fan at seven, but once the Beatles came along, I saw the horror on my parents' faces," explains Cooper. "I figured if they could affect my parents that way, I wondered what I could do to affect an entire nation. I always had this vision; if you were going to do rock 'n' roll, why not use the entire stage? Since I liked these horror creatures and was attracted to them, I thought that was a great way to do the stage thing."

Succumbing to these mischievous impulses, Vincent assembled his first band, the Earwigs, in 1964. Imitating the Beatles, and using a hastily constructed guillotine as a prop, the group appropriately debuted on Halloween Night to anguished howls of disapproval.

Recognizing that the Earwigs were "pretty awful," Furnier tried to work some magic. After conferring with playing partners, Glen Buxton and Dennis Dunaway, he changed the group's name to the Spiders, then adopted a harder, Yardbird-edged sound. This shift soon paid off. The Spiders became a regular act at Phoenix's VIP club. Once they began attracting "thousands of people" every weekend, Vincent's imagination ran wild.

Envisioning stardom, he renamed the band the Nazz (after a Yardbirds' song), and moved to Los Angeles in 1967. The group quickly distinguished themselves, as many critics dubbed them, as "the worst band in town." This didn't worry Furnier, however. He had a more pressing concern: Todd Rundgren's band was already called the Nazz. So, deciding that the "Beatle peace-love thing was over," Vincent went for the jugular.

"I had to come up with something that would get us press, and Alice Cooper just came along," recalls Coop, who legally changed his name in 1975. He snickers as he talks about manipulating the media, and his deep, dark eyes take on a playful, yet disturbing glint. Perhaps it's the result of one's own overactive imagination, but with the fog rolling in off the lake, his horseshoe-shaped apartment is suddenly shrouded in mist, which makes him seem very sinister.

"I could've said Mary Armstrong or anything. But the name Alice Cooper came up, I don't know why, it just sounded like some sick little girl. The name was perfect. People, the media, are going to expect a blond folksinger, and they're going to get this *Clockwork Orange* kind of band. It worked; no one could understand what was going to happen. Everyone was taking acid, and peace and love, but when they got us, we were anything but peace and love [he chuckles, chillingly]. We were militant rock.

"I was bored with all the flowers, with the peace and love. I didn't think it was exciting. There was nothing exciting about 'Saving the Whales' or legalizing grass. What was thrilling to me was getting on stage, and turning the volume up past people's limits. And blowing everyone out of the room."

When asked about this urge, Cooper defiantly continues, "Why not? We were pretty much punks. The band was like a motorcycle gang. We were there just to raise hell. We were rebelling against everybody. We felt the only way that we were going to get press, the only way we'd be recognized, was to upset the entire apple cart."

That intensity first flared with a vengeance at Lenny Bruce's Memorial Birthday Party (Halloween night 1967, in a club called the Cheetah). Borrowing Janis Joplin's gold lamé pants, and wearing high-heeled boots, the black-mascaraed Cooper ignited a near riot, as the stoned crowd was repulsed by his assault on the sound barrier. After having heard the Jefferson Airplane and the Grateful Dead play more familiar songs, and shocked by this frightful apparition, most people scurried to the exits.

Frank Zappa remained seated. Seeing a kindred spirit at work, he soon concluded a deal with Cooper's manager, Shep Gordon, that brought Alice to Straight Records. "Frank loved us. He thought our ability to drive people out of there was great," exclaims Cooper joyously. "He said anybody that has this much energy can turn things around. He understood us, and why we threw so much at people, musically and visually, that they overdosed. We bombarded their senses. The critics said we couldn't play, but Frank said, 'Whatever you're doing, keep doing it.' He had never seen anything like us. Our arrangements were so weird, within two minutes there were thirty-five arrangements, so he'd sit there and say, 'I don't think I could even teach the Mothers [of Invention] with this material, that's how strange it is.' "

Cooper's first two albums, *Pretties for You* and *Easy Action,* had an even stronger effect on the record-buying public. They were so outrageously "different," that both works died on the racks. Admitting that they were "terrible" (one reviewer called *Pretties for You* "a tragic waste of plastic"), Cooper adds, "I could see what they [critics] were talking about. There was no handle to the music; it was like early Devo. People wanted to like us, but they had no reason to."

Hoping to widen his appeal, Cooper switched to Warner Records in 1970, where he worked with producer Bob Ezrin. They were in the studio together for six months, refining certain production techniques, and finally, a handle was found. In *Love It to Death,* the work that featured the million-selling single, "Eighteen," Cooper spoke directly to teenagers' discontents. He was an avenging angel against a morally bankrupt system, the voice—and stage act—which trumpeted a Nietzschean brand of anarchism.

Alice didn't do this by aping the "messagy" radicals of the 1960s. There was no spiritual absolutism or revolutionary preaching in his lyrics. Everything was more free-form than that. While far from subtle, Cooper's imagery was highly evocative and grotesquely sensational. He wanted people's imaginations to run wild, like the distorted subliminal messages on a Salvador Dali canvas.

"What would you rather read, *The Wall Street Journal* and a story about a tax cut, or a paper announcing, 'Man Born with Dog's Head'?" asks Cooper, underscoring his philosophy about show business. "No matter what had happened in the past, I didn't feel that people went to rock shows to be preached to. I go to shows to escape. I hated the idea of going to something, and having people tell me what I should do about Vietnam. What we were doing was saying, 'Go have fun.'

"I was rebelling against any form of authority. We had one song, 'Don't Talk Old to Me,' and there was one line in it that said, 'Don't shake that finger in my face no more, 'cause I might bite it off and spit it on the floor.' That's what the Alice Cooper thing was all about."

Since "Eighteen" and "School's Out" (a 1972 hit) echoed this rebellious note, horrified parents understandably viewed Cooper as either "a drug addict, a homosexual, or a deviant from another planet." Recognizing the PR value of being America's black sheep, Alice didn't do anything to soften this image. In fact, he milked it, and by the time of his notorious 1973 Billion Dollar Babies tour, Cooper's ever-evolving stage act had become "fully perfected." It went beyond "the little horror movies" of the late 1960s, to incorporate all the carnality of an orgiastic blood rite. Now, he was ready to drive a stake into America's heart.

By bringing Dracula to life.

At every Babies performance, a thick vapor enveloped the stage, and as the music grew deafening, Cooper leaped into view, outfitted in black leather, with "Eva Marie Snake" wrapped around his neck. Then the hijinks began. Using a real guillotine with a forty-pound blade, he slipped his head into the contraption, and *Zap!* While the whistling hatchet missed Alice's throat by eight inches, a "bloodied" plaster of Paris head would bounce onto the floor. Next came the gallows. Cooper stood on the platform, the floor dropped out, and by the use of an ingenious parachute device concocted with piano wire, he seemed to be actually hanging in suspension. A smoking electric chair and coffins were also on stage, but, even more striking, Cooper played the vampire, bludgeoning dolls and mannequins to pieces. Each dismembered item was splattered with blood, and in the spirit of Bram Stoker's famed character, Cooper feasted on the red liquid.

Besides insisting that these theatrics were straight out of the American mainstream, Coop proudly credits himself with "liberating the stage." That's undeniable. The Babies tour, which grossed $6 million in a few months (in 1973, the band's revenues totaled $17 million), revolutionized the production of rock shows. It was unprecedented to employ forty full-time technicians, to use such sophisticated props, and to spend over a million dollars on special effects. Cooper felt the acid-rock shows of the past were primitive, that bands "merely played," so he saw the need "to thoroughly open up the stage."

But to middle America, Alice was only flirting with the devil. Since every Babies performance celebrated raw, brutal sex, deaths, and destruction, Cooper was seen as another Charles Manson. How could people think otherwise? At one show, he threw parts of a hacked-up watermelon into the audience, prompting one newspaper to announce, "Cooper Drenches Crowd with Blood." He was also denounced for killing live chickens and drinking their blood on stage. In truth, the birds that were thrown at him were flung back at the crowd—only then were they destroyed.

Yet reality didn't matter anymore. Taking advantage of the rumors, or starting his own, manager Gordon planted stories with the press. Blindly cooperating, the media portrayed Cooper as the Son of Satan, the demonic figure who ate raw flesh, threatened the young, and violated America's most sacred taboos.

Vincent Furnier would have objected to these media fabrications. While loving the horrific, he was too straight to flail out at the system. The Vincent persona loved America, for "this is the only place in the world where you can go out for pizza at five in the morning, or have TV on all night long."

But Vincent wasn't in control anymore. Alice, or the Dostoevskian dark side of his personality, was calling the shots. For Vincent couldn't have staged such an extravagant, high-powered show. Something far more perverse was needed, something that wouldn't be created by a few hours in a makeup room. He had to actually *be* Alice.

Admitting that this psychodrama smacked of Dr. Jekyll and Mr. Hyde, Cooper says, "I had to drink two bottles of whiskey a night just to cope with Alice. I say cope, because I felt I had to be Alice all the time, otherwise the audience would lose their love affair with Alice. What I didn't realize was that you can't live an intense character like that all the time—that's what happened to Jim Morrison and Keith Moon. I don't think I'm crazy now, but I was unbalanced for a while, and that's putting it mildly.

"It's not because my ideas were wrong, but because the alcohol was distorting them. When I play Alice I let all of the insanity that is stored up in me be part of the adrenaline, the catalyst; so there were periods, years, when I didn't see anything of Vincent. I was totally Alice. At that point, there was no time not to be Alice. I just became Alice *all the time.*"

This is hardly an exaggeration, for in the mid-seventies, Cooper rarely took a break from touring. He had the money to buy mansions in Beverly Hills and Phoenix, but his life was nothing more than a string of Holiday Inns (the Babies tour, for example, traveled to sixty-five cities in seventy-two days). Though this was grueling, to say the least, the band had become one of the top drawing acts in the world. So rather than risk any loss of popularity, Alice kept the show on the road. Having always dreamed of being "the act that everyone was talking about," Alice was not ready to give it up, even if it eventually cost him his physical and mental well-being.

In the meantime, Cooper's near-dictatorial rule came under fire. The other band members grew tired of the theatrics. Feeling that enough barriers had been broken, they wanted to move away from the violence, so critics would view them more seriously.

Cooper thought they were crazy. "While everyone was trying to sound like us, the band suddenly wanted to sound like Pink Floyd or the Doors," recalls Cooper, thirty-eight, brushing back his black hair, which is highlighted with henna to camouflage the gray. Moving over to a window to hide his disgust, he crisply continues, "There was a giant insecurity in the fact that we were successful—they didn't feel as good as 90 percent of the bands. But they *were.* I said 'Wait a minute, guys, you have this backward, we're number one right now, everybody's imitating us.' I believed in the sound [Bob] Ezrin had created, while everyone else drifted away from that."

The group disbanded in late 1974, but Cooper formed a new unit for his 1975 *Welcome to My Nightmare* tour. Except for Alice's becoming even more of a daredevil (he was now propelled out of a cannon), the act remained basically the same.

Changes would have been foolish. More than ever, Cooper's violent skits mirrored events in the nonrock world—North Vietnam's brutal, *1984*-style takeover of South Vietnam, and the continuing Watergate nightmare. "Shock rock" had become more than a battle cry of a few deviates, as evidenced by legions of chain-wearing, leather-clad adolescents. Cooper tapped into a distinct, ever-widening subculture. These teenagers were so disgusted with society, they dropped out, turned punk, and adopted Cooper as their spiritual guru.

Yet the system has a way of dealing with rebels. Just as the Beatles were co-opted into the mainstream, Cooper's growing acceptance ironically led him into America's true heartland—the *Nightmare* tour played Las Vegas and Lake Tahoe casinos.

Not wanting to be coupled with the Establishment, Cooper tries to dismiss the significance of this "breakthrough," insisting "we still played for the kids, not for the gamblers. We only played there one time."

Despite these disavowals, Cooper wasn't the outsider anymore. Besides playing Las Vegas for week-long stretches, he was nominated for a Grammy, and even appeared in an hour-long ABC-TV show, "Alice Cooper—the Nightmare." Outlaws aren't treated with such respect. Nor are they allowed to sit next to America's most beloved icons—on the "Tonight Show," or "The Hollywood Squares."

Alice (or Vincent?) made a few appearances on that game show, and when asked about this strange character switch, he stammers, "Well, that was, you know, that was—the funniest thing about that, I figured, eh, everybody would get the joke of Alice Cooper showing up on 'Hollywood Squares.' I sort of overestimated the sense of humor of the public."

After giggling nervously, he continues, "Well, I figured it would be the funniest thing in the world to be on there. It's an All-American thing. The same people that wouldn't let their kids go to see Alice Cooper would be asking me questions to win their refrigerator. It was hysterical because I was very good at these shows; at home I watched them constantly. It was hysterical. These same people had me for their partner on a quiz show.''

Though Cooper laughs heartily now, back then rock critics weren't amused. They assailed him for selling out. Remembering these blistering attacks, he soon adds, "It was so tongue-in-cheek. I would look out at the camera, and I was like sending out mental messages to the kids, 'Look at these jerks up here, can't they tell that they're being infiltrated by us.'

"My audience didn't get it, they did not get the joke. They thought I was selling out [Cooper's cheeks redden, and his voice bristles with anger]. I didn't want to be on 'Hollywood Squares,' but I thought it was a real slap in the face to the public—the older generation—that I would turn up on the show."

Cooper would like us to believe that he was still "goofing" on the media—that Alice was his villainous self—but, at the same time, the public also heard about his socializing with Groucho Marx, Perry Como, Fred Astaire, and other Establishment figures. But Mr. Evil Incarnate admittedly enjoyed being on 'Hollywood Squares.' "I had a great time . . . I think it's an American's God-given right to watch quiz shows." Only one conclusion can be drawn from these reflections —by 1976–77, Vincent was battling Alice for supremacy.

After working so strenuously for several years, Cooper could no longer cope with Alice. That character demanded too much of him. His alcohol consumption had reached a point where he "couldn't cross a room without taking a drink." The act had grown so large, he was now responsible for the livelihood of over fifty people. And since he insisted on working six nights a week ("Once you're so successful you can't give it up"), the strain simply overwhelmed him.

Depressed and exhausted, Cooper voluntarily entered a New York psychiatric clinic in 1978. He underwent months of therapy, hoping that would clear up his drinking problem. "I wanted to see if I could play Alice straight," says Coop, as his pregnant wife, Sheryl, and four-year-old daughter, Calico, enter the room. After eyeing them affectionately, he returns to his tormented past.

"I was used to Beverly Hills, right, my Rolls-Royce and stuff, and suddenly here I was in this little room. There were some real cases in this place, it was a haven for a writer. You could sit there and observe people who were really out of their minds. These people had some serious problems, and you had to talk to them about it. That gave me a different perspective.

"I had this doctor who didn't allow me to blame Alice for the drinking. 'Cause when you look at it, Alice doesn't drink, when I'm on stage I don't drink. So the doctor asked me, 'Who's doing the drinking, you or Alice?' And I'd always blame everything on Alice, and he'd say 'No, Alice doesn't drink, Alice performs.' I had to digest that. I totally understand that now, and that's why I can talk about Alice in the third person. Before, I'd call myself Alice all the time."

Cooper managed to lay off booze for over a year. During that time he did two confessional albums, *From the Inside* ("How You Gonna See Me Now" brought him back to the charts) and *Flush the Fashion*. Both records re-created his hospital experiences, but Cooper wasn't content with writing vinyl history. Desirous of reenacting his "Cuckoo's Nest" confinement, he took the "Madhouse Rock" tour onto the road, complete with surgical outfits, scalpels, and oxygen tents.

By 1980, the charms of the Seagram's bottle again proved irresistible. "I started out real simply, real dumb, like a complete jerk," says Cooper, a frown on his tanned, wrinkle-free face. His drinking didn't return to the two-quarts-a-day level, but the more he worked, the more he drank. That realization, coupled with the birth of his daughter in 1981, forced him to give up touring. "I just wasn't interested in working, so I didn't do anything at all."

A self-confessed TV junkie, Cooper watched soaps and reruns of "Father Knows Best" for over three years. His Chicago apartment has eighteen TV sets, all of which are constantly turned on.

Finally tiring of this life in late 1984, Coop surveyed "the new technology" around him, and has since restyled his stage act to resemble Mel Gibson's *Road Warrior*. Insisting that he has total control over Alice now, Cooper confidently adds, "The new Alice is much more of a killer, he's combat ready. He's more vicious than ever. My show is eighties' insanity. It's high tech, but it looks postnuclear.

"I think there's going to be a real breakdown in techno stuff. I can see thousands of TV sets piled up as art, piles of broken aerials and transistors. I've been thinking of doing the 'Ultimate Killing Machine'; the whole stage would eat everything, the band, anyone near the stage. It would be a machine that has gone totally out of its mind, but it would be under the control of Alice."

Violence is Alice Cooper. The stage act has undergone several transformations, yet the "bloody" mutilations remain a constant. Cooper says it's now therapeutic for him to vent this "craziness," that these gross, often frightening displays keep his "split personality" in balance.

Vehemently insisting "There'd be no psychiatrists if everybody had an Alice character," he calls his outrageous behavior "innovative," and delightedly credits the violence for "blowing the sissy rockers off the charts. It made me the Francis Scott Key of the punk generation."

Yet if Cooper is indeed saner, certain questions naturally arise. Assuming that he's given up drinking, and *is* in control of Alice, doesn't this bode ill for his stage show? If he isn't crazy anymore, how can those diabolical forces be unleashed?

When asked to respond, Cooper stops watching "The Honeymooners" on an imposing five-and-a-half-foot TV screen, raises his eyebrows, and grins demonically. "Vincent and Alice used to be involved in a friendly war with each other," he says, "but at this point, I can't figure out who's more dangerous. When I play Alice on stage, the personality that makes him work is the one that watches TV shows. Vincent loves 'Father Knows Best.' I'm a real good daddy—I'm Ward Cleaver in that respect—but when I think 'Where does that insanity come from?' then I wonder about Vincent's sanity."

An eerie chuckle punctuates these remarks, and once again, Vincent (or Alice?) falls under the spell of Jackie Gleason.

James Brown

The Artist of the Century

"Soul Brother Number One" has a brand-new bag. Once the fiery crusader against heroin, ghetto poverty, and racism, he's now styling himself as an Angel of Peace, the Kissinger of the music set.

Ethiopia is his first concern. Joining the international relief effort, Mr. Soul has donated his talents to OXFAM, an organization that raises money for food and medicine. Through a series of benefits, in clubs and theaters, he's already raised thousands of dollars, in the hope of alleviating human suffering.

Appearing at a wild, hastily arranged City Hall press conference with New York Mayor Ed Koch, James Brown eyes the throng of reporters, and announces, "I want to feed human beings—kids—they have no choice, they can do nothing about it. I believe in OXFAM, what they're doing. I saw the things they were doing, and feeding people is one of my pet projects. I called the White House to see if they were legit, so this made sense to me. Ethiopia is where Christianity comes from, but whether people are Russians, Jewish, Italian, German, Arabic, African, it makes no difference—they're human beings—and helping people is one of my pet projects."

After alluding to the riots in the wake of Martin Luther King's assassination and his efforts to defuse the violence, Brown continues, "With something like this, you forget rhetoric, politics, or a man's reputation. Whether it's a Nixon, or a [Jesse] Jackson, or whether it's a Reagan, a Mayor Koch, a James Brown, a Michael Jackson, or a Boy George, or whoever it is, you have to forget the rhetoric and do something good.

We're talking about feeding people, we do that first. I take my music from God. I've been lucky enough to be the artist of the century, but thank God, because that came from God, it didn't come from me. I never had any formal training in my life, and I put it [the music] all together in my head."

In apparent deference to Brown's lofty stature, Mayor Koch puts his arm around the Soul King, and whispers a few pleasantries. Looking like the Odd Couple, they give new meaning to the phrase, "Politics makes strange bedfellows." For the avuncular, serious-faced Koch is anything but funky. Dressed in a camel-colored cardigan sweater and tie, the mayor is a pale ghost compared to the flamboyant Brown, who's decked out in a pinstriped suit, turquoise shirt, and a gleaming Navajo Indian medallion. Their worlds are as different as their hairdos; Brown's is an inspiration, slicked back into a shiny pompadour, while the mayor comes up empty. Koch might also draw a blank if asked to talk about Brown's major hits, "Papa's Got a Brand New Bag," "It's a Man's, Man's, Man's World," "I Got the Feeling," and "Say It Loud, I'm Black and I'm Proud."

But no matter. Once the two men embrace, cameras flash. To better capture this memorable moment, reporters and photographers scramble for position. The pushing and jostling are reminiscent of an opening night at the Apollo. And warming to the occasion, J.B. gives the mayor more than a radiant smile. Aware that an election is coming up, Brown declares, "Mayor Koch is a good man, a very good man. I really believe in the man, I may make enemies by saying that, but I believe in Mayor Koch. He's good for the city. He exceeds everybody as far as I'm concerned, and I'm not saying this because I'm here. My wife can attest to that, so you know I'm legit. She hears it all the time."

Everyone laughs except for Koch. Surprised by Brown's foray into New York politics, he simply beams, and thinks about the endorsement's impact on the black vote.

The Soul King meanwhile continues to rhapsodize about his new role on the international scene.

"I've just been asked [by President Reagan] to represent our country, to go to the Soviet Union and also China. It's in the plannin' stages. I'm not gonna be talking, I'm gonna be entertaining. I'm gonna be somebody who takes a good feeling to them. I'm gonna try to help the relationship between both countries. Hopefully they won't start a nuclear war. I have a new song out called 'Unity,' that's going throughout the world, all countries, that's all the world is—[we have] to come forward and sit down and talk of a way to get away from nuclear warfare, because I think that's somethin' we all want to get away from. It's the *last* thing we want to think about. We want to think about livin', not dyin'. So, we'll use that kind of message to impress upon them our wish to extend life.

"I feel honored that I can be a representative, not just of the United States, but of all people. I'm glad the United States wants me to go. I'm glad I've kept myself in the people's eye, and in a position where my government wants me to go. I'm glad that all people here want me to represent them in a lot of different things. I'm glad that they feel I've been that type of fellow—faithful and dedicated to humanity. If I don't like somethin', I speak out on it, whether the president wants me to say it or not, whether the mayor, whether the governor, don't make no difference. But I think we, as citizens, have that right, we, as citizens and human beings, have the right to bring people together. And I've done that all through my life. I'm here because I can help."

Why should J.B., the man known around the world as "Mr. Dynamite," stick to music? Already a larger-than-life figure, he could warm the hearts of Kremlin bosses with his "bad ass" lyrics, and whirling-dervish stage acrobatics (he says he loses eight pounds during every twisting, body-jerking show). Haven't ghetto-toughened black youths responded in the past to such funkified pleas as "King Heroin" and "Don't Be a Drop-Out"? And while the East-West chill is a crisis of a far different sort, Brown shouldn't be quickly dismissed as just another dreamy-eyed goodwill ambassador. He's already done the impossible.

A shoeshine boy during the Depression who sang for pennies in the streets of Augusta, Georgia, Brown is now credited with selling over 75 million records. Before embarking on a career that would chalk up twenty gold singles, he spent three years in a reformatory for armed robbery. Instead of surrendering to the despair that entraps most poor, uneducated blacks, the nineteen-year-old Brown escaped his surroundings by becoming a professional boxer. When that didn't pan out, he turned to baseball, but a leg injury soon ended his pitching career. Shrugging off these disappointments, Brown returned to Augusta, put together a gospel group called the Swanees (they later became the Famous Flames), and in 1956 recorded "Please, Please, Please," a regional hit that propelled him onto the "chitlin' circuit."

In segregated Southern clubs and outdoor tents, Brown played the fire-breathing, sinners-be-damned preacher, whipping audiences into an orgiastic frenzy with his hip-swinging, leg-flailing contortions. Part of this act is captured in *The Blues Brothers,* as J.B. is pictured in front of a congregation shouting Hallelujahs to the Lord. But this scene, even if it's the Blues Brothers' (Belushi and Ackroyd) "baptism" into soul, doesn't do Brown justice. It's too tame. The *real* Brown enthralled those early audiences by slithering across the stage, collapsing as if from a heart attack, and "miraculously" reviving to sing an encore.

Such hijinks secured his reputation as "the Hardest Working Man in Show Business." Performing with the James Brown Revue dancers and musicians, he broke black box-office records across the country. And after his famous 1962 *Live at the Apollo* album (one of the first soul albums to sell over a million copies), there was no denying his boast— he was indeed "Soul Brother Number One."

But beyond the ghetto, Brown was a virtual nobody. Even into the mid-sixties, white stations ignored him and his R & B vocals. There was more money and fame on the other side of the color line, yet J.B.'s attempts ("Out of Sight" and "Prisoner of Love") at reaching a wider audience only had limited success.

Moving more into polyrhythmic funk by 1965, Brown finally won white acceptance with "Papa's Got a Brand New Bag." Then came "I Got You (I Feel Good)." There was no stopping him now, as each of his subsequent singles—"Cold Sweat," "It's a Man's, Man's, Man's World," and "I Got the Feelin' "—went gold.

Befitting his new stature as a black role model, Brown joined Martin Luther King, Jr., and Muhammad Ali in the crusade for racial pride and justice. Besides exhorting youths to "Say it Loud, I'm Black and I'm Proud" and "Don't Be a Drop-Out," he sponsored several black businesses and social service programs in the late sixties. And when the ghettos exploded in the wake of King's assassination, J.B. showed just how far he had risen since his days as a shoeshine boy. Appearing on TV in a few riot-torn cities, Brown made an emotional plea for peace, and was subsequently commended by President Lyndon Johnson.

This political involvement would continue through the Nixon years, into the Carter administration, and during the Reagan era. Brown has been a "friend" to all these presidents. Because of his connections and investments (radio stations, a publishing and production company), J.B.'s influence on the American sociocultural scene widened. Whether it was disco tunes, or more "bad ass" funk, he kept minting gold records—"Give It Up or Turn It Loose," "Get on the Good Foot," "The Payback," "Hot Pants," "Get Up I Feel Like Being a Sex Machine," and "My Thang."

The magic lasted until the mid 1970s. Then, personal problems turned Brown's world upside down. His second wife divorced him, a son died in an automobile accident, and J.B. was suddenly faced with financial ruin, as the IRS demanded millions of dollars in back taxes. Compounding these difficulties, competition from newer, equally energized funk groups grew stiffer. Brown could no longer generate hits at will.

The Blues Brothers (1980) sparked a resurgence of interest in him. And he even made it back to the charts with "It's Too Funky in Here." But forced of late to play small clubs and theaters, Brown could be running out of comebacks. Even *his* legendary legs have to grow tired. Yet as demonstrated at City Hall, Soul's Elder Statesman can still dazzle an audience with wit and charm.

Upon leaving the mayor's office, he shares a few jokes with the police commissioner, then moves from desk to desk, to give each of Koch's secretaries a kiss on the cheek. While posing with them for more photos, J.B. is again the showman, exclaiming, "People want to see James Brown, and James Brown is saying the right thing. He said it on the railroad tracks [as a kid], and he's saying it in Russia."

Explaining that this trip is "special," even though there've been other "peace missions," Brown continues, "If I can go there and get them to do like I did at the Apollo Theater, or the Brooklyn Fox, it'll make me feel good. It'll show that everybody has a soul. The power's from God, not from my music. I might have influence, and I think people love me, but I don't want any power. Oh no! Nobody needs power."

Brown then cites "It's a Man's, Man's, Man's World," "Please, Please, Please," "Don't Be a Drop-Out," and "Say It Loud . . ." as his favorite tunes. Quickly adding his latest work, "Unity," to this list, he says that song has a vital message for humanity. "It's very, very important because we're asking people to get away from nuclear energy, and to use it to extend life, to press on, not to destroy."

His face now turns somber, and he plaintively insists, "People come first, people come first, people come first . . ."

These remarks trail off, as Brown slips on his brown mink coat and walks out the door into the wintry twilight's chill.

Petula Clark
A Happy Trip Downtown

Shirley Temple, move over!

To the British in the 1940s, the daughter of a would-be Errol Flynn was the reigning queen of baby-faced entertainers. The adopted "mascot" of British World War II troops, she became a silver-screen idol in the 1950s, starring in some twenty-five films. This blond little darling then conquered another country, singing her way to the top of French pop charts. After Germany was similarly bewitched, the whole world soon came to know her. In 1965, Petula was "Pet" to millions, the songstress who took us on a bouncy jaunt "Downtown."

That Grammy Award-winning number one tune was followed by other million-sellers, "I know a Place" (number two), "My Love" (number one), and "Don't Sleep in the Subway" (number three). She was on a roll and as popular as the Beatles and Stones in 1965–66. Pet had mounted her own British invasion. We were all whistling or humming her songs. The future looked bright.

Petula Clark is of a rare breed. She wasn't dizzied by the heady adulation, the Johnny Carson show appearances, or the twenty-five-thousand-dollar-a-night engagements. When confronted with the dilemma that pits career against marriage and family, she chose motherhood over glamour and opted to live with her husband and three children in Switzerland. Clark totally disappeared from the limelight. Raising children instead of signing autographs was a difficult adjustment, but Pet has no regrets. Still married to the same man, she has lived one of rock's few love stories—and is of an even smaller minority that has emerged unbloodied and unscarred.

"I was torn, the people who were booking me in America wanted me here . . . but the personal side won; there was no way I was going to watch my family be unhappy," says Clark, in her Radio City Music Hall dressing room, after rehearsing "Downtown" for the 1985 production of "A Night of 100 Stars." "In the 1960s, I suddenly found myself catapulted across the Atlantic into this really crazy world, which I also loved, but eventually I had to say no to it. It's very difficult to have a career and a personal life, and to do it all well is virtually impossible."

Clark admits to certain doubts—wonders if it was indeed the "right decision." That's only natural for a performer who thrives on singing.

But she also talks proudly of her children, especially of two grown daughters, ages twenty-one and twenty-three, who now have their own professional, nonmusical careers. *Their* successes—not "Downtown" or any other platinum record—make her blue eyes sparkle. Not only because her sacrifice was worthwhile, but, of even greater importance, Petula has honored a certain spiritual commitment, a veritable pact with the past. For her father was also selfless. He, too, gave and gave of himself, to further his daughter's career.

Petula's father, Lesley, was once an aspiring albeit frustrated actor. Though the dark, ruggedly handsome youth looked a lot like Errol Flynn (this resemblance once led to his being bitten on the leg by a female admirer), his parents disliked theater people, and wouldn't allow him to act. He was forced into the business world, but his dream didn't die. It simply found a different expression when he began working at Ventalls' Department Store, outside London in 1941.

While Lesley and eight-year-old Petula were shopping, they were drawn to a band hired by the store. Impulsively, Lesley asked the bandleader if his daughter could sing a song. The little girl was hesitant at first. But she was soon persuaded, and as a reward, the store gave her a handful of toffees. As for Lesley, he was exultant. His daughter's "professional debut" had been a smash success. After years of waiting, he finally heard the crowd's cheers.

Continuing to live vicariously through his daughter, Lesley took her to various talent shows. And by 1942, Petula had her own weekly radio program, "Pet's Parlor," during which she sang and spoke encouragingly to the troops stationed in England and abroad. Her popularity soon brought her to as many bases as Bob Hope.

"I did about five hundred shows for the troops," says Clark, blushing as she combs her sandy blond hair. "I was something of a mascot; I sort of represented the children that were left behind. This was a special type of atmosphere, you know, England was at war, we all had to do our part."

Managed by her father during this period, she began appearing in films, debuting in *A Medal for a General*. She also continued to sing on TV, and in vaudeville shows because, "I enjoyed that more, it was less rigid than films." But by the mid-1950s, she was a genuine movie star, having been featured in over fifteen films.

Her interest in "white rock 'n' roll" was minimal at this time, although these sentiments would change drastically in the sixties, once the Beatles "started to happen." Bill Haley didn't impress her, and Elvis was just "okay." She was fascinated, however, by Ray Charles. According to Clark, he bridged the gap between rock and pop. There was real feeling, or a romantic bent, to his music. And it's understandable why Petula was charmed by this. While pursuing her singing career in France in the late 1950s, she had fallen in love with Claude Wolff, the publicity director of her French record company, Vogue Records.

Their relationship survived the tribulations of stardom: the constant traveling, the long hours, the loss of personal privacy, the fending off of an adoring, yet merciless public. Claude and Petula's love for one another even flourished. They married in 1961, a year that gave Petula several pop bestsellers, including "Sailor" and "Romeo."

This fairy tale had only one hitch. As the nuptial bells sounded, one heart was broken: her father's, for Wolff now replaced him as Petula's manager.

Pet *had* been managing her own affairs for a few years, but Lesley always assumed that their business split was a temporary thing. Once she married, he had to face the truth; the break was final. He was a virtual nonentity, as far as her career was concerned. This made him resentful, and he eventually became estranged from his daughter.

"Once again it was the personal life versus the public life. It was very difficult for him being my manager," Clark says, her voice growing faint. "I loved him very much, but as I got older, and started having my own ideas, maybe not the best ideas, I wanted to make my own mistakes. This put a strain on our personal relationship, and I"—she hesitates—"I wasn't quite sure who I was talking to, my manager or my father. Eventually, when we split, it was not an easy moment for either of us; suddenly I was on my own, and he didn't have this thing in his life, which was very important to him. So there were a few years of being uncomfortable together.

"When Claude took over my career, there was discomfort there, too.

My father could've been jealous, but later on, when he saw what a marvelous job Claude was making of my career, he was delighted. When it was all happening, I brought my father over to America. He felt good. He saw it was a good marriage."

After settling in France, Petula sang in the most "bizarre" places, from circus tents to bullfight arenas. She had her own band, and was recording exclusively in French. Adored by much of Europe for songs like "Chariot" and "Casanova," she was content with her life in Paris.

Recording in English didn't even interest her. Not until she heard a now famous melody.

"Tony Hatch [her French studio engineer/producer] told me I should do something in English, but I told him it had to be a really good song," recalls Clark, referring to their fateful 1964 meeting in Paris—a meeting that eventually resulted in her recording "Downtown." "Well, he said he had this song, and while I was in the kitchen making tea, he started playing 'Downtown' on the piano. I loved it right away. I was very enthusiastic. And I said 'Listen, if you can write a lyric that's up to that melody—as good—I'll do it. I don't know if we have a hit, but I certainly want to do it.' We were in the studio a week later."

Smiling broadly, Petula seems to be thinking about how she became synonymous with the pulse of city life. More than an international celebrity in 1965, she symbolized the supercharged pace of New York, London, Los Angeles, and every other urban mecca. Downtown was here, it was happening, and that's where she took us.

The song, according to Clark, mirrored our fascination with cities, for "It was exciting, it was never flat. It had dynamics, it went somewhere, it went up and down, it had climaxes."

Yet true to its soul, "Downtown" also meant complications. International fame swept Petula into a frenzied, dizzying world.

"I was already working very hard on a career that included not only France, but all the French-speaking countries, North Africa, parts of Dark Africa . . . my life was already very full. I also had two children by then. The song was a hit in England, which was fine. But when it became a hit in America, I started getting these offers from America. It was exciting, but I couldn't see how I was going to do it all. I had to make a decision; would I go to America, and make the most of this marvelous opportunity, or say no?

"You don't say no when that sort of thing happens. So I came over here, and did the usual things, "The Ed Sullivan Show," the Johnny Carson show. I did it because no matter how successful you are in the rest of the world, the United States is still the most important thing for a career. You haven't really made it until you've made it here."

When Petula first came to the United States to play Las Vegas and Lake Tahoe nightclubs for a week or two, her family came with her. After repeated successes with "I know a Place" (1967), "Don't Sleep in the Subway" (1967), and "Kiss Me Goodbye" (1968), she was booked into so many clubs that traveling *en famille* became far more complicated. Movie offers also came streaming in. The family lived together during Petula's filming of *Finian's Rainbow,* but, while she enjoyed living in the United States, the rest of the family didn't. This polarization eventually forced Petula to give up her American career, although she still shuttled back and forth between the United States and Europe in order to play certain clubs or hotels.

But in 1977, after a few years of this madcap pace, she was finally worn down.

"I'd get over here two days before I was supposed to open, and leave immediately after I finished the date. It was not very satisfactory, I wasn't getting any feedback from the work, and I was getting tired. One day I said 'No, that's it, I'm stopping now. I've had enough of this . . .' When I got back home [she was living in Geneva by the mid-1970s] I just said, 'This isn't working anymore, I'm not getting any joy from it anymore.' So I just stopped."

Pet didn't return to the stage until 1979 when she formed her own band, and appeared almost exclusively in Great Britain, which didn't necessitate much traveling.

She dipped into Julie Andrews's songbook, and starred in a "gusty" version of *The Sound of Music.* It ran for thirteen months in one of London's biggest theaters, and as Clark delightedly exclaims, "I hadn't done a stage musical before. It gave me a taste for that medium. I would like to do a new one, a modern one. I write, and at the moment I'm writing one myself."

A triumphant return to the United States is another ambition. When she sang a few bars of "Downtown" at Radio City, she was well received, but it was basically a cameo role. She's hoping to land a Las Vegas engagement, and that this will serve as a springboard to other bookings. "It would feel really good going back there [Las Vegas] . . . I would do it differently, though. My act's much more compact now; before I had a big orchestra, but now I work with nine musicians. I sing some of the old songs, but I don't do them the way I used to. They sound very contemporary, and I do all kinds of things, classical, rock . . .

"I like the business of making music. I've done it all my life, it's part of me. It's not separate from the rest of my life, although I have tried to separate it, to have some kind of private life. You have to do this. But it's in me all the time, there's music going on in my mind all the time."

Saying this as she adjusts the collar of her white silk blouse, Petula then dons a stylishly tapered black jacket. She looks ready to go "downtown" herself. But before leaving the dressing room, she mentions one of her old leading men, seemingly to put her continued use of the song "Downtown" into the proper perspective.

A distinct note of exasperation in her voice, she passionately declares, "I don't want to be remembered for 'Downtown,' for I find that a bit limited. When people see me perform, I think I give them a feeling of hope . . . But it's like what happens to actors, they can make masses of valuable films, and it's just that one, like Peter O'Toole [she starred with him in *Goodbye, Mr. Chips*]. He'll always be remembered for *Lawrence of Arabia*. I think he's proud of that . . . and I think 'Downtown' is a good song. It's a song that deserves to live, but I think I've done a lot of better things. Sure I have. I can't single out a favorite, but even if I had another big hit now, there are still people who would only remember me for 'Downtown.' "

Petula shrugs. As she walks to the door, her face sparkles again. She's meeting her husband for dinner, and one's left with the feeling that Pet Clark is still on her honeymoon.

Levi Stubbs of the Four Tops

A Unique Friendship

Ever since *The Three Musketeers,* popular mythology has been rife with images of male bonding. We thrill to the exploits of Robert Redford and Paul Newman; laugh with the Blues Brothers; and buy countless six-packs of beer hustled by incongruous teams of Miller Lite spokesmen. In our imagination, all these figures have found a fraternity that is sorely missing from modern life. So we lionize them and yearn for a similar comradeship.

Rock 'n' roll, for the most part, isn't conducive to such lasting, uplifting friendships. It is a far more atomized world, where egos dominate and rivalries are the rule. Artists do come together and support one another as they make it to the top, but with success, mutual struggles are forgotten, and sharing gives way to destructive factional battles. There's little longevity in music circles. Of the groups that do survive personnel changes, very few can actually say, "We Are Fam-i-ly."

One group has preserved this "one for all, all for one" spirit. Thirty-one years after their initial engagement, the Four Tops are still wedded to one another. The bonds between them remain unshakable. The proverbial roller coaster that heaves groups through success and failure hasn't dizzied them. Not in the slightest. They've discovered a special harmony, a love that infuses their music with the essence of soul.

"After seeing how performers were taken advantage of by managers, agents, etc., we decided to put all our eggs into one basket in the middle of the Four Tops," says lead singer Levi Stubbs, while breakfasting in a New York hotel room. Dressed in a flowing Japanese kimono, and wearing a diamond ring that's big enough to mash potatoes, the forty-seven-year-old Stubbs clears his hoarse throat before continuing. "No one was going to penetrate our little circle, because we had, and still have, a great love for each other. There's a complete faith and confidence between us. We trusted each other with our lives. Why, I know more about the Four Tops than I do about my own brothers."

This unity has produced a stream of catchy, emotionally charged love songs. Stubbs, Lawrence Payton, Renaldo Benson, and Abdul "Duke" Fakir consistently broke onto the charts in the 1960s with "Baby I Need Your Loving," "I Can't Help Myself (Sugar Pie, Honey Bunch)," "Reach Out I'll Be There," and "Standing in the Shadows of Love." They drifted into obscurity in the early seventies, when Sly Stone's "acid-soul" dominated the industry. But the Tops "smoked" with so much power, the venerable Phil Spector called their work "black Dylan."

Where did this passion spring from? Why does love have a unique potency among the Four Tops?

These answers are found in the Tops' roots, the ten years of suffering they endured before recording their first hit. During that stressful period in the 1950s, while growing up in Detroit ghetto clubs, they were so poor that they shared five pairs of raggedy pants among them. Numerous record deals fell apart, as these four teenagers hopscotched from one record company to another. And while they grew frustrated, playing in no-name bars or all-black resorts on the Michigan shore, they refused to quit. True to their name at that time—the Four Aims—a lofty sense of purpose kept them plugging away.

"We were aiming for the top, it wasn't important enough just to get a record or a flash of success," reflects Stubbs, stroking his neatly clipped black beard, which is distinguished by a silver-gray border. "The emphasis of black performers in the 1950s was on 'show,' instead of on the business." He proudly eyes his ring and a gold ID bracelet that's studded with diamonds which spell LEVI. "Consequently, they never accomplished anything. They had a few limousine rides, champagne, and late-night snacks, but what's that? Nothing! These things are façades, there's more to life than the glitter. Those things cost; someone has to pay for it. In the final analysis, the people doing the limousine riding are the ones doing the paying."

Levi becomes even more emphatic, as he crisply continues, "We didn't want that to happen to us, we didn't want to be flash-in-the pans. In those days we greatly admired the Mills Brothers; they were mainstays, they were entrenched. *That's* what we wanted. We didn't care about getting it all, we just wanted it all the time."

Upon signing with Chess Records in 1957, Levi and Company felt they were finally on their way. With fame and fortune apparently beckoning, they confidently changed their name to the Four Tops. But success still proved elusive. Their Chess single "Kiss Me Baby" flopped. Then they moved to Red Top Records, to Riverside, and to Columbia, with equally disastrous results. And, as the failures mounted, more than their hopes were dashed. "Those times were so bad," sighs Stubbs, "we literally had nothing, I mean nothing to eat. We were doing well when we had a dollar or two to buy baloney sandwiches."

In 1963, after years of playing the "chitlin' circuit," or rinky-dink segregated clubs in the South, the Tops came limping back to Detroit. "Let me tell you, the South was *rough,*" says Stubbs. "Being from the North, we couldn't understand that there were bathrooms for whites and bathrooms for so-called 'coloreds.' Well, there were times we'd walk into the white bathroom, and sure enough, the police would catch us. With their guns drawn, they'd remind us, 'Niggers, don't you know we have segregation down here? You better learn that for your own good.' This finally sank in, but we were often very scared, very frightened."

Once the Tops settled in Duke's parents' basement, they discovered that an old acquaintance had gone on to glory. Berry Gordy had built a veritable empire, a recording colossus that included many of the Tops' friends from the north end of Detroit. The Tops had also been asked to join Motown in the late 1950s, but, thinking Gordy didn't have a chance against the giant labels, they refused. So now, with their own future looking bleak, the Tops were compelled to swallow some of their pride and, in a sense, go begging.

"We had no idea that Motown was going to be what it was. It was unheard of for a black guy to start a record company," exclaims Stubbs, still enthralled by Gordy's achievements. "Berry really did it, but back in the fifties we didn't want to make a record for a local company. No one would hear it and you'd be stuck there. Finally, though, we just saw what was happening.

"Let's face it, at all these other companies the executives would sit you down, and they'd have this look in their eyes. You knew that if you did get lucky with a record, you weren't going to get anything from it. It just made sense to go with Gordy; we had nothing to lose—99 percent of the black stars were making records and not seeing *any* of the money."

When the Tops joined Gordy's stable, he shifted them from R & B to jazz for one album *(Breaking Through)*. The group felt comfortable with the change ("We would've gone along with anything that put shoes on our feet"), but the record died. Astutely recognizing that soulful R & B was gaining popularity among white Americans, Gordy then made another change. He coupled the Tops with Motown's most talented writing team, Holland-Dozier-Holland, who produced the group's first hit, "Baby I Need Your Loving" (number eleven in 1964).

Though there was an initial rush of excitement that saw Stubbs buy a Pontiac Bonneville and a new wardrobe, he says, "After a little of this craziness, we just stopped. The four of us sat down one evening and said, 'Things are happening for us. All these cars are fine, but what are we doing? What had we talked about doing ten years ago?' So we just backed up, and started putting our few pennies aside. This eventually made it possible to survive the lean years."

Without being asked, Stubbs then explains why the Tops reacted so rationally—why they weren't intoxicated by success. "We came from such impoverished backgrounds; we were the hope of our families, and that kept our heads screwed on tight. We wanted to do something for each other, for our parents, and when that thought is in your head constantly, it brings you back to earth. It doesn't let you wander far away. So if one of us was going off the deep end, one of the guys would throw him a rope. We sacrificed, and with each hit we saved a little more to buy our parents homes."

Over the next few years, those chart-hitting songs included "Ask the Lonely," "I Can't Help Myself (Sugar Pie, Honey Bunch)," "It's the Same Old Song," "Something About You," and "Shake Me, Wake Me (When It's Over)." These urgent, deeply emotional love songs, together with their elaborate stage routines and choreography made the Tops one of Motown's most popular acts. Only the Supremes, the Temptations, and perhaps the Miracles won more acclaim. So, as Stubbs enthusiastically points out, the Tops played a vital role in the revolution Motown was leading.

"Because of Motown the music merged, black and white music was brought together and solidified. This mixture was a turning point in our country—the music melted together, and that was great for social relations. Now when you turn on the radio, you don't know if an artist is black or white.

"The Tops helped bring this change about because we had a pop sound. It caused a lot of people to focus in on black music. Our visual performance, especially the dancing, was such that people were comfortable with us. Audiences relax with us, so, in my opinion, we, too, allowed people to merge together. When you start dancing with one another, those racial barriers disappear."

While Stubbs derives a great deal of satisfaction from the "history" the Tops made, he speaks even more passionately about another achievement—the group's "unrivaled" togetherness. "Being on the cutting edge of social change is great, but knowing how hard it was for us to survive, that really makes me proud. Do you know that before they filmed *Lady Sings the Blues,* Berry called to offer me the part Billy Dee Williams played? But, since there wasn't any place for the other Tops, I refused. If they couldn't be involved, I didn't want it. You go through life, and you're extremely lucky if you have one friend. I've had three.

"We have a respect for each other that's unique. Ego has never threatened to disrupt what we have. We've seen people that could take others down the drain with them. We call them 'Egors.' We don't have 'Egors.' "

These ties weren't tested during the glory years. Through the late 1960s into 1970, the Tops continued to score with "Bernadette," "Seven Rooms of Gloom," "It's All in the Game," and "I'll Turn to Stone." The Tops were making a lot, "a real lot" of money and also, as Stubbs admits, "We thought the hits would go on forever."

But they didn't.

Holland-Dozier-Holland, the triumvirate Stubbs calls, "the Tops' true heart and soul," left Motown to establish their own company in 1967. In the wake of that departure, the Tops went on to more hits, but their successes weren't as monumental as before, and these successes were now mixed with failures.

"Things had to change after these guys left; they were unique, real beautiful people," muses Stubbs, a perceptible note of sadness creeping into his voice. "No one felt any awe at Motown, because we were all in there grinding and struggling together. But you could see where these guys were going—Brian [Holland] would be doing something on a piano, Lamont [Dozier] would walk in, and say 'Hey, that sounds great, man. Listen, what do you think about this with it?' And all of a sudden [Levi snaps his fingers], they'd have something. They'd call Eddie [Holland], and he'd come up with the damnedest lyrics. They were quite a marriage. You just knew that these cats were special."

Other Motown writers tried to duplicate H-D-H's artistry, but as Stubbs admits, "They were an impossible act to follow, so there were bound to be problems. These guys had produced one hit after another. How could anyone equal that? There was much too much pressure on these other writers, and eventually [1971–72] our record sales fell off tremendously."

Though Stubbs insists that the Tops were mentally prepared to accept "the calm which sooner or later affects all artists," the slump prompted their switch to ABC Records in 1972. There, they quickly soared to the top of the charts with "Ain't No Woman Like the One I've Got." Their follow-up effort, "Keeper of the Castle," also sold well, as it reached the number eleven slot in 1973. Suddenly "hot," the Tops left the small clubs they'd been playing in for Las Vegas casinos and Europe. They were rolling again.

Or so it seemed.

Starting with *Main Street People* in 1973, the Tops bombed. They did seven more albums for ABC/Dunhill over the next five years, and each of them suffered the same fate—total failure. So those years were more than a "calm." This cold spell was the Tops' own Ice Age.

If Stubbs is to be believed, however, this wasn't a painful period, or a time for self-doubt. Despite these seven successive flops, he says the Tops retained their composure. No one thought about a solo career, or questioned their respective talents. "It was calm, real calm, sure it was. But it wasn't the end of the world. Life went on. I had a lovely family; I wasn't at a point where if I didn't sing tomorrow I'd be hungry. That won't happen in my life. I prepared for misfortune. So things continued to be fine, no matter what was happening with business."

Stubbs raises four of his fingers, flicks them in the air several times, then continues, "The others felt the same way. We were together—the four of us. That kind of unity goes back to the strengths we developed early on."

The Tops wrestled with adversity until 1981, when they had their comeback hit, "When She Was My Girl." "That song put pep in our step, slide in our slide," says Stubbs, his previously subdued voice suddenly filled with emotion. "Our dates improved, everything got better. Coming back again is the greatest feeling in the world."

Since that success, the Tops haven't returned to the charts, even though they rejoined Motown in 1983. Yet that "calm" hasn't engulfed them again. In addition to playing the Vegas Strip, and Broadway theaters, they've formed their own production/management company, which Stubbs says, "is developing and nurturing young artists" in Detroit. "We want to groom talent the right way, really let them know what this business is all about. They shouldn't have to spend half their lives learning from mistakes. Right now Lawrence [Payton] is working with his son, who's tremendously talented, and I'm grooming my younger sister and two nieces. This is going to take some time; cultivating talent can't be rushed, but we want to put something back into this business, because we've gotten a lot out of it."

To better serve these young performers, Stubbs will retire from the stage in 1990. And, as is customary with the Four Tops, the other members will also repair to a quieter life. "We're all looking forward to stepping back. Don't get me wrong, singing is still a joy. We still get off on the fact that people love us. When the Tops perform, people are still dancing in the aisles."

Savoring this image of frenzied crowds, Levi chuckles heartily and adds, "We've really done it, we've gotten people to connect, and that's a wonderful feeling." Levi then shakes his head, as if the Tops' "power" still amazes him.

Yet after a short silence, Levi's face turns somber. "We have done quite a lot, we helped merge the world musically. Blacks and whites came to see us, and Motown's artists made it possible for black performers today to make loads of money. The Tops' dream, though, was always to be the best. And I guess we only made 65 percent to 70 percent of that, because we haven't kept a string of big records going like we did in the beginning. We're hoping to have another hit, but we've been singing the same stuff for years. That's what people want. They love the oldies-but-goodies stuff."

Levi's eyes brighten now, and he smiles impishly.

"Yeah, that's been a problem, but guess what? the Tops aren't finished yet! No one's getting into any wheelchair. There's still time for a hit—or two!"

Otis Williams of the Temptations

Frosting on the Cake Comes in Many Flavors

During the height of the Vietnam War, a young soldier approached the Temptations' Otis Williams in Hong Kong, and told him, "The only thing that's getting some guys through this war is the Temps' music. We're in those trenches dying, while your music is playing. The Temps make us think of home, and they give us a little hope."

There have been other dramatic moments in the Temptations' illustrious career. The Motown ambassadors have entertained presidents at the White House, traveled overseas to lighten the load of American soldiers, and, in the racially torn 1960s, forced Southern officials to integrate concert halls.

On the top of the charts for over a decade with such standards as "My Girl," "I Know I'm Losing You," "Cloud Nine," and "Ball of Confusion," the Temps symbolized Black Power. They made white America (and the world) dance to *their* tunes. They established themselves as the most popular black vocal group of the 1960s and early 1970s, which caused commercial history to be recorded. The Temps sold over 75 million records.

Their spotlight has dimmed of late. Besides suffering a huge dropoff in sales, the Temps have lost some of their old bounce. Once viewed as the Fred Astaires of soul, for their dizzying, synchronized choreography, they don't cook with the same heat anymore. So instead of appearing on the Bob Hope show, or alongside the likes of Cher and Diana Ross, they must be content with less soulful fare. Today, the Temptations turn up as passengers on TV's "The Love Boat."

A faint reminder of their former glory, such cameo slots, in the severest sense, are a rite of passage. The Temps have entered the twilight stage; their biggest moments are behind them.

But that doesn't demean the legend, or in any way diminish the group's legacy.

As one of the Temp's founding fathers, Otis Williams once dreamed of a special type of power. And as evidenced by that American soldier's poignant declaration, Williams's hopes were fulfilled beyond his wildest expectations.

"When I was a kid, I saw how crowds reacted to Frankie Lymon, La Vern Baker, and the Cadillacs, so I said to myself, 'I want that adulation, I want that kind of mass control,'" reflects the stockily built Williams, wearing a T-shirt that accentuates his bulging biceps. The forty-five-year-old Texas-born baritone, understandably nicknamed "Oak," sits next to a window in a New York hotel room, with both of his massive legs propped on the bed. His feet have been bothering him lately, and the pain makes it difficult for him to relax. Yet after a few complaints, his voice markedly softens, as he again recalls the past.

"These performers had a power. I became aware that music is a universal language, that it sweeps over people, and really controls them. The Temptations have had an influence on people that even politicians couldn't have. In Mississippi, and in all kinds of other places, we overcame the black-white thing. We made sure people sat where they wanted. We did have influence; the Temps had the power I always wanted."

Before reaching this magical plateau, Otis left Texarkana, Texas, in the early 1950s with his mother and moved to Detroit. By his seventeenth birthday, in 1958, he was singing doo-wop harmonies in a group called the Distants, alongside three other future Temps: Richard Street, Melvin Franklin, and Eldridge Bryant. They had a regional hit with "Pecos Kid" on the Northern Records label, but their manager, who was also a DJ, couldn't work for them full-time. So the Distants found another manager, MJ for short, and took a walk on the funkier side of town.

"Old Miltie was a *player,* you know," explains Otis, rolling his eyes good-humoredly. "He was a suave kind of guy, who was always surrounded by beautiful women. The prettiest girls you ever did see. His sideline was managing acts. He had the Supremes, who were then the Primettes, the Primes (Paul Williams and Eddie Kendricks would leave that group to become charter members of the Temps), and us. At that time we were Otis Williams and the Siberians. We'd all rehearse in the same building, so that's how we got to know Paul and Eddie. The Temptations finally emerged in 1960, but by then Milt was out of the picture. We just weren't getting enough attention with him; I guess he had to take care of his other thing. But let me tell you, whenever he'd show up at an engagement, Miltie would always have a pretty young lady by his side. He traveled first class, that man, he sure did."

While Williams was singing lead for the Distants, he met Berry Gordy at a record hop. The Motown *wunderkind* had just started to groom Smokey Robinson and the Miracles, and was looking to produce other acts. After watching the Distants on this particular occasion, Gordy asked Otis to come see him whenever he wanted to make a management or label change. So a few years later, in 1960, when the Siberians sought to escape their own wilderness of third-rate clubs, Otis finally responded to Gordy's invitation.

"I saw Brian Holland, Marv Johnson, Smokey, and Lamont Dozier going into Mr. Gordy's building, and was really intrigued by all this activity," says Williams, his already husky voice growing more strained. "It was really happening there. Gordy had written 'Reet Petite' for Jackie Wilson, 'Lonely Teardrops,' 'You Got What It Takes' for Marv Johnson; he had a track record. So when we became disenchanted with Northern Records over not seeing any royalties or statements, we went over to Motown.

"One of Gordy's groups was already called the Elgins. So one summer day, while standing in front of his place on West Grand Boulevard, we were kicking around names, and I said, 'What about the Temptations?' We didn't look too good at the time; everyone was wearing secondhand clothes. It would've been pretty hard to tempt anybody. But the name sounded good, and it stuck."

Once Otis signed a contract with Gordy's Miracle label, Paul Williams and Eddie Kendricks were brought into the group. The Temps then had a local hit with "Dream Come True" in 1962, but they were still playing "sawdust joints." At one of these gigs, the frustrations of the past few years spilled over, and a beer bottle was smashed into Paul Williams's face.

After Eldridge Bryant was replaced by David Ruffin in 1963, Gordy made one of the decisions that would establish Motown as "Hitsville, U.S.A." Assuming control of the Temps' development, he assigned Smokey Robinson to write a song for them. And in 1964, that collaboration led to the Temptations' first major hit, "The Way You Do the Things You Do."

When Williams recalls the night they recorded that song, he closes his eyes, and murmurs, "Once the session was over I knew this group was going to make history. I just knew it. We had recorded eight songs in those four years and they didn't do too much. So, we'd have to play in places like Saginaw, Michigan. But this time, after we got back to Detroit from one of these trips, a few guys at Motown came up to me and said, 'You've got one.' I said 'Got what?' They'd been telling us we'd have a hit for years. And nothing ever happened. Now though, they told me to look at the trades. I said, 'You mean we really made the newspapers?' And sure enough, 'The Way You Do . . .' was number ninety-four nationally. I'll never forget. Ruffin, who was singing lead with Eddie, sat down and cried."

There'd be more soulful celebrations. For Otis was right. The Temps *were* ready to make Top 10 history.

It started with "My Girl" in 1965.

Another inspired piece of writing from Smokey Robinson, "My Girl" catapulted them to the number one spot on both the pop and R & B charts. They registered three more Top 20 hits that year, including Robinson's "Since I Lost My Baby," as America began to associate the group with earthy, up-tempo harmonies.

Norman Whitfield replaced Robinson as the Temps' producer in 1966, but the group's hold on the charts wasn't weakened. In quick succession, the Temptations minted such platinum classics as "Ain't Too Proud to Beg," "Beauty Is Only Skin Deep," "(I Know) I'm Losing You," "You're My Everything," and "I Wish It Would Rain."

Though the Temps eclipsed other Motown acts, Williams firmly insists, "No one was jealous, there was a great feeling of camaraderie between the different groups. Smokey would have us over to his house, he'd come to ours. There was that kind of familyness. It was all genuine and poor. And a lot of honesty. We wanted anyone connected with Motown to make it."

Referring to Robinson's 1963 "Mickey's Monkey" to emphasize this point, Williams continues, "Smokey is the only Miracle on that song. I'm on it and some of the other guys who were in the studio at the time. That was always happening at Motown. In those days there was a real closeness. Business hadn't changed mental attitudes yet. So you'd see people helping out. We [the Temptations] would wax the floors, Martha [Reeves] was a secretary. You could see the Miracles or the Contours taking the trash out, or cleaning up. That's when there were bonds between people. Isn't that what the sixties were all about?"

For most of those years, the Temps were united in spirit. Success didn't inflate their egos, and they remained loyal to Motown.

Naturally, in the wake of so many hits, Williams's material life changed. As he laughingly admits, "I didn't have to press my nose on store windowpanes anymore, I could go in and buy four or five suits. Or even five or six pairs of shoes."

Yet Otis insists, "Emotionally I kept myself in check. I didn't put on airs, or act like I was full of myself." Avoiding this type of behavior was important to Williams, for as a teenager he had been disappointed by his boyhood hero, blues singer Marv Johnson. Having seen him mistreat a waitress in a bar, Otis attributed this conduct to an "ego gone wild," and swore to himself, "No way was I ever going to act like that. No way. Forget that kind of stardom, I wanted to be a real person."

According to Williams, however, one member of the Temps did succumb to the Star Syndrome. Speaking in a soft, muffled voice, Otis clearly wants to mute his criticism. But judging by the pained expression on his face, he's still annoyed by David Ruffin's leaving the group in 1967.

Repudiating reports that Ruffin quit because of a financial dispute with Motown, Williams says, "We were riding a very high crest, and we all handle success differently. Some of us can be appreciative, others can think 'I'm the only game in town.' In the beginning we said we were going to stay together, because we had heard about other groups getting big and splitting. We were going to be different. It's sad it didn't work out that way, because we had a really good lineup. People loved the hell out of us. But there are just some things you can't help. It was very sad. Ruffin and I were very tight at one time."

After Dennis Edwards moved into the lineup, the Temptations made two albums with the Supremes in 1968 and, even more important, restyled their music. Echoing the psychedelic arrangements of Sly and the Family Stone, the Temps adopted an "acid-soul" sound and also sang about social issues. Vietnam. Black ghetto life. The international political situation. Each of these concerns became the focal point for a song. And while the switch from mellow ballads to socially relevant lyrics gave the Temps a whole new image, they retained their old magic.

"Cloud Nine," "Run Away Child, Running Wild," "Psychedelic Shack," "I Can't Get Next to You," and "Ball of Confusion" were all smash hits.

"Voicing these songs differently, with the ensemble kind of thing and abstract harmonies was an adjustment, but we were glad to take on a new challenge," says Williams. "Before, one guy would sing a song all the way through, now it became a multilead kind of thing. Sly had started it, and we picked up on it. We were also getting a tremendous amount of TV exposure, "The Sonny and Cher Show," Dean Martin, Ed Sullivan, so we took this quantum leap. It was exciting, real exciting."

As Williams continues to talk about the late sixties, and the Temps' role in "bringing people together," his dark eyes mirror a certain wistfulness. Now that the worldwide tours and cheering crowds are merely memories, feelings of regret are inevitable. But as Otis soon explains, this grieved expression points up an even greater loss. By 1971, conflicts splintered the group. Both Kendricks and Paul Williams (as a result of illness) quit. So in spirit, the Temps weren't the Temps anymore.

"Once again, that ego thing took over," sighs Williams, "Eddie wanted to do an album on his own. His thing was 'I wonder how I would be on my own.' He started drifting over to that, and, in a group, if five guys start thinking like that, you'd never get anything done. So we had to let him go."

For a few years, the new lineup (Damon Harris and Richard Street) kept the Temps on the charts, with "Papa was a Rollin' Stone," "Masterpiece," and "Hey Girl (I Like Your Style)."

But after *A Song for You,* an album that sold millions of copies in 1975–76, the group slumped badly.

Attributing this fall from grace to "politics," Williams sadly says, "Motown released two albums that shouldn't have been released *[House Party* and *Wings of Love].* This did more harm than good. The material just wasn't up to the quality we had tried to maintain. We then did an album by ourselves, *[The Temptations Do the Temptations]* but it didn't get any support from Motown.

"The company was being run by some guys who were alienating Motown's top acts. It just got to be a bad thing. No way *House Party* should've been released. I told them that, but I guess they felt the Temps were hot, that they could capitalize on the momentum. *Wings of Love* didn't have the Temptations' sound either. I kept telling this to Gordy: 'You have all that choralizing on there, you have no Temptations harmonies, the colorings we're noted for just aren't there.' But he was impressed with the record's producer, Jeffrey Bowen . . . And sure enough, when the album came out, it died."

Angered by Motown's intransigence, the Temps signed with Atlantic Records in 1977. Instead of getting more promotional support, however, they were again ignored. Their record sales continued to plummet, as two more [disco-flavored] albums failed. As Otis admits, the personnel changes had also blurred the group's "true identity." So falling out of favor with the public, they moved from fifty-thousand-dollar-a-night clubs to five-thousand-dollar shows on the sleazy side of town.

"With these new members in the group, we had a much different sound. Our old gospel throatiness was missing," Williams says, grimacing, as he removes his legs from the bed, and hunches over a table covered with tapes and paperbacks. "Whew! It was tough back then. We played some pretty rough gigs. Places we'll *never* go back to—clubs that weren't set up for our kind of movements, and that had the filthiest dressing rooms imaginable. Urine on the floor, cushions spotted with semen . . . it was rough."

The Temps endured these indignities for four years. Forced to tighten his belt during this period, Williams couldn't go on those clothes-buying binges anymore. The financial pressures weighed on his marriage as well, and he was eventually divorced for the second time. Worst of all, however, Otis was no longer the star, the person everyone pampered. This could easily have embittered him, but displaying remarkable inner strength, he turned adversity into a learning experience. "I discovered that no matter who the artist is, everybody will have highs and lows, from the Sinatras to the Elvises. Everyone catches hell at one time or another, so I came to appreciate the success I did have a lot more."

Interrupted by a knock at the door, Otis ushers a friend into the room before continuing, "No matter how bad things were, I didn't question my talents. I did this when the Temps were first making it, I asked myself if I was worthy of the success—so much was happening, so fast. But even in our bad period, I didn't have those insecurities. I knew how hard the Temps worked . . . people out there were paying good money to see us, and we discovered that we were satisfying them. That showed us there was a legitimacy to what we were doing."

So the Temps persevered.

After recording a third album for Atlantic in 1980, they met with Smokey Robinson, who raised the possibility of a reconciliation with

Motown. When the Temps responded positively, a meeting was arranged with Gordy.

"Since we had left on such a sour note, I just let it all hang out when we got together," says Williams soberly. "I felt we'd been humiliated before . . . and for an artist to really create, he has to be free of mind, he can't sing his heart out if something's gnawing at his soul. The rest of the group whispered, 'Oh my God, we're not going to get back into Motown now,' but I just spoke my mind . . ."

Gordy apparently respected Otis's honesty, for he subsequently cowrote "Power," the album title song that brought the Temps back to the charts.

"I was told that Berry just sat on the song until we returned, he felt the Temps were the only group that could sing it . . . And the song was really doing it until the Miami riots broke out. White stations backed off it then—they were afraid of 'Power's spread-the-wealth message. The DJs thought we were talking about power to the people . . . *zap.* The record just fell off. It was too touchy for white DJs."

Williams's voice again cracks with emotion. For the early 1980s were another drought period. Nothing clicked. They released several records, all to mixed reviews. And each successive failure was another humbling experience that tested their resolve.

The Temptations, though, are the Muhammad Ali of Soul. They always seem to come back for one more flash of stardom.

In late 1984, they rebounded with *Truly for You,* the gold record that brought them more than another wall plaque.

"My heart still races when I think of our being asked to appear on 'The Love Boat,' " says Otis, gleefully recalling how *Truly for You* sparked renewed interest in the group. "That was such a helluva challenge, for normally we'd go on TV shows, and just sing our songs. That was it. But here we actually had lines and we acted, that added another dimension. Why, this is more exciting than our going to the White House—there you only act cordial, say 'Mr. President . . .' it's not like 'Action, roll 'em, sing!' You have to know your lines, you're primarily noted for singing, but now you're stepping over into acting. That's another challenge.

"I think we came off real good. We breezed through certain scenes, and even the director told us we were fantastic. I'm as proud of this as some of our songs, because when people see it, they're going to think we're impressive . . . and that's how I want the Temps to be remembered, that we are men of purpose and quality. We're not just shallow people of song and dance—there are several dimensions to the Temptations. We're thinking people of sensitivity and concern, and we want to meet new challenges."

Besides envisioning more TV appearances for the Temps, Otis is planning to steer the group into movies. His biggest dream, in fact, is to help produce a film based on the Temps' career.

For most stars, these aspirations could simply be attributed to ego—that recurring need to validate their identity. But this doesn't seem to be the case with Williams. There's no urgency, or desperation in his voice when he talks about the future. As he says, "Doing something in Hollywood would just be frosting on the cake."

Williams's calm, reasoned attitude is easy to understand. He has nothing to prove. A movie, or TV guest appearances would only reaffirm the fact that the Temps have already made history—that they have touched people's hearts.

"Why should ego be important to us?" asks Otis, staring ahead intently. "We don't need that, we've found a different satisfaction."

His eyes look a little moist now, as he continues, "We were there for those soldiers who were putting their lives on the line. The bullets were whirling past them while our music was playing. They were dying, and yet they gave us that kind of importance. That's the biggest compliment we could ever receive."

Marty Balin of the Jefferson Airplane

Airsickness

Seated under a golden Chinese Buddha, garlanded with yellow flowers, Marty Balin slips into a yoga-inspired trance. Wearing only the bottoms of a black exercise outfit, he fixates on a mantra, oblivious to the passions swirling around him. The real world has grown too frustrating, too explosive for his tender spirit. Dreams, youthful loves, friendships, his beloved Airplane, they've all been snatched from him. So off he goes, to a calmer, less cluttered landscape, where the past gets lost in a world of plaintive "oms."

The sun streams onto Balin's tanned face during this reverie, and his soft smile has a virginal, innocent quality. He seems at peace on the top floor of his Marin County A-frame, surrounded by photos of an Eastern mystic and stacks of philosophical readings. Here in this Northern Californian retreat, with Mount Tamalpais looming in the background, discordant notes are seldom heard. For this is the land of herbal teas, health foods, and hot tubs, where only harmonies prevail.

Yet Balin, Jefferson Airplane's principal founder, is the extreme exception. Meditating is only a temporary escape. Once the spell is broken, the spirits of Hesse, Gurdjieff, and Krishnamurti give way to base, uncontrollable demons. Balin acts like a man betrayed, a wounded renegade, seething with anger.

"It was fucking appalling, there was no band, no communication, the

Airplane just became a group of egocentric moneygrubbers," rails Balin, describing the disaffection that led to his leaving the band on two occasions (in 1971 and 1978). Still embittered by their giving him "blood money," to hasten his exit, he steps up the attack, blistering, "We were the biggest band in the world, except for the Beatles, and then it was nothing but ego, everyone stopped working together. We became prisoners of fame, the knife stabbing began, *eeech!* As long as everyone had their drugs and cars, they didn't care about making music, our visions, or the shit I was taking from record-company people.

"We once made great music, there were a lot of good years . . . But after a while I couldn't talk to Grace [Slick]. I used to go to her with my songs, and she'd look at me and say the most outrageous, stupid things. I couldn't even get Paul [Kantner] there to rehearse. Eventually, I just gave up, I couldn't get anyone to change. Yet I was always the one who was seen as stubborn. So I said 'Fuck you, assholes, you're ruining *my* band.' I didn't believe in doing it just for the money. I had to leave. It was like Che Guevara leaving Castro. I didn't want to be associated with tyrants."

In 1965, at the height of a more innocent time in his life, the twenty-three-year-old Balin was determined to study glassblowing and painting in Florence, Italy. Leaving his native Cincinnati to pursue an acting career in San Francisco, he had fallen under the spell of such Italian artists as Botticelli, Masaccio, and Michelangelo. These geniuses were far more intriguing to him than the Everlys or Little Richard. And he hoped to work in a Tuscan factory or a quarry outside Florence, "so I'd get a real feel for the Italian temperament."

There was only one major problem. Balin didn't have the money to go abroad. He had been supporting himself by painting portraits, but this wasn't even lucrative enough to get him out of his Haight-Ashbury digs.

So Balin came up with a novel scheme. Noticing the Bay Area needed a club that echoed the music of the rising hippie movement, he put together a group of investors and restyled a folkie hangout into a psychedelic dance hall, the Matrix. Now, only one more hurdle had to be crossed. If Balin was going to make enough money to get to Europe, the place had to offer unique entertainment. A band was necessary that featured a "totally new sound."

"There was something happening in San Francisco at the time, I didn't exactly know what it was, but I knew the energy on the streets demanded a different type of music," says the taut-lipped Balin, his bronzed face as pensive as the Sphinx. "When I put the band together I found Paul first at a hoot, he had two guitars, and there was something about him that I really liked. I told him how I wanted to use drums— back then, they were an anathema in folkie circles, because you couldn't get a pickup on the guitar. But I wanted to use a lot more electricity; I knew the English sound was popping.

"Later on, I was at Paul's house, and I saw Jorma [Kaukonen, another Airplane guitarist] coming down the stairs. He just looked great, and when he told me about his guitar playing, I asked him to play with us. Soon Signe [Anderson] and Skip [Spence, the group's drummer] came along, we'd see them sitting in clubs. And about two months later, [Jack] Casady joined us. He was still going for a [college] degree at the time, but I was sure he was the bass player we were looking for. I called him solid for two weeks . . . we'd always wake him up . . . I kept telling him, 'Come on, man, we're going to turn the world on.' "

The emotion wells up in Balin's voice, even though he now has mixed feelings about these people. They were his soulmates, the folks who shared his dream. Through countless love-ins, acid trips, and incense burnings, they were together, Balin's veritable second family. It's therefore disturbing to listen to him, for his tale of a love gone sour encapsulates the death of an era—a loss that affects us all.

"We were really tight back then, very close," sighs Balin. "Jorma thought of a name for us, he had a friend with a dog who was called Thomas Jefferson Airplane, so he mentioned it, and we all cracked up . . . The first night we used it, Paul yelled to the crowd, 'Jefferson Airplane loves you,' and everyone wanted to know what the name meant. So we were immediately a mystery, the flower children that people wanted to know more about.

"Then Ralph Gleason [the celebrated *Rolling Stone* critic] did a piece on us for a San Francisco paper, and the record companies started offering us the moon. I told everyone, 'We're not signing anything until Phil Spector comes.' The next night, his sister came to the club, to invite us to his place in L.A. . . . Those were some times, everything was working for us, *real* fast. We went down there to see him, and would you believe, the guy was out to lunch. I didn't even wait around for his offer. He was a joke, he was too much the star for me . . . He didn't offer us one joint, and he had the fucking nerve to keep talking about his great stashes."

Instead of marijuana, the band received twenty thousand dollars from RCA to do their debut album, *The Jefferson Airplane Takes Off*. While that work had only limited commercial success, Balin's songwriting, especially "It's No Secret," won highly favorable reviews. The band's style was also a hit with hippies, as their penchant for blending group vocals with folk, jazz, and blues motifs reflected the era's emerging eclecticism—with its new emphasis on personal freedom.

Life with the Airplane, though, wasn't simply a psychedelic high. There were problems right from the outset. While Balin was thrust into a leadership role, the other members questioned his making all the decisions. He felt the band would self-destruct if there were too many spokespeople. And tempers flared when he unceremoniously dumped Signe, to bring "Miss Ice," Grace Slick, into the group.

"No one likes to be the bad guy, but it was a decision that had to be made," explains Balin, firmly and crisply. "Signe's husband was a jerk, but Signe loved him, and couldn't see what he was really like. She didn't want to travel too much, either . . . I only had one option, she had to go.

"Anyway, I was attracted to Grace. She was already in a band [the Great Society], and I knew she was the only person I could sing with. Jack approached her about it one night, and the next day she joined us. Grace is like that, she is one cold-blooded lady . . . And in the beginning we never had any problems. We'd rehearse together, bounce ideas off each other, and I really loved the way she sang. It was only later, when I had to go through entourages and a fleet of lawyers just to talk to her, that there were problems."

As Marty suggests, the Airplane's rising popularity was a mixed blessing. Once *Surrealistic Pillow* (1967) became synonymous with the burgeoning drug culture, egos began to dominate. Various members now saw themselves as larger-than-life figures, celebrities on a glittering world stage. Balin describes himself as "a lone wolf," the one who didn't need plush hotel suites or fancy limousines. Yet his ego was also on the line. He had been the driving force behind the group, their chief songwriter, and sensual vocalist. But once Slick arrived (she refuses to be interviewed), his most celebrated *Surrealistic Pillow* songs, "Plastic Fantastic Lover" and "3/5 of a Mile in 10 Seconds," were overshadowed by her raspy, red-hot vocals. She was a stinging, all-consuming presence on stage, whose slithery moves oozed S-E-X. And once her contributions to the album, "White Rabbit" and "Somebody to Love" leaped onto the charts, there was bound to be friction.

"Everything lost its flavor, I started to pull away," confesses Balin, biting into a cookie, while waiting for a pot of tea to cool. A kitchen wall is covered with photos of rock stars who have died, and echoing the gloom of that collage, Balin continues, "Before we got popular, we'd all sit on the floor, put in riffs, and construct something together. There was a grand idea, a purpose behind our music. We were always working on things, late into the night . . . oh, we could've made such boss music . . . but once we made it, everything fell apart. We were always keeping Grace together, protecting her from the fame, the alcohol . . . or giving her a setting . . . Then there were the coke users, once you start sniffing it, you never think of others. You just whine, constantly, 'I want my way . . . I want my way . . .'"

In a faltering, subdued voice, Marty then adds, "I loved the music we did—rock 'n' roll is the sculpturing of our day. It's a high art form . . . there's a darkness above the audience when you look out from the stage, and I love filling in the void.

"Geez, it was difficult to walk away. I built that band. We were important to people, we had vision. With that came a tremendous amount of power and responsibility, but I couldn't live out a lie. All that sixties' crap—love, peace—was a lie. There was no sharing, no higher principles, everyone was so insulated, they couldn't share an idea. Grace was the worst of all, she'd sit there like Edgar Bergen, and her boyfriend [drummer Spencer Dryden] would do all the talking. She just wouldn't talk, it was so damn infuriating. We had this love affair on stage, our moves were so hot, everything was so volatile we made great music. But offstage there was nothing, no communication at all . . . no one gave a good god damn about anything, just as long as they got their fucking money."

This estrangement continued over the next few years. The Airplane appeared at Woodstock, and other giant love-ins, yet Balin was progressively ostracized from the group. Now that Slick was the dominant figure, Balin's contribution to the heavily psychedelic *After Bathing at Baxter's* was limited to one song. He wrote four tunes for *Crown of Creation,* but hostilities peaked after Dryden left the band in 1970. Then, Slick gave birth to a daughter by Kantner, which forced the group to stop touring. That angered Kaukonen and Casady, who split to form Hot Tuna, and the ensuing fragmentation left Balin totally alone. The Starship now came into existence, with the release of *Blows Against the Empire.* But Balin had nothing to do with that sci-fi-influenced work, and in October 1970, he sorrowfully quit.

"I had to get back onto the streets, and just be normal again," admits

Balin, who wrote a rock opera after leaving the Starship. "Getting back into life was very difficult, it took me years to come down. I was depressed, how could I not be? We had so much there for a while. But the music we were doing was horrible, I thought the band was atrocious. I just didn't want to play that lousy shit."

During the early seventies, Balin also got involved with the American Indian Movement. After reading *Black Elk Speaks,* Marty was inspired to do a film on the famed Indian warrior, to educate other "unfortunate tribespeople" about genocide. "I wanted them to know how the white businessman had trampled on their rights. It's still going on. I felt so bad about being a white man, even though my friends, War Eagle and Thunder Cloud, had made me a brother. It sickened me to see what whites were doing . . .

"While I was with the Airplane I put aside a small fraction of my royalties for these Indians. It wasn't anything much, maybe ten to fifteen thousand. They had some great Thanksgiving Day meals with it. I even thought the Airplane would get involved, but like I said, that peace and freedom thing was a bunch of crap. They didn't have it together to do something like that. They were only interested in their drugs, and forty-thousand-dollar cars."

Voicing such hate, Balin wouldn't be expected to rejoin Slick and Company. Almost every pronouncement is an assault on the group's integrity, a venomous affront to their very being. Any kind of relationship would seem out of the question, especially one that brought him into close daily contact with his former friends.

Logic was not operative here, however. This was a matter of the heart. Acting like a headstrong, lovesick teenager, Balin ignored "the odds that were stocked against it, and rejoined the Starship in January 1975. The band had survived several permutations by then. And despite its all-star lineup, which included Turtles drummer John Barbata and the legendary Papa John Creach, the band had three successive failures, *Thirty Seconds Over Winterland, Early Flights,* and *Flight Log.*

Balin quickly turned things around. Abandoning the political, drug-glazed themes of the past, he wrote soft, endearing love songs. Ballads like "Miracles" reinstalled the Starship on the charts for the first time in years *(Red Octopus,* Balin's comeback effort, went double-platinum, selling over 3 million copies in 1975).

The uneasy truce between him, Slick, and the rest of the group (especially manager Bill Thompson) lasted for three years. None of the old problems disappeared, they were just shoved under the rug. So Balin kept writing about love, (his "With Your Love" was another major hit), while pretending "the revulsion and sadness inside me didn't exist."

Ultimately, that sickening discontent couldn't be dismissed. It kept throbbing, swelling like a neglected abscess. When the hurt of "everyone going back to Ego City" proved too devastating," Balin left the group again. Only this time the denouement was doubly painful.

"I brought them back to the top, but did that matter? Shit, no one gave a damn," flails Balin, his face reddening. "They said they'd listen to my ideas, that we'd get back to our old vision, and principles. I thought eventually I'd see some moral fiber, but it never happened. Nothing would ever be done. I got tired of the disappointment, they were just a bunch of egocentric crazies . . ."

Marty shakes his head disgustedly. Looking confused and emotionally drained, he stammers, "I really thought that when you were in a band it meant love, an unshakable bond. But I guess that's only the way I looked at it. Bill Thompson would keep reiterating to me, 'This is a business, this is a business.' And that's how things worked out; when I quit, no one could care less. Not one person asked me to reconsider. I was amazed. No one tried to stop me. They were glad that they were finally rid of that 'asshole.' "

Though traumatized, Balin did go on to other triumphs. In 1980, his opera *(Rock Justice)* was finally released as an LP by EMI-America, and his first solo album, Balin (1981), included the bestselling single, "Hearts." That song made him an international star, and over the next few years, he toured extensively in the Far East and Europe.

Most importantly, the forty-four-year-old Balin is not hurting for money. Heeding his father's advice, he didn't "go through the royalties like everyone else." A large portion of his earnings was invested, and as a testament to this sagacity, he recently added a floor to his pyramid-shaped house.

Adjourning to that upstairs retreat, Balin sprawls out on the floor, in a room that holds only a flower-bedecked Buddha and a few odd photographs. Ordinarily, he does most of his meditating here. So it's not surprising that he again waxes philosophical.

"The Airplane was just one of those unfinished things you leave in your life," says Balin, staring at a wall, as if this will block out the past. "I don't care about the rumors, the Airplane, the real Airplane won't resurface. I won't go back . . . No one ever wanted to complete what we had going, and now that era is gone. We had our time . . . there's not much meaning out there anymore. People are just into trivial pursuits. It's like Hemingway said, life is nothing but a moveable feast."

Paul Kantner of the Jefferson Airplane

There Were Bumpy Flights, but . . .

Darting through San Francisco traffic in his turbo-charged Porsche, Paul Kantner narrowly misses hitting a truck, before stopping at a secluded spot near the Oakland Bay Bridge. Here, he lights a joint and starts to talk about Marty Balin and the Airplane.

"It's true, each member of the group did get insulated, there were power fiefdoms, but the group died a natural death. If we didn't have egos we wouldn't be in this business. We got caught up in the tide of having fun. We went through a hell of a lot while breaking down barriers. Rock groups in the sixties were just like SDS [Students for a Democratic Society], the Berkeley Free Speech Movement, and other political activists; we expanded the limits, we were freedom fighters. In finding our own parameters, we made lots of mistakes as anyone would. But we also made a whole lot of nonmistakes that helped keep people alive, from ending the Vietnam War, to the cutting back of repressive drug laws."

Looking out at the bay through his metal-rimmed glasses, the blond, long-haired Kantner then smiles knowingly. "If you want to talk about legacies, with Grace [Slick] it was simply standing up and doing things her own way. We just had such a good time that a lot of people noticed us. I don't know why we never got arrested. Jorma [Kaukonen] always thought a CIA experiment had gone awry, and that they just wanted to observe us, so they kept police agencies away.

"We were outrageous. We'd walk down streets in Hollywood smoking marijuana. When we went to RCA, we went with a black janitor into his broom closet to smoke a joint. RCA executives were afraid to come into the studio; they were afraid they'd have to deal with it.

"Drugs were just another act of rebellion, like acupuncture, communism—all the things we weren't supposed to look into. I still think drugs are an opener; I gained respect for the environment through LSD.

"But at the end, when we couldn't agree on anything, speed and cocaine accelerated that splitting into fiefdoms. It's like Marty said, no one wanted to give. Speed and cocaine just built that up. 'Fuck you, I don't have to give, I'm king of the world.' "

This is said sharply. Usually easygoing and flip, often referring to himself as "a bozo," Kantner now seems genuinely serious. "Marty," Kantner says the name with real affection and a trace of annoyance, the kind of tone a person uses when discussing a mischievous child.

"Marty, he's such an idealist, he can't get through to anyone on a lasting basis. No one tried to buy him off, or wanted to get rid of him. Marty had honorable feelings, but they weren't realistic. Once he said, 'Paul, let's fire the whole band and go write songs for a year, then we'll come back, and do it again—as if the whole band would be there a year later.

"I'm very idealistic too, but when something doesn't happen, it doesn't happen. With Marty, when things don't work out, he takes it as a personal insult. After a while I couldn't deal with that. A lot of what Marty says has merit. Everyone has egos, but the Airplane did get egoed out. But, at one point, the drugs, the egos, they were the group's strength. I wouldn't want a bunch of wimps who just followed along. So you go for people who are strong, independent. That fire or bubbling was vital at one time. A band is just a collection of people with similar interests; it's not love all the time. People have conflicts, and you compromise at times. Maybe those clashes, that fire, killed the group. But so be it. The Airplane had its day. Nothing goes on forever. I wouldn't want it to."

Despite a straitlaced, Catholic military-academy education, Kantner hasn't always been such a cold pragmatist. Not knowing what to do after attending the University of Santa Clara, he fantasized about becoming a bank robber. Intrigued by a book, *The Life of Willie Sutton,* he was swept away by the romance of a life on the run. So instead of emulating Elvis or the Everlys, Kantner planned to follow Sutton ("a real cool guy"), on the path to adventure and daring escapades.

Eventually, deciding that a life of crime was a little too risky, Kantner did the next best thing. He hooked up with a rock band. Upon Balin's urging, he joined the Airplane in 1965 and managed to pull off that much dreamed-about "caper."

"I'm still amazed that I was able to get rich from singing," says Kantner, innocently grinning. He discounts the fact that the Airplane's surrealistic sound made the group the voice of the counterculture. They were the first San Francisco band to have a major national hit, but he persists, "Grace thinks that everything we've done is a pile of shit, and I agree with her. To get paid what we do is obscene. I've just gone along with it; we're all bozos on this bus."

Believing that members of the Starship take themselves too seriously, he's left the group to help an aspiring San Francisco band, the Mutants. By so doing, he seems to be in agreement with Balin, for the conversation again focuses on ego.

"Unfortunately, egos have broken the whole thing up. They've gotten out of control on the Starship. But I'm not a guy who wants to control things. When Grace was around and having her drinking problem, everyone was asking, 'Why don't you take care of her?' I said, 'Fuck you, I'm not her babysitter or zookeeper.' It didn't matter, she was still the consummate professional on stage.

"I'm not going to complain the way Marty did. People screw up, but so what? He just amplified things too much. He's focused too much on the last years. It's his nature to complain. There were problems, but rather than quitting, he should've come to me, we should've talked. I was sad and hurt by the fact that he said 'I'm leaving,' instead of saying 'I want to leave.' He didn't come to me, didn't give me the option of trying to change things. In true hippie fashion, he wanted things to just happen. We were able to rehearse, to do all kinds of things. He's just focusing on the shitty."

There's a reason for Kantner's positive thinking. He's survived a brush with death.

In 1981, while he was making love to "the mother of his latest child" (the forty-four-year-old guitarist has three children, including Slick's fourteen-year-old daughter, China), a blood vessel burst in his brain. Kantner was rushed to the hospital, where he was observed by neurosurgeons for several days. Remarkably, they didn't have to operate on the aneurysm, and as Kantner quips, "I'm my asshole self these days."

Nonetheless, Kantner has become more philosophical since then, and increasingly tolerant. Despite his differences with Balin, he recalls "the great fire, the connection" that existed between them, and speaks wistfully of resuming their partnership.

"I know Marty's afraid of bigness—the organization, the planning—but I think we can do it together. Our getting back together has been bubbling for a while. This time there won't be any managers, and maybe we'll do it for just one record. That way we won't get too big. Who knows?"

Staring at an oil tanker moving under the bridge, Kantner draws heavily on his joint, then offers a closing thought on the Starship.

"I had to leave. Some of the band members are just not very original at all; I'd rather not sell records and be original, than sell 40 billion records, and sound like Van Halen."

Bryan "Chas" Chandler of the Animals

Good-bye, Eric Burdon—Hello, Jimi Hendrix

Once the conversation turns to Jimi Hendrix, and to that "dreadful" subject of drugs, the gray-haired woman eavesdropping from a nearby table gulps her tea. Trying not to look nonplussed, in a typically British sort of way, she takes a bite of her scone and looks nervously around the Kensington tearoom. She might not know about Hendrix, or of his magical guitar, but for her, this acid-laced tale is an uncomfortable one, so she finally moves away, to another seat, as soon as an opportunity presents itself.

Ignoring this little sideshow, Bryan "Chas" Chandler, the former bass player for the Animals, continues to speak of Hendrix's drug problem, and how it spoiled their brotherly friendship.

"We were so close; my first wife and I shared an apartment with him for two years, and we were always talking music late into the night," says Chandler, somberly reflecting on the days he co-managed Hendrix, along with Michael Jeffrey. "After all the aggravation I had with the Animals, it was great fun to be with him, concentrating on putting his act together, cooking up ideas. I was fortunate to set up the Experience, but the drugs, the acid, I spent half my time trying to convince him not to do it. After a while it disgusted me. I couldn't stand to see such talent go to waste.

"We finally had to split when he went ahead with his plans to buy this New York club (the Generation club). The acid convinced him that he could turn the place into a recording studio. I couldn't talk him out of that or the acid. So after about four weeks of working on *Electric Lady-land,* and seeing he'd only done a few takes, I got tired of the whole thing. I had to get away. My wife was expecting a baby, and I just didn't like the hangers-on he was with. It was a druggy, sick scene. I always think that if I had stayed around he might still be alive—and that gives me nightmares sometimes. But I had to get away from him, there was no other way."

Unfortunately, the sixties were also a tangled time for Chandler. There were more disappointments, other anguished leave-takings. Far from being a blast, success with the Animals threw him into an ever-swirling maelstrom of ego conflicts, financial disputes, and ugly back-stage politicking. Even as the hits kept coming—"House of the Rising Sun," "We've Gotta Get Out of This Place," and "Don't Let Me Be Misunderstood"—the tensions sapped the group's energy. Various members split. Others fixated on drugs. And as Chandler's dream of "making important music" died, his frustration spilled over. He left an American tour prematurely and has come to regard the Animals' legendary Eric Burdon as less than an outstanding human being.

Chandler's six-foot-four-inch frame seems to twitch when he says this. The words come slowly out of his mouth, as if they're causing him a great deal of pain. His freckled, fair-skinned face also looks drawn and tired. Understandably, he finds it difficult to continue talking, for the criticism of Burdon underscores not only the disintegration of a rock group, but, more important, signals the death of a vital partnership—a fraternity that once prompted great dreams. "With Eric talking so much about our making it big, I eventually forgot about his ego, and started to take him seriously."

In the early 1960s, the Animals (then known as the Alan Price Combo) needed such a catalyst. Up until then, under various names, they'd been limited to playing small clubs in remote Northern England, near their hometown of Newcastle-upon-Tyne. Content with this local notoriety, they didn't envision broader horizons of success. As Chandler indicates, instead of thinking about London or a stab at a record contract, hitchhiking to a Glasgow or Edinburgh talent show "was about as daring as we ever got. Doing anything more was just out of the question. It never dawned on me, or on any of the other guys, that we'd play music to make a living."

While Chandler couples these remarks with a hearty chuckle, he forgets that the early sixties were a difficult time for him. Of working-class origins, with little formal education, he was then drifting from job to job. This had more than merely financial implications, for with England sending military troops to Burma and Cyprus in those years, twenty-year-old men without government-approved employment were subject to the draft.

"After worrying for months that I'd have to go into the Army, I finally found this factory work that offered a way out, but was it boring, goddamn!" complains Chandler, again breaking the hush of the staid London tearoom. "For ten to fifteen hours a day, I had to work on this lathe. I didn't know what else to do. The routine was terrible, but it was either that or getting shot at."

Since Chandler was tied to his lathe for the next few years (in 1962, at the age of twenty-four, he would become draft exempt), he didn't care about the band's future prospects. Nightly relief from the day-long grind was a more important concern. As he points out, "I just wanted to have a few beers with the guys, and play my guitar. If we got a booking, great. I'd play wherever they'd have us. And if things didn't work out, that was okay too. I only wanted to have some fun."

Sneering, Chandler hints at what happened next.

Eric arrived on the scene. The fun ended, as ambition engulfed them.

Returning to Newcastle after he had failed as a solo performer in London, Burdon was asked one night to fill in for a missing band member. He immediately impressed Price with his bluesy, "black-flavored" vocals. So much so that other group members not in synch with him were replaced. For instance, guitarist Hilton Valentine was brought in, to give the quintet a blacker, more pronounced rock sound, while the "jazzier" Nigel Stanger was dropped—a change that didn't go over too well with Chandler.

"I knew right then and there that we weren't just out for a good time anymore," recalls Chas, lighting a cigarette. "We wouldn't have gone anywhere with Nigel, we didn't have any commerciality, but I preferred his being in it. There was a loose, easygoing feeling with him around. Once he left, everything got very serious. We were suddenly out to become big stars."

In pursuit of this goal, the newly christened Animals grew more adventuresome, and moved to a new lair. Renting a small, badly heated flat in London, they made their local debut at the Scene Club in December 1963. And while Chas glowingly says, "We virtually took off

straightaway," success didn't bring much joy. They were too busy
snarling at one another.

"Living in one flat was a big mistake; we were continually fighting,
and at each other's throats," admits Chandler, through gritted teeth.
"We saved money, that's for sure, but being together twenty-four hours
a day had to lead to fights. You know, over petty things. There was no
privacy. It was like I was living in Alan's or Eric's pocket. No wonder
everyone was always threatening to quit. It was no way to start down
that so-called 'magical' road."

Perhaps not. Their quarreling over spilled toothpaste or dirty ash-
trays boded ill for the future, when money and managers would complicate matters even more.

But in the early days, these angry exchanges had a positive side.
There was a wild energy here, and if it were harnessed, it could be used
to turn on crowds—a fact which didn't escape producers. With the
Animals causing near-riots at the Scene Club, these honchos flocked to
the place in droves. The boys listened to all their promises, and, to
Chandler's later chagrin, they eventually tabbed Mickie Most as their
manager.

Quickly showing he was one of rock's smoothest operators, Most got
the Animals a slot on Chuck Berry's 1964 European tours. The Animals' ambitious mix of blues and soul, which contrived to attract frenzied crowds, evolved out of Berry's ringing, electrified licks on the guitar. So the boys were delighted to appear with him—especially
Chandler. That tour, in fact, is still described by Chas as "one of the
greatest experiences of my life."

"Playing with him symbolized that I was finally making it. I didn't
feel that way up until then, even with the successes we were having in
London. All of us felt these crowds were easy, that they'd applaud for
anything. But the Berry tour was different. Here he was, the great
antihero [Berry had served two years in jail for transporting a minor
over state lines], the coming of a legend, and we were part of one of his
first public appearances. It was great. We did twenty-minute spots, and,
best of all, we were stopping audiences dead with 'House of the Rising
Sun.' That tour showed us we had a major hit on our hands."

Most wasn't as enthusiastic. He didn't want "House of . . ." to be
recorded as a single, and according to Chandler, tried to "sabotage"
interest in the song.

"He put the 'mockers' on it. He kept telling us the song wouldn't
work, that it would hurt us, that we were wasting our time," bristles

Chandler, his cheeks flushed with anger. "But we knew that was a lot of bull. We gave him this ultimatum that we either record it, or we wouldn't do another song. We knew it was a great song, but he was so damn shortsighted, so straight-music oriented.

"We finally convinced Most that we weren't going to change our minds, so grudgingly, he told us we'd get one hour in the studio if we got to London. We were in Liverpool doing a gig on a Friday night, but we made it down there, and we did one take on the song, in twenty minutes it was done. The recording bill was about four pounds (ten dollars), and three months later it was number one all over the world."

The feuding continued, however. Now that the Animals had a monster hit, the writing credits (which are the basis of future royalties) became the focal point for another battle with Most. He had listed only Price as the song writer, and this infuriated the others. Insisting the song was a collaborative effort, they argued that Price had made only a token contribution and had even failed to appear at rehearsals. And while they pressed their case for months, the only result of this skirmishing was more bad feelings. This divisiveness eventually led to Price's leaving the group in 1965.

Still embittered by that controversy, Chandler sarcastically says, "I guess it would've meant too much work for Most to put five names on the record. That [song] was a five-man arrangement. The way it was handled had to create troubles. It was always a source of contention between us.

"We were finally led to believe that we'd still share the royalties. Maybe it was naïve, but none of us ever thought that anyone would pull a 'runner.' Well, I'm still waiting for the money."

After snickering loudly, he adds, more cheerfully, "The one good thing about the whole mess was that the four of us drew closer together. We weren't about to let the Animals fall apart just because of Alan. The first thing we did was '. . . Gotta Get Out of This Place' [the song made it to number thirteen in 1965]. There was a lot of good feeling then, a determination that lasted eight to nine months. We felt we had to prove ourselves all over again, so the acrimony was replaced by this 'do it without him' attitude."

While the honeymoon period generated several time-honored standards, pieces like "It's My Life" and "I'm Crying," which underscore the group's indebtedness to Berry and Bo Diddley, money continued to be a problem. Whether it was their extravagant spending habits (on booze and drugs), or, as Chandler maintains, "We were simply ripped off," the Animals were constantly strapped for funds. Chandler often thought about suing Most for a better cut of the royalties, while drummer John Steel took more drastic action. Unable to support his wife, he quit, thus changing the entire dynamic of the group. Suddenly, it didn't matter to Chandler whether they recorded a few more hits. He had lost a friend, and playing became a "rotten drag."

"From that moment on I stopped enjoying it, the performing was like a job, and I felt like I was back in the factory again," complains Chas sourly. "I had an understanding with Steel; we were partners out there. He was the only guy I could really be close with.

"Do you understand what I'm saying? It wasn't fun anymore. I think Eric felt that way too. We got to talking one night in a hotel, and decided to just call it a day. There was nothing left for us to accomplish together. We were tired of the hassles, fed up with Most, so we did one more American tour [1966] and that was it. The Animals had had it."

The day before that tour began, Chandler went to the Cafe Wha? in Greenwich Village, and met this "wild-eyed kid" named James Marshall Hendrix (he was performing as Jimmy James). "The only thing he wanted to talk about was the English scene," recalls Chandler. "Once he heard that I knew [Eric] Clapton and [Jeff] Beck, he wanted to know everything about them, what they were 'really like,' what kind of amplifiers they used. He was very concerned about amplification. Well, we talked for about half an hour, and he finally asked me if I'd introduce him to them.

"I wanted to try my hand at producing and I was convinced he could make it really big. So I told him I'd come back and take him to England. He had nothing then—he was sleeping wherever he could, doing these twelve-dollar-a-night gigs. I guess he was desperate for a change, so that was it, everything was signed, sealed, and delivered in that quick meeting."

After bringing the twenty-two-year-old to England in the fall of 1966, Chandler gave his discovery a new name. While the guitarist would later be heralded as "the most innovative instrumental genius" of the rock era, Chas simply dubbed him Jimi Hendrix. He then put the Experience together, installing Noel Redding on drums, Mitch Miller on bass—and used the last six hundred dollars of his Animals' money to take them all to France.

There, they hooked up with the self-proclaimed "French Elvis," Johnny Halliday. The European star wasn't known only for covering others' hits; he also knew, according to Chandler, how to manipulate an audience, how to "whip them into a frenzy." Of course, Jimi had some ideas of his own along these lines. He already had a soul education, having played behind Little Richard and the Isley Brothers. But Chandler insisted, "It was time to go to school again.

"We watched Halliday, and made notes on what we'd steal. Later, the psychedelic stuff came out of the science-fiction books I gave him, songs like 'Stone Free' [the flip side of 'Hey Joe'] and 'Purple Haze,' where the sound effects are so important. But in the beginning, Jimi's act just evolved out of that French tour. He learned a lot from Halliday."

Over the next two years, the Hendrix-Chandler friendship flourished. The two men were constantly together, rehearsing songs in the studio, and, as Chas says, "spending twenty-four hours a day talking music." They would drift apart by 1968, as Jimi began to hang out with a heavy-drug crowd. But these all-night talks, which are recalled in near whispers, were clearly productive. From 1966 to 1968, Hendrix released two albums, *Are You Experienced?* which critic Dave Marsh labeled "the most stunning debut album of all time," and the equally memorable *Axis: Bold as Love.*

Since both of these albums were done in a matter of weeks, Chandler couldn't tolerate the delays in recording *Electric Ladyland.* As already noted, he attributed this change to Hendrix's new friends; the people he holds responsible for "twisting Jimi's head with all kinds of crazy ideas." So when Hendrix remained adamant about opening a studio, Chas felt "It was a time for a vacation. I was totally disillusioned, and thoroughly burnt out."

Three months later, not knowing what else to do, Chandler got back into the business. Forming a production company with Robert Stigwood, he again scouted new talent—and eventually restyled a group which would go on to twenty-three hit singles in England, the heavy-metal-sounding Slade. Though the quintet was ignored in the United States, "Slademania" gripped Europe for several years. As Chandler likes to remind people, "Their songs were recorded in fifteen different languages. They had plenty of number ones, and, through it all, I was dealing with honest people for a change. Stigwood was the greatest.

"Here's a group that was making a lot of money, and he allowed me to buy the management rights for only five thousand pounds (1972). That was a very generous gesture. He said I'd done all the work with the band, so I should have them. He's one of the few gentlemen in the business."

Chandler managed Slade until 1982. He was operating five studios at the time and the workload finally unnerved him. Once again he wanted to break away, to "do something completely different." And for a few months he actually succeeded at dropping out. Isolating himself in front of a word processor, he began to fulfill his long-standing ambition of writing a novel.

Chandler, however, never got a chance to finish that work. He had to write the ending to another story.

"Just when I started to get going, the boys called and asked me to do an Animals reunion tour," says the forty-eight-year-old Chandler, before cursing himself for never learning. "I really thought the tour would be fun, but, except for a few good moments on stage, it was sheer hell.

"Eric had become a legend in his own mind, and he made the tour miserable for us. He felt everyone should bow down to him. It was sheer unpleasantness on his part. He went out of his way to be rude to people. He just hadn't grown up. I don't know why—maybe he realized he was in the spotlight again, and that frightened him. His nerves must've cracked. He was probably afraid he'd blow it."

Shaking his head in disbelief, Chandler then exclaims, "God, what a tragedy that was! He was better than ever; he was absolutely magic out there on the stage. But I don't know what happened to him everywhere else. He was always pissing me off with his attitude, like he was doing us a favor by showing up. I couldn't take that, it was plain crap."

Once the six-month tour ended in December 1983, Chas returned to his hometown in Northern England, to manage another young band, the 21 Strangers. After refining their bluesy sound, which was reminiscent of the Animals, he recently secured their first recording deals. That contract has apparently taken the edge off the past, for judging by Chas's smiles, he's been reinvigorated by the Strangers' early successes.

"I'm absolutely tingling right now, I'm enjoying life very much," exults Chandler, finally taking a bite of a raspberry tart. "It's a tremendous challenge working with these young kids, so I don't have any time to think of what's past. Besides, I know all the crooks now, I know how to avoid them. You get a second sight, you walk away from the bad guys. And let me tell you, there sure are a lot of these phonies around."

Why is he different from them?

When asked this question, Chandler gives it a moment's thought, then jokingly replies, "Maybe it's because of my clean living. I've always taken a better kind of acid."

Martha Reeves
of the Vandellas
Triumphantly Walking the Tightrope

Vengefully, life has mirrored art for Martha Reeves.

Her romances have been like heat waves. Searing. Intense. All-encompassing. They've swept her to peaks of ecstasy, only to leave her emotionally spent, and cynical about love.

Two marriages have wound up in failure. The heat couldn't sustain itself. Not with her on the road, away from husbands who didn't understand the demands of a rock life. Young newlywed passions, the joys of setting up a home, even the satisfaction of having a baby, succumbed to male jealousy and suspicion.

Reeves's love for her son has withstood the traumas. Although she's still on the road, singing standbys like "Love Is Like a Heat Wave," and "Dancing in the Street," her fourteen-year-old is her prime concern. His needs will be met, even if it costs her another shot at glory. Whatever it takes, she's "going to be there for my baby."

But here lies the dilemma, the balancing act that bedevils many career-minded women: Can a woman sustain a professional life, without sacrificing her home, husband, and children? Or are these pursuits mutually exclusive, with only regrets and frustrations in the offing for those who walk the tightrope?

Bewitched by "a dream, a conviction that I could be a star," Reeves never considered the dangers of a life in the spotlight. Eager to escape the Detroit ghetto, she just plunged ahead in the late 1950s, wildly and naïvely, like a starry-eyed schoolgirl.

Sharing her mother's interest in gospel, she first joined a church choir, then graduated to the Del-phis, a high school all-girl group that cut a few records on the Check-Mate label. None of these singles dented the local charts, so between weekend engagements, Martha ("Mickey" as a teenager) worked for a dry cleaner.

"I was still confident. I wasn't discouraged at all, since I had won some amateur contests that year [1960]," recalls Reeves, smiling at her mother, who sits nearby in a wheelchair, watching an afternoon soap opera. The seventy-one-year-old woman recently suffered a paralyzing stroke, and now that she's confined to her Detroit home, Martha is frequently found by her side. "My whole family believed in me, and one weekend, while I was performing at a local club, William Stevenson, the A & R director at Motown, approached me. I didn't know a thing about Motown, even though they already had some big hits. But he said I had something, so instead of going to the dry cleaner, I went down to the studio the following Monday morning, thinking this was my big chance."

Chuckling, Martha takes off her running shoes, and stretches out on a couch. Dressed in a baggy purple jogging suit, she smoothes her curly brown hair, then sweetly tells her mother, "I took some food out of the freezer. I'll make it in a few minutes. Mom, do you remember my first day at Motown? How it all began?"

Disappointed by the ensuing silence, Martha pinches her lips into a girlish pout. When her deep, dark eyes also narrow, the wrinkles on her forehead become more pronounced. But, with that kittenish expression seemingly engraved on her otherwise smooth, mocha-colored face, she hardly looks old enough to have a teenaged son. Still slender and sensuous at forty-three, she's retained her sultry sexiness; that fire which once engulfed men like a mind-numbing afternoon in the tropics.

"Well, when I got to Motown, I was immediately disappointed," continues Reeves. "The audition wasn't going to be held for another month. But they asked me to stay there, to answer the phones. I had some secretarial skills from high school, so I became a secretary to about twelve writers, including Smokey Robinson, Stevie Wonder, Lamont Dozier, Brian Holland, Eddie Holland—the people that made history.

"Motown was full of surprises then. There were so many talented people in one small area. And everything was shared. Writers would assist other writers, artists would assist other artists. We'd go into the studio together, not knowing whose product it was; we just wanted to lend our voices to making good music. Berry Gordy was the captain of the whole ship, he knew what he wanted, and insisted we produce it. The experience was fun, adventurous, and educational."

A big "sister" in those days to Stevie Wonder (ten years old in 1960), Martha laughingly recalls, "What a sweet baby. He was so talented, but we really didn't know what to do with him at the time. We had to find out where his talents lay. We'd bring him in every day after school, and I'd be with him, not to baby-sit, but I'd follow him around all day, and I was just amazed at his talents. He'd go from drums to piano, piano to guitar, anything you put in his hands the baby could play. It was amazing to see him develop. He was just a genius—every time he came to the studio he'd come up with something very creative."

Memories of another Motown legend, Smokey Robinson, also bring a smile to her face. "Oh, Smokey, what a sweetheart he was to me. He was easygoing, always pleasant, and really, he's one of the most creative people I've ever had a chance to work with. Back then he was kind of my older brother, although he had a baby face, he had a lot of authority, a lot of creativity, and he always came up with winner songs."

Enjoying the camaraderie at Motown, Martha was content with being a secretary for over a year. She talks proudly of buying the company's first clock, filing contracts, and arranging recording sessions for girl groups that would one day compete with her for recognition.

Insisting "I wasn't jealous, not at all," Reeves remained the company loyalist—the good soldier who believed in Motown's fabled future.

But she still dreamed of a singing career, and in late 1961, her big break came.

Marvin Gaye was set to record "Stubborn Kind of Fellow," but his customary backup group, the Andantes, were out of town. Remembering the demo Reeves had cut in 1960, Bill Stevenson asked her and the Del-phis to fill in at the sessions. Gordy was immediately impressed, and in a few months, Martha, Annette Sterling, and Rosalind Ashford signed a Motown contract.

Calling themselves the Vandellas, because Martha idolized Della Reese, and lived near Van Dyke street ("Gordy wanted to name us the Tillies, or something else that was corny, so we quickly came up with the Vandellas"), they were soon touring with Gaye. It was his Motown debut as well, and as Martha points out, "Since we shared so much on that trip, we all got to love him. He was very special.

"In the beginning, at the studio, he was very shy, you could hardly get a word out of him. He'd do the sessions, and leave. He wouldn't hang around, like other artists. I guess he was hiding all that talent under his shyness.

"But I got to know him," continues Reeves, her voice cracking. "And I'm very, very touched and moved by his passing from this earth. I don't feel he's gone. He's left enough music and enough talent here for us to know that he has been here. He holds a very special place in my heart."

After that tour, the Vandellas' first record was released, "I'll Have to Let Him Go." It didn't sell too well, but Motown didn't lose confidence in the group. The girls had a fiery stage presence, a raw sex appeal that distinguished them from the rest of Gordy's stable. As the Motown Master had presumably noticed, the Vandellas' exuberant blues-oriented music made people stand up and dance. "Even early on, we hit a groove that was a precursor to disco," says Martha triumphantly.

Perhaps that's true.

But Gordy had higher ambitions for his girls. He always did. So their act was refined at the Motown "charm school"; they were educated, to a certain extent, about the business; and then it was time for their fateful "marriage" to Motown's illustrious writing team, Holland-Dozier-Holland.

Their first hit together was "Come and Get These Memories" (1963), a soft, bluesy ballad that lacked the energy of the group's later successes.

Then, in 1964, H-D-H came up with a more inspired effort—the brassy, pulsating dance tune that made the Vandellas a household name.

" 'Heat Wave' opened so many doors for us, it was amazing," raves Martha, while running into the kitchen. "That song was the key, all right. We got our first Grammy nomination, and all of a sudden, we were appearing all over the place. We went to Europe, as sort of the exchange act for the Beatles. They were here making their splash, while we were in London getting our flowers and our fan clubs. With 'Heat Wave' our life really began. That was the start of the big time."

There's an ambivalence in Martha's voice, and her unsmiling face is fixed on the stove. As she soon explains, success had its drawbacks, its empty side. Her dream was far better than reality.

"Any woman who takes on a career such as show business is taking on the life of a gypsy," says Reeves. "And some of that is hardships, the romance is taken out of it. You don't exactly have time for the meaningful relationships that you want. And you get a little depressed and lonely at times—that was the hardest thing I had to deal with.

"I was always the leader of the group, so I had the responsibility of leading all the songs, and making all the arrangements, checking the costumes . . . I'm proud of the job I did. We stayed out front for a long time [through 1965, the Vandellas had such hits as "Quicksand," and "Dancing in the Street"]. But socially, I wasn't successful."

Showing no sign of emotion, except for her silence, Martha walks around the kitchen, making last-minute preparations for her mother's meal. A question about her first marriage is ignored, but upon returning to the living room, she finally says, "The marriages I've had haven't been the romantic relationships someone would picture. They were, I guess, business deals for ambitious guys. You can fall prey to that if you're not aware of what's going on around you. Those are some of the things that I could throw back at the biz bag.

"But on the whole, I feel we [she and the Vandellas] were some of the blessed of our generation. We were singled out, selected—I walked through a door that was open to me. We found success and gold in there.

"I really don't want to talk about the other stuff; that was just part of the experience of being a woman on the road, and details can be left out. I just found it difficult to have a career and a marriage, because they [her husbands] weren't involved in the business, and had no idea what a tour is about, or what a one-nighter is, or what a promoter's job is, or what an artist is obligated to do because of a contract. That can cause problems, and it did in my life."

While Martha's love life was in disarray during the mid-sixties, the H-D-H triumvirate could do no wrong. Surviving several changes in the group's lineup, the Vandellas were consistently on the charts, with "Nowhere to Run" [Martha's adopted theme song], "I'm Ready for Love," and "Jimmy Mack."

But by 1967 priorities had changed at Motown. A tamer, less explosive group gained ascendancy, as Gordy had fallen under the spell of Diana Ross. Now the Supremes received preferential treatment at shows, in promotional campaigns, and, most important, with the writers. Martha and the Vandellas could no longer depend on Holland-Dozier-Holland, or on having any more hits.

Still the Motown loyalist, Martha denies there was any competition between her group and the Supremes. Though it's well chronicled that Gordy pushed Ross, to everyone else's disadvantage, Reeves adamantly insists, "We were all part of a big company, and everyone had a turn to be number one. When I signed my contract, Mary Wells was coming off being the number one female vocalist with 'My Guy.' Everyone had a turn to be exposed to the public, the Marvelettes, Wells, so there was no competition. It was like seeing a new baby being born into the family. I was glad to see new artists cutting their teeth, learning to walk, and becoming part of Motown. We didn't have the competition there is today."

Her voice growing more strident, in response to the suggestion that the Vandellas were eclipsed by the Supremes after 1967, she quickly continues, "We had our own fans, and they had theirs. We shared fans. We have an identity, just as they do. And we can be proud of each other. We associated with one another; there was no way you could separate us. The competition might've been something that someone around us created, but we helped each other grow. I sang on Supremes sessions, on Marvelettes sessions, it was a matter of accepting the fact that we were all talented, and we all worked and went to school together. That we all grew together, and had life and death situations together."

Then, in a softer tone, she sighs, "It was an innocent time, there was a pure family spirit, one could get to the truth, real feeling. At Motown, we were urged to help each other. It was like we were in a winning situation, and we were all one. In '61, '62, '63, it seemed as if Motown had hit a pot of gold. Then, Motown was the sound of young America."

Reeves won't ever admit to feeling frustrated; she's too iron-willed to pity herself. Yet there must have been a crisis of faith in the late sixties, or a large measure of anxiety. In her search for serenity, she became dependent on tranquilizers.

Referring to 1969, the year she suddenly left the touring circuit, Reeves says, "I had run into a lot of street people, and they introduced me to amphetamines. Drugs were flowing about, and, being young and adventurous, I had a couple of drug-related illnesses. Fortunately, I've overcome that. Now I can just use yoga or meditation to keep a calm mind.

"I'd say I had a six-month bout with tranquilizers, that went from five milligrams to twenty. When I got to the Thorazine, I stopped. I said 'No, this is not the way to go.' I got them from doctors, but they were detrimental to my health and career. I couldn't perform, so I had to find other ways of relaxation. 'Nowhere to Run' would be an apt title for this period, but, thankfully, I wasn't engulfed by drugs, I found a better way."

During Reeves's absence, the Vandellas experienced more personnel changes (Martha's sister Lois joined the group), and were relegated to opening for other Motown acts. They finally disbanded in 1972, after Martha had a son, and moved to Los Angeles.

"For a while I thought about totally leaving the business," recalls Reeves, her eyes sparkling again. "But if talent is given to you by the Almighty, it will go away if it isn't utilized. I didn't want to make that sacrifice, I felt honored to be a singer. I didn't take that for granted. I felt blessed to have a talent, that I was part of a select group. I thought I had an obligation to God."

So, still believing in the "dream," Reeves tried to make "the right career moves" in Hollywood. Leaving Motown upon the urgings of her sister's manager, she switched allegiances to MCA, and even appeared in an X-rated movie, *Fairy Tales* ("I didn't take my clothes off"). It was admittedly painful not to be in the Top 10 anymore—and thrust into a new world by herself, she had a stream of managers who "weren't too interested in furthering my career, they only wanted to get what they could."

When reminiscing about this "growing" period (1972–75), Martha remains calm, often measuring her remarks, or punctuating them with laughter. Instead of lashing out at deceitful managers, she talks of her own "raw" innocence, and of the Motown environment, which fostered "creative artistry," unspoiled by business dealings.

While insisting "I'm well educated now," she declares, "at Motown, I didn't have any cares or worries. After I signed a contract, and went onto the road, I was an artist, not a business person. By seeking my own destiny, I've learned a lot. But back in the sixties, the whole Motown roster was innocent. Creatively, that was good, because I was free. I could put a lot of my emotions and personality into the songs. Had I been a businesswoman, I probably wouldn't have given all that I did. I appreciate listening to those records now, because I know I did the best I could.

"Once you become a business person, you lose some of that fire. The enthusiasm for the work changes, you want to see a return, you want to cover yourself all the time. At Motown, I didn't have any concern about finances. I know there are a lot of horror stories in this business, but my story wasn't, because I won't accept the fact that I was ignorant. Considering what Motown had to work with when I came to them, they did an uptight, profound job of exposing us, establishing us, and producing us."

Not receiving the same type of treatment at MCA, or subsequently at Arista or Fantasy, Martha returned to Detroit in 1982. This move was not meant to signal "a surrender," even though her hits had become distant memories. Instead, her "dream" took a different form. Increasingly independent, she formed her own corporation ("I love the control"), which not only handles Martha's solo engagements, but also "advises" young Detroit talent.

"I'm not really a manager, I don't want to be a business tycoon, I'm only interested in being a friend to performers," says Reeves. "I don't think I could've made it with Motown, if people hadn't encouraged me, or personally tutored me in their spare time. Now I want to help others."

A few years ago, Martha was giving private vocal lessons, but she's abandoned that to work on a "pet project": recreating the Motown sound. "It's a hard task; most musicians today are either disco-minded or playing too loud. But there's an art to playing together and I'm working with young people I'm very proud of. I've seen them develop. My younger brother is my drummer, and he's helping me bring this music, in its truest form, close to the uniqueness and magic of Motown."

One young person won't be encouraged to join this effort. Although Martha speaks warmly of Motown, and the "business," she's firmly opposed to her son Eric's being a musician. While saying, "I'm going to live this dream out, I'm going to be Martha Reeves of the Vandellas as long as I live," she wants Eric to have "a life of his own," one that gives him "the freedom to choose." So, tacitly, this is an admission of a certain sadness, a recognition that she always had to put her career before her personal life.

"His happiness can come from a college crowd, or from friends—mine was put on a wide, broad scope, but his can be as he chooses. He can have a freer life, where mine wasn't. I don't know if I'd be happier now if I wasn't in show business, but if he has a choice, let him choose. Right now I'm not going to have him programmed as a performer. He sings, and has a lot of talent. But I don't want him to be known as a singer. I want him to be known as a young man whose career is open, who can be anything he wants to be.

"My son has been aware of my career the whole of his life, because I've had to sacrifice being with him for the road. He's a sturdy child, and we're making it really well. I don't want this to sound as if show business is bad, but I don't want it for my son. The more I can keep him away from the business, the better."

Frowning, Martha continues, "My life just wasn't my own. I've basically been under contract for the past twenty-five years. I never had a chance to make personal decisions, or to think completely of myself. I've always had to have other people in mind. My girls came first, and my husband last. Because my real marriage was to the two girls I had a contract with. The Vandellas were considered before my husband."

Opening a curtain as she says this, Martha looks across the street, at a group of youngsters playing basketball in a schoolyard.

She doesn't have to say anything more. Judging by her radiant smile, it's apparent that Eric is among them.

And that Martha Reeves has finally come home.

Mannfred Mann

A Ravaged Land, A Son's Lament

In Francis Ford Coppola's epic movie *Apocalypse Now,* Martin Sheen takes a journey into the heart of darkness. It's an agonizing passage, up a river into the dense jungles of Vietnam, past charred corpses, devastated villages, and sampans carrying the scared and homeless. Amid this desolation, another war rages. Sheen, in the role of Captain Willard, is a tormented assassin, struggling with a host of inner conflicts that divert him from murdering the notorious Green Beret renegade Colonel Kurtz. The bloodletting finally takes place, but like America after that ill-advised war, Willard's soul is transformed. Having traveled to the darkest reaches of his being, he discovers aspects of himself that demand further exploration.

To his ultimate horror and disgust, Mannfred Mann learned that a visit to South Africa is also an existential journey. Returning to his native land in 1982, after a long absence, Mann didn't have to dodge bullets or war-crazed villains. Yet that might have been easier for him. For the British rock-scene veteran of "Do Wah Diddy Diddy" fame was a stranger in his own land, alienated and dispossessed from a landscape rife with racism. Here, he too was forced to grapple with his emotions, beliefs, and with realities that defy reasonable explanations. How could he not suffer? Every segregated bus ride and trip to the Bantustans, that remote expanse south of Johannesburg where the families of black city workers are banished, affronted his sense of justice. And as he also admits, mocked his otherwise liberal Jewish heritage.

"The incidents you see all the time; people are humiliated, talked down to, the economic oppression, it's just awful," seethes Mann, while walking his Bernese mountain dog in a London park. "It's wrong. These people are human beings. I've always seen it as a question of dignity. You're perpetually seeing blacks as servants, fetching and carrying.

"There are whites opposed to the system, and a lot of Jewish people fall into this category, but much to the discredit of the Jewish community in South Africa, I have to say that as a race that suffered to the extent they did in World War II, to find them in any sense condoning that same [racist] principle is a great shame. For me it's something to be ashamed of. It's the most awful thing to see, people defending racialism, and not seeing, unable to see the parallel. It's as if some of them feel Jews are so special that when the Nazis persecuted Jews it was wrong, because they were Jews. But if other people are put down—I don't mean put down. There isn't genocide in South Africa, so it isn't an identical parallel—but when other people suffer under the identical master-race principle, you embrace the master-race principle yourself by calling yourself Jews who are leaders, intellectuals, scientists, as if you were different. It's really awful to see. I particularly abhor racism, in any form."

Out of this *angst* came *Somewhere in Afrika*, Mann's well-received political statement that saluted the "brothers and sisters of Azania" (the black-power name for South Africa), and called for their freedom. The Arista release does have a jazzy rock side, with such commercially successful tunes as "Demolition Man" and the "Runner." These Top 10 songs overshadow the more exotic African Suite pieces like "To Bantustan?" and "Koze Kobenini," which feature surreptitiously recorded Zulu chants (tribesmen can be arrested for singing rebellious songs). But the album's popularity pales in significance to Mann's return to Africa, utilizing the mournful tribal tempos that influenced him as a youngster. Once again, Mann steps into his own heart of darkness, and distances himself from rock's traditional borders. The resulting musical triumph, or personal breakthrough, shouldn't be surprising. Mann has always dared to be different. In his own cerebral fashion, he remains the rock rebel, the intellectual who's consistently questioned the meaning of pop stardom.

Even as a teenager in the late 1950s, Mann (born Mannfred Lubowitz) was at odds with his surroundings. Initially, this only meant a refusal to take piano lessons. Against his mother's entreaties, he insisted on plunging into the world of Errol Garner, Oscar Petersen, and other jazz musicians by himself. But as his interest grew, it also became more isolating—and dangerous. For in the fifties, there was no bohemian scene in South Africa. Whites could be jailed for playing with black musicians. Grudgingly, Mann recognized the limitations. Not seeing a future for himself in music, he worked with his father as a printer. It was the only "practical" thing to do.

"The work was challenging for a while. I stayed with my father for three years, from the time I was seventeen till I was twenty [1957–60]," says the bearded Mann, buttoning his leather jacket, as a chilly late-afternoon breeze sweeps through the park. "But in the end I realized that you only have one life, and you've got to try and do what you want to do. Because the only time you can afford to fail at something is in your early twenties. As you become older, a failure becomes much more disastrous. So I figured if I was going to fail as a musician, I might as well try it early. And if I wasn't going to succeed, there'd be time for me to do something else. And you must remember, I was a jazz musician. The gap between me and Oscar Petersen, or someone like Bill Evans was tremendous. It didn't inspire much confidence."

Nor did South Africa. Faced with the restrictions of that society, Mann had only one choice. If he was going to pursue a music career, that meant leaving the country. This wasn't an easy decision, South Africa was still home. His friends and family were here. Yet in 1961, overcoming this initial reluctance, Mann surrendered to the musical charms of John Coltrane and Ornette Coleman. He emigrated to England.

Settling in London, Mann lived like other struggling artists, on the edge. While playing jazz made him feel part of an *avant-garde,* the income from these small club dates was so paltry that he also had to give music lessons. Neither of these gigs was steady. So for nearly two years, there was little certainty in his life. In fact, the only thing he could be sure of was recurring self-doubt, which inevitably arises when one is barely surviving.

To earn a better living, Mann was forced to change his musical direction. Abandoning jazz, he moved closer to a rock sound in late 1962, by switching to rhythm and blues. Remembering that his newly formed Mann-Hugg Blues Brothers band played to overflowing crowds in clubs outside London, he chuckles, "The R & B became more and more enjoyable as it went on. We (Mann, Mike Hugg, and six other musicians) had some anxious moments in 1963, but it was a time of building toward a bigger and bigger following. All the places we played—the

Concord, Marquee, the Richmond Athletic Club—there were more and more people around. People queuing up around the block couldn't get in. We were becoming more and more popular. We were a very good live rhythm and blues band."

That memory is savored for a moment. Then, as he talks about the emotional adjustments the switch to R & B demanded, the smile vanishes from his face. And while he weighs this trade-off between artistic purity and financial stability, one aspect of his personality becomes strikingly clear. He's disposed to see the flip side of what life has to offer. To him, nothing is ever a simple matter of black and white. In his complex, highly serious world, there are nuances, ambivalences. He's thus reminiscent of Captain Willard, a Hamlet-like figure, wrestling with existential dilemmas.

"We were more successful all the time, but I set out to be a jazz musician, so there were mixed feelings about that. I was in England, and earning a living, and that on its own is an achievement. But R & B wasn't what I always wanted to do. Of course there were certain doubts."

These ambivalent feelings toward success would sharpen in the years ahead. Mann would have to make further compromises, especially in his private life, that posed an even greater philosophical quandary.

But in late 1963, as the renamed, reconstituted Mannfred Mann band grew more popular, there was little time for reflection. Everything was moving too fast.

Influenced by the international hysteria over the Beatles, the quintet made the leap from R & B to rock and increasingly appeared in some of London's hottest clubs. Consequently, the producers of a forthcoming rock TV show, "Ready Steady Go," heard about them. Though Mann is a bit hazy about the exact details, he was asked to write a theme song for the show, a tune which was entitled "5-4-3-2-1." And as that TV program became *the* showcase for the elite of British rockdom, the Mannfred Mann band was catapulted into the spotlight.

"From being successful on a smaller level, we became famous," says Mann, with a pungent note of sarcasm in his voice. That has some things going for it. In other words, instead of being liked by perhaps a few thousand people in the areas you play, you are now known to millions who know nothing but the one song you've done. That's what being famous means—unless you become very, very famous—then everybody knows everything you've done. That's different.

"But we became very well-known. People asked for autographs, people knocked on your door. You couldn't go out in the street; little girls were screaming. That's what happened. And so we became famous." More somberly, he continues, "But the other side of that is you lose your loyal following in places where you were playing before."

Then, without any hesitation or prompting, Mann angrily adds, "We earned more money, but we never really . . . the way the music business was set up in those days, we were just pawns for other people. The kind of royalties being paid by EMI at that time was ludicrous, inequitous (sic). I can't find the words to describe how we were paid for what we did. We were getting something like 1 1/2 percent. The average band now is getting between 8 percent and 15 percent. A lot of people on their first deals are getting 8 percent and 10 percent. If we sold over a certain amount, or if EMI picked up certain options, we went up to perhaps 1 3/4 percent. Five people were sharing that, and there was a manager taking *25 percent* off the top."

When asked if this was a festering sore, Mann spiritedly replies, "It wasn't initially, but as the years went on, and you realized you could only afford a small car after a few years of international success, it was irritating. It rankles me now, as well.

"I've survived that. I'm not in any financial trouble. Overall, I feel I've been rewarded for my years in the music business, more than adequately rewarded for what I've done. But think of the people who had their most successful period at that time. I'm not sure that they got enough. That just isn't right."

The whimsical nature of success also grated on him. For after "5-4-3-2-1" peaked, Mann discovered that he was playing to a fickle public. "It had all seemed so easy. We wrote '5-4-3-2-1' and it was a hit. So we wrote 'Hubble Bubble (Toil and Trouble),' expecting another hit. It was, but it was so quick, the effect of it was as if we had failed. It went up in three weeks, and straight down. Then one realized that this was a deadly serious thing, you can't fail. We sort of thought that once you succeed, you somehow succeed, like a solicitor, or a doctor. But it didn't work that way. [His voice rising bitterly] You have to keep succeeding over and over again."

This realization prompted Mann to give up songwriting. Feeling he couldn't keep churning out hits, Mann convinced the group to cover other artists' songs. In 1964, this meant adding an R & B flavor to an old Exciters' tune, "Do Wah Diddy Diddy"—the single that gave the group the credentials (the song topped the charts for months) to join the British Invasion.

Again, though, the fame was bittersweet. More than ever, Mann's life was no longer his own. "To me the 1960s was something more than having a hit record," he fumes, reluctantly adding that he then had a wife and two daughters. "My life didn't revolve around 'Do Wah Diddy . . .' It revolved around being a father. Everyone always assumes that one lives because you're in the public eye, as if you live totally through what the public sees. That to me is a much more important part of the sixties—the records and the fame spoiled my ability to take my children for a walk in the park, because everyone was asking for autographs and bothering me. That to me is my abiding memory of the sixties.

"It's just being bothered, and not being paid enough for that amount of hassle. It isn't even ego-satisfying. Having 50 million people know you means that you have 50 million people who have a passing, peripheral interest in you, and remember your name in amongst the names of soap powders and chocolate bars. That's what being a household name is. It's much much better to have fewer people who really like your work, buy the album, come to the concert, leave you in peace. That's a far, far preferable situation."

This "lesser" type of fame that Mann so fervently desires he attained in the seventies with the heavy rock Earth Band. Playing to older, more subdued audiences, he could enjoy gigs, for there was a greater feeling of privacy.

But Mann still had to survive the sixties. The Mannfred Mann band continued to chart hits—"Pretty Flamingo" (1966), "Ha Ha Said the Clown" (1967), Dylan's "The Mighty Quinn" (number ten in 1968), "Ragamuffin Man"—and all the while, Mann's disenchantment intensified.

"There was a feeling that I started off being, you might say, an idealistic young guy being a jazz musician, and I landed up being somebody who was a figure and face in the background, hitting an organ that was an awful instrument. Nobody could hear my contribution, I was just some sort of figure there helping to make a record. As a musician, I felt my contribution just had nothing to do with music. In the beginning we were a very, very good rhythm and blues band, but as the sixties wore on, as we got to '67, '68, I began listening closely to the way other people were making records, and they seemed to be making much better records than we were. By the time '69 came around, there was a feeling I had, as well as the other people, that we had reached our creative peak."

The denouement came when "Ragamuffin Man" was still in the Top

10. Mann and Mike Hugg disbanded the group, and formed the jazz-oriented Chapter Three unit, which included a five-man horn section. In the spirit of the Blues Brothers, Mann could play "pure" music again. So despite the financial risk involved, he was convinced that the gamble had to be taken.

Showing no remorse over that decision, Mann sounds a theme that could be called the guiding principle of his life. "You only have one life, and there are times when you ask yourself 'What am I trying to do?' So you get the feeling if you don't do something you'll regret it forever."

Speaking more and more passionately, he continues, "Hugg and myself started off being very cautious. We started off trying to run two bands. We'd leave the Mannfred Mann group running, and we'd have the jazz-rock unit on the side. The manager said to us, 'Don't do it halfheartedly—if you're going to do it, damn well do it!' He had a point. There's always an appeal in that kind of risk-taking. Don't play it safe, go for it. That's what we did. We had reached the end of our creative road, and the only reason for staying together would've been financial."

Up until the split, Mann had lived like a country gentleman, secure in recording studios, producing music for TV specials.

Chapter Three, though, meant live performances. As Mann explains, the world of sweaty dressing rooms was far more "dangerous." "I never ever thought I would want to go back to this, but when I did, I found it very, very good. We did things the way we wanted."

This adventure lasted for nearly two years. Then, in 1971, Mann insisted on "getting rid of all preconceptions." After working with Hugg for over a decade, he'd become too reliant on his partner's "considerable talents." Now Mann "wanted to be free to do any songs I wanted to do, anything." So the two men parted, as the Earth Band was formed.

Though Mann dislikes the term "cerebral," the group played a brand of music that was akin to later Pink Floyd efforts. This made them popular with a rather select crowd. The glitz of conventional success was missing, but that was fine with Mann. Finally, he could play to people who weren't intrusive, genuine fans who simply appreciated the music.

This appeal widened in 1973, when the Earth Band had a British Top 10 single with "Joybringer," a rock adaptation from Gustav Holst's *The Planets.* And they had another bout with glory in 1976, upon releasing a version of Bruce Springsteen's "Blinded by the Light." This was the

Earth Band's first number one hit in the United States, and it was soon followed by another big seller, "Davy's on the Road Again."

The band's alignment changed over the next four years, and subsequent recordings were only moderately successful. But commerciality, or the lack of it, hardly affected Mann. The ensuing serenity allowed him to pursue his craft, to experiment with various musical formulas. And by 1981–82, it was time to take another risk.

"We were going to sing all the lyrics and African words (to 'Redemption Song'), but then I thought 'Hold on, it's a bit like Chapter Three—if you're going to do it, do it properly,'" says Mann, referring to the genesis of *Somewhere in Afrika.* "So I decided to get African guys to sing it, to get a choir going. The thing really expanded from that. But again, being very pragmatic, I wasn't prepared to throw away other things like 'Demolition Man,' and stuff that I thought were good tracts [laughing now], so then the idea became a mishmash, or perhaps not a totally conceived activity. One side is rock, the other African.

"At one time we were mixing the African stuff with the rock stuff, trying to make it palatable. But then I thought, 'No, hold on again, go for it. Don't sit around saying people will get bored with the African music . . . just put all the African stuff together on one side . . .'"

Initially, Mann wasn't concerned with "changing [South African] society, or the way people think. I only wanted to achieve a good piece of music." But the album's political messages can't be ignored. And as Mann admits, "It was like my chance to say my little piece for once, instead of making a collection of songs.

"And I think it [the album] was the end of the period of Mannfred Mann's Earth Band being a slightly intellectual band, in the kind of music it did, and the sounds and stuff. I thought I'd do this [wax political], and then I'd play straight rock music from now on. And that's probably what we're doing. It's not really part of my makeup to tell other people how to think, because I know in the real world people don't listen to you. They make up their own minds. You can go along and make a political album, but the truth is, very few people change their minds."

Mann still has no intention of surrendering to what's commercial, or conforming to the public stereotype of a fast-living rock star. Despite his cynicism, he remains the "artist" of the 1960s, preoccupied with turning out a high-quality product. Because his music has been "intellectual," the public often views him as a solitary, cerebral type, apart from the rock 'n' roll mainstream. He has taken a different road to success. But Mann objects to being categorized as an aloof, quixotic figure, insisting he simply wants to avoid the glare of notoriety.

"The funny thing is, if you do things that ordinary people do, like walk the dog in the park, sit around with your friends, talk, play squash, but don't hang around clubs, and don't particularly like cameras popping . . ." He lets the thought trail off, then continues, "I'm just doing what the rest of the world does, I'm not really a solitary figure. But it always sounds pretty glamorous, 'Mannfred Mann solitary figure, lonely, lonely figure out in the wheat fields on his own, communing with nature.' I'm not like that at all. But I am very intolerant of the pizzazz bullshit that goes with being a musician, or a public figure. I get tired of it and not because I'm the big intellectual and it's all shallow. I just get bored with it."

As Mann watches his dog, Cissy, scampering around the park, he says squash is a "release" from these rock world pressures (of two hundred players in his local club, Mann's rated #100), and adds, "I just want to make good records. That's hard enough—you don't have to do anything too adventurous. It's hard enough to be competitive with all the guys around who are very talented. It's kind of hard operating on that level, which I try to do."

He has survived. Unlike most sixties artists, he's evolved, and has shown remarkable longevity in a business that mercilessly destroys people. Mann is proud of this staying power, and credits his work for allowing him to remain active.

But when asked to delineate his greatest accomplishment, Mann again turns philosophical. Soberly, and in a voice choked with emotion, he concludes, "I'm especially proud of my decision to leave South Africa. I have a love-hate relationship [with the country]. Part of me still belongs there, I spent twenty years of my life there. But for me, at the time, to leave my father's business, and to take a chance on being a musician in London, that was an incredibly frightening thing to do. I'm proud of having done that."

Mann whistles for his dog, and turns toward home.

Dion
A Heroin Nightmare
and the Road Back

One Sunday afternoon in the spring of 1959, the DiMucci clan sat around their Bronx kitchen table, listening to the Top 10 countdown. Once it was announced that their twenty-year-old *bambino* had moved into the number one slot with "Teenager in Love," pandemonium broke out. Meatballs started flying. Dion's parents wept. His aunts hugged each other, and ran to the windows to share the good news with the neighborhood.

This scene repeated itself several times over the next few years. Dion had a string of international hits—"Where or When," "Runaround Sue," "The Wanderer," "Donna the Prima Donna"—that made him the Michael Jackson of his day. With him around, Fabian and Avalon had to stand aside. In bobbysoxers' hearts, he was It.

Especially in his own neighborhood. Whenever he returned from a show at the Brooklyn Fox or some other rock palace, the girls mobbed him. They'd wait outside his house just to smile at him. Or to get an autograph.

Even the local storekeepers stopped him in the street, as did priests, and the guys hanging out at the corner candy store. "Everyone," says Dion, "treated me like I was a Super Bowl hero. I was so special to these people. Sure, they'd say 'Hey, meatball, don't forget where you came from.' But overwhelmingly, there were mostly cheers, my success was a neighborhood deal. Everyone was into it. And that was so neat, for like most kids, I was still wondering about who I was, where I was, and where I was going. Their praise gave me a feeling that I was connecting, that I had an identity. I needed that. I said to myself, 'Wow, I must be good at what I'm doing.' "

The adulation continued. Dion was so esteemed that DiMucci clan members told their children, "Look at your cousin Dion, he's such a success I pray to God that you'll be just like him."

How unsuspecting everyone was. They never saw anything amiss. Even Dion's closest relatives assumed he was happy.

They didn't realize he was truly the Wanderer, traveling a lonely, aimless road that led straight to hell.

For even as a fifteen-year-old, Dion was snorting heroin. Smack softened the insecurities of growing up. It was a release from the pressures of making it. And for a while, the white stuff was a dreamy good time.

Until it became an addiction.

By the 1960s, Dion was mainlining.

Tormented by the drug's deadly grip, Dion went into seclusion, his career seemingly finished. That period was so nightmarish, so stained with grief, Dion has trouble remembering its grimiest details. Only one thing is for certain, he'd hit rock bottom.

But unlike Hendrix, Elvis, or Janis, Dion was blessed. Miraculously, he had escaped death once before, having refused to go on the flight that crashed with the Big Bopper (J. P. Richardson) and Buddy Holly aboard. Destiny mercifully gave him a reprieve in that instance—and again in 1968, his death sentence was commuted. For after falling to his knees, in anguished supplication to the "Man above," Dion rose from his bedroom floor freed from drugs.

Though dismissing the "born again" tag, Dion is now involved with several Miami, Florida, churches, in their crusade against drugs. Hoping to steer young people away from "the mistakes I made," he lectures to church groups, and appears on religious TV shows, "essentially to help youngsters find themselves."

Apparently, the identity crisis that first led him to heroin is finally over. Now, at forty-six, he's found new purpose. No longer nagged by insecurities, he's content with himself. In a sense then, he's come home, his wandering has ended.

So why should we retrace that journey? What purpose does it serve to dredge up old hurts and horrors?

In Dion's case, such probing is crucial, since it destroys the myth of some Rock Babylon. Contrary to popular thinking, success isn't just glitz, glamour, and good times. Being Mr. Teen to millions of young girls was a burden for Dion. It prevented him from defining his own life. He couldn't *be*. Nor could he talk about these frustrations to his friends and relatives. They believed in the mythical Dion. He became the vicarious fulfillment of their own dreams. To avoid disappointing them, he kept everything inside. Only now can he bare his soul—or as was once pointed out, remember where he came from.

The Bronx . . .

In the early 1950s, the borough was still Yankee land. Most boys dreamed of wearing the famed pinstripes and following the footsteps of Joe DiMaggio and Yogi Berra. Except for the weirdos who harmonized on street corners, or in subway entrances, youngsters weren't involved with music. Since the transistor-radio fad—and the rock explosion— were still years away, street kids focused on baseball, batting statistics, and driving a stickball over a schoolyard fence.

The Yankees won the pennant again in 1950, but the "doo-woppers" gained another convert—a soft-spoken eleven-year-old with the angelic good looks of a choirboy.

"I remember the day I was first attracted to music," says Dion wistfully. "It was a Sunday, and I remember the aromas in the kitchen, the spaghetti, the meat sauce, the whole bit. There was a show that came out of Newark, the Don Larkin show, and while I was sitting in the kitchen, I heard this Hank Williams song, 'Honky Tonk Blues.' Then they played 'Be Careful of Stones That You Throw,' and I said to myself, 'Who is this guy?' I did a little research, and became a big Hank Williams fan. By the time I was thirteen, I had two hundred of his seventy-eights. I also got this little guitar, and on Friday nights my uncle would take me down to this club that I wasn't allowed into. They'd hide me in the kitchen, just in case the police came in . . . and they'd bring me out a couple of times a night to sing a few songs. People would stick money into the guitar, so I'd come back home with about thirty-five dollars."

Sitting in the den of his North Miami Beach ranch house, Dion props his legs on a big antique desk, and then points to a photograph on the wall. This particular photo of his mother and father is set apart from the gold records and other memorabilia. Before continuing, he stares at it and smiles.

"After a few years of hiding out from the law, I taped this demo, as sort of a Valentine's Day gift for my mother. It was 'Wonderful Girl,' the back side of an old Five Satins record, and an original song, 'We Belong Together.' I think that's it. Well, there was a song writer in the

neighborhood who knew people at Laurie Records, and they were looking for a singer. I went down there and they wanted to put my voice on
this recording; it was called 'The Chosen Few.' But the background was
so sterile, so polished. It was bad, so I said 'If you want to listen to real
music, I'll round up some guys.' "

That song was released in 1957, and the backup group that he never
met, the Timberlanes, became part of the Dion legend.

But he still went back to his neighborhood, to "the Belmont Avenue
candy stores where the guys buried themselves in the jukebox," and put
together the Belmonts.

"These guys could really harmonize," continues Dion, proudly pointing to another photograph. "They were the best singers from each
candy store, Carlo [Mastangelo], Freddy [Milano], and Angelo
[D'Aleo]. So we went down to Laurie, and started fooling around . . .
there was no fear in us, we were just goofing. Eventually we came up
with this song, 'I Wonder Why' [a typical 'doo-wop' mix of nonsense
syllables, falsettos, and cappella vocalizing, that made it to the Top 20
in 1958] . . . that impressed a lot of people."

Once they became local celebrities, the group left the candy stores for
a more private "studio." They did their riffs behind abandoned tene-
ments, or on subway platforms. Here, they could escape envious neighborhood gangs, and as Dion relates, "It's in these places that we did our
best music.

"We'd also have bashes on Saturday night, these parties where we'd
bang on beer bottles and cardboard boxes. We'd get riffs going, and
those are the kinds of things that I'd put lyrics to, and bring to Laurie.
That's how most of our songs started, 'Runaround Sue,' 'Donna the
Prima Donna' . . . But every time we made a record [he chuckles], the
guys would signal thumbs down; they felt it was better the time we did
it at a party, or in the tenement."

Admitting that Laurie's writers sharpened this street material into
recordable songs, Dion praises the company for their early help. Unlike
most artists of this era, he doesn't have any complaints about being
bilked out of money. And he even commends Laurie executives (particularly owners Gene and Bob Schwartz) for treating him squarely once
they learned about his heroin problem.

"I started to snort heroin even as a kid," admits Dion, his tanned face
beginning to tighten. "First it was pot and stuff, then snorting heroin,
then it was skin-popping heroin, and finally mainlining. A lot of the
guys I hung out with, even Frankie Lymon, died very young . . . my

parents didn't know anything about it . . . at first I was just dabbling in it, I wasn't full-blown. But once it grabs you, it's a career. I didn't have that, not at first. I had a problem that I knew of, and it was kind of periodic. I'd leave it [the heroin]. I'd think, 'Thank God, I can get off.' But it's progressive, if you don't deal with the problem, with the root of the sickness, it keeps surfacing, it just keeps progressing . . ."

The Schwartz brothers, and one of their investors, Alan Sussel, urged Dion to seek medical help. But once "Teenager in Love" soared to the top of the charts in 1959, Dion joined Buddy Holly, Ritchie Valens, and the Big Bopper on their ill-fated Winter Dance Party tour. This bus caravan moved slowly through the Midwest that winter, because of subfreezing temperatures in the cranky old school bus. It often broke down between towns, so the older band members, worried about freezing to death, complained to Holly.

As Dion sadly recollects, "Buddy got tired of the whole thing, and besides, he liked to rent planes . . . On this particular night [the caravan had reached Clear Lake, Iowa by February 1], he was kind of recruiting, offering places on the plane. The more people you got on the plane, the less it would cost. I wasn't going to go for the money; since the Belmonts and I were splitting the paychecks, I didn't want to spend anything extra. I don't know, but I was cheap. I turned it down."

Shuddering, Dion shifts uncomfortably in his chair.

"Afterward, I wasn't only thinking that I could've been on it [the plane]. It was just that three guys I was traveling with were gone. When something like that happens to you when you're only nineteen years old, it's baffling. One day it's just rock 'n' roll, having a lot of fun, the girls screaming, and sharing chords with three friends. While the next day these three guys are just taken away, that's it . . . you wonder what life, death, and everything's about. You start asking yourself some deep questions; it baffles you at nineteen. I don't know if it affected my singing . . . I was just struck with a deeper sense of reality. We did go on, we finished the tour. But, to be honest with you, I was puzzled, I was in a state of shock."

Though Dion's drug dependency worsened, he continued to work. In 1960, he had another hit with "Where or When." But this would be his last record with the Belmonts until 1973. Egos and "instincts" started to clash, so feeling "the old tightness just wasn't there," Dion decided to go solo.

"We had a lot of internal problems," confesses Dion. "Everyone was very strong in what they believed. With our creative juices flowing, there were bound to be collisions. I think we just had to pursue different avenues . . . it's easy to make it, but once that acceptance comes you sometimes have differences. There wasn't any hate there, but the other guys were into harmonies, jazz, and Freddy was really a rock 'n' roll fanatic.

"I liked rock 'n' roll, no doubt about that, but a different approach. I just couldn't get into the high-low harmony thing, they wanted to go more that way. I guess it's an ego thing, or there was just something inside me that I wanted to communicate. I wanted to do more rhythm things. I couldn't identify with four guys singing harmonies. I was hoping to share my experiences with people, that's it, maybe the music I wanted to do should be called 'Bronx Blues.' "

With songwriter Ernie Maresca's help, Dion's "autobiography" took shape on the bestselling "Runaround Sue" (number one in 1960) and "The Wanderer" (number three). Admittedly, these songs don't have any profound existential themes. Based simply on Dion's adolescent experiences, they were vinyl pictures of teenagers in the Bronx: the girl who was making it with everyone but Dion, and the neighborhood macho guy with girls' bodies tattooed all over his chest. And while the lyrics often lacked sensitivity ("It was sick to blame the girl for my own promiscuity," admits Dion, referring to "Runaround Sue"), they weren't just catchy numbers to dance to. Suddenly sex-conscious teenagers could identify with the infidelities of a "Wanderer"; there was a desperation in these tunes that underscored young love.

"Lovers Who Wander" (number three in 1960), and "Donna the Prima Donna (number six in 1963), were variations on the same love-is-tormenting theme. And as Dion tightened his grip on the charts ("Little Diane," "Ruby Baby," and "Drip Drop" also made it to the Top 10 by 1963), he left Laurie for Columbia Records.

That 1963 switch, however, was his undoing.

"Once I got that Columbia contract, or the guarantee of money, it allowed my drug addiction, or my obsession to surface. Not having to worry about earning a living, I could go full time with the drugs. It got bad, it became a daily thing, all kinds of drugs. It became a full-time heroin thing by '64."

What drove Dion into the sordid world of smack, syringes, and street-corner pushers?

When asked this, he winces, and murmurs, "I don't have all the answers . . . I always wondered who I was, and where I was going. I thought when I got fame, fortune, and romance, I'd be happy. After eight gold records, a couple of million dollars, marrying my childhood sweetheart, a beautiful house, and material security, I still felt there was something missing. I didn't know what it was.

"People can look at you and think you've got it all—yet I was into a slow suicide. I've seen friends of mine and contemporaries die every year; they've just gotten fried in the spotlight . . . When things got really down, when my life was in this bleak valley, I never dealt with the root of my problems. I used different formulas to avoid things . . ."

Like a man squirming in a straitjacket, Dion ricocheted off the walls of that valley for four years. All the joy in his life dissolved, as he lived in seclusion, tormented and fearful.

Finally in 1967, after being told by his wife, "Dion, I can't help you anymore, I don't know what to do," he was forced to pray for guidance.

"I just got on my knees, and said, 'God, I have some questions, I just can't handle life anymore,' " sighs Dion, standing up, and moving to another corner of the room. Looking vacantly at his gold records, he continues, "I came up lacking, empty, so I had to know if God was real. I asked him to come into my life, to direct me. I needed a wisdom beyond my own . . . I was looking for peace of mind, I had reached the end of my life, I felt like I knew absolutely nothing . . .

"I had broken so many promises to myself, it was insane to do the same actions and to expect different results. I promised myself that tomorrow would be different—and I was so devastated, the more you break the promises the more you lose faith in yourself. I felt I didn't have power, I kept asking myself, 'Why am I on this merry-go-round?' You keep saying, 'How did this happen?'

"The moment I got on my knees is the moment I ran out of excuses. Before, I was so frustrated, I'd blame people for my problem. I'd accuse them, and fight everybody and everything. I had just had it. I couldn't make excuses anymore, I didn't know what to do, so I got on my knees."

From that moment on, Dion says he was "released." Purged of self-doubt and other fears, he immediately renounced all drugs. A calm came over him, as he felt like a new person. And while this turnaround sounds too fantastic to be believed, Dion insists, "The need for drugs was lifted right out of me. I've never done drugs since then."

Besides seeking "more of God," Dion then tried to revitalize his sagging career. Up until this spiritual "commitment," he had released several singles, and an album with the Belmonts *(Together Again),* which went nowhere. In a vain attempt to score another hit, he also moved back to Laurie. But nothing clicked. Overly romantic love-rejection songs were out of date by 1967. Political protest sounds were fashionable, a fact which Dion couldn't recognize.

At least not until 1968.

Influenced by Dylan, Baez, and other folksingers, he came up with a "monster" ballad, "Abraham, Martin, and John," his tribute to three assassinated American leaders.

"The country was going through a restlessness, an emotional upheaval," says Dion, who then appeared in coffeehouses, armed with an acoustic guitar. "The Kennedys had gotten shot, Martin Luther King . . . the song was an attempt to make something good out of a bad situation. I do believe that in God's economy there's no waste. You can turn everything for good. And that song was an attempt to say, 'Hey, these guys had a dream. The dream didn't die.' Maybe the Kennedys died but we could pick the ball up and go on."

Written by Richard Holler, the song was clearly a radical stylistic change for Dion. The mood was so gentle, critics didn't believe this was the "old" Wanderer. Yet, according to Dion, the song was "the natural result of spending years in seclusion, of a lot of years quietly working on a guitar [around that time, he was also working on an antidrug song, 'Clean Up Your Own Backyard']. I didn't only like Dylan, I was also listening to Lightnin' Hopkins, John Hammond, Jr. . . . It seemed at the time that this music was at the roots of what I'd been doing earlier, only I had never heard it. It was like 'Where did this stuff come from?' This is my grandfather, and I didn't even know it. It was a great discovery."

Though Dion feels the song was "a step toward a higher reality, a search for love" that was far different from his "putting down women," this quest took a U-turn in 1972. Slipping back into the past, he joined the Belmonts for a reunion concert at Madison Square Garden, only to recognize, "the show was a disaster . . . the fans gave us more than we gave them." Admitting that such nostalgia shows are a "rip-off," he quickly adds, "It's sweet for the first hour, talking about memories, but you can't stay there [in the past], it soon turns bitter."

An album marking that event, *Reunion,* was issued in 1973, but there were no more Belmont concerts. Over the next two years, Dion continued on the coffeehouse circuit, enjoying "the creative excitement of working with so many writers." In 1975, though, Dion broke with this cerebral world, to enter a playground that was hardly spiritual.

Along with his new Street Heart band, he regularly appeared in Las Vegas casinos. "It wasn't as intimate as the coffeehouses," says Dion, "but Dick Clark called me, and he had started to do some things in Vegas. I guess it was a time I wanted to get back with a band. I wanted to integrate and incorporate some of the things I did in coffeehouses [with rock] . . . I did this for three years, I did Cher's TV show, 'The Dinah Shore show' . . ."

There is an edge of doubt in his voice, a hint of defensiveness. Vegas, a return to rock—this was more wandering, the antithesis of Dion's current crusading. Sensing the contradiction, Dion grins sheepishly, then tries to clarify matters.

"I know this is going to sound wild, but after all these years I really felt I found myself, I realized what I wanted to do. I always had this sense that I wanted to share what God had done for me on a personal level—and not just for entertaining people. I loved rock 'n' roll, and I loved music, but there was a lack of motivation, there was a lack of direction. I didn't know why. I saw these covers coming out, I became very unimpressed with what people were selling [he still released *Return of the Wanderer* in 1978].

"So I thought it would be nice if I could share something of worth with people, to show what God had done for me. He had released me, given me life, love, and a deep sense of who I was. I said to myself, 'Gee, it would be nice to express this in a happy, joyous, and free atmosphere, that didn't require my wearing a three-piece suit on the pulpit.' So I went into the music ministry."

Focusing on the upbeat and inspirational, Dion now sings praises to the Lord, that can best be described as "good news," or "contemporary Christian" music. Besides appearing on radio and TV broadcasts, he has recorded *Inside Job, Only Jesus, I Put Away My Idols,* and most recently, *Kingdom in the Streets.* Passionately insisting "I haven't had to change musically," he says that only his lyrics have taken a new direction.

"God has refined my lyrics, and given me words of life, and has just made me part of the solution. I can share real neat things now. I've done the '700 Club' and other religious TV shows, but I don't like preaching, I just see myself as a ministry of encouragement. I want to bring hope, life, and love to people. God has brought me through so much, I see people like Presley, Jackie Wilson, and Bill Haley dying, and he's saved me from that. Without his grace I wouldn't have gotten through the sixties. And what I'm doing in song is just passing on, I just hope I'm passing it on."

Hearing his eleven-year-old daughter, August, in the kitchen (he has two other girls, aged eighteen and sixteen), Dion nods emphatically, and his face brightens. Acting as if he just discovered another "truth," he says, "You know, I've done so much to mess my life up, but in spite of me, I now think that I'm standing on the rock, and my name is on the roll. I pray I can be a bridge for people, because there's so, so much more to life than rock 'n' roll."

Mitch Ryder of Mitch Ryder and the Detroit Wheels

Miss Molly Rides Again

It's been a long journey, from leather motorcycle jackets, through a heroin habit, to impassioned songs about sexual politics and other controversial issues.

No wonder Mitch Ryder's face is heavily lined. The road to rebellion has been a hazardous one, replete with dizzying skids and soul-scarring collisions.

Ryder once rode on air, as his Detroit Wheels carried him to the top of the charts with "Jenny Take a Ride," "Devil with a Blue Dress On," "Sock It to Me, Baby," and "Good Golly, Miss Molly." Powered by "white soul," this mid-sixties stuff mirrored our fascination with two-toned Chevy convertibles, rocket-shaped tail fins, souped-up V-8s, and drive-ins. These songs were fast-moving blasts of urban energy that roared defiance. Like other children of the sixties, Ryder didn't care about limits. Pushing down hard on the gas pedal, he recklessly believed that success would be everlasting. Never slowing down, he didn't know he was playing chicken with destiny.

Mitch eventually kicked amphetamines, hallucinogens, and heroin. In the process, he also became "a lot smarter" in business dealings—he had only pocketed fifteen thousand dollars from his string of hits. Ryder now puts records out on his own label, Seeds and Stems, and carefully avoids signing any managerial deal. "All this is part of my getting politicized, educated, and pissed off at the way this society worked," notes Ryder, sounding more weary than angry. "I was once sucked into something, and my attitude is just a backlash at what happened to me. I failed myself back then."

After releasing *Never Kick a Sleeping Dog* in 1983 (it was coproduced by John Cougar), Ryder regained some of his former prominence. Riding a wave of new publicity, he was seen as an early-day Springsteen, and a spiritual father of punk.

But this sudden burst of acclaim was of small consolation. What do legacies mean when one is battling to survive? Ryder's "nose dive" was so all-consuming that recalling the past only evokes terrible memories. Why think about the "glory days"? All that's lost. The "mistakes" he made in 1967–68 still gnaw at him, and eventually they resulted in his going to Denver to get away from drugs. All of this is apparent in his cynical, angry remarks, and the sardonic jokes that tend to be self-mocking. They belie his saying "I'm happy, because I'm able to write." Ryder should be more content—he's had the courage to kick. Yet, the pain that first turned him to drugs hasn't totally disappeared. Instead of attributing his loss of fame to youthful innocence, he keeps blaming himself, again and again.

"I just failed to educate myself, I failed to protect myself from the rape that was going on," says the forty-one-year-old Ryder, referring to the bad business deals he made. "Everything fell apart in my life, my marriage. There was a lot of mud-slinging [against his producer, Bob Crewe], and everybody just got into my shit. Record companies blacklisted me. It was fucked."

Admitting that drugs were an escape from these problems, he continues, "Heroin didn't get real big in my life until '71, '72. Before then it was a lot of ups, downs, grass, psychedelics. I was pretty heavy into all this stuff. But in '71, I broke up the group, and went to see J. Geils in New York. I was invited to sing with him at a Central Park concert, and was approached by these idiots from Bud Prager's office, who handled Mountain at the time. They offered me a contract, and I was pretty screwed up. I never should've signed it, but I did. I toured with Leslie West for about four months, but finally the drugs and the situation I was being manipulated into became too much. Prager tried to break me. I wanted a contract so bad, so bad. Finally in '73, I gave it up, I got myself off the stage."

Ryder's face pales. Getting up from his chair, he moves over to a window in a New York hotel room and stares out at the skyline. In town to do a one-nighter at a local club, he mumbles a few words about the city "falling apart," that it only has "twenty years to survive." And, as he talks about other more heralded visits to the city, one can't help but pity him. The road back to the stage has been a rough one—a passage from innocence to hard-edged realism is always traumatic.

In the past, ambition shielded William Leavis, Jr. (renamed Ryder in 1965), from reality. Able to dream, he was protected, even from the grayest of surroundings.

As a child, growing up in a poor Polish section outside Detroit, he watched his father, a factory worker, struggle to meet the rent. The family house was barely big enough for the eight Leavis children, and there wasn't always ample food. But William, even at fourteen (1959), found an escape.

"Mysteriously enough, I got my own radio," says Mitch dryly. Agreeing that was a "big" event, he continues, in a deep, throaty rasp, "Then, after everyone went to bed, you could lay in bed and tune in to whatever you wanted. I used to pick up this show out of Nashville, 'Randy's Record Mart'; there was one out of Memphis too. And I also listened to black stations in Detroit. That really started telling me that there was something more to music than watching Fabian come out on 'American Bandstand' and lip-synch. The black stuff was more vital, more potent. That cheap little Japanese job [his ten-dollar transistor] really did it for me."

At fifteen, Billy got wheels and the freedom to explore that inviting black world. Hooking up with older boys who could drive, he started going downtown to ghetto clubs where his new idols (Jimmy Reed, Little Richard, Smokey Robinson and the Miracles) were appearing. "At this one place, the Village, I'd meet people. It didn't take long to make friends. I'd go down there on the weekends, while most of my peers were watching football games, getting drunk, or trying to get girls. Checking out the music was more important to me—I wanted to sing there. Finally, I got the courage up to ask if I could try out, and I did.

"That was satisfying, very much so. Why? Well, number one, singing set me apart from all the other people in high school. And number two, folks really showed up there. So that kept me apart. I just wanted to be away from that high school scene. The music was also a little more potent than the kind we were being force-fed in the 'burbs."

Joining an all-black group, the Peps, in 1961, the sixteen-year-old began to sing his own brand of white soul. Not even out of high school, he cut his first record, "Fool for You," which appeared on a gospel label after his family scraped up enough money for him to do the demo. This song was only played by black stations, but as Mitch laughingly remembers, it led to a recognition of sorts. "After the Peps did this black social function one night, this old lady came up to me and said, 'We sure like the way you sing, and you're sure light, too.'"

The strictly rhythm and blues Peps gave Billy a valuable education. During his year and a half with them, he learned the rudiments of soul, and how to work a crowd. For most of that time, though, the group's income barely covered expenses.

So Billy also did a few solo gigs. These local shows didn't amount to much, maybe ten to twenty dollars a night. And now knowing much about rock, he stayed with rhythm and blues.

Until a group called the Rivieras came to the Village. Filling in for the house band, they asked Billy to do a few rock numbers with them. Like a chain reaction, the ensuing chemistry brought the crowd to its feet. The music was so "neat," Billy agreed to do an encore with them the following weekend. Then the deal was struck, Billy Lee and the Rivieras came into being in 1964.

"Over the next six months we were the hottest band in the area," says Ryder, pulling the brim of a New York Yankees cap over his forehead. A few strands of gray hair are still visible, and his voice has grown strained. But he proudly continues, "We took a basement tape to Bob Crewe [the Four Seasons' producer] and he arranged for us to open with the Dave Clark Five. I guess we tore him up enough so that he wanted to sign us."

A master of promotional gimmicks, Crewe then made a move that would have warmed Lee Iacocca's heart. After leafing through a local phone directory, he renamed the group Mitch Ryder and the Detroit Wheels.

"At first, Crewe wanted to change my name to Michael Rothschild," laughs Mitch, "but we decided that wouldn't be too nice. The switch to Ryder didn't affect me, not until I saw it on records. Then it took on a whole new meaning."

Judging by the glint in Ryder's eyes, he's referring to his first hit, "Jenny Takes a Ride." Essentially a spin-off of Little Richard's "Jenny,

Jenny" and Chuck Willis's "C. C. Rider," that song climbed to the
number ten slot in 1966, after Crewe bounced the original studio cut
from two tracks to four. "I'm still trying to figure out how he got a
writer's royalty for that, but it was exciting. 'Jenny' was a smash."

That same year, the Wheels had two more chart-busters—"Devil
with a Blue Dress On," and "Good Golly, Miss Molly" (number four).
Predictably, fame changed Ryder's life. He still didn't have too much
money, but that didn't prevent him from having a good time. "We were
quite young, so we chased women wherever we went. That was the only
thing that kept us from doing our shows—we were tired. It was just a
little early for us to get into drugs."

The Wheels had a few more minor hits in 1967, such as "Sock It to
Me, Baby," a sexually suggestive tune that was banned by several radio
stations. "It was just about making love, lyrically it was pretty wild,"
insists Ryder, shrugging his shoulders. Prodded to sing a few bars, he
chuckles, " 'Every time you kiss me it hits me like a punch' . . . we
took out a four letter word and put in punch, but the KKK, or whoever
the hell they were, had a real problem with it. They wanted to burn all
Beatles and Mitch Ryder records. 'Gimme, gimme, gimme, gimme,
gimme something sweet, knock me ooh off my feet, sock it to me baby
. . .' that's the first verse. The PR people liked it [the controversy] a
lot, but we didn't pay any attention to it."

Ryder was too preoccupied with other problems at the time. After
three years of harmony, Mitch began to fight with Crewe, and with a
few of the other group members over "musical policy." Management
wanted to expand the act to make it more viable in places like Vegas; I
think Crewe was under the impression that all the big money would
come from there. In the meantime we saw other groups getting
stronger, so I tried to talk him into adding some horns, keeping it
R & B instead of a Vegas thing. Some of the guys didn't want to expand
the band. I wanted to expand the band, but I didn't want to do the
glamour deal—my thing was getting back to an R & B, horn-type
sound because I thought that was the way to progress. That split the
group, so I cut a solo album *[What Now My Love]* and did a nose dive."

Trying to hide his disgust, Mitch looks away, to stare at a cheap copy
of a Renoir hanging on his hotel-room wall. This is the period in his life
that he wants to forget. For then, he was forced to pump out albums on
any label that would have him. There was no getting out of this skid.
With everything in his life falling apart, Ryder became increasingly
confused, and vulnerable to all sorts of demons.

"I went through a bankruptcy, I lost a lawsuit against Crewe [he had previously signed away all future royalties for fifteen thousand dollars], I got divorced . . . I had just failed myself. I tried to blame Crewe, but I simply failed to protect myself."

During this 1969–72 period, Ryder re-formed the Wheels, only to break them up again after one album *(Detroit)*. He signed a managerial deal with Bud Prager that now prompts him to say, "Prager uses people, he hates artists. You're going to hear his name a lot when I kill him." And of course, there were the drugs. Moving away from amphetamines and grass, he used more and more heroin.

Eventually forced to give up singing, Ryder settled near relatives in Denver, where he painted houses and worked in a warehouse. "It wasn't easy, but in my two years there, I didn't touch anything. I found the strength to give it up and I found myself missing the creative part [of the business], so I started writing at night. I devoted my time totally to creativity."

Ryder married his present wife in 1975, then moved back to Detroit. Still wary of managers and other business people, he formed his own record company, Seeds and Stems. "We tried this for two and a half years and came up with some good product. We had *How I Spent My Vacation* [1978], and *Naked But Not Dead* [1979]. I wrote all the songs. We followed that with *Got Change for a Million,* that was recorded in Germany. Then we did *Live Talkies* [1981] and *The Legendary Full Moon Concert.* I finally broke up with my partner, and did *Smart Ass* on my current label, the Michigan Broadcasting Corporation."

Besides being autobiographical, these hard-rock albums detail another journey: Ryder's political evolution. Turning to radicalism after the "establishment" nearly destroyed him, he wrote songs about homosexuality, the "welfare state" in Detroit, gun control, and abortion. Two tunes, "The Jon," and "Cherry Poppin'," have prompted the most attention because of their sexual references. But, disagreeing with the critics, Ryder insists that these works weren't a prohomosexuality statement.

Referring to the lyrics in "Cherry Poppin'," he says, "It's just that I take on the persona, or give the female viewpoint." He then sings, " 'Honey, I don't need no man that can't make up his mind. If you want to sleep with me tonight, better stay in line . . .' What does that say about homosexuality?

" 'The Jon' is just dealing with a statement that communism is not the answer, communal living is not the answer, violence isn't the answer. I just say 'keep the change,' meaning the revolutionary change. But people read so much stuff into that, it's so weird, that song, it's classic."

Despite this transformation from white soul artist to political activist, Ryder angrily adds, "I only want to be known as a good writer, not as a political one." Yet at best, acclaim has been fitful. Except for the excitement over *Never Kick a Sleeping Dog* (Riva/Polygram), Ryder has fallen back into the shadows, unrecognized and ignored. Booked for only nineteen dates in 1984, he understandably told a Philadelphia newspaper, "I feel I'm a neglected artist. There are things on those earlier records that no one else has done, and of which I'm very proud. You read histories of rock 'n' roll, and they say something like 'Mitch Ryder was a big star for two years. He had a couple of hits and did a lot of oldies material and that's it.' Well, that's a lie. The work I did had an impact on a lot of people."

Asked to comment about this statement, Ryder again responds in a fiery manner. "I hear the shit they put out for hit records today, while I'm trying to write something informative, or at least something that will cause discussion. I guess people want to be entertained, they don't want to think. And I guess that's the reason I'm neglected. I insist on doing material that causes controversy.

"My sexual stuff could be accepted now—look at Prince, he's very sexual. But as far as politics go—I mean actually making changes in such matters as abortion, war—it just doesn't happen. Everything's just too conservative. Duran Duran does political material, but they have the big budget. They're cute young boys and they can say things, because nobody cares what the fuck they're saying. They're cute and they have a beat. But I don't have the budget to shove it down everyone's throat."

In the face of the yuppie eruption and the Reagan groundswell, Ryder's rebelliousness does seem out of date. So why does he stubbornly insist on challenging this conservatism? Isn't he setting himself up for more frustration?

Pondering these questions while getting ready to leave his hotel room, Ryder changes into a different pair of jeans and a plaid flannel shirt. His sixties leather jacket, motorcycle boots, and silver chains are long gone. But as Ryder soon suggests, he's still ready to tough it out, to ride it on the edge.

"I'm committed to taking chances, to pushing the music to extremes. None of the big labels will touch me. They want to play it safe, they don't want any trouble, and they know I've caused trouble in the past. But that doesn't bother me; I'll get my hit one way or another. The political songs will continue, if they like it or not. My duty is to myself. I'm doing what I believe in."

ED SANDERS

Tuli Kupferberg and Ed Sanders of the Fugs

The Revolt Spreads to Czechoslovakia

Years before Chairman Mao Tse-tung's "Little Red Book" became a sixties phenomenon, satirical pamphlets calling for free sex, an end to American racism, and "killing for peace" were inflaming minds in New York's East Village.

These tracts attacked everything that was once held sacrosanct, in scathing, scatological terms. The presidency, America's war dead, the "martyrdom" of Adolf Eichmann, even the Crucifixion, were targets for bitter, sardonic barbs. Essentially, war had been declared against the Square World. Society was seen as too limiting, too fraught with misery. And according to this polemic, until man regained his freedom, the lurching toward global destruction would continue.

Still recovering from the torpid "I Like Ike" years, people were hardly ready for this inflammatory message. They shuddered at every four-letter word. And even the Beats were unimpressed. Rebellion was one thing, anarchism quite another.

But the author of these salvos, Tuli Kupferberg, remained unperturbed. He kept grinding them out with a mounting intensity that paralleled the escalation of the Vietnam War. For five years, this crusade for "peace, love, and freedom" was a one-man show.

Then in 1964, Tuli met fellow iconoclast Ed Sanders, and they decided to put these diatribes to music. Neither of them could sing on key or play any instrument with precision. But that didn't really matter. In tune with calling themselves the Fugs—a takeoff on their favorite expletive—they put together a ragtag group of poets-cum-musicians who echoed the rage of the times. Never shying away from any taboo or totem, the Fugs shattered the restraints on "political" music with a brand of profanity that has yet to be rivaled. And by enlarging the boundaries of what was musically acceptable, the Fugs twisted rock 'n' roll inside out. They gave it such a new shape that Bill Haley and Buddy Holly must have been turning in their graves.

"We were freeing everything up, there was nothing subtle about us, but we were raising consciousness, and warning people to watch out for the bastards in power," muses Kupferberg, standing near a stove in his SoHo loft while preparing a pot of chicken soup. Now sixty-three, he gives every indication of having lost that battle against the establishment. His tweed jacket is badly wrinkled and tattered. Both his beard and his hair, unkempt and streaked with gray, give him the look of the stereotypical doddering professor. And even sadder, as he recites an old poem, a satirical blast at Richard Nixon, his teenaged son turns up the volume on a TV set.

Ignoring the banter of two sports broadcasters, the same way he used to shrug off hostile audiences and police, Tuli relentlessly continues, "I think of all the musical groups, and except maybe for Dylan, our message was the most direct. No one was talking about high school sex, masturbation, drug addiction, oral sex, the killing in Vietnam. There was a silence about these things, they weren't in the popular culture. But the Fugs took poetry off the printed page and got people to question what was going on. We created an attitude, an anti-authoritarian feeling, that convinced people to enjoy themselves. We just didn't want the herd to dominate."

The songs heralding this "new freedom" never made it to "American Bandstand." Such works as "Supergirl" (an ode to feminine perfection) were too obscene for the average rock 'n' roller; while the more melodic "Star-Spangled Bomber" or "Kill for Peace" assaulted long-cherished notions of patriotism. "Coca Cola Douche" and "New Amphetamine Shriek" not only lacked commerciality but, much like the wit of Lenny Bruce, enraged people and have since been forgotten, along with our "Dump LBJ" and "Make Love, Not War" buttons.

But the Fugs didn't care about "bourgeoisie" popularity in 1964–65. They wanted to incite strong feelings, raise political/social consciousness—and it's here that they succeeded. By encouraging audiences to "enjoy sex," "have more of it," and to oppose the draft (Country Joe and the Fish didn't voice these cries until late 1965), the Fugs broke ground for the then-blossoming flower-child movement. Their brand of anarchism, in fact, was at the crux of the hippie phenomenon—as were their outrageous pantomime skits, theater-of-the-absurd dramatizations, and soon to be echoed calls for "love-ins"—which would later influence Frank Zappa's Mothers of Invention, Alice Cooper, and current punk-rockers.

"I guess the most theatrical piece we did was our anti-LBJ number, when I dressed up in this shredded, 'blood-stained' army uniform," chuckles Kupferberg, recalling how his outfit was splattered with tomato paste to "bring home the horrors" of the Vietnam War. "I'd roam around the stage, like a soldier dazed from battle, and I'd find this doll that was supposed to represent a Vietnamese child. I'd fondle it, try to give it candy, but of course the kid wouldn't take it . . . the child was dead. So I'd angrily smear the candy in the doll's face . . .

"Like I said, we weren't very subtle, but stuff like this worked. Ed would be singing, I'd get around to playing the tambourine or the maracas . . . it was cultural politics in action. I think we had an effect. The beatniks took poetry off the printed page, and we took this one step further, by combining music and poetry. You still see that today, and we were certainly a liberating influence on groups back then."

While agreeing with this assessment, Ed Sanders takes a less cerebral view of the group, pointing out that the Fugs were "a randy lot," intent on satisfying the most basic of urges. "We were testosterone-maddened, we were driven to meet girls, and playing music let us do that. And besides, we all felt we were geniuses, with a message for the world. On a primitive level the Fugs were good, we turned on a bunch of kids to look at the world from a rebel stance. A lot of people were touched by our songs. Those people are now doctors and lawyers. The whole thing was a lot of fun, but it was also a struggle . . . These crackers would come up to us and say 'I don't mind these dirty songs, but if you jerk off on that microphone one more time, I'm going to bust you.'"

As Sanders pungently suggests, once the Fugs left the friendly confines of New York (where they did more than eight hundred performances at various Greenwich Village theaters) and hit the road, there was trouble on several fronts.

In the Midwest, most notably in Appleton, Wisconsin (the hometown of right-wing Senator Joseph McCarthy), after bomb threats failed to cancel a concert, the group was forcibly thrown out of town by the police.

Their 1968 "From Russia with Love" encounter was equally hair-raising. Czechoslovakia was then being overrun by Soviet troops. To show their disapproval, the Fugs traveled to one of the borders on their own "peace mission." When they tried to masturbate on the road near a convoy of tanks, the Russians quickly escorted them to the airport.

Closer to home, there were serious philosophical differences between Sanders and Kupferberg. While Tuli was primarily interested in fomenting the "hippie revolution," Sanders felt the group's future survival was dependent on their expanding "a very narrow performance base." The only way to reach more people, he reasoned, was to play in bigger theaters, and to do this, the group was urged to go electric. But content with "political buffoonery," Kupferberg resisted this switch to the psychedelic, and the two men clashed. Or as Sanders puts it, "We had a bifurcation."

Now living in Woodstock, New York, and describing himself as "a mad poet-inventor," who likes to "tinker around with wild contraptions," Sanders still feels the Fugs had the potential to be a top-quality rock act. "We were getting real good, we just had to take that next step. And that meant our purchasing a professional sound system so we could play bigger places. Bumping the sound up to the next level would've gotten us outdoor gigs, stadiums . . . there's no telling how far we could've gone . . ."

But the disputes discouraged him, as he sadly adds, "I wanted to be a beatnik poet, yet here I was making decisions about road crews, talking about bank loans, retaining lawyers [always subject to arrest, the Fugs needed an attorney] . . . I got tired of running the whole show and having to justify whatever I did to the others. I was convinced that if we didn't become electric, we'd wind up in clubs for twenty-five dollars a night."

By 1969, the Fugs, or "the first All-American-Skin-Rock-Peace-Sex-Psychedelic-Tenderness-Society-Group," disbanded.

After releasing a few solo albums, *Sanders' Truckstop* and *Beer Cans on the Moon,* Ed went on to write *The Family,* the bestseller about Charles Manson and the Sharon Tate murder trial.

Tuli, meanwhile, remained loyal to his anarchist convictions, forming another political satire group called the Revolting Theater. Directing this "very underground, very nonprofit" troupe for five years, he supported his wife and three children by writing poems and books—didactic works like *Newspoems,* which have the redundant ring of the sixties.

"Life was open in the sixties, the whole country was being bohemianized, and it seemed like everything was getting better and better," sighs Kupferberg, moving from the kitchen to an office space crammed with leftist literature. "Hippies almost pulled off the revolution. What a letdown! Who would've dreamed that Reagan would be here. Right now we could be at the end."

To get even for this disappointment, Tuli, the self-anointed "oldest rock star in America," has launched another attack on the establishment. Only this time it's a two-pronged effort. Besides drawing heavy-handed political cartoons, he's haunting us again with his music. The "Thing That Wouldn't Die" is on the comeback trail.

According to the latest reports, Tuli has only been seen in New York clubs. There have been no repeat performances in Czechoslovakia, and up until now, the madness hasn't spread to other American cities.

But there's still reason for alarm. The usually level-headed Sanders has forsaken his laser beams and poetry to join Kupferberg. What started out as a mere "reunion concert" in the spring of '84 has turned into a more permanent arrangement—and the consequences could be devastating. For after defiantly insisting, "I will not be burnt out," Sanders likens the Fugs' rebirth to the ghostly apparitions of a Samuel Beckett play.

"There's this wall. First your skin, teeth, and fingernails fall off . . . then you use your bones . . . you either get through or you die. You just chew through it, and dodge the galactic ice pick . . ."

Sanders's voice then trails off. And his cryptic words hang perversely in the air.

Ricky Nelson

The Prodigal Son Goes Home

It could have been too much Mary Lou. A plain case of overdosing on white bread. Or perhaps those 1950s critics of rock 'n' roll were right, and rock's evil chant would lead us straight to the devil.

Well, whatever the reason, everyone's All-American boy, the angel-faced Ricky Nelson, owns the actor Errol Flynn's La-La land home (a retreat nestled in the Hollywood hills, where all sorts of Bacchanalian rituals were once held), this would-be Elvis is hoping to revive his acting career.

Recapturing that old "Ozzie and Harriet" magic won't be easy. For fourteen years, the Nelsons were America's favorite TV family. Yet the mellow-voiced crooner who sent hearts fluttering in the late fifties with such classics as "Travelin' Man" and "Poor Little Fool" hasn't been content with being a standard on the revival circuit. Small theaters and county fairs aren't enough for him. He wants a bigger spotlight; his own TV show, or, at least, another shot at the movies. For who can forget his film successes, *Rio Bravo* and *The Wackiest Ship in the Army?*

"David and I were born into TV, it got us going, so that's a natural place for me to be," says the forty-five-year-old Nelson, after donning a shirt his girlfriend has just ironed. Though his stomach has ballooned a bit over the years, Rick (he dropped the "y" at age twenty) still has an image to protect, so he fidgets with his shirt collar, opening one more button to display a little chest hair, and then sits down under a wall case of ten gold records. It's an impressive display, representing sales of 50 million units. But his appearance is even more eye-catching, since he remains basically the Ricky of old. Every hair on his head has been meticulously slicked into place, the wave is still pronounced, and as for that legendary boyish face, just the right amount of makeup has been applied.

"Yeah, I owe everything to TV. It gave me an edge on [Buddy] Holly, Fabian, and the Everlys, and it sustained me for several years. Besides, I really enjoyed it. That's why I want to get back. Or do some movies. I recently did a pilot for a TV show where I play the principal of a high school. Boy, that'll be great if I get it."

As viewers rush to their dials, they should also prepare themselves for another treat; brother David (now a film director) owns hundreds of Ozzie and Harriet tapes, and is hoping to screen these fifties' gems. If he's successful, we'll quickly learn why the Eisenhower years put people to sleep. In these shows the Nelsons debate such burning issues as who gets the car keys, Ricky's senior prom and his high school grades. Yet the show also produced a string of million-selling records and a seventeen-year-old rock 'n' roll star. The first hit was "I'm Walking," a Fats Domino song which hit number four on the charts in 1957.

"I had never thought of singing on the show, but I went out one night with this girl from Hollywood High, Arlene, and everything changed," recalls Nelson buoyantly. "We were driving over Laurel Canyon, and all of a sudden, Elvis's 'Blue Moon of Kentucky' came on the radio. She went wild, and kept talking about how great he was, so I felt I had to say something. I told her I was going to make a record. She only laughed, so I said to myself, 'I have to do it.' "

That same night Ricky went to his father and asked permission to do a recording of "I'm Walking." A twenty-year veteran of the Hollywood entertainment scene, Ozzie was more than supportive. Taking advantage of his connections, he soon took a demo to record companies, and landed a deal with Verve. Then he suggested that Ricky do the song on national TV.

Thanks to good old Dad, the record was an immediate hit. In a week it sold over 300,000 copies. Yet even more important, the Nelsons had discovered a unique formula for success. Unlike other budding stars, who had to go on tour to promote their records or pay homage to Dick Clark on "American Bandstand," Ricky was "coaxed" every week into singing a new song on his family's TV show. This wholesome, noncommercial approach distinguished him from his rock contemporaries, and it wasn't long before he became Middle America's antidote to the cruder, more threatening Elvis.

"It was a real rush; the girls took me a little more seriously, and there were all these fan clubs that treated me like some god," Rick admits, moving uncomfortably in his chair. "But quite honestly, none of that stuff really changed my life much. I was still living at home, and, except for a new car, I only got my regular allowance. I didn't even have time for much socializing or parties. I was just too busy with the show."

By the early 1960s both "Poor Little Fool" and "Hello Mary Lou" (written by Gene Pitney) had reached the top of the charts. Ricky now did a little touring with a band that featured James Burton (later Presley's lead guitarist). But for the most part, he stayed close to home. The "Ozzie and Harriet" show was delighting the nation, and public appearances couldn't have made Ricky's life any sweeter. He already had one of the greatest deals in rock history.

Again, Ozzie was the guiding genius. An attorney before getting into show business, he had the foresight and skill to work out a twenty-year deal for his son with Decca records in 1963. While other artists of this era were getting ripped off constantly, Ricky had a fixed yearly income, video rights (virtually unheard of then), and a hefty royalty percentage. All of this constituted a set of guarantees that were only matched by Elvis's.

Rick shakes his head in disbelief when talking about this pact, and an awe-struck look, reminiscent of young Ricky Nelson's TV persona, returns to his face. "Dad was amazing; he was always doing things to protect my interests. Things that hadn't become standard yet. I don't know what would've happened to me without him. That twenty-year contract gave me a certain security; I could experiment. I didn't have to worry about my career. Thanks to him there was always money coming in, and that took the pressure off."

Presumably, the Wizard of Oz looked into the future, and realized his son would need to be protected in the fickle world of rock. A revolutionary new sound, the "Mersey beat," was already gathering force abroad. This would mean radical changes for the old order, even in America. Ricky *would* need some insurance, and Ozzie's great deal would provide it. But it was only a cushion. Nothing could stop the inevitable fall. By 1964 the Beatle Invasion had begun. And as the mania spread, from swooning girls to sold-out stadiums, Ricky was suddenly forgotten, a has-been at age twenty-four.

One would assume this was a troubled period for Rick, a time of painful reevaluation and confusion. He had had it all: sprees in the soda shop, beach parties galore, fan clubs, and sing-alongs with Bing Crosby's children. But now, that was all behind him. America's bobbysoxers had found another love, and this could easily have broken Rick's heart.

True to his smiling, ever-innocent image, Rick insists this wasn't a "negative" period. He describes the sixties as a "time of experimentation," and flatly dismisses any notions about his being traumatized. "It didn't hurt to see the girls screaming for others. It only pushed me to find something new. The most important element here is the music, my own creativity. So I never felt envious about anyone. I thought the Beatles were great. I never viewed them as a threat. I just wanted to be myself, and to do my favorite songs."

Yet after his family's TV show went off the air in 1966, Rick did change. With his brand of gently sung rock 'n' roll (and Edd "Kookie" Byrnes-styled hairdo) now passé, he adopted a new country-rock style, and even let his hair grow. This remodeling led to *Bright Lights and Country Music* and *Country Fever,* two albums which were later combined on the double-record *Rick Nelson Country.* However, after having his own TV show, and over forty entries on the singles chart, poor Rick was relegated to making the rounds at the county fairs and nightclubs.

His fortunes didn't improve until 1969, when he covered Dylan's "She Belongs to Me" (number thirty-three). Despite James Burton's leaving him for Elvis (the King resumed live performing), Rick was so happy about being on the charts again that he viewed the loss good-naturedly as a "tribute" from his longtime idol. "We'd often wind up in the same hotel and talk about music," Rick says reverently of Elvis. "You couldn't help but be influenced by him." Rick then put together the Stone Canyon Band with Tom Brumley and Randy Meisner (of Poco and Eagles fame), and stopped playing nightclubs. It was time to hit the revival circuit, with some hard-driving rockabilly.

Initially, this strategy proved disastrous. Backed by his souped-up band, his hair still long, Rick came to New York's Madison Square Garden in the fall of 1971. The crowd expected him to be the old Ricky, the squeaky-clean teenager who was eons removed from the torn America of the Vietnam War era. But since this strange-looking Rick was wired into the rebellious seventies, the crowd mercilessly booed him. The din cut through Rick, shocking him, and would eventually prompt "a spiritual rebirth." But Ricky had to pass through the fire, before the true rock 'n' roller could be born again.

"I needed a little straightening out; I had lost my direction," says Rick, looking to his girlfriend for support. Seeing her smile encouragingly, he nods his head, and turns around, to stare at the "wall of gold."

"I had forgotten my roots, and besides, rockabilly wasn't right for the Garden. Originally I didn't even want to do the show. I talked myself into it. I had the new band, and had never played Madison Square Garden. It just went against my instincts; it didn't feel right. I'm not good at doing things I don't feel deep, deep inside."

Grinning broadly now to change the mood, Rick moves over to a different seat, and thumbs through a box of old photographs. This trip into the past elicits a lighthearted chuckle, and he says, "The Garden crowd wanted the old Ricky Nelson. After a while I realized that, so the hurt went away. I had disappointed them. That booing wasn't a putdown, it was just a tribute to what I had done in the past."

Yet Rick wasn't so forgiving in 1971. He was so dispirited by the Garden reception that he retreated to England—and wrote "Garden Party," his emotional, often embittered reply to the folks who jeered him. The song's message was clear: despite his 1950s image, Rick was going to be true to himself before he tried to please anyone else. This newly found spunkiness apparently touched the right chords, for the song rose to the top of the charts. For the first time in a decade, Rick went platinum.

"It was an important song for me, I was able to express my real feelings, and the public accepted it. You'd think that MCA would've been happy; they had themselves a big seller. In fact, though, I created a monster with 'Garden Party.'

"Just when the record was doing real well I got this call from Mike Maitland, the MCA [Decca] president. I thought he was calling to congratulate me, but instead he tells me 'You spent too much money, you need a producer.' I couldn't believe it. Not only did they stop promoting the album, but they also wanted to limit my freedom. I had always worked best when I had a free hand, and now that was going to stop. It was clearly the beginning of the end of our relationship."

The bitterness in Nelson's voice reflects the lean times that followed. MCA/Decca released him from his contract after one more album, the poorly received *Windfall* of 1974, and when *Intakes* met a similar fate in 1977, his subsequent relationship with Epic also fell apart. Not knowing what to do, and facing a barrage of criticism in the music press, Rick again went abroad. But this time there was no escape. While European audiences continued to appreciate him, their enthusiasm didn't soften the pain of two straight failures, nor could Rick look to his father for help; Ozzie had recently died. So, as Rick now recalls, "Things got very confused. Nothing much was working. I kinda had to get it together."

Aside from admitting that he had to look for "new musical formulas," Rick won't discuss how these setbacks affected him or his family. Was this a period of uncertainty, depression, inactivity? How did his family react? Were relations strained at home, or did someone provide a measure of relief? Instead of addressing these concerns, Rick looks away, shakes his head, and finally dismisses them with "Everything worked out for the best. My private life is going to remain my own business, and as for that period, I'll only say it was a learning experience that helped me in the future."

Despite these soft words, it is clear that the late seventies and early eighties were a difficult time for Nelson. After two unsuccessful LPs, record companies were reluctant to deal with him, and, as evidenced by his drifting between country and pop rock, that "right formula" remained elusive. He didn't strike it right on *Playing to Win,* a 1981 Capitol release that was described by *Rolling Stone* reviewer Dave Marsh as "marginally listenable." And he was soon forced to tour county fairs again, where standbys like "Hello Mary Lou" had to compete with the frenzy of hog calling and cattle trading.

At the present, Nelson does two hundred one-nighters a year. Wherever nostalgia is popular—dank little theaters, small Vegas clubs, amusement parks—Rick is there. It's not known if he needs the money. He won't talk about his finances. But this grueling schedule, that would wear down even a younger person, must be getting to him. While he's not one to complain (the strong moral fiber of the Ozzie and Harriet home wouldn't allow that), his revived interest in acting speaks volumes. It's his way out, his escape from the defeats of the past ten years. Inside Rick Nelson, beneath that calm, ever-cheerful aura, lies a demon that has to get out.

"Right now I don't care what critics say about me, or whether *Rolling Stone* lumps me with Fabian and Avalon," Rick blurts, when asked to assess his legacy. His face reddens despite the makeup, as he angrily squints, and he continues, "I know I was good, I know that each one of my songs had a certain positive feeling. That's all that counts.

"The only people I really care about are other musicians, they're the ones playing my songs. They're the real experts, not the critics. The musicians remember me. Doesn't that say something about what I've accomplished?"

Rick paces around the room for a while, then stares at a family picture. Speaking more to the photo than to his guest, he sounds a plaintive note. "Dad did everything for us. He was always there when you needed him. Things really changed after he died. Boy, they sure did. I know where I want to go now, though. I have a new direction. I just hope Dad was proud of what I accomplished. I think he was."

On New Year's Eve 1985, Ricky was once again flying to one of those many one-night stands. His small plane crashed and he died in the blaze. A few days later, a throng of fans came to pay their last respects. Clearly, these were people who appreciated his accomplishments.